D0679124

WILLIAM F. MAAG LIBRARY
YOUNGSTOWN STATE UNIVERSITY

Y 10 5

Behavioral Assignments and Treatment Compliance

A Handbook of Clinical Strategies

WITHDRAWN

John L. Shelton
Rona L. Levy

and contributors

RESEARCH PRESS
2612 North Mattis Avenue
Champaign, Illinois 61820

Advisory Editor, Frederick H. Kanfer

Copyright © 1981 John L. Shelton and Rona L. Levy

9 8 7 6   89 90 91 92

All rights reserved. Printed in the United States of America. No part of this book may be reproduced by mimeograph or any other means without the written permission of the publisher. Excerpts may be printed in connection with published reviews in periodicals without express permission.

Copies of this book may be ordered from the publisher at the address given on the title page.

Cover design by Jack W. Davis

Composition by Custom Graphics

ISBN 0-87822-255-3
Library of Congress Catalog Card Number: 81-51872

RC
489
.B4S5
1981

To Cynthia Shelton and Diane & Eddie Isenberg,
and in memory of Rona's Bobe, Sophie Isenberg

WILLIAM F. MAAG LIBRARY
YOUNGSTOWN STATE UNIVERSITY

CONTENTS

FOREWORD

Clinicians know that it is not enough for clients to make progress during therapy sessions—clients must translate that progress into action in their daily lives. But in order to accomplish this, clinicians must teach clients how to transfer skills and knowledge from the consulting office to the real world. They must also motivate clients to use their therapeutic experiences to change their lives. These tasks demand the use of strategies for transfer and generalization *throughout* treatment, not just as an afterthought at the end of therapy. They also require strategies for gaining client cooperation and compliance with the therapeutic program. To obtain lasting benefits, it is essential to bridge the gap between what the client says during therapy and what he or she actually does after the session.

Most current behavior change programs include some components directed at one or the other of these critical treatment aspects. But they are rarely applied systematically or integrated into each step of the treatment processes. In this book, Shelton and Levy have compiled techniques for enhancing treatment compliance and developing behavioral assignments that they and other experienced clinicians have used to help clients generalize their skills and remain motivated to continue using them. But more than that, they have shown how these methods can become an integrated part of the change process.

Systematic homework assignments benefit the clients by stressing the centrality of self-management. They let clients gradually try newly developed skills and knowledge in real situations and allow them to see the effects on their own problems. In this approach the goal is not to improve the client-therapist relationship, but to strengthen the client so that he or she can function independently. Systematic utilization of behavioral assignments can also minimize the buildup of many common client problems: excessive dependency on the therapist; restriction of change to the therapeutic milieu; and reluctance to put skills and insights to work in day-to-day activities. Client contracts, behavioral assignments, and related therapeutic strategies are presented for a variety of common behavioral disorders.

Practicing mental health workers from various disciplines should find this book useful in helping their clients to plan, try out, and evaluate new behaviors. Numerous methods for various presenting problems are to be found here, and many can be applied to both individual and group treatment with only minor modifications. Research-based rationales and related studies are included to support the use of the methods and to give clinicians a basis for making treatment decisions. However, the book's major contribution is not in the compilation of methods that can be interwoven into the readers' current practices. Its major impact is in the demonstration of how such diverse methods can be carefully woven into systematic and interrelated sequences throughout the change process—for it is this consistency and continuity that gives the total fabric its power as a tool for behavior change.

Different chapters will appeal to different readers, depending on their interests; but all readers should come away from this book with new perspectives on their own practices in formulating and handling clinical cases.

Frederick H. Kanfer, Ph.D.
University of Illinois
Champaign, Illinois
April, 1981

PREFACE

All experienced therapists know that success in clinical practice depends heavily on the activities of the client when he or she is not with the therapist. This dependence on outside activities is particularly true for behavioral practice, for which it has been said, "In probably no other treatment approach is the patient's participation more sought."*

Each therapist, through experience, develops his or her own ideas both about what to ask the client to do outside of treatment and how to increase the likelihood that the client will follow through with these activities. Indeed, individual experiences are usually all a therapist can rely on, since outside activities as a central focus are rarely discussed in publications on treatment procedures. This peripheral placement is unfortunate because outside practice activities, to be effective, must be systematically built into the therapeutic process as homework assignments. Only by carefully structuring all aspects of these assignments—from their type to their form and to the context in which they are given—can the therapist and client move purposefully toward a specific goal, and only by such structuring can the therapist have any degree of assurance that the assignments will be carried out as planned.

This book addresses the lack of focused discussion on homework in the literature on therapy methods. Using information drawn from the authors' and other clinicians' experience, it discusses homework assignments and the enhancement of compliance with homework. In Section I, Chapter 1 covers the importance and history of homework in clinical practice. Chapter 2 presents a general framework for clinical practice and the place of homework within this framework, and Chapter 3 provides a series of practice recommendations that should enhance the likelihood that clients will complete homework assignments as planned. Section II in this book contains 10 chapters on specific treatment problems. Each chapter was written by one or more clinicians who are highly experienced with the problems in their particular area.

---

*McNamara, J.R. *Behavioral approaches to medicine.* New York: Plenum, 1979.

It is hoped that this book will serve two purposes: first, to share information about specific assignments and compliance-enhancement strategies among clinicans; and second, to encourage other writers to describe homework-related activities in more detail.

ACKNOWLEDGMENTS

The first acknowledgment is to Fred Kanfer, whose early writings with Jeanne Phillips provided the authors with much of the basis for their ideas on the importance of systematic behavioral assignments. More recently, Fred Kanfer's support and encouragement have greatly helped in the completion of this book.

Dr. Shelton would also like to thank J. Mark Ackerman, who introduced him to the concept of therapeutic homework and provided an important early role model for the effective use of behavioral assignments in clinical practice. Cynthia Shelton is thanked for her love and support throughout this project.

Dr. Levy acknowledges the continued support of Deans Scott Briar and Naomi Gottlieb, who help create a school where scholarly activity is encouraged. Steven Hayes is also thanked for his much-needed boost of noncontingent reinforcement during the final manuscript preparation phase.

Finally, the editorial work of Lesley L. Link was essential to combining the various sections into a complete manuscript.

SECTION I

This section contains three chapters that provide a foundation for understanding and using systematic behavioral assignments. In Chapter 1, homework-based therapy is contrasted with traditional practices, the development of the concept of systematic behavioral assignments is traced, and the advantages of using homework in therapy are highlighted. In Chapter 2, a model of the use of systematic behavioral assignments in all stages of therapy is outlined. Finally, in Chapter 3, the crucial concern of enhancing client compliance is addressed.

CHAPTER 1

The Use of
Behavioral Assignments in
Clinical Practice

Almost every therapist in an outpatient setting assigns outside activities to clients as part of treatment. Undoubtedly, many have observed the advantages of having clients work on their problems outside the formal consultation hour. It accelerates the clients' progress toward therapeutic goals, increases their powers of generalization and their ability to maintain the effects of treatment, and allows them to work on problems such as sexual dysfunction and insomnia in which the therapist's presence would be awkward, impractical, or ill-advised.

This chapter and this book present a simple message: *systematic behavioral assignments should be the focus of treatment.* This new focus shifts responsibility for treatment from the therapist to the client.

DEFINITION OF SYSTEMATIC BEHAVIORAL ASSIGNMENTS

Systematic behavioral assignments are therapeutic home-practice activities that are carefully integrated into the therapeutic process. Each treatment session begins and ends with a discussion of these outside practice tasks, which are specifically designed to achieve therapy goals. As therapy proceeds, a large part of each session is devoted to preparing the client for the next homework assignment, and the difficulty of each task is gradually increased as therapy progresses. *Systematic* also means that the manner of giving homework is carefully thought through. Assignments are never given "off the cuff," but follow a standardized delivery format that follows the week-to-week developments occurring during within-office treatment. Finally, guidelines for checking on whether the client is doing his or her assignments are built into the assignment process. This last feature demands that the therapist use a number of compliance-enhancing tactics.

In the systematic behavioral assignment model, the therapist is seen as a facilitator, consultant, or educator, and the heaviest responsibility for change rests on the client (rather than the therapist), who completes the therapy by carrying out assignments. Homework assignments are therefore seen as *the* goals of therapy, not adjuncts to those goals, as they are seen in traditional therapy.

Other distinctions between the systematic behavioral model and the traditional model are important as well. For example, the systematic behavioral assignment model employs a standardized delivery format, whereas its more traditional counterpart does not. Descriptions of outside practice activities are made specific and clarified to insure that the activities will be carried out constructively. Nor does this model assume that compliance will occur automatically; rather, it emphasizes the responsibility of the therapist for seeing that the client actually follows through. Finally, this model recognizes that some assignments may bring on aversive consequences and that the client should be prepared for them, rather than being left to struggle and perhaps give up. Table 1.1 summarizes some of the important distinctions just raised. The table depicts the essential elements of the systematic behavioral assignment model and contrasts it with an alternative model involving the nonsystematic use of behavioral assignments.

EXAMPLES OF SYSTEMATIC
BEHAVIORAL ASSIGNMENTS

Most of the activities performed within the office can also be done by the client in his or her natural environment. For example, the client may be given assignments that involve pinpointing and counting, relaxation, assertion, sensate focus, mutual masturbation, participation in pleasant events, or wheelchair pushups. The next two figures give two actual examples of systematic behavioral assignments.

Table 1.1

Contrast between the Systematic Behavioral Assignment Model and the Nonsystematic Model

	Treatment Program Outline Using Systematic Behavioral Assignment Model	Treatment Program Outline Using Nonsystematic Model
Integration into Treatment	Outside practice is carefully integrated into treatment. Each session begins with a discussion of last week's assigned task and concludes with a new homework plan for the coming week.	Outside practice activities are rarely planned carefully or fully integrated into therapy. Outside practice may be urged but is not *the* focus of treatment.
Role of Therapist	The therapist gives assignments, but responsibility for change is heavily on the client.	The therapist is seen as the person primarily responsible for change.
Role of Assignments	Assignments are criterion tasks of therapeutic goal(s).	At their most influential, assignments are viewed as a helpful adjunct, but not a critical part of the therapeutic process.
Purpose of Treatment	Performance attained through assignments is the targeted goal of therapy.	Assignments may be seen as helping to reach goals, but they are not seen as goals themselves.
Standardized Format	Systematic behavioral assignment delivery typically contains six standardized elements: 1. Do Statement 2. Quantity Statement 3. Location Statement 4. Record Statement 5. Contingency Statement 6. Bring Statement Furthermore, the behavioral assignment is described, rehearsed, and written for the client.	Behavioral assignments seldom contain any standardized elements. Instead, clients are urged to practice, with little attention given to the manner of assignment delivery (where, when, how frequently, and with whom to practice). Assignments are seldom rehearsed in advance and are rarely written down.
Compliance	A careful check is made to minimize all factors that may diminish adherence and to enlist all available compliance enhancers. The therapist recognizes that some behavioral assignments may have very severe side effects, such as punishments from homework "target" people. Consequently, steps are taken to prevent or cope with this problem.	No attention is given to whether or not the client will practice whatever the therapist suggests; failure to comply is thought of as the client's "problem" and is not the responsibility of the treating professional. The therapist who uses homework in a nonsystematic fashion assigns tasks with little recognition of the dangers inherent in some outside practice activities.

Figure 1.1 shows the first assignment for a man who entered treatment complaining of "an overeating problem." This assignment, which involved a self-diagnostic task, had to be completed before any treatment intervention could be designed and implemented. The assignment was also "bilateral": in other words, it gave the therapist something to do as well. This bilateral aspect helps the client feel that the therapist is involved and underlines the contractual nature of the treatment process.

Figure 1.1   Example of a systematic behavioral assignment for an obese client

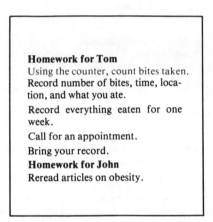

Homework for Tom
Using the counter, count bites taken. Record number of bites, time, location, and what you ate.
Record everything eaten for one week.
Call for an appointment.
Bring your record.
Homework for John
Reread articles on obesity.

Figure 1.2 shows a homework assignment for a recently divorced man who was learning how to behave more assertively with his friends, boss, and lover. In this particular case, care was taken to minimize the potential effects of punishment that might occur as a result of completing the prescribed task. Particular care should be taken with behavioral assignments that involve assertion tasks because the "targets" of some assertion responses may punish the client severely for open and honest expressions or opinions (Shelton, 1976). Figure 1.2 illustrates such a precaution. Again, a bilateral agreement was used.

THE ORIGINS OF SYSTEMATIC BEHAVIORAL ASSIGNMENTS

A number of writers have developed treatment models that use home-practice activities to some degree or another. Among the best known models are Directed Learning (Kanfer, 1970), Directive Therapy (Haley, 1963, 1976), Guided Practice (Deffenbacher, 1976), Instigation Therapy (Kanfer & Phillips, 1966, 1969), Programmed Psychotherapy (Sulzer, 1965), Systematic Homework (Shelton & Ackerman, 1974), and Rational-Emotive Therapy (Ellis, 1970; Maultsby, 1971).

Figure 1.2   Example of a systematic behavioral assignment for a nonassertive client

Homework for Ed
Discuss your job dissatisfaction
with Mr. James on Monday.
Prior to your meeting (5 min.):
   Relax.
   Rehearse what you will say and do.
   Do it!
Call me immediately after for a briefing and to schedule your next
appointment.*
Homework for John
Be available Monday evening.

*This approach was utilized for two reasons. First, in all behavioral assignments where the possibility of punishment is high, the therapist is responsible for designing some sort of a safeguard to aid the client if the need arises. Usually being available for a phone call is sufficient. Second, the agreement to call the therapist on a certain day often prompts homework completion.

However, long before the work of these contemporary writers, many of whom we will soon discuss, a small number of psychotherapists were discussing the use of assigned practice activities designed to augment psychological treatments. Among the first were Dunlap (1932), Herzberg (1941), and Karpman (1949), all of whom pointed out the advantages associated with putting clients to work outside the therapy hour. For example, Dunlap's (1932) home-practice activities consisted of patient-managed extinction trials, which he called "negative practice." Herzberg (1941) and Karpman (1949), on the other hand, were analytically oriented writers who explored the worth of homework consisting of free association activities that were recorded by the analysand and brought back into therapy for discussion.

George Kelly

From a historical perspective, the work of George Kelly (1955) represents a cornerstone for all recent work done in the area of prescribed assignments. Although his approach to homework was not fully systematic, Kelly did carefully integrate outside practice assignments into therapy. Kelly's approach consisted of urging clients to define appropriate target identities and to act out those roles in the social environment. For example, a shy client would be urged to formulate an

WILLIAM F. MAAG LIBRARY
YOUNGSTOWN STATE UNIVERSITY

identity opposite to his or her current self-image. Discussions with the therapist, movies, and books were all used to provide data from which to construct the target identity. Once selected and discussed, Kelly would then rehearse the role with the client again and again until it was mastered. The client was frequently instructed to forget about him or herself and pretend that he or she was an actor playing a certain role. Assignments were then given in which the client went into the environment to practice the new role. An assumption underlying Kelly's work was that reinforcement from individuals in the client's social environment would maintain the new behavior.

The parallels between Kelly's work and modern-day behavior therapy are striking. Behavioral rehearsal, cognitive control, and behavioral assignments all played a large role in his fixed-role therapy model. Since then, a number of developments have occurred that have taken homework and prescribed activities from the occasionally used adjunct to the point where it is *the* central focus of treatment around which all interventions within the office are aimed.

Kanfer and Phillips

The first of these developments was the work of Kanfer and Phillips (1966, 1969). These writers provided the critical first step in the development of homework-based therapy by presenting a conceptual model around which systematic behavioral assignments could develop. They coined the term "Instigation Therapy." In essence, they argued that Instigation Therapy could be differentiated from other approaches in its reliance on outside activities and its shift of responsibility for change from the therapist to the client. In contrasting Instigation Therapy to other approaches, they state that "the main feature of this technique lies in its use of the therapeutic relationship for joint planning of a program which *the patient executes in his daily environment in the absence of the therapist*" (Kanfer & Phillips, 1969, p. 453, italics added). They further argued that, in some instances, prescribed outside behavioral assignments in which the client engaged in behavior change could and should be the entire focus of therapy.

Sex Dysfunction Therapy Pioneers

By-and-large, sex dysfunction clinicians and researchers were the first to carefully integrate home practice into treatment. Both Masters and Johnson (1970) and LoPiccolo and LoPiccolo (1978) gave homework a central place in treatment. Their behavioral assignments (discussed in Chapter 10) involved improvement of verbal communication, relaxation, sensate focus, and the control of faulty cognitive patterns such as "playing the spectator role" (LoPiccolo & LoPiccolo, 1978).

WILLIAM F. MAAG LIBRARY
YOUNGSTOWN STATE UNIVERSITY

Therapeutic homework for couples suffering from sexual dysfunction focused both on skill enhancement and on the change of sexual attitudes and cognitive sets. The enhancement of skills was brought about by carefully structured homework assignments that involved practicing sexual behaviors in a nonthreatening home environment. Performance anxiety was eliminated by teaching clients to concentrate on physical sensations and to avcid worrying about reaching performance standards. In the basic Masters and Johnson approach, changes in attitude often resulted from discussions surrounding sexual issues, but a great deal of change was also achieved by homework assignments involving reading books and listening to audio tapes.

Modern sex dysfunction clinicians have thus made prescribed homework the focus of therapy and have incorporated it into therapy in a systematic manner. This systematization is a hallmark of sexual dysfunction treatment.

Shelton and Ackerman

A recent emphasis on prescribed outside activities has come from the work of Shelton and Ackerman (1974). For these writers, behavioral assignments are the core of successful therapy. Borrowing from the conceptual framework provided by Kanfer and Phillips (1966,1969), Shelton and Ackerman took the concepts of Instigation Therapy and translated them into more than 150 examples of homework assignments that could be used with a wide number of common behavioral disorders. Their work was the first to address itself to therapeutic homework per se and to propose a standardized format by which home practice should be given. They also discussed contraindications for its use and provided detailed examples of how to integrate systematic behavioral assignments into the therapeutic process.

THE CONTEMPORARY USE OF THERAPEUTIC HOMEWORK

It is now time to turn to the question of the extent to which therapists make use of homework in their treatment with clients today. The authors surveyed all the outpatient treatment articles published from January 1973 to January 1980 in eight popular behavior therapy journals.* In all, a total of 500 articles were reviewed. In particular, the

---

*Those journals are *Behavior Modification, Behaviour Research and Therapy, Behavior Therapy, Biofeedback and Self-Regulation, Cognitive Therapy and Research, Journal of Applied Behavior Analysis, Journal of Behavioral Medicine,* and *Journal of Behavior Therapy and Experimental Psychiatry.*

survey was done to see whether homework was used, which type of behavioral assignment was most typically assigned, and what types of problems most frequently lent themselves to some form of homework-focused treatment. Information was also sought as to the extent to which reported behavioral assignments were systematically prescribed and whether or not efforts were expended to assure adherence to the assignments after they were given. More details are listed in Table 1.2.

Table 1.2

Incidence of Reported Therapeutic Behavioral Assignments for Adult Outpatients as Found in Behavioral Journals

Category	Number of Articles Reviewed	Number of Articles Using Homework	Percentage of Articles Using Homework
Anxiety	140	79	56%
Nonassertiveness	34	25	74%
Depression	20	10	50%
Insomnia	18	14	77%
Obsessions and compulsions	29	23	79%
Obesity	28	21	75%
Physical illness and rehabilitation	117	83	71%
Sex disorders	33	16	48%
Sex dysfunction	41	32	78%
Stuttering	11	6	55%
Social skills	15	13	87%
Smoking	14	9	64%
TOTAL	500	331	68%

The results of this survey were surprising. Of the hundreds of outpatient articles reviewed, 68 percent reported the use of assigned home practice to promote treatment gains. In addition, as Table 1.2 reveals, the frequency of prescribed outside activity usage was extremely high for most problem areas. Treatment for such problems as nonassertiveness, insomnia, obsession-compulsion control, obesity, physical illness and rehabilitation, sex dysfunction, and social skills were recorded as relying on outside behavioral assignments to promote treatment outcome more than 71 percent of the time. Furthermore, if, as we mentioned previously, many therapists do not use homework systematically or do not consider it central to treatment, they would probably not report it. This table may then represent a minimal estimate of the use of homework assignments.

Another question the survey sought to answer was the degree to which assigned home practice was given in a systematic fashion. To answer this question, some of the criteria for systematization of homework listed in Table 1.3 were used. The criteria of most interest were the extent to which authors reported telling their clients when and where to practice, how long to practice, and how frequently to practice, as well as the extent to which compliance with the assigned activity was monitored.

Table 1.3

Amount of Systematization Found in Articles Reporting the Use of Behavioral Assignments

Reported instructions		Compliance Data	
Frequency of assignments per day	10%	Reported	5%
Frequency of assignments per week	11%	Not reported	95%
Duration of each practice trial	4%		
Where to practice	5%		
Frequency of assignment per day and week, duration of each practice trial, and where to practice	2%		

Table 1.3 shows the results of this aspect of the study. It appears that even though behavioral assignments are frequently reported, they are rarely given systematically. Table 1.3 reveals that less than 2 percent of all the articles that included outside practice assignments reported telling clients when, where, how frequently, or how long to practice. Hence it appears that clients are often encouraged to practice but rarely given guidelines to follow regarding common-sense parameters such as how frequently to practice. Of additional concern are the data contained in Table 1.3 that show that only 5 percent of all articles that used homework reported compliance-rate figures. Thus, we found that although 68 percent of all behavior therapy articles involving outpatient treatment reported the use of outside practice assignments, only about 1 in 20 reported efforts to ascertain whether or not the subjects complied with the assignment.

In summary, it appears that behavioral assignments are frequently reported as a component of outpatient behavior therapy and are reported across most problem areas. Despite the heavy use of assignments, however, little is known regarding the specific components of homework assignments and the methods of assignment delivery. Furthermore, no current evidence exists to suggest that behavioral assignments are given in a systematic fashion by most practicing therapists.

THE ADVANTAGES OF USING SYSTEMATIC BEHAVIORAL ASSIGNMENTS

Why do many professionals — even if they do not use assignments systematically — make use of outside practice activities in their work with clients? The fact is that behavioral assignments, if carefully integrated into psychotherapy, can result in a number of useful benefits. Some of the most important of these follow.

Access to Private Behaviors

A treatment approach that allows for therapy to continue even in the absence of the therapist is especially useful for problems that cannot be readily observed or treated in the therapist's office. For problems such as sexual dysfunction, insomnia, or obesity, the therapist's presence in the client's natural environment would prove impractical and, in some cases, unethical. Systematic behavioral assignments allow the therapist to design home treatments that would not interfere with a normally private activity or an activity which is generally confined to certain locations or behavioral settings.

Efficiency of Treatment

Most new patterns of behavior need to be practiced repeatedly and tried out in different settings. Practice that is limited to the in-the-office therapy hour will not finish the job. In fact, individual psychotherapy is quite inefficient when viewed from the perspective of how much time is needed to produce the necessary change. Systematic behavioral assignments overcome this problem because they allow for unlimited practice in a number of settings. Use of the other 167 hours of the week not devoted to formal therapy can mean a big savings in time, money, and health-care utilization.

One recent study (Shelton, in press) strongly supports the view that therapy is made more efficient by the use of outside-of-therapy practice assignments. This particular study was designed to explore the impact of systematic behavioral assignments on overcoming conditioned urinary retention, or shy bladder syndrome. Two groups of patients were given treatment consisting primarily of *in vivo* desensitization. In essence, treatment demanded that the client report to therapy under high-drive conditions and progress through a series of rest-room-related situations involving the client and therapist. In each case the client urinated in a nearby rest room immediately adjacent to the treatment office. Anxiety was reduced by having the therapist gradually approach the client. In addition to *in vivo* systematic desensitization, one group was given systematic behavioral assignments consisting of urinating in public rest rooms under various stimulus conditions.

Both groups improved in onset to urination, but the group given in-the-office treatment plus outside therapeutic assignments improved almost twice as fast. The group receiving only in-the-office treatment took an average of 10.5 weeks, or 17 sessions, to complete treatment, while the group receiving both in-the-office treatment and systematic behavioral assignments took an average of 5.8 weeks, or 9 sessions.

Increased Self-Control

The instigation of homework-focused procedures may increase the client's self-control. Secord and Bachman (1964) have noted that clients who perceive themselves as the principal agents of behavior change develop more self-control skills. A more recent study by Bandura (1975) found that self-control behaviors decreased when clients thought treatment gains were due to group support rather than their own resources. These studies show that involving clients in their own treatment outside the therapy hour may help them see themselves as the principal agents of change and may thus motivate them to act in their own best interests (Lefcourt, 1966; Rotter, Chance, & Phares, 1972).

Research involving pain control has supported this same conclusion. In one study, Staub, Tursky, and Schwartz (1973) found that clients who could control the intensity of shocks rated them as less painful. It thus appears that merely believing that one is in control — regardless of the true situation — is sufficient to increase motivation to change and control oneself.

Transfer of Training

One of the biggest tasks facing the psychotherapist is helping the client transfer what he or she has learned during therapy to the outside world (Gruber, 1971). Transfer can occur in three dimensions: across situations, across responses, and across time. The transfer of training across situations refers to the fact that many learned behaviors become situation-specific. For example, the formerly nonassertive client can now assert him or herself but only in specific situations (with the therapist or in a therapy group). Transfer of training across responses refers to the fact that some clients learn a behavior but fail to generalize from it. Thus, the nonorgasmic woman may learn to have an orgasm with her vibrator but not with her husband, or the client with a spinal cord injury may learn skin care but fail to brush his teeth. Transfer of training across time refers to how well the patient is able to maintain therapy gains once treatment is terminated. As in the case of the other two classes of generalization just discussed, the evidence in support of effective transfer of training across situations is not good (Fordyce, 1976; Kazdin & Wilson, 1978).

As a result of the transfer of training problem, many therapists may become frustrated by their seeming lack of effectiveness. In fact, they may be highly effective in the office setting but fail to actively program for transfer to the client's social environment and therefore observe no changes outside of therapy. As Gruber (1971), Fordyce (1976), Shelton (1976, 1977), and Stokes and Baer (1977) have all noted, the effective therapist cannot assume that skills acquired during the formal consultation hour will automatically transfer to the client's social environment. The research literature on this issue is clear: treatment effects will not transfer or be maintained unless systematically planned by the professional (see Goldstein & Kanfer, 1979, for an extended discussion of this issue). Hence, even therapists with outstanding relationship and behavioral change skills may fail to produce transfer and maintenance of therapeutic gains if they fail to systematically program for them.

How can transfer be programmed? A good way is through systematic behavioral assignments, which can greatly enhance the generalization of treatment effects from clinical settings. The capacity for therapeutic assignments to foster generalization is based on several aspects of the assignment process. For example, since many prescribed behavioral assignments can be practiced in settings other than the clinic, they maximize the likelihood of generalization. Thus, the client can be given systematic behavioral assignments that involve practice in a number of settings and with a number of targets. The greater number of practice trials in new settings and with new targets greatly increases transfer across classes. Broadening the response class may be a goal of homework as well. For example, clients who can be taught to "make small talk" can, using systematic behavioral assignments, learn to broaden their repertoire to include longer and longer conversations involving increasingly intimate topics. Similarly, chronic pain patients who learn the value of "well behaviors" such as walking may broaden the response class to include other similar activities such as jogging, tennis, or bike riding.

An example of the use of systematic behavioral assignments to enhance transfer follows. In the study cited earlier, one group of "shy bladder" clients was given a traditional *in vivo* desensitization approach, and the other was given the traditional approach plus prescribed behavioral tasks consisting of urination in public rest rooms. In this particular study, the clients were instructed to practice certain urination-related tasks on progressively more difficult bases, beginning with assignments involving urinating in little-used rest rooms where the threatening presence of others was minimal, and culminating weeks after treatment in the client urinating in a public rest room at a sports event (the Transfer Condition). The improvement of transfer as a result of this practice is shown in Figure 1.3.

As the figure shows, clients who were treated only in the office were less able to transfer their acquired skills than were those who practiced in numerous settings.

Figure 1.3   Level of transfer of skills for clients with shy bladder syndrome*

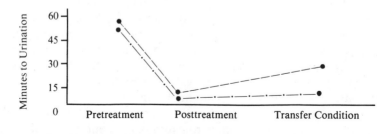

—.— In-the-office treatment and systematic behavioral assignments
——— In-the-office treatment only

*Reprinted by permission from J.L. Shelton. Using systematic behavioral assignments for the treatment of shy bladder syndrome. *Journal of Behavioral Medicine,* in press.

Systematic behavioral assignments can also be programmed to increase the chance for maintenance to occur once therapy is terminated. For example, the therapist can assign homework that involves periodic monitoring of some aspect of behavior that was formerly the focus of therapy. He or she may send a postcard to the client with the understanding that the results of the assessment will be returned for review. In other instances, the therapist can assign some activity that is especially designed to maintain therapeutic gains. For example, attending a couples workshop conducted by another reputable therapist can help maintain improvement if the assignment is to be done twice a year. Likewise, the obese client can be encouraged to attend booster sessions at Weight Watchers once every 2 months. In other instances, the client can return to the therapist at periodic intervals for a brief assessment and assignment of additional maintenance activities.

In addition to these strategies, the *process* of homework-focused therapy itself may enhance maintenance. Davison (1968) demonstrated that clients who were involved in their own treatment planning were more likely to maintain therapy gains over time. Thus, clients who are put to work outside the formal therapy hour may acquire skills during the process that will continue to be used long after formal therapy is terminated. Davison's work supports that of Secord and Bachman (1964), who showed that new behavior was more apt to be maintained when individuals perceived that they were responsible for the change.

Another advantage of homework in the transfer of training is the opportunity it provides for correction and feedback via assignments *during* therapy. This aspect helps the client note and prepare for problems and also gives the therapist a better picture of what demands may be made on the client, or what deficits he or she may have.

Finally, planning for transfer of training, the therapist and client may become aware of areas in the client's environment that do not reinforce or that even punish the client's new skills. Similarly, the client has the opportunity to practice newly acquired behaviors and discern areas that need further practice or more flexible or generalized responses.

In conclusion, the possibilities of improving generalization across time, place, and activities are extensive once the therapist uses the systematic behavioral assignments model for enhancing transfer. The key point is the fact that transfer is not likely to occur automatically. The therapist *must* take an active role in programming these outcomes. A carefully planned use of systematic behavioral assignments with an eye toward promoting transfer is one effective way of achieving this result.

SUMMARY

In this chapter, the fundamental idea is introduced that systematic behavioral assignments should be the *focus* of treatment. Differences between homework-based therapy and traditional therapy are summarized. Homework-based therapy calls for carefully and systematically planned outside assignments, which are seen as criterion tasks toward therapeutic goals. The assignments are delivered in a standardized manner and clarified for the client. Steps are taken to enhance client compliance with assignments, but the responsibility for change is seen as the client's. Traditional therapy, on the other hand, rarely requires planned or integrated outside assignments, and views them as adjuncts to treatment. These assignments are not offered in a standardized format and often not clarified for the client. No attention is given to enhancing client compliance, and the therapist is seen as the person responsible for bringing about changes in the client.

It is then briefly shown how systematic behavioral assignments are used in therapy, and both the historical origins and current usage of this therapeutic approach are presented. The roles played by several key therapists in developing the use of systematic behavioral assignments are explained. A survey of the recent literature is described that outlines the extent of present use of behavioral assignments.

The last portion of this chapter is a short discussion of the advantages of using homework in therapy. Some advantages listed are the access gained to private behaviors normally done at home, the improved efficiency of treatment, the increased self-control fostered in clients, and the effective transfer of training.

The advantages of systematic behavioral assignments will be illustrated in more detail by the chapters in Section II. The next chapter will show exactly how the use of assignments is integrated into all phases of therapy.

REFERENCES

Bandura, A. Generalizing change through participant modeling with self-directed mastery. *Behaviour Research and Therapy*, 1975, *13*, 141-152.

Davison, G.C. Systematic desensitization as a counter-conditioning process. *Journal of Abnormal Psychology*, 1968, *73*, 91-99.

Deffenbacher, J.L. Relaxation *in vivo* in the treatment of test anxiety. *Journal of Behavior Therapy and Experimental Psychiatry*, 1976, *7*, 289-292.

Dunlap, K. *Habits, their making and unmaking*. New York: Liveright, 1932.

Ellis, A. *The essence of rational psychotherapy: A comprehensive approach to treatment*. New York: Institute for Rational Living, 1970.

Fordyce, W.E. Behavioral concepts in chronic pain and illness. In P.O. Davidson (Ed.), *The behavioral management of anxiety, depression, and pain*. New York: Brunner/Mazel, 1976.

Goldstein, A.P., & Kanfer, F.H. *Maximizing treatment gains: Transfer enhancement in psychotherapy*. New York: Academic Press, 1979.

Gruber, R.D. Behavior therapy: Problems in generalization. *Behavior Therapy*, 1971, *2*, 336-368.

Haley, J. *Strategies of psychotherapy*. New York: Grune & Stratton, 1963.

Haley, J. *Problem solving therapy*. San Francisco: Jossey-Bass, 1976.

Herzberg, A. Short treatment of neurosis by graduated tasks. *British Journal of Medical Psychology*, 1941, *19*, 36-51.

Kanfer, F.H. Self-monitoring methodological limitations and clinical applications. *Journal of Consulting and Clinical Psychology*, 1970, *35*, 148-152.

Kanfer, F.H., & Phillips, J.S. Behavior therapy: A panacea for all ills or a passing fancy? *Archives of General Psychiatry*, 1966, *15*, 114-128.

Kanfer, F.H., & Phillips, J.S. *Learning foundations of behavior therapy.* New York: John Wiley & Sons, 1969.

Karpman, B. Objective psychotherapy. *Journal of Clinical Psychology,* 1949, *5,* 140-148.

Kazdin, A.E., & Wilson, G.T. *Evaluation of behavior therapy.* Cambridge, Mass.: Ballinger, 1978.

Kelly, G.A. *The psychology of personal constructs* (Vol. 2). New York: Norton, 1955.

Lefcourt, H.M. Internal versus external control of reinforcement: A review. *Psychological Bulletin,* 1966, *65,* 206-220.

LoPiccolo, J., & LoPiccolo, L. (Eds.). *Handbook of sex therapy.* New York: Plenum, 1978.

Masters, W.H., & Johnson, V.E. *Human sexual inadequacy.* Boston: Little, Brown, 1970.

Maultsby, M. Systematic written homework in psychotherapy. *Rational Living,* 1971, *6,* 17-23.

Rotter, J.B., Chance, J.E., & Phares, E.J. *Applications of a social learning theory of personality.* New York: Holt, Rinehart & Winston, 1972.

Secord, P.F., & Bachman, C.W. *Social psychology.* New York: McGraw-Hill, 1964.

Shelton, J.L. Homework in AT [assertive training]: Promoting the transfer of assertive skills to the natural environment. In R.E. Alberti (Ed.), *Assertiveness: Innovations, applications, issues.* San Luis Obispo, Calif.: Impact, 1977.

Shelton, J.L. The elimination of persistent stuttering by the use of homework assignments involving speech shadowing. *Behavior Therapy,* 1977, *6,* 392-393.

Shelton, J.L. Using systematic behavioral assignments for the treatment of shy bladder syndrome. *Journal of Behavioral Medicine,* in press.

Shelton, J.L., & Ackerman, J.M. *Homework in counseling and psychotherapy.* Springfield, Ill.: Charles C. Thomas, 1974.

Staub, E., Tursky, B., & Schwartz, G.E. Self-control and predictability: Their effects on reactions to aversive stimulation. *Journal of Personality and Social Psychology,* 1973, *18,* 157-162.

Stokes, T.F., & Baer, D.M. An implicit technology of generalization. *Journal of Applied Behavior Analysis,* 1977, *4,* 200-216.

Sulzer, E.S. Behavior modification in adult psychiatric patients. In L. Ullmann & L. Krasner (Eds.), *Case studies in behavior modification.* New York: Holt, Rinehart & Winston, 1965.

CHAPTER 2

A Model of Practice for Using Behavioral Assignments

This chapter presents an overview of the therapeutic process in order to provide a background for the application of systematic behavioral assignments. Steps in that process are discussed as if they occurred sequentially, even though each of them may recur at any point in treatment. For example, although it is certainly important to establish a positive relationship at the beginning of therapy, relationship building and enhancement should continue throughout treatment. Similarly, target problems, once defined, may often need to be redefined as new problems or information emerge.

RELATIONSHIP BUILDING

All therapeutic interventions can be seen as a process of interpersonal influence, in which one individual seeks to change his or her own behavior, thoughts, or feelings, and another tries to facilitate that change. Such intervention cannot succeed without a good working interaction between the client and the therapist. If the client does not trust the therapist, he or she will withhold crucial information early in therapy and will probably not follow through on recommendations and strategies for maintaining desirable change later. From the perspective of this book, of course, the client's willingness to follow through with homework assignments is especially critical: if assignments are seen as successive approximations to therapeutic goals, it logically follows that unless they are carried out, those goals cannot be reached.

One ethical caveat should be noted here. The approach just described assumes that all therapists are operating from a basis of acceptable ethical conduct: that both client and therapist have agreed on the overall goals of therapy and the general means to achieve these goals. To this end, early in the therapeutic process clients and therapists should work together to discuss the client's problems and related goals. (This process is described later in this chapter.) The relationship between client and therapist should not be abused by asking clients to do anything inconsistent with responsible practice.

The client-therapist relationship has been shown to change as the therapeutic process itself progresses. Goldstein (1975) describes a chain reaction in which the therapist engages in interaction-enhancing activities that encourage liking, respect, and trust. These three components lead to communication, openness, and persuasibility, which in turn affect client change (see Table 2.1). Goldstein outlines several relationship-enhancing qualities, including increased perception of the helper as a warm person, as an individual similar to oneself, and as an expert professional. Perceiving someone as likeable, credible, or similar are thus three important factors in building a relationship. The influence of likeability, or source attraction, on behavior change has been explained from a behavioral perspective by Lott and Lott (1968): "Learning to like a stimulus person

Table 2.1

Progression from Relationship Enhancement to Client Change*

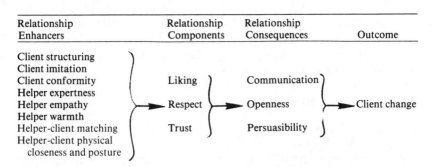

Relationship Enhancers	Relationship Components	Relationship Consequences	Outcome
Client structuring Client imitation Client conformity Helper expertness Helper empathy Helper warmth Helper-client matching Helper-client physical closeness and posture	Liking Respect Trust	Communication Openness Persuasibility	Client change

*Reprinted by permission from A.P. Goldstein. Relationship enhancement methods. In F.H. Kanfer & A.P. Goldstein (Eds.), *Helping people change: Methods and materials.* Elmsford, N.Y.: Pergamon Press, 1975.

is essentially learning to anticipate reward when that person is present" (p.68). Studies on verbal conditioning (Sapolsky, 1960) and on modeling (Bandura, 1969, 1971; Bandura & Walters, 1963) also demonstrate the positive relationship between a source's potential to influence a client and whether that source is perceived as an attractive or positive (nurturing) source or model.

A number of studies have also investigated the effect of source similarity on patient influence, most of them concluding that a client is likely to comply with a source who he or she feels is similar to him or herself (Hayes, Note 1). Ragaa and Leventhal (1972) found exceptions to this idea in their study. In a 2 x 2 design, pregnant black woman were encouraged to breast-feed and room-in when having their babies by a source who was pregnant and one who was not. Race of the source was also varied, with the source either being black or white. The content of the message given the subjects varied by the inclusion of personal endorsements or merely factual information. Ragaa and Leventhal found that although more women complied when the sources were seen as similar, there was no difference between groups receiving different message content. They went on to examine their findings more closely and raised the point that although more women breast-fed when the source was of a similar race and pregnancy condition, they did not necessarily room-in more when the source was of the same race. Therefore, the relationship between similarity and compliance is probably not a simple one and should be considered with caution.

The variable of credibility has also been investigated. Karlins and Abelson (1970) state, "There will be more opinion change in the desired direction if the communicator has high credibility than if he has low credibility" (p. 108). This conclusion has been upheld in the general literature on influence as well as in the therapy literature (Higbee, 1969; McGuire, 1969). Bandura (1969) has shown that the more prestigious the model, the more likely will be the desired behavior change by the client. However, the way these findings could be used in clinical practice is, as with similarity, not immediately apparent. Most research utilizes attitudinal rather than overt behavioral measures. This weakens confidence in any findings. Strong (1968) notes a second problem: "Few investigators have developed perceived expertness behavior, that is, with communicator rationale and knowledgeable arguments and confidence [being manipulated]" (p. 217). Rather, the method of establishing credibility has been direct (the subject is informed that he or she will like the partner or experimenter in the study) or indirect (the subject is informed of certain characteristics of the source that are assumed to have an effect on credibility), with the occasional use of physical props (such as degrees or journals posted around the room). Thus, although there has been some work on general source characteristics and interpersonal influence, the results must be extrapolated with some caution. Further research is needed in which variables are more clearly specified and results are replicated over time.

Perceiving someone as likeable, similar, or credible may also be related to positive interactions with that person, which in turn can be related to compliance. There is some evidence in the medical literature that supports the notion that the patient is more likely to comply when, in simple terms, the health-care provider and patient get along well. Positive perceptions of the clinic and the friendliness of the therapist have been shown to affect patient compliance (Hagen, Foreyt, & Durham, 1976; Hulka, Zyzanski, Cassel, & Thompson, 1971; Hurtado, Greenlick, & Colombo, 1973; Korsch & Negrete, 1972). In addition to patient-reported perceptions, the frequency of observable positive behaviors in the interview, such as laughter and affective tone, have also been shown to be related to compliance (Davis, 1971; Freemon, Negrete, Davis, & Korsch, 1971; Svarstad, 1974).

Gambrill's (1977) recommendation to start "where the client is" is another method of encouraging positive interactions with the client which may lead to client perceptions of the therapist as likeable and trustworthy. She also recommends structuring client interactions. This practice may convey to the client that the therapist knows why the client is there, has a purpose in mind, and is a highly credible professional.

A final caveat should be added here. Because of variability across experimental situations, some correlational studies have not been able to demonstrate relationships between compliance and the variables just discussed. In any case, the reader should keep in mind that recommendations for influencing the client are based on considerable, but not necessarily consistent, findings. As Garrity (Note 2) states: "No intervention trials have yet attempted to manipulate the affective quality of the clinician-patient interaction to influence compliance" (p.22).

Relevant Homework

In the early stages of the client-therapist relationship, the therapist may choose to give the client homework assignments that may enhance relationship-building. Having the client fill out pretreatment questionnaires and read educational materials are both good assignments for this purpose.

Pretreatment questionnaires, such as Stuart's (1973) Marital Pre-Counseling Inventory, Cautela and Kastenbaum's (1976) Reinforcement Survey Schedule, and problem lists, are typically used to obtain information that may be useful at various stages in therapy. Although these techniques are discussed later, they are mentioned here because they may also be used to enhance the client's perception of the expertise of the therapist. A questionnaire received prior to treatment may help the client feel that the therapist is prepared, organized, and knowledgeable in his or her field.

Literature, tapes, and other educational activities may be seen as forms of "structuring" as described by Goldstein (1975).

> Structuring a client so that he will like or be attracted to his helper is, quite simply, a matter of: (1) telling him that he will like his helper ("direct" structuring), (2) briefly describing to him certain positive characteristics of his helper ("trait"structuring), or (3) clarifying what he may realistically anticipate will go on in his meetings with the helper (role expectancies structuring). Each of these three structuring procedures seeks to mold the client's expectations and feelings about his relationship with his helper. (p.18)

Basically, such literature can inform the client that he or she is likely to be pleased with the therapy and that the therapy has been effective with others. It also shows what is involved in the therapeutic process.

The compliance enhancers discussed in the next chapter should also increase the quality of the client-therapist relationship. For example, learning the client's expectations about treatment, structuring homework around these expectations, and giving assignments that are easy or likely to be completed will increase compliance and the opportunity for the therapist to award praise. Praising the client may then in turn help establish the therapist as a reinforcing stimulus.

The focus in this brief description of relationship-building activities has been on factors that most directly affect liking, trust, and respect in the therapy and therapist. Again, if change is to occur the client must believe in both the therapeutic process and the therapist throughout the treatment, not merely at the beginning of therapy.

PROBLEM SELECTION

The next major phase of the intervention process involves specifying a problem profile and selecting a target problem. This phase can be seen as having three steps: selecting a problem, determining assets and deficits of the client and his or her environment, and forming a hypothesis that will underlie the treatment plan.

Kanfer and Grimm (1977) present five categories of complaints that may serve as examples of the first step. The first category is *behavior deficits*. It includes problems with inadequate knowledge, skill deficits, inadequate self-directing responses, deficiencies in self-reinforcement, deficits in self-monitoring, inability to alter responses in conflict situations, restricted number of reinforcers, and deficits in cognitive or motor behaviors. The therapist may determine which specific areas are problems by thoroughly assessing the client's activities in the outside environment and his or her thoughts or behaviors connected with a particular activity, such as decision making.

The second category, *behavior excesses,* includes problems of inappropriate anxiety and self-observational activity. Understanding the situations in which the client experiences anxiety and engages in self-monitoring are critical to determining this problem.

In the third category, *environmental stimulus control,* the client may show undesirable affective responses, may be in an environment that is not supportive of his or her behavior, or may organize his or her time poorly. Again, knowledge about the client's responses, environment, and potential alternate environments is critical for an adequate assessment of the problem.

The fourth category described by Kanfer and Grimm is *inappropriate self-generated stimulus control* and focuses specifically on problems in self-description that lead to negative outcomes, verbal or symbolic activities that cue inappropriate behavior, or faulty labeling of internal cues. Again, the therapist must have a thorough knowledge of the client's internal responses at the time at which a problem occurs.

The final category covered by Kanfer and Grimm is that of *inappropriate contingency arrangement.* The environment may not support appropriate behavior, it may provide too much reinforcement for desirable behaviors (thus leading to satiation), or it may reinforce inappropriate responses. Here, as in all other areas discussed above, the therapist needs to know such factors as the type, frequency, and timing of reinforcement.

Given this array of potential problems, Gambrill (1977) selects several criteria that aid in selecting a target problem. Her list follows:

1. Annoyance value of the current situation to the client

2. Danger value of the current situation

3. Interference of the current situation in the client's life

4. Likelihood that the outcome will be attained with intervention

5. Centrality of the problem in a complex of problems

6. Accessibility of the problem (Can you get at it?)

7. Potential for change (Can you do something about it; do you have the resources and skills?)

8. Probable cost of intervention (time, money, energy, and resources)

9. Relative frequency, duration, or magnitude of the problem

10. Ethical acceptability of the outcome to the counselor

11. Likelihood that new behaviors will be maintained in the post-intervention environment (p. 140)

After the therapist and client have agreed on a particular problem, they must proceed with the second step — delineating the assets and deficits of both the client and the environment that are important to the treatment process. Key questions here include the following: What skills does the client have that can further the treatment process? What factors in the environment can be used for treatment — for example, who can be enlisted to monitor, cue, or reinforce the client? Finally, the therapist and client should work together, as Gambrill states, to form hypotheses about functional relationships that will serve as the basis for the intervention plan.

Several aspects of the interview situation make it desirable to obtain information that is gathered when the client is in his or her natural environment. In the interview, clients underreport poor compliance and overreport good compliance (Dunbar, Note 3). They often forget information on such parameters as frequency or detail; also, they may be biased by the interview process itself. Finally, they may be affected by the way questions are asked (Thomas, 1973). One source of information that avoids such problems may be the preinterview checklists mentioned in the last section on relationship enhancement. These checklists provide much information that is crucial in the problem selection phase of treatment, such as behaviors to be increased or decreased, situations of relevance, and information on reinforcement.

A client may also be asked to keep ongoing records on relevant thoughts and behaviors and the situations in which they occur. For example, the client may be asked to report on situations that occur before the problem situation or on the response of someone to a particular action of his or hers. The client may also be asked to list information needed for treatment, such as foods currently in the home (in the treatment of obesity).

One useful recording sheet simply consists of a three-column page where clients are asked to record relevant behaviors (actions, thoughts, or feelings), antecedents to the behaviors, and consequences of the behaviors. This sheet is often called the ABC (antecedents, behaviors, consequences) file. As an example of its use, a client may report a problem such as excessive outbursts by his or her son. The assignment in this case might be to ask the client to record under B (behavior) each time a form of the behavior, such as shouting or temper tantrums, occurs. Under A, the client would record what occurred just before the incident and, under C, what occurred just after the incident. A sheet such as this provides information on the type of behavior to be targeted for change, as well as the factors that may be controlling the behavior.

In another example, a client may say that self-critical thoughts are his or her problem. The assignment for this client might be to record under B (behavior) when he or she has such thoughts and what they are about. Under A, the client would record what happened and what he or she thought just before criticizing him or herself and, under C, would record what occurred and what his or her thoughts were immediately following self-criticism.

Information is a major product of these early assessment activities. The therapist learns about the selected problem and discovers directions for potential intervention, and the client assesses what he or she wants out of therapy.

Homework during this phase in effect "trains" the client for important homework that will be assigned later. At this point the client learns that homework is central to therapy, and also learns how to do it.

THERAPEUTIC INTERVENTION

The next phase involves selecting an intervention, then implementing it and monitoring the client's progress. Guidelines are offered regarding the structure of the therapy session during this time.

Step 1 — Selecting an Intervention

As already discussed, the therapist chooses an intervention strategy by determining the variables that cause and are caused by the chosen target problem. (Selection of a strategy should of course be based on the ethical guidelines presented by the Association for Advancement of Behavior Therapy.) Four broad types of intervention that may be selected are (1) giving the client new information, (2) having the client alter his or her physical environment, (3) changing the existing reinforcement, and (4) having the client either learn a new skill or extinguish an old one.

The client may be provided with new information by being given reading materials or audio tapes, asked to attend lectures or movies or watch television programs, or referred to consult with persons whom he or she already respects as expert. Therapists, however, should approach giving clients "self-help" books with caution. Glasgow and Rosen (1978, in press) have carefully reviewed the evidence on the efficacy of self-help behavior therapy manuals and found considerable variability in the manuals and types of target problems that have been studied. In their latest review, they concluded that manuals for fear reduction, weight reduction, physical fitness, child behavior problems, academic performance, and some general problems have been found to be helpful. Self-help manuals in many other areas, such as assertiveness, smoking reduction, and sexual dysfunction, have not been studied adequately to merit their recommendation without caution.

Assignments for changing the physical environment may also be given to the client. For example, the client with weight problems may be asked to buy certain new foods or to remove other foods from the kitchen. For a client who has difficulty sleeping, the assignment may be to sleep in a different room in the house or change the lighting or sound-proofing arrangements in the bedroom.

Changes in reinforcement are given as assignments directly to clients or mediators. These changes may pertain to client behavior skills or thoughts. For example, a client working on a weight reduction program may be assigned to reward him or herself with $1 towards a new smaller-sized garment for every day he or she adhered to the prescribed diet. A client practicing assertiveness may be assigned to give him or herself points on a wrist counter for assertiveness with a coworker.

Finally, although clients may be taught new skills in the intervention setting, the homework activity or practice of these skills is typically a key ingredient in learning the new skill. A client learning to reduce self-criticism may be assigned to write five positive self-statements each evening. A parent wishing to stop a child's whining may be asked to practice praising the child every time he or she speaks normally and ignoring the child when he or she whines during mealtimes.

Step 2 — Monitoring to Determine
Client Progress

Monitoring can be accomplished in several ways, again often with homework assignments.

Dunbar (1979), writing on the assessment of medical compliance, discussed the following ways to measure compliance: (1) clinical outcome, (2) clinician's ratings, (3) self-report, (4) pill counts (permanent product), and (5) direct observation of behaviors. All of these, with the exception of pill counts, would also be appropriate for the nonmedical setting. Pill counts could probably be replaced by a more general "permanent product" measure (to be explained later). A sixth measure — mechanical or electronic devices — can also be added.

Clinical outcome. Weight control is one area where clinical outcome can be used as a measure of progress. Clients typically weigh themselves and/or report in for periodic weighings by the therapist. Dunbar (1979) cautions against the use of weight or any other outcome measure such as this partly because it is based on the assumption that compliance and the measure are directly related. Since individuals respond differently to dieting and exercise, however, the correspondence may be difficult to determine. This problem aside, a biological indicator like weight may not necessarily provide information on whether or not the client has complied with the assignment as given. For example, dramatic weight loss may result from a crash diet rather than a more desirable reduction plan.

Clinician's ratings. Studies have shown that clinicians often overestimate compliance (Caron & Roth, 1968; Gordes & Peterson, 1977; Mushlin & Appel, 1977; Paulson, Krause, & Iber, 1977; Roth & Caron, 1978; Weintraub, Au, & Lasagna, 1973). It may be that they are as prone to mistaken expectations as all other people. They have been working with a client, and they believe themselves to be sympathetic, perceptive people. Expecting them to believe that their clients are noncompliant may be unrealistic.

Self-report. Usually the therapist asks the client to fill out some form of monitoring sheet in the natural environment and to bring it back to the office. Clients may also either be interviewed about the extent of their compliance, or be asked to reconstruct a compliance history by completing a chart in the therapist's office.

Barlow's (Note 4) recommendations on the enhancement of compliance with self-monitoring parallel the present recommendations. They are as follows:

1. The client should be motivated to comply. He or she may be so motivated if he or she is reinforced for accuracy and sees the therapist as a positive stimulus.

2. The client should be able to discriminate the behavior to be recorded and must also understand the monitoring assignment.

3. The therapist should use easy recording procedures. For ease of remembering and simplicity, recording should be done over short spans of time and for relatively simple responses. Self-monitoring should also cost the client little time or trouble.

4. The need for training in self-monitoring should be assessed. If necessary, training should be implemented.

5. Recording should take place as soon as possible before and after the response.

6. Feedback on the accuracy of self-monitoring should be available.

7. Recorders should be aware that accuracy will be checked.

8. The number of behaviors monitored should be gradually increased. Clients should not be asked at first to monitor several different behaviors.

It should be noted here that client self-monitoring of compliance with assignments may increase the rate of compliance (Nelson, 1977).

Thus, self-monitoring may act as a compliance enhancer as well as a progress measurement.

Permanent product. Many times clients are asked to perform actions that, if complied with, would produce a physical change in their world. This change may be called a "permanent product." For example, a depressed client may be instructed to buy a new and long-desired item of clothing, or an obese client may be instructed to rearrange the kitchen. Both of these events would produce a "product" that the therapist could observe and use as a fairly valid measure of compliance.

Direct observation. When practical and ethical considerations permit, the therapist or trained observers can directly observe the client. Of course, the client's behavior in the presence of an observer may not accurately reflect his or her performance in the observer's absence. Furthermore, the therapist using trained observers must take into account all of the recommendations made above, such as training, monitoring, and reinforcing their accurate performance.

If the systematic behavioral assignment involves some kind of skill practice, the therapist may choose to use a simulation situation to determine if the client has mastered the skill. Simulations raise concerns about whether the observed behavior is a valid representation of the behavior in the real world. However, they avoid many of the ethical and practical problems of direct observation in the client's home environment.

Mechanical or electronic devices. Several monitoring devices, such as wrist counters (standard golf game scorers), may be useful aids to treatment (see Haynes, 1978, for information on available methods). Fowler (1977) reported the use of a counting device in an assignment in which an obese client was asked to report the number of swallows of food consumed per day. Numerous other uses for monitoring devices have been tried or could be conceived.

Structure of the Therapy Session during this Phase

The following guidelines may serve as a format for the interaction between the therapist and client.

1. *First part of the session.* The therapist reviews the homework of the previous week, praising successes and discussing problems.

2. *Second part of the session.* Preparation for next week's homework begins. The therapist engages in several compliance-enhancement strategies (to be elaborated on in the next chapter) to increase the likelihood that these assignments will be completed. Most important among these is assuring the client that he or she is able to carry out the assignment. During this part of the session, the therapist should teach the

behavior that is to be enacted in the natural environment. The training might consist of instructions, modeling, guided behavior rehearsal, corrective and reinforcing feedback, and returning to earlier activities if the behavior does not meet the criteria.

3. *Third part of the session.* The therapist should review the assignment for the next week, distribute written material describing the assignment, and obtain a commitment from the client to carry out the new assignment.

MAINTENANCE

The final phase of the treatment process is the maintenance of the changed behavior and the transfer of the therapeutic process to variables occurring naturally in the client's life. Obviously, the extent to which such transfer is needed will depend on how focal the therapist has been throughout the treatment process. For example, treatment that originally relied heavily on training mediators to distribute reinforcement will be less in need of transfer than treatment programs where the therapist was the central distributor of reinforcers.

The basic goal of this phase is for the client to maintain desirable changes that have occurred during the intervention phase. Stokes and Baer (1977) list several specific tactics for generalizing behavior:

1. Look for a response that enters a natural community [those the client normally interacts with]; in particular, teach subjects to cue their potential natural communities to reinforce their desirable behaviors.

2. Keep training more exemplars; in particular, diversify them.

3. Loosen experimental control over the stimuli and responses involved in training; in particular, train different examples concurrently, and vary instructions, S^Ds, social reinforcers, and backup reinforcers.

4. Make unclear the limits of training contingencies; in particular, conceal, when possible, the point at which these contingencies stop operating, possibly by delayed reinforcement.

5. Use stimuli that are likely to be found in generalization settings in training settings as well; in particular, use peers as tutors.

6. Reinforce accurate self-reports of desirable behavior; apply self-recording and self-reinforcement techniques whenever possible.

7. When generalizations occur, reinforce at least some of them at least sometimes, as if "to generalize" were an operant response class. (p. 364)

With maintenance as the goal in therapy, assignments can be designed to rehearse future problem situations, seek out critical problems, learn coping strategies, and prepare for relapse (as in alcoholism or other addictive behaviors).

SUMMARY

This chapter shows how homework fits into the four stages of therapy: relationship building, problem selection, therapeutic intervention, and maintenance. The first section on relationship building is based on a model by Goldstein (1975), in which liking, respect, and trust of the therapist by the client are seen as relationship components essential to bringing about client change. Supporting evidence is given, and the role of homework in developing these three relationship components is discussed.

The problem-selection phase is broken up into three steps: selecting a problem, determining assets and deficits of the client and his or her environment, and forming a hypothesis. Five categories of common problems delineated by Kanfer and Grimm (1977) are set forth. Guidelines for problem selection by Gambrill (1977) are offered, and relevant homework assignments are presented.

Under therapeutic intervention, the selection of an intervention and its implementation and monitoring are described. Four types of intervention are listed: giving the client new information, having the client alter his or her physical environment, changing the existing reinforcement, and having the client either learn a new skill or extinguish an old one. Ways to monitor an intervention suggested by Dunbar (1979) are elaborated upon, which include clinical outcome, clinician's ratings, self-report, pill counts (permanent product), and direct observation of behaviors. A sixth way — mechanical or electronic devices — is also added. The structure of the therapy session during the therapeutic intervention is then outlined.

Maintenance is the final phase of therapy covered. Some tactics for behavior generalization by Stokes and Baer (1977) are given.

Specific ways of enhancing client compliance and their integration into homework assignments will be the subjects of the next chapter.

REFERENCE NOTES

1. Hayes, M. *A study of the relationship between the type of behavior to be modeled and the model's similarity to the observer.* Unpublished manuscript, University of Michigan, 1972.

2. Garrity, T.F. Medical compliance and the clinician-patient relationship: A review. In *Patient compliance to prescribed antihypertensive regimens.* NIH Publication No. 81-2102, October 1980.

3. Dunbar, J.M. Assessment of medication compliance: A review. In *Patient compliance to prescribed antihypertensive regimens.* NIH Publication No. 81-2102, October 1980.

4. Barlow, D.H. *Self-report measures.* Paper presented at the High Blood Pressure Education Program Meeting, New Orleans, 1976.

REFERENCES

Bandura, A. *Principles of behavior modification.* New York: Holt, Rinehart & Winston, 1969.

Bandura, A. Psychotherapy based upon modeling principles. In A.E. Bergin & S.L. Garfield (Eds.), *Handbook of psychotherapy and behavior change.* New York: John Wiley & Sons, 1971.

Bandura, A., & Walters, R.H. *Social learning and personality development.* New York: Holt, Rinehart & Winston, 1963.

Caron, H.S., & Roth, H.P. Patients' cooperation with a medical regimen: Difficulties in identifying the noncooperator. *Journal of the American Medical Association,* 1968, *203,* 120-124.

Cautela, J.R., & Kastenbaum, R.A. Reinforcement survey schedule for use in therapy, training, and research. In E.J. Mash & L.G. Terdal (Eds.), *Behavior therapy assessment: Diagnosis, design, and evaluation.* New York: Springer, 1976.

Davis, M.S. Variations in patients' compliance with doctors' orders: Medical practice and doctor-patient interaction. *Psychiatry in Medicine,* 1971, *2,* 31-54.

Dunbar, J.M. Issues in assessment. In S.J. Cohen (Ed.), *New directions in patient compliance.* Lexington, Mass.: Lexington Books, 1979.

Fowler, R.S. The mouthful diet. In E.E. Abramson (Ed.), *Behavioral programs for the treatment of obesity.* New York: Springer, 1977.

Freemon, B., Negrete, V.F., Davis, M.S., & Korsch, B.M. Gaps in doctor-patient communication: Doctor-patient interaction analysis. *Pediatric Research,* 1971, *5,* 298-311.

Gambrill, E.D. *Behavior modification.* San Francisco: Jossey-Bass, 1977.

Glasgow, R.E., & Rosen, G.M. Behavioral bibliotherapy: A review of self-help behavior therapy manuals. *Psychological Bulletin,* 1978, *85,* 1-23.

Glasgow, R.E., & Rosen, G.M. Self-help behavior therapy manuals: Recent developments and clinical usage. *Clinical Behavior Therapy Review,* in press.

Goldstein, A.P. Relationship-enhancement methods. In F.H. Kanfer & A.P. Goldstein (Eds.), *Helping people change.* Elmsford, N.Y.: Pergamon Press, 1975.

Gordes, E., & Peterson, K. Disulfiram therapy in alcoholism: Patient compliance studies with a urine-detection procedure. *Alcoholism: Clinical and Experimental Research*, 1977, *1*, 213-216.

Hagen, R.L., Foreyt, J.P., & Durham, T.W. The dropout problem: Reducing attrition in obesity research. *Behavior Therapy*, 1976, *7*, 463-471.

Haynes, S.N. *Principles of behavior assessment*. New York: Gardner Press, 1978.

Higbee, K.L. Fifteen years of fear arousal. *Psychological Bulletin*, 1969, *72*, 426-444.

Hulka, B.S., Zyzanski, S.J., Cassel, J.C., & Thompson, S.J. Satisfaction with medical care in a low-income population. *Journal of Chronic Diseases*, 1971, *24*, 661-673.

Hurtado, A.V., Greenlick, M.R., & Colombo, T.J. Determinants of medical care utilization: Failure to keep appointments. *Medical Care*, 1973, *11*, 189-198.

Kanfer, F.H., & Grimm, L.G. Behavioral analysis: Selecting target behaviors in the interview. *Behavior Modification*, 1977, *1*, 7-28.

Karlins, M., & Abelson, H.I. *Persuasion*. New York: Springer, 1970.

Korsch, B.M., & Negrete, V.F. Doctor-patient communication. *Scientific American*, 1972, *227(2)*, 66-74.

Lott, A., & Lott, B. A learning theory approach to interpersonal attitudes. In A. Greenwald, T. Brock, & T.M. Ostrom (Eds.), *Psychological foundations of attitudes*. New York: Academic Press, 1968.

McGuire, W.J. The nature of attitudes and attitude change. In G. Linzey & E. Aronson (Eds.), *The handbook of social psychology* (2nd ed., Vol. 3). Reading, Mass.: Addison-Wesley, 1969.

Mushlin, A.I., & Appel, F.A. Diagnosing potential noncompliance: Physicians' ability in a behavioral dimension of medical care. *Archives of Internal Medicine*, 1977, *137*, 318-321.

Nelson, R.O. Methodological issues in assessment via self-monitoring. In J.D. Cone & R.P. Hawkins (Eds.), *Behavioral assessment: New directions in clinical psychology*. New York: Brunner/Mazel, 1977.

Paulson, S.M., Krause, S., & Iber, F.L. Development and evaluation of a compliance test for patients taking disulfiram. *The Johns Hopkins Medical Journal*, 1977, *141*, 119-125.

Ragaa, J., & Leventhal, H. The influence of communicator-recipient similarity upon the beliefs and behavior of pregnant women. *Journal of Experimental Social Psychology,* 1972, *8,* 289-302.

Roth, H.P., & Caron, H.S. Accuracy of doctors' estimates and patients' statements on adherence for a drug regimen. *Clinical Pharmacology and Therapeutics,* 1978, *23,* 361-370.

Sapolsky, A. Effect of interpersonal relations upon verbal conditioning. *Journal of Abnormal and Social Psychology,* 1960, *60,* 241-256.

Stokes, T.F., & Baer, D.M. An implicit technology of generalization. *Journal of Applied Behavior Analysis,* 1977, *10,* 349-367.

Strong, S.R. Counseling: An interpersonal influence process. *Journal of Counseling Psychology,* 1968, *15,* 215-224.

Stuart, R.B. *Marital pre-counseling inventory.* Champaign, Ill.: Research Press, 1973.

Svarstad, B. The doctor-patient encounter: An observational study of communication and outcome (Doctoral dissertation, University of Wisconsin, 1974). *Dissertation Abstracts International,* 1975, *35,* 6254-A. (University Microfilms No. 74-26, 513).

Thomas, E.J. Bias and therapist influence in behavioral assessment. *Journal of Behavior Therapy and Experimental Psychiatry,* 1973, *4,* 107-111.

Weintraub, M., Au, W., & Lasagna, L. Compliance as a determinant of serum digovin concentration. *Journal of the American Medical Association,* 1973, *224,* 481-485.

CHAPTER 3

Enhancing Compliance with Behavioral Assignments

DEFINITION OF COMPLIANCE

Compliance may be defined as carrying out an assignment in the way described by the assignment giver(s). Ideal compliance would thus mean carrying out the assignment at the time, in the place, and in the manner prescribed.

The word "compliance" was chosen rather than alternatives such as "adherence" or "cooperation" merely to be consistent with much of the literature. It is not meant to imply a particular form of interaction. Indeed, while many may see compliance as a one-way activity, we specifically note in this chapter that one way to increase the likelihood of assignments being completed is for both the therapist *and* the client to be assignment givers. In addition to compliance-enhancement reasons, ethical clinical practice dictates such mutuality. In this context, the definition of compliance may be interpreted to mean the client's carrying out an assignment in the way originally planned, discussed, and agreed upon by both him or herself and the therapist.

THE PROBLEM OF NONCOMPLIANCE

A number of investigators (Dunbar & Stunkard, 1979; Epstein & Masek, 1978; Haynes, Taylor, & Sackett, 1979; Levy & Carter, 1976) have recently recognized noncompliance with assigned therapeutic regimens as one of the most serious problems facing health care professionals, and some professionals consider noncompliance to be the *most* serious problem they have. What can therapists do to anticipate noncompliance, understand its causes, and reduce its occurrence?

Predicting noncompliance is unfortunately not yet possible. However, a few rudimentary guidelines, based solely on clinical observations, can be given here. For example, it has been observed that any condition that interferes with the client's ability to remember, respond to visual cues, and carry out complex behaviors without the active, direct intervention of a professional will seriously interfere with the effectiveness of systematic behavioral assignments. Hence, those who suffer from an active psychotic process, are intellectually retarded, or have brain damage often have trouble complying with assignments.

Another population of clients who may fail to complete homework is those who have "hidden agendas." These clients are often the most frustrating to work with because although they appear to have the necessary skills to successfully complete the home treatment regimens, they will not comply for unexpressed motives (hidden agendas). Clients with hidden agendas based on litigation (such as the client with low back pain who plans to sue his or her former employer for total disability payments) typically torpedo attempts at home treatment. Early determination of these issues will save considerable time.

Researchers are still investigating the many factors that can affect compliance. These factors are probably specific to individuals, situations, and assignments, a specificity which can to some extent explain the often contradictory findings in the compliance literature. Nevertheless, some common reasons for noncompliance and general recommendations for maximizing the possiblity of compliance can be developed. The following modification of a model by Munjack and Ozieo (1978) describes several reasons for noncompliance. The reasons are listed in Table 3.1 along with corresponding compliance enhancers (presented in more detail later) that address these problems.

Reasons for Noncompliance

Following are some of the ways that the three reasons for noncompliance listed in Table 3.1 may manifest themselves.

Type 1: The client lacks the necessary skills and knowledge to complete some or all of the tasks in the assignment. A frequent error

Table 3.1

Reasons for Noncompliance and Recommendations for
Compliance Enhancement

Reasons for Noncompliance	Recommendations for Compliance Enhancement
Type 1: The client lacks the necessary skills and knowledge to complete some or all of the tasks in the assignment.	The therapist should be sure assignments contain specific detail regarding response and stimulus elements relevant to the desired behavior. (Proposition 1)
	The therapist should give direct skill training when necessary. (Proposition 2)
	The therapist should begin with small homework requests and gradually increase assignments. (Proposition 4)
	The therapist should use cognitive rehearsal strategies to improve success with assignments. (Proposition 8)
Type 2: The client has cognitions that interfere with completion of the assignment.	The therapist should have the client make a public commitment to comply. (Proposition 6)
	The therapist should help the client develop a private commitment to comply. (Proposition 7)
	The therapist should try to anticipate and reduce the negative effects of compliance. (Proposition 9)
	The therapist should use paradoxical strategies when necessary. (Proposition 11)
Type 3: The client's environment elicits noncompliance.	Compliance should be reinforced. (Proposition 3)
	The therapist should use cuing. (Proposition 5)
	The therapist should try to anticipate and reduce the negative effects of compliance. (Proposition 9)
	The therapist should closely monitor compliance with as many sources as possible. (Proposition 10)

made by therapists using instigation procedures, or assigned home practice, is to assume that the client has the necessary skills and knowledge to complete the prescribed outside therapeutic assignment. The therapist should *never* make that assumption. A few minutes during the therapy hour can allow the therapist to observe the desired target behavior. If the client has a skill deficit, measures can then be instituted to correct the problem before the client attempts the assignment in his or her natural social environment. Or the therapist may decide to consider a different way of structuring the assignment.

Failure to check for deficits typically retards the pace of successful therapeutic outcomes. In some cases the consequence of not making a skill assessment can even be harmful. The nonassertive client who is told to engage in an activity that he or she is not prepared to handle can experience disastrous consequences. Confronting one's boss in an inappropriate manner, for example, can cost a job. The same is true of the client with social skill problems. Prescribing a homework assignment that involves a 3-hour date with an attractive woman may be beyond the skill level of the socially anxious man and may result in such extreme anxiety as to cause a setback in therapy.

As we have said, some client populations such as brain damaged, retarded, or psychotic persons present the therapist with special problems in planning systematic behavioral assignments. In many cases, it is necessary to program small concrete steps, involve other family members in facilitating homework, and devote much more time to planning prehomework antecedent controlling events than would usually be the case with less difficult populations. In some cases, various intellectual deficits will present such difficulties as to make instigation procedures nearly impossible.

In all cases, the therapist first needs to take a realistic look at the terminal goal and determine if it is appropriate for the client. He or she should then break this goal into steps that can be feasibly attained. These steps become the systematic behavioral assignments.

Type 2: The client has cognitions that interfere with completion of the assignment. The client's cognitive processes can add to or detract from the completion of instigation procedures. Those that create problems may take many forms. For example, certain beliefs regarding the seriousness of the condition, the ability of the therapist to offer effective aid, and the value of the recommended treatment can interfere with the completion of assignments. Clients may consider their psychological condition to be more or less serious. Those who believe that they are "in a bad way" are more likely to comply than those who do not think of themselves as having serious problems. Some clients have experienced many frustrations and failures with therapy. Having had numerous failures, they are skeptical about the ability of the therapist to provide appropriate treatment, and understandably reluctant to engage in directives designed to be carried out at home. Finally, there are those clients who may believe that they are in a serious fix and who trust the therapist, but who doubt the worth of the treatment regimen. Various combinations of these beliefs will greatly increase resistance to prescribed instigation procedures.

The client's expectations of the therapeutic process may also interfere. Many clients expect a relationship with a professional to focus on understanding the causes of target behaviors. Other individuals seek a relationship with the professional in which the therapy relationship is the central focus and all behavior change occurs as a result of open and honest discussion of feelings and thoughts between the two participants.

Some clients have magical expectations. They come to be "treated" by a doctor or a healer who will work some medical, technological, or mystical miracle. These clients are looking for eloquent assurances, pills, or something like laying-on of hands. To them, healing comes from the therapist and occurs during the therapy hour or soon after, and they are the passive recipients. Their only contributions are keeping the appointment, having faith, accepting the cure, and hopefully, paying the fee.

Finally, to many clients homework makes therapy too much work. An hour of work per week is what they seek and no more.

Type 3: The client's environment elicits noncompliance. Noncompliance may be primarily a result of variables in the client's social or physical environment. For example, Fordyce (1976) has shown that pain behavior can be maintained for years by environmental consequences that reinforce its occurrence. In some instances, clients receive a tremendous amount of attention because of their pain and thus are positively reinforced. Even more common is the case where the client is able to avoid some unpleasant duty by having a chronic pain problem, and thus is negatively reinforced for displaying pain behavior. Many other problems are maintained in a similar way. They can be viewed as essentially avoidance behaviors that are maintained by the decrease in anxiety resulting from avoiding stressful situations.

There may also be competing, stronger stimuli which outweigh the client's desire for compliance. Homework may represent a set of behaviors so incompatible with those maintained by the home environment that a therapist's instructions may be insufficient to give the client the control needed. The therapist may therefore have to carefully analyze the client's environment before beginning to identify and plan the homework procedures. Since most new behaviors require a specific set of skills, and a place and a time for their practice, if these are not present, homework may never be attempted.

One good example of competing stimuli is the client's family. Patterson and Gullion (1968) describe some families as having a "diffusion environment." There seems to be little consistency and regularity in the discipline of children: many competing cues and consequences surround behaviors, and behavior is erratic. Such a disorganized family environment may exist in the homes of clients who are unable to do their homework. The major problem with the diffusion environment is the cues, the events that tell the client to engage in the prescribed homework activity. If they are highly visible and specific, the client will probably comply. If, on the other hand, they are invisible or ambiguous, the probability of adherence to the instigation procedure is low. Zifferblatt (1970) notes that cues for compliance must be salient, must have significance for the client, must be compatible with the client's daily routine, must require only a short latency period between the cue and the compliance behavior, and must be clearly related to the behavior in question. Table 3.2 illustrates the relationship between various cue dimensions and the probability of compliance for an instigation procedure involving relaxation practice.

Table 3.2
Various Cue Dimensions and Their Relation to
Probability of Compliance

| Cue Dimension | Probability of Compliance | |
	High	Low
Visibility	Relax as soon as the buzzer sounds.	Have your spouse remind you to relax the night before.
Compatibility	Relax in your office.	Relax when lecturing.
Latency	Relax as soon as the buzzer sounds.	Have your spouse remind you to relax the night before.
Relevance	Relax whenever you feel tense.	Relax whenever you can.

Recommendations for Compliance Enhancement

Following are explanations of the propositions to enhance compliance listed in Table 3.1. Clinicians should view this list of 11 propositions as a checklist of options. However, compliance seems more likely to increase as more of the first 10 propositions are integrated into therapy. The eleventh proposition is particularly useful in situations "when all else fails."

Proposition 1: The therapist should be sure assignments contain specific detail regarding response and stimulus elements relevant to the desired behavior. Depending on the nature of the assignment, messages to clients should specify how, when, for how long, and in what circumstances the behavior is to be performed. Studies in the medical literature show that there is considerable variation in interpretation of instructions regarding timing and sequencing of instructed behaviors (typically medication taking) (Malahy, 1966). For example, in one interesting study (Mazzulo, Lasagna, & Griner, 1974) it was found that patients had very different ideas of what a simple instruction such as "take four times a day" meant. Written instructions specifying in detail the desired behavior may also serve as prompts for action (Leventhal, 1967; Thomas & Carter, 1971) and greatly enhance the likelihood of compliance.

Empirical support for Proposition 1. Understanding of instructions has been shown to be related to compliance (Kincey, Bradshaw, & Ley, 1975; Ley, Jain, & Skilbeck, 1976; Ley, Whitworth, Skilbeck, Woodward, Pinsent, Pike, Clarkson, & Clark, 1976), and a substantial amount of research on compliance with instructions supports the notion that specific instructions are more likely to be followed than those that are less specific (Doster, 1972; Kanfer, Karoly, & Newman, 1974; Liebert, Hanratty, & Hill, 1969; Rappaport, Gross, & Lepper, 1973; Svarstad, 1976). The success of contracting procedures (Steckel & Swain, 1977) may also be taken as evidence of the value of explicitness. To meet all contingencies, contracts require clear and specific descriptions of the required behaviors.

It must be remembered, however, that specificity should not result in making the behavior too complex or too difficult. Haynes et al. (1979) note that more complex and demanding prescriptions are met with greater noncompliance. This is also supported by the research on concept formation (Flanders & Thistlethwaite, 1970). In short, simplicity should not be sacrificed in the search for specificity.

Proposition 2: The therapist should give direct skill training when necessary. As already mentioned, a frequent mistake made by therapists who utilize outside therapeutic home practice is the assumption that the client has the necessary skills to complete the target task. It is therefore wise to practice the target behavior in the consultation office before asking the client to engage in the task in the natural social environment. This practice is particularly recommended in cases where the target behavior is so complex that verbal instructions alone are inadequate, when the client has the necessary skills but is inhibited in performing them because of intense emotional arousal, or when the behavior is likely to be extinguished or punished by target persons involved in the therapeutic homework.

Regardless of which of these reasons prompts the therapist to consider direct skill training, such training should proceed in a systematic manner. Direct skill training involves a chain of events that, depending on the skill level of the client, may need repeating. In its complete form, an instructional chain consists of the following therapist behaviors:

1. The therapist assesses the level of client skills relevant to the upcoming behavioral assignment (skill training is not always necessary).

2. If the decision is made to proceed with skill training, the therapist begins by giving the client verbal and written instructions as well as a rationale for why the target behavior is important.

3. The therapist models the skill.

4. The client then imitates the skill, with coaching, prompting, and reinforcement for approximations toward the desired goal being provided by the therapist.

For example, consider the case of a client who suffered from social inhibition. The therapist's first step was to assess the extent of the skill deficit. A brief period of roleplaying was sufficient to make a quick determination of the client's skill level. In this case, when asked to roleplay the task, the client mumbled his words, spoke very softly, and avoided eye contact. As a result of the assessed social skill deficits, it was decided that a systematic behavioral assignment involving strangers would be potentially punishing. Thus, treatment began with a less risky assignment for the client.

The therapist began with a straightforward skill-shaping routine that consisted of first allowing the client to follow him across campus as he briefly stopped a half-dozen people separately and asked directions to a common landmark. After each interaction, which the client observed, the therapist briefed the client on how the interaction went and which particular behaviors were effective. This entire sequence of social interactions took slightly more than 30 minutes.

Therapist and client then returned to the office and continued to practice the skills just modeled. With the therapist playing the role of the stranger, the client conducted several brief encounters in which he asked questions similar to the ones just observed. The therapist provided immediate feedback and reinforcement for appropriate improvements. This session ended with the systematic behavioral assignment shown in Figure 3.1 (Bob is the client; John is the therapist). As mentioned in

Figure 3.1   First homework assignment for shy client and therapist

Homework for Bob
For 10 minutes each day of the week, stand in front of the mirror and practice the skills we reviewed.

Call for an appointment when you have practiced for 7 days.

Homework for John
Read workbook on shyness for treatment options.

Chapter 1, the therapist's homework is also listed in the assignment as part of this bilateral agreement.

This assignment allowed the client to practice the target skills without the potential threat of interacting with a stranger. The activity was an easy first step, had a very likely outcome of success without any adverse side effects, and was simple in nature. This assignment also illustrates that some form of homework, even if very simple, can always be given during the week.

During the first half of the next session, the therapist and client reviewed the behavioral assignment and briefly practiced the "initiating-conversation-with-a-stranger" task. The second half of the session was spent out of the office, where the client actually interacted with strangers *but* with the therapist present. Feedback and reinforcement from the therapist immediately followed. After the therapist was convinced that the client acquired the necessary skill, the systematic behavioral assignments shown in Figure 3.2 were given. The rest of the treatment progressed in a similar manner. In each case no behavioral assignment was prescribed regarding interaction with others before it was first determined that the client had the necessary skills to proceed.

Empirical support for Proposition 2. A significant body of research has demonstrated that use of participant modeling and behavior rehearsal enhances learning behavior (Bandura, 1969; Lewis, 1974; McFall & Marston, 1970). Feedback and reinforcement during practice sessions may also augment the learning experience (Locke, Cartledge, & Koeppel, 1968; Leitenberg, 1975). In medical programs, supervised practice of assigned tasks also has been used as a compliance enhancer (Bowen, Rich, & Schlatfeldt, 1961).

Figure 3.2   Second homework assignment for shy client and therapist

> **Homework for Bob**
>
> For each day during the week, stop five strangers and ask them for instructions to the Student Union. Be brief, repeat what you have heard, thank them, and leave.
>
> Record the number of daily interactions you have had and the amount of anxiety felt for each.
>
> Call for an appointment when you have talked to 35 people. Call me at home after 7:00 on Thursday for an update.
>
> **Homework for John**
> Be home Thursday after 7:00.

Proposition 3: Compliance should be reinforced. The rate of compliance is influenced by the consequences that immediately follow compliant behavior. Any missed opportunity to reinforce compliance may lead to a decrease in the frequency and duration of home practice activities and an overall reduction in effectiveness.

A number of reinforcement opportunities exist for encouraging the client to adhere to the prescribed task. The sources of reinforcement can be the therapist, the client him or herself, and significant others.

Therapist reinforcement. Since the client may not gain immediate reinforcement from persons in his or her social environment, he or she should always be told in advance that the criterion for success is the execution of the behavior (compliance) and not the outcome of performance. The therapist, at least initially, is frequently the most important source of reinforcement. The therapist should keep a careful record of all prescribed homework assignments so that compliance with these can be reviewed and, if appropriate, rewarded at each contact. By using commercially available NCR (no carbon required) paper, it is simple for the therapist to have an immediate record of the client's assignments. Clients should never have to fish for reinforcement by reminding the therapist of what they were asked to do.

Initially, clients should be reinforced for *all* approximations to desirable compliance efforts. For example, if a client were assigned to keep a daily journal of food consumed for 1 week but completed only 1 day's record, he or she should be reinforced at first for this approximation to carrying out the assignment. Shaping of the client's performance can then be carried out by reinforcing gradually closer approximations to the assignment.

Therapists should also make use of the telephone to deliver reinforcement, either by calling clients or having them call in. Since newly acquired behaviors may be specific to the reinforcers, setting, and discriminative stimuli around which they occur, a telephone call can provide the therapist with an opportunity to provide social reinforcement to the client in a natural setting. Phone calls are also a handy and useful tool when homework may not lead to immediate reinforcement in the environment, as in the case of newly acquired assertive behaviors. In this case the therapist, alert to the possibility that the client may possibly run into trouble because of external variables impossible to predict, such as the boss's reaction to a demand for a raise, may elect to phone the client after the scheduled homework attempt in order to provide support and reinforcement for successive approximations.

Phone calls should be carefully used because some clients may use homework failure as an excuse to obtain more contact with the therapist.

Whenever possible, phone calls should therefore be made at a scheduled time, preferably after completion of a task rather than when there is difficulty in doing the task. Clients can be instructed to call when they finish a difficult assignment, not "whenever the homework doesn't go well." Thus, although problems arising from homework should be understood and empathized with, the emphasis remains on the positive aspects of performance of assigned tasks.

In addition to the therapist's praise, other avenues of therapist-initiated reinforcement exist. A contingency statement in the homework format is one good way of assuring that the homework will be completed, and several contingencies can be designed to increase adherence. Rather than seeing the client on an interval schedule of appointments (for example, Tuesdays at 10:00), the therapist may not schedule the client for the next appointment until he or she calls to say that the behavioral assignment is done. This contingency is based upon four assumptions: clients (1) accept the homework as relevant to their needs, (2) find it manageable in quantity, (3) share enough rapport with the therapist that they will do their homework in order to see him or her again, and (4) are reinforced by the act of calling in (an assigned task, itself).

Such contingencies should be carefully planned so none of these assumptions are violated, or the assignments may not be completed. For example, the act of calling in for an appointment may change from a reinforcing to a punishing experience if the client must always call repeatedly to get through to the therapist. He or she may become frustrated and stop complying altogether. In such cases it might be easier to simply have the client come to the office to sign up for the next appointment after the homework assignment is completed.

Other reinforcement contingencies can also be considered. For example, the therapist may give a money rebate contingent upon the completion of agreed-upon homework. Or he or she can make a regular appointment with a client but reduce the length of the session if the client does not attempt the homework. This latter reinforcement intervention is useful for agency workers who cannot manipulate the fee and also for situations in which the therapist chooses to make some contact with the client, albeit for a short period of time.

Reward structures should be clearly outlined. One way to do this is to use a behavioral contract. Although contracts require time and effort to construct, they can provide the additional structure and contingencies needed to foster the completion of home activities. Behavioral contracts generally emphasize the positive contingencies for achieving compliance with assigned behavioral tasks, and, as stated previously, are particularly useful in helping the client to complete greatly needed behavioral assignments. In addition, they help clarify the consequences of completing the systematic behavioral assignment, and they provide clear-cut criteria for achievement of the stated therapeutic activities.

Behavioral contracts can be unilateral or bilateral. A unilateral contract is one in which the client obligates him or herself to complete the homework and is rewarded for such completion. Bilateral contracts, illustrated in Figures 3.1 (p. 44) and 3.2 (p. 45), specify the obligations and the mutual reinforcements for each of the parties involved. Bilateral contracts for behavioral tasks can be made with family members, spouses, and therapists.

Contracts should be very specific, determined by negotiation, and fully understood and accepted by the client. Successful behavioral contracts should have short-range goals: 2 or 3 weeks between appointments is maximum. To be fully understood, they should be written down, preferably on NCR paper, so that both the therapist and the client have a copy at all times. Again, it is especially important that behaviors specified in the contract be rehearsed before engaging in the assigned task. Great effort should be expended to avoid giving assignments that might be difficult to perform or might be punished by persons associated with the home-practice activity.

Other elements of a successful contract include the following:

1. A very clear and detailed description of the homework should be stated using the standardized homework format listed in Chapter 1 (see Table 1.1).

2. The contract should specify the positive reinforcements gained if the homework is completed.

3. Some provision should be made for some consequence for failure to complete the behavioral assignment within a specified time limit or behavior frequency.

4. The contract should specify the means by which the contracted response is to be observed, measured, and recorded.

5. An arrangement should be made so that the timing for delivery of reinforcement contingencies follows the response as quickly as possible.

The contract shown in Figure 3.3 was devised to implement an outreach program involving systematic behavioral assignments for the treatment of chronic lower back pain. In each case, the specific task, e.g., getting out of the house, was preceded by careful plans regarding where to go, how long to stay, and other details. In some cases, rehearsal was done in the office.

Client reinforcement. Another important source of reinforcement is the client him or herself. Self-reinforcement is vital to the success of

Figure 3.3   A behavioral contract

I agree to do my assigned homework involving (1) walking every morning twice around my block; (2) doing 15 situps; (3) taking the pain cocktail* before going to sleep at night; and (4) getting out of the house at least once per day for a half hour or more. Harold (my husband) will monitor my progress and report it to Dr. Shelton on Mondays and Thursdays. The reward for completing all homework as assigned will involve a choice of the following:

A. Attending a movie
B. Riding in the car for a short drive
C. Having Harold join me for TV†
D. Having Harold give me a back rub †

I get one of these rewards for each day that I complete my homework assignment. This contract will be renegotiated and new homework added in 2 weeks during my next scheduled appointment.

Signature   _____

Signature   _____

_____

*The pain cocktail is a strategy for gradually decreasing the amount of pain narcotic used by chronic pain patients. It is not a standardized commercial commodity that can be purchased, but instead is prepared individually for each patient depending on his or her former drug usage pattern. For more details of the pain cocktail intervention the reader should see Chapter 9.

† These rewards were previously negotiated with Harold, as was his participation in the role of "monitor."

homework and may actually be the key to maintaining therapeutic behaviors after treatment has been terminated. The possibilities are limited only by the collective ingenuity of the therapist and the client.

Conceptually, it is helpful to look at a model first provided by Johnson (1971), in which overt and covert behaviors can be reinforced overtly or covertly. The reinforcement possibilities and contingency relationships generated by this model are extensive. Examples of the practical applications associated with this model are listed in Table 3.3.

Example 1: An assertive response (overt behavior) could be reinforced by a self-administered token that is later redeemed for a ticket to a movie, a play, or a basketball game (overt behavior).

Example 2: An assertive response (overt behavior) is followed by self-praise (covert behavior) such as "I did a beautiful job on that assertive response. Dr. Shelton would be proud of me."

Example 3: A thought such as "I will be successful as long as I concentrate on the task" (covert behavior) could be reinforced by a pleasant activity, such as having a pop or coffee (overt behavior).

Example 4: A thought such as "I am very attractive when I smile" (covert behavior) could be followed by an instance of self-praise (covert

Table 3.3

Four Possible Combinations of Behavior and Consequence Types

Behavior	Consequence
overt	overt
overt	covert
covert	overt
covert	covert

behavior) such as "Keep up the good work of thinking good self-thoughts. It will help prevent depression."

Reinforcement by significant others. Another successful means of insuring adherence to assignments is to involve other significant persons from the client's social environment in prompting, assisting, and reinforcing compliance. These persons often have control over a greater number of more powerful reinforcers than does the therapist. In addition, they are more likely to be near the client when he or she performs the homework, and can observe and reinforce compliance when it occurs. As always when mediators are used, the therapist must be careful to reinforce the mediators for *their* compliance as well.

Several final points need to be made about reinforcement of compliance with homework assignments. As with other tasks, success breeds success. Therapists should therefore ask clients to begin with assignments that are likely to be successful.

The early success notion was investigated during a pilot study by Shelton. He compared the dropout rate for clients with early compliance success to that for clients with early compliance failure. Figure 3.4 shows the results of this pilot study.

The figure reveals that clients whose initial behavioral assignment ends in failure are far more likely to drop out of treatment than those who succeed in their first homework task. Although the number of clients followed was small ($N = 10$) and the number of weeks the clients were followed was short (3 weeks), data suggest that clients who fail are more likely to drop out. Failure may lead to discouragement or reduced expectancy. We cannot, however, rule out the possibility that failure and dropping out may also be an indication of poor effort to begin with. Experimental research will need to address these questions.

The length of time between completing prescribed systematic behavioral assignments and seeing the therapist for review and reinforcement should initially be quite short. The longer the interval between assigned activity and therapist contact, the further away is the opportunity for reinforcement. Exact time recommendations will need to be a matter of clinical judgment. When assignments are to be conducted

Figure 3.4   Dropout rate of clients whose initial assignments end in failure

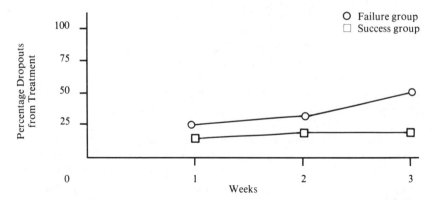

every day (such as in self-monitoring or monitoring a child's or spouse's behavior), some form of initial contact is desirable (for example, a telephone call) 2 or 3 days after the assignment is made. If a "big assignment" such as confronting one's boss is to occur on a given day, the therapist may want to call, or ask the client to call, that day. As therapy progresses, the intervals between reinforcements by the therapist may be extended, since the source of reinforcement is hopefully transferred to the client or his or her environment.

Empirical support for Proposition 3. Justifying the effect of reinforcement seems almost unnecessary. A vast body of literature demonstrates that the systematic application of positive reinforcement can alter behavior in a range of settings to alleviate many problems.

In the area of medical problems, where much of the work on compliance has been done, positive reinforcement has been incorporated into several weight-treatment programs. Mahoney, Moura, and Wade (1973) found that positive reinforcement had more effect than other strategies in their program, and Agras, Barlow, Chapin, Abel, & Leitenberg (1974) showed the power of positive reinforcement in the treatment of anorexia nervosa.

Other compliance-enhancement studies in the medical literature have used positive reinforcement. In a program for an antihypertension regimen, Haynes, Sackett, Gibson, Taylor, Hackett, Roberts, & Johnson (1976) combined positive reinforcement with monitoring, home visiting, and tailoring a regimen to a client's daily activities to increase compliance in medication taking. In dentistry, Reiss, Piotrowski, and Bailey (1976) demonstrated that a monetary incentive increased the number of parents who brought in their children for dental care, and Iwata and Becksfort (Note 1) demonstrated that home dental care improved when monetary reinforcement was used.

Data also exist attesting to the value of a contract technique. Eyberg and Johnson (1974) demonstrated the effect of promising in advance, and delivering contingently, rewards for successful performance. In their study, parents in a family behavior modification program were asked to participate in such contingency contracting to increase completion of weekly assignments. Experimentation in other clinical areas has supported the use of written contracts (Kanfer, Karoly, & Newman, 1974), and many of the positive reinforcement programs in obesity have also been based on a contract structure (Harris & Bruner, 1971; Leon, 1976; Mann, 1972).

Work on systematic behavioral assignments per se has produced some interesting results. For example, in a pilot study to test the effects of verbal reinforcement on homework compliance, Shelton compared compliance rates for six clients who received reinforcement for adherence and six who did not. Figure 3.5 shows the results of this study.

The data illustrated in Figure 3.5 seem to reveal that clients who are asked to engage in simple home practice activities but are not reinforced will gradually decrease the extent to which they adhere to prescribed activities. The group that was reinforced for complying with task assignments completed more and more of the assigned activities as time passed. After 7 weeks the positive reinforcement group was completing three times the number of assignments as those completed by the nonreinforcement group. In an effort to control differences in assignment difficulty, prescribed tasks were deliberately set well within the

Figure 3.5   Psychological assignments completed

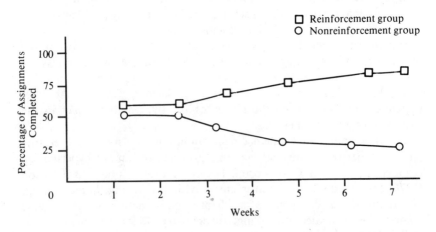

ability level of each client. In every instance, clients rehearsed their homework in the therapist's office before attempting it. As is always the case, each client could veto any assignment that seemed too difficult.

Many studies (Becker & Green, 1975; Blackwell, 1979; Brownlee, 1978; Christensen, 1978; Stokols, 1975; Stuart & Davis, 1972) report that mediators from the client's natural environment are important in both monitoring (see Proposition 10) and delivering reinforcement. Several studies also demonstrate a relationship between social support and compliance (Caplan, Robinson, French, Caldwell, & Shinn, 1976; Earp & Ory, 1979; Haynes, 1976; Kar, 1977; Mahoney & Mahoney, 1976; Nessman, Carnahan, & Nugent, in press).

Experimental data are available as well. In two reports on a weight reduction program and its follow-up results, Israel and Saccone (1979) and Saccone and Israel (1978) found that monetary reinforcement by spouses was the most effective incentive for producing and maintaining weight loss. Zitter and Freemouw (1978) investigated whether individuals complied more when they themselves received a reward, or when they saw that someone else suffered by their noncompliance. In this experiment, subjects in one group lost money if their partner did not lose weight. Partners were friends chosen by the clients. Interestingly, weight was kept off more in the individual than in the partner-consequated condition. The authors suggest that partners may have reinforced client noncompliance.

Environmental mediators have been used in several nonobesity programs as well. Dapcich-Miura and Hovell (1979) used a multiple baseline/reversal single-subject experimental design to demonstrate that a token reinforcement contingency administered by a subject's grand-daughter could be used to increase juice and medication consumption and walking. Tokens were redeemable for the subject's dinner selection. Lowe and Lutzker (1979) also used a multiple baseline design to demonstrate that a point system with backup reinforcers could be effective in motivating a 9-year-old female diabetic to comply with dieting, urine-testing, and foot-care regimens. The child's mother both monitored compliance and delivered prompts and reinforcement.

In another study, Brownell, Heckerman, Westlake, Hayes, and Monti (1978) compared three groups in couples training for weight reduction. Twenty-nine subjects with cooperative spouses were placed in either a couples-training group or a contrast group where spouses did not receive training. Subjects with an uncooperative spouse were placed in another contrast group where the subjects received training but the spouses did not. These two contrast groups provided controls for possible confounding due to spouse cooperation. Spouses were present at all meetings in the training condition and were given the *Partner's Weight Reduction Manual* (Brownell, Note 2). They also were instructed in specific behaviors such as reinforcement, mutual monitoring, and stimulus control. At a 10-week, posttreatment measurement time, subjects in the couples-training group did significantly better than the subjects in the two contrast groups, both in weight loss and change in percentage overweight.

This study had two strengths. First, the author standardized the significant other (the spouse). Second, this study provided the couples with several behavioral suggestions and a monitoring system that the experimenter could use to determine if the suggestions were met.

Unfortunately, in another study, Wilson and Brownell (1978) failed to obtain similar findings. Overweight women with cooperative family members were randomly assigned conditions in which the family member was either present in treatment sessions or not present. Out of 32 cases, all but 3 of the family members were again spouses. The goal of having family members present was to:

1. Acquaint them with the principles of behavior change. . .;

2. Instruct them to cease criticizing their partner's weight and/or eating behavior;

3. Teach them to provide positive reinforcement for improved eating habits; and

4. Provide assistance in their partner's attempts to monitor eating activities and restrict some of the conditions and consequences of eating. (p. 944)

No differences in weight loss between groups were found when the partner was present or absent.

Proposition 4: The therapist should begin with small homework requests and gradually increase assignments. Closely related to Proposition 3, this technique is sometimes referred to as "the-foot-in-the-door" technique. Clients are first asked to comply with a small request. If the request is complied with and reinforced, they are then more likely to comply with a subsequent larger task.

This technique may succeed in part because it provides for the use of some of the other compliance enhancers mentioned earlier. For example, adherence to the first task can be reinforced, thereby increasing the likelihood of subsequent compliance and making the therapist a potential source of positive reinforcement.

Some examples of first behavioral assignments appear in Figure 3.6. Note that all are in the bilateral agreement form discussed earlier.

It is important for the reader to note that in each case the beginning behavioral assignment was simple and required relatively little effort on the part of the client. Each assignment was carefully planned to be within the client's skill repertoire. When possible, other persons were included in the therapeutic homework, because close supervision improves self-observation recording and often enhances compliance with the prescribed activity. Each behavioral assignment was written on NCR paper, with the original for the client and a copy for the therapist.

Empirical support for Proposition 4. Techniques of minimal initial demands that gradually increase over time have found some support in the literature on attitude change, and three experiments have strongly supported the effectiveness of the "foot-in-the-door" effect. In two experiments, Freedman and Fraser (1966) showed that suburban housewives were more likely to submit to a major request (such as allowing a large unattractive billboard to be placed on their front lawn, or allowing a survey team to enter their homes and catalog their household products) if they had first complied with a simple request like signing an innocuous petition, answering a few survey questions, or placing a sign in their window supporting safe driving or a beautiful California. In a later

Figure 3.6   Examples of initial behavioral assignments

For Depression

Homework for Jim
With your wife, take 30 minutes once during the next week and list five ways you used to spend your leisure time.
Bring your list next Thursday at 3:00.
Homework for John
Reread paper on depression.

For Sexual Dysfunction

Homework for Bud
During one occasion with Grace, take 60 minutes and listen to sexual satisfaction tape. Record your feelings, call for appointment when done, and bring your list.
Homework for John
Obtain sexual anatomy diagram for the next session.

For Anxiety Management

Homework for Cynthia
Take 30 minutes a day prior to bedtime and read assigned book on relaxation. Practice exercises in book as needed. Write down questions or interesting points and call for appointment.
Bring your list.
Homework for John
Dub relaxation tape.

For Chronic Pain

Homework for Dan
Ride fixed bicycle for .10 of a mile once daily. *Do not* exceed this amount. Record progress and bring back to 3/14/81 session. $5 subtracted from bill for following agreed-upon instructions.
Homework for John
Call Dan to check progress.

study, Lepper (1973) helped extend the generality of this effect in an experiment on the resistance to temptation of second-grade children. As predicted, children who resisted the temptation to play with an attractive toy under minimal-threat conditions tended to resist the temptation to cheat in a game played 3 weeks later more than children who were not exposed to the initial situation or who were exposed to it under high-threat conditions. Lepper stresses the importance of the initial compliance being obtained under relatively low demand conditions. Minimal initial demand may be related to one of the processes involved in creating cognitive commitment (see Proposition 7). If the client is an active participant in determining the therapeutic activities rather than a respondent to heavy demands from the therapist, the chances for compliance are increased.

Proposition 5: The therapist should use cuing. The therapist should take steps to insure that the client is reminded, cued, or prompted to carry out an assignment at the appropriate time and place. One cue to assignment compliance that can be carried into the natural environment is the client's copy of the written assignments (mentioned in Proposition 1). Clients should be encouraged to place this in a convenient and visible location. Phone calls by the therapist, in addition to being reinforcers, may also be used to remind and prompt the client. Significant others can be helpful here by providing needed reminders at appropriate times. Finally, various devices and other forms of environmental manipulation have been used as aids to compliance, including timed buzzers, calendars, and dated pill dispensers. A systematic behavioral assignment illustrating the use of cuing as a compliance enhancer can be seen in Figure 3.7.

Empirical Support for Proposition 5. In studies in the medical literature, patients frequently report "forgetting" as a reason for noncompliance (Alpert, 1964; Badgley & Furnal, 1961; Harfouche, Abi-Yaghi, Melidossian, & Azouri, 1973). Some experimental studies have tested the effects of reminders on appointment keeping. Shepard and Moseley (1976) and Gates and Colborn (1976) compared compliance rates for subjects who received mail or phone reminders to compliance rates for those who received no reminders. Both types of reminders significantly improved the appointment-keeping rates for these subjects over the rates for subjects in the control condition.

Finer discriminations on the type of cues and the effect of cuing over time have also been made. Nazarian, Machuber, Charney, and Coulter (1974) compared the effect of two types of reminder cards on appointment keeping. Both cards indicated the date and time of the appointment, and one card also noted the physician or nurse and the

Figure 3.7   Example of a behavioral assignment using cuing

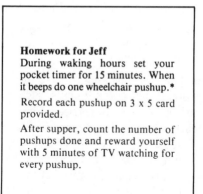

> **Homework for Jeff**
> During waking hours set your pocket timer for 15 minutes. When it beeps do one wheelchair pushup.*
> Record each pushup on 3 x 5 card provided.
> After supper, count the number of pushups done and reward yourself with 5 minutes of TV watching for every pushup.

---

*Severe skin ulcers can occur when wheelchair patients do not occasionally reduce the pressure due to sitting for hours on end. In some cases, such ulcers can become life-threatening; pushups are, therefore, important to the patient's health.

reason for the appointment. No difference in compliance was found when one or the other type of card was used. However, both groups receiving cards had a significantly higher appointment-keeping rate than the control group.

Also interesting was the indication that the reminders seemed to have a greater effect as the interval between appointments increased. The smallest appointment interval in this study was 12 days. Adding to this the study by Levy and Claravall (1977), who tested the effect of reminders on patients with between-appointment intervals of as low as 3 days, it is possible to compare the effect of reminders with a wide range of interval periods. In the Levy and Claravall study, reminders had a significant effect on patients whose appointments were more than 2 weeks apart, but no significant effect on patients whose appointments were scheduled within a 2-week period.

Further research is needed on the many parameters that will influence the effectiveness of a cue on compliance. For example, we do not know what the optimal interval is between when a reminder is delivered and when compliance is to occur, or how the content of a reminder could influence compliance. Some studies have failed to show that reminders enhance appointment-keeping rates (Barkin & Duncan, 1975; Kidd & Euphrat, 1971; Krause, 1966). In a review of this literature, Frankel and Hovell (1978) suggest that the negative results may be due to variations in the clinics or in the selection of patients to be reminded (for example, Kidd and Euphrat, 1971, only looked at subjects who had previously failed).

In conclusion, therapists should carefully consider how reminder procedures are implemented and whether they are relevant for their clients. For example, mailed reminders may not reach intended clients if the population is mobile.

Proposition 6: The therapist should have the client make a public commitment to comply. Public commitments, such as verbalizations of a concrete plan, can serve two purposes. First, they can provide considerable evidence on how someone intends to behave. Such information can provide a basis for further discussion if it appears that the client may not intend to adhere to prescribed behavioral assignments. One of the best ways to predict compliance behavior is to simply ask the client whether or not he or she intends to comply with the intended assigned outside activity. A question from the therapist such as "What is it you are going to do?" can provide a final check as to whether or not the client is willing to adhere to the assignment. The therapist may also ask for specifics such as frequency and duration.

An overt, publicly given commitment may also serve to enhance the likelihood of compliance. In many situations such a commitment, if given verbally and written down, is sufficient to insure completion of systematic behavioral assignments. However, despite assurance from the client that he or she intends to comply with the stated assignment, the therapist may doubt the accuracy of the prediction. In some cases, the client may have repeatedly promised to complete the assignment only to not follow through. Further intervention may be needed, such as appointments contingent on compliance.

Empirical support for Proposition 6. Concerned with low correlations between standard attitude measures and external behaviors, social psychologists have turned to alternative ways of measuring attitude change. Although there is no pervasive consensus, convergence on one simple idea has emerged: if we want to know how an individual may perform in a specific situation, we can ask him or her. In the literature on attitude change, this has come to be known as the elicitation of a behavior intention (BI).

Evidence is accumulating that by focusing on BI as opposed to more global attitude measures, correlations between verbal behavior in an assessment situation and external behavior in another situation can be appreciably strengthened. A number of studies provide convergent confirmation for this view (Ajzen, 1971; Ajzen & Fishbein, 1970; Fendrich, 1967; Kothandapani, 1971; Ostrom, 1969; Wicker, 1971). By asking subjects what they will probably do in a performance situation, one is obtaining specific information in the inquiry situation (Fendrich, 1967). Further, by asking specific questions about kinds of external performance situations, one provides the subject with concrete detail that he or she can use in providing a more accurate response.

There is also some reason to expect that the verbalization of an intention may alter compliance — in other words, that BI may be linked to the simple concept of social commitment. Kothandapani (1971) suggests, "When a person agrees with an intention-to-act statement, he, in effect, is committed to act in a specific manner. Such a commitment to action cannot be confidently inferred from a person's agreement with belief and feeling statements" (p. 332). Similar thoughts are expressed by Fendrich (1967) and Greenwald (1965). This concept also can be found in Kanfer and Karoly's (1972) idea that intention statements may play a crucial role in response execution. Indeed, another reason for the effect of contracts (Propositions 1 and 4) may be that they provide an opportunity for an explicit intention statement.

Levy has conducted a series of experiments to test the effect of public commitment on compliance. In the first (Levy, 1977), clients in an outpatient behavior therapy setting were asked to phone the therapist in a few days to set up a subsequent appointment. Subjects in a "verbal commitment" experimental condition were given the assignment and asked if they would comply. In addition to asking for a verbal commitment (or a head nod) to indicate intended compliance, subjects in a second experimental condition — the "verbal and written commitment" group — were also asked to sign a form indicating that they would comply. Subjects in the control condition were merely given the assignment. Subjects complied more in the commitment conditions than the control condition, with the highest compliance rates in the verbal and written commitment condition. In a second study (Levy, Yamashita, & Pow, 1979), patients reporting for a flu inoculation were asked to return a postcard within 48 hours that indicated whether they were experiencing any symptoms. Experimental subjects again were asked to verbally (or by nodding) indicate their intention to comply. Again, experimental subjects returned more cards and at a faster rate than control subjects.

In a final study (Levy & Clark, 1980), however, the effect of a public commitment was not replicated. Subjects given a reappointment time and randomly placed in a commitment experimental or a no-commitment control condition were compared on appointment keeping rates. No differences between the experimental and control conditions were found.

Replicating the series of studies by Levy and her colleagues, Wurtele, Galanos, and Roberts (1980) also found that both verbal and verbal plus written commitment conditions were positively associated with compliance. Patient return rate for a skintest reading during a TB detection drive was the major dependent variable.

This series seems to be weighted in favor of the positive effects of eliciting a public commitment from clients. Further research will be needed to specify the parameters — such as the type of assignment, the setting, and the client population — where this compliance enhancer is most effective.

Proposition 7: The therapist should help the client develop a private commitment to comply. This proposition actually covers a class of recommendations. Other ways writers have phrased it is that the client should "want" to carry out the assignment, the client should be motivated, and the client should believe in the assignment and the therapeutic intervention. Simply put, the client must believe in the value of the assignment in treating his or her problem.

First the client needs to have a belief structure that supports the task. He or she must believe that the assigned task is useful, that it is acceptable to others, that it has a high degree of successful completion, and that the entire treatment program is valuable. Therapists should take considerable time to elicit the client's beliefs, fears, and expectations regarding compliance. Question-asking should be encouraged, and good rapport, as always, is critical. After giving any assignment, the client should be questioned regarding his or her reaction to the assignment. This intensive discussion will also provide the opportunity to further enact other enhancers, such as more intensive direct training, if needed. Well-chosen bibliotherapy regarding the benefits of treatment or the evils of the client's problem may alter beliefs. In addition, some people benefit immensely from listening to audio cassettes designed especially for therapy clients.

Therapists should also consider that when clients experience problems large enough to bring them into therapy, they have probably already tried a number of remedies related to their particular problem. In many cases, the spouse, friends, or relatives may have offered suggestions and advice; in other instances, the clients may have sought relief from other professionals. However, to some extent the previous interventions have fallen short of meeting their needs or they wouldn't be seeking the services of a professional. Thus, the therapist who replicates earlier approaches will likely foster client thoughts such as "I have tried this before and it didn't work. Why should it work now?" These thoughts will, in turn, lead to lack of cooperation.

One approach for this type of low expectation begins in the office during the first or second visit. The therapist asks, "Could you please tell me what things you have tried that were unsuccessful?'' This will enable the therapist and client to pinpoint previously attempted procedures that failed, and assess reasons for these failures. The detailed information is crucial in planning which intervention to implement with the client. In addition, having the client speak about previously tried procedures may give the therapist information about the client's likelihood of compliance with new assignments.

Second, clients should be prepared for potential problems. They may have early negative reactions or evaluations to systematic behavioral assignments. By pointing out those reactions in advance, the therapist may demonstrate his or her empathy and competence. For example, the therapist might say, "You will probably find this assignment difficult" or "I suspect you are thinking, 'This homework is superficial and misses my real problems.' " If the client does have difficulty with the prescribed homework, then the therapist's prediction reduces the possibility that the client will use the difficulty as an excuse for not completing the assignment. Once a negative reaction on the part of the client has been recognized, the therapist then, of course, needs to pursue the nature of the difficulty. If the client discusses obstacles, the therapist may be able to suggest how these problems can be overcome. If the client says, "I feel this is silly because. . .," the therapist may be able to explain why the assignment was given and how assignment completion will work, report successes with other clients, or give other encouragement. Saying the homework will be difficult may also function in a paradoxical intention way (see Proposition 11), as the client may choose to prove the therapist wrong by not finding the homework difficult at all.

Therapists may also find it useful to predict other problems. For example, when working with the parents of a spoiled, uncooperative child, the therapist might note that the parents have used sporadic extinction and punishment in their earlier attempts to control the child's behavior. Knowing that the child is on a variable ratio schedule of reinforcement allows the therapist to predict the extinction curve of the target behavior. In short, the therapist can predict that the child's noncooperative behavior will get substantially worse before it gets better, especially for the 2 or 3 days following the implementation of the project. The therapist thus prepares the parents for the worsening effects of treatment and decreases the chance that they will discontinue treatment because the child's inappropriate behavior temporarily becomes more intense. Ironically, if the child's behavior worsens in line with the therapist's prediction, this change will only demonstrate that the treatment plan is working and will enhance the parent's perception of therapist credibility. If the prediction is wrong and the parents are imme- diately successful with the intervention, then both parties profit.

As mentioned earlier, clients have often previously undergone treatment procedures that failed and may understandably feel wary about committing themselves to such procedures if they are again proposed by the therapist. By carefully paying attention to what procedures have been unsuccessfully used before, the therapist can avoid using those procedures in the new intervention. It is probably best to choose a new intervention that is easily distinguishable from the old one, since the more similar the new and old approaches are, the more likely the client is to resist commitment. However, if a previously tried intervention still has merit, the therapist should show the client the critical elements left out of the previous attempt and reassure the client that these elements will be used in the new presentation of the procedure.

A final recommendation within this proposition is that clients should also help select homework assignments. Rather than just hand out assignments, therapists should work with clients to develop assignments, perhaps using phrases such as "Now, what do you think is a good way to keep track of ...?" Or the therapist may offer a range of assignments from which the client can choose.

Two important results may occur. First, clients should have an increased perception of control. No one is *making* them do this — they have chosen to do the assignment, and are thus more likely to follow through. (Cognitive dissonance may also be put to use here. A client may think, upon hesitation on doing an assignment, "Well, I thought once I could do this. Maybe I can.") Second, clients will have selected assignments that they can imagine occurring in *their own* world. This fact reduces the possibility that, after reflecting on an assignment, a client will think, "He (or she) doesn't really know how difficult it would be to do that," and then not comply.

Empirical support for Proposition 7. The Health Belief Model, developed early by Rosenstock (1966), outlines several areas of patient beliefs that are believed to be important in increasing compliance with medical regimens (Becker & Maiman, 1975; Maiman & Becker, 1974; Maiman, Becker, Kirscht, Haefner, & Drachman, 1977). Several studies have demonstrated relationships between health beliefs and medical compliance, and much of this information would be useful for extrapolation to the therapy situation. Included in health beliefs are perceptions about one's own sense of control, the priority one puts on health in one's life, the perceived severity of the illness, and the cues for action that are available to the client. Again, although several studies support the Health Belief Model, a large number have not found relationships between compliance and health beliefs (Haynes et al., 1979). Variation across situations may be a critical factor here.

Several writers in the behavior therapy literature have discussed the role of expectation in treatment (Wilson & Evans, 1972). Expectation, as these authors point out, may bridge the gap between present difficult tasks and ultimate success. It may also help keep clients in treatment. Finally, treatment that is inconsistent with a client's expectations of it may result in reduced compliance (Davis, 1968; Francis, Korsch, & Morris, 1969).

Some studies have supported the value of client participation in decision making. Kanfer and Grimm (1978) found that subjects who were given a choice of several behavioral methods designed to increase reading performance did significantly better than those who had no choice. Lovitt and Curtiss (1969) found that children showed higher rates of academic behaviors such as studying when they were allowed to participate in their own treatment plan. A similar study by Brigham and Bushell (Note 3) revealed that children would work to earn control over their own rewards. In this particular study, the authors found that individual response rates were higher even when the self-imposed reinforcement conditions were identical to those imposed by a teacher. Likewise, Phillips (1966) was able to demonstrate that clients who helped in the design of their own treatment were more motivated to change.

Schulman (1979) developed a measure of Active Patient Orientation (APO) that determined the extent to which patients perceived themselves to be "addressed as active participants, involved in therapeutic planning and equipped to carry out self-care activities" (p. 278). High APO was associated with greater blood pressure control, adherence, and understanding, and fewer medication errors. Since contracts, discussed in Proposition 3 (pp. 47-48) as a tool for establishing a contingency relationship, may also be effective because they give patients an opportunity to discuss treatment options and participate in treatment decisions, it is not surprising that patients assigned to a contracting group in a larger study showed higher APO scores.

Proposition 8: The therapist should use cognitive rehearsal strategies to improve success with assignments. The efficacy of cognitive strategies for enhancing human performance is now well supported in the research literature (Mahoney, 1977). Numerous research studies have been published that demonstrate the positive impact of cognitive-behavioral interventions on clinical problems ranging from the treatment of depression and pain to enhancing athletic performance. Several different procedures surrounding the theme of controlling or modifying cognitions have been developed and assessed. For example, Beck (1976), Cautela (1971), Ellis (1962), Lazarus (1976), Meichenbaum (1977),

Suinn (1972a, 1972b), and Turk (1977) have all produced procedures that have been proven to be very useful clinically. However, two of the procedures just listed are particularly effective in enabling the client to rehearse a homework assignment prior to engaging in it. These procedures are Suinn's (1972a, 1972b) Visual Motor Behavior Rehearsal and Meichenbaum's (1977) Self-Instructional Training.

With Suinn's (1972a, 1972b) approach, the client is asked to carry out a specific cognitive strategy just before engaging in a self-directed behavioral assignment. This procedure asks the client to:

RELAX
VISUALIZE (the successful completion of the assignment)
DO (the behavioral assignment)

For example, the client who is fearful of failure in some athletic event would be asked to first relax immediately before the event, then visualize being successful in the event, and then do, or initiate, the athletic response.

Meichenbaum's (1977) Self-Instructional Training approach is considerably more complex than that just discussed, and it has shown a great deal of merit. His approach is essentially based on the premise that individuals fail to perform well because they do not concentrate on the task at hand. Thus, the preorgasmic woman may not experience an orgasm because she worries about an upcoming exam instead of paying attention to the physical sensations occurring as a result of coitus. The student with "test anxiety" may do poorly on tests when he focuses on the consequences of not doing well rather than the task at hand. And, more to the point, systematic behavioral assignments are likely to fail if the client is unable to focus on what he or she is supposed to do.

Meichenbaum's approach is designed to teach clients to focus on the assigned target task. The strategy consists of the following:

1. *Preparing for a stressor.* In this first step the client is urged to prepare a "game plan" for later anticipated anxiety and inability to focus on the assigned task, e.g., taking an exam. The client might, for example, rehearse the more frequent distractors likely to be faced when the stress mounts. The client would then remind him or herself what he or she plans to do when the distractors occur, e.g., "I must remember to read the directions twice and do the easiest questions first."

2. *Confronting the stressor.* In this second phase, the client actually activates the coping strategies rehearsed earlier. Cues such as written notes can be used as reminders of what self-control interventions to employ during the stressful time. Self-statements such as "Don't worry about the clock; just concentrate on the exam" and "Don't worry if they are already finishing; that doesn't mean they have done well" may be

useful. Virtually any self-statement can be made during the course of stressful homework that can enhance performance.

3. *Reinforcing self-statements.* This third step requires the client to reinforce him or herself for the successful completion of homework. The importance of this tactic can be overlooked until one realizes that some clients have a tendency to focus on the relatively poor aspects of their homework performance instead of giving themselves credit for progress.

Empirical support for Proposition 8. Several studies have shown the worth of using cognitive rehearsal to improve targeted behaviors. In one study Nesse and Nelson (1977) utilized between-session rehearsals of covert modeling scenes to examine the effectiveness of several variations of covert modeling on cigarette smoking reduction. In covert modeling the client is asked to imagine a competent model engaging in the behaviors he or she wishes to develop. In this particular study subjects were asked to imagine themselves feeling an urge to smoke, making an alternative nonsmoking response, and then receiving a favorable consequence for not smoking. This study found that covert rehearsal combined with self-reinforcement was more effective than covert rehearsal alone in reducing cigarette smoking.

During the 12th Winter Olympics, Suinn (1977) worked with the athletes of the United States' cross-country skiing and biathlon teams. Suinn developed a package composed of his Visual Motor Behavior Rehearsal, thought stopping, and covert positive reinforcement to counteract pain sensations. The athletes' self-report indicated that this behavioral-cognitive treatment package improved their performance. Interestingly, one of the skiers won a silver medal, the first medal won by an American in Nordic racing. However, because of the lack of objective controls, the conclusions of this research should be taken as suggestive rather than definite.

Other research articles have confirmed the importance of using covert rehearsal as a means of enhancing subject behaviors outside the therapeutic hour. For example, this technique has been shown to be effective in reducing fear (Cautela, Flannery, & Hanley, 1974; Kazdin, 1973, 1974a, 1974b, 1974c), in increasing assertive behavior (Kazdin, 1974d, 1975, 1976a, 1976b), and in decreasing alcoholic and obsessive-compulsive behavior (Hay, Hay, & Nelson, 1977).

Proposition 9. The therapist should try to anticipate and reduce the negative effects of compliance. Efforts should be made to anticipate barriers to compliance in the natural environment and facilitate the integration of the assignment into the client's normal activities. In behavioral terms, the response cost for compliance should not be high.

Thus, problems in areas such as transportation and finances should be anticipated and worked out in advance. Minimal disruption in normal activities should be the goal in planning assignments.

With some assignments, there is the very real possibility that compliance may initially be punished by persons or events in the natural environment. This is true of almost any treatment in which the client is assigned practice activities involving other human beings. Because of the unpredictability of others, one can never be sure when an assignment may backfire.

The problem of how to control others' responses is difficult. Some work, such as that done by Pendleton, Shelton, and Wilson (1976), has attempted to overcome the problem by "programming" trained targets in the client's social environment. Similar work has been done by Christensen, Arkowitz, and Anderson (1975). But despite efforts to train confederates or others in the client's environment to interact with the clients, most therapists must face the fact that they cannot control the responses of others to their clients' homework-related behavior.

Although the therapist using a systematic behavioral assignment approach cannot control the consequences that may befall the client when conducting a homework assignment, he or she can take precautions to minimize problems. First and foremost, the therapist can reduce potential difficulties by carefully planning the behavioral assignment. There is no substitute for caution when prescribing therapeutic outside activities. When designing homework, the therapist should always take time to run through the whole sequence in a "cognitive rehearsal," search for possible negative consequences or obstacles, and then alter the plan to avoid or handle them. He or she should integrate prescribed behavioral assignments carefully into the treatment program and be careful about tacking on an assignment hurriedly at the end of the hour without carefully thinking through all its implications. About three or four assignments should be planned at a time so that the therapist knows in advance what next week's assignment will be (assuming that last week's activities went according to plan).

The potential for problems is increased if the client does not have the skills to do the prescribed assignment. The therapist can decrease the likelihood of adverse consequences by engaging in skill training before the prescribed activity. (Skill enhancement was discussed earlier under Proposition 2.)

Another measure that can forestall punishment for compliance is having the therapist accompany the client on difficult assignments, such as those where there is a lack of environmental reinforcement. Therapist coparticipation in assignments with the client provides support and may allow the therapist to model behavior that the client can then imitate outside the therapist's presence. An example is a therapist teaching a parent techniques to manage a child's temper tantrums. A home visit, with the therapist modeling management techniques for the parent, will lessen the potential for punishment when the parent tries out these same techniques with the child.

When the therapist cannot accompany the client, he or she may wish to prepare the client for occasional failure by rehearsing cognitive strategies designed to remove the sting from negative responses to homework compliance. Thinking reassuring cognitions such as "What counts is that I complete the assignment, not the response I get" is a coping strategy that can be rehearsed in the therapist's office prior to homework attempts. In a situation where the assignment is to ask a coworker to share a coffee break, the client may then be able to reinforce him or herself by thinking, "What is important is that I *ask,* not whether he (or she) says yes or no."

Another useful safeguard is to arrange for the client to call the therapist after each assignment or whenever a problem is encountered (also discussed under Proposition 3). Again, one must be cautious not to establish a contingency that encourages reports of disaster in order to gain access to the therapist's support and care. The client should not develop a pattern of calling the therapist for each failure.

An example of an assignment for a client in a potentially punishing situation appears in Figure 3.8.

Figure 3.8   Example of a potentially punishing behavioral assignment

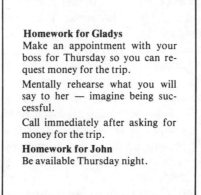

> **Homework for Gladys**
> Make an appointment with your boss for Thursday so you can request money for the trip.
>
> Mentally rehearse what you will say to her — imagine being successful.
>
> Call immediately after asking for money for the trip.
>
> **Homework for John**
> Be available Thursday night.

Empirical Support for Proposition 9. The basis for this proposition is actually derived primarily from client self-report data. Clients have given various barriers to compliance as reasons for not complying. These barriers include finances (Alpert, 1964; Caldwell, Cobb, Dowling, & DeJongh, 1970), transportation (Abernathy, 1976; Alpert, 1964), and employment (Abernathy, 1976). However, experimental data to support these reasons have been less than overwhelming. For example, Sackett et al. found no increase in compliance by locating client treatment centers on the worksite as opposed to the usual community-based treatment (Sackett, Haynes, Gibson, Hackett, Taylor, Roberts, & Johnson, 1975). Further experimental work is needed to test their findings in a variety of settings with different patient populations.

Support for enhancing compliance by counteracting potential punishers is derived from the almost self-evident position that behavior that is punished is likely to decrease. Again, a vast number of studies support this position. Clients complain of punishment following assertive responses or cite side effects as another reason for non-compliance with medical regimens (Ballweg & McCorquodale, 1974; Caldwell et al., 1970). Exactly how much reinforcement, of what kind, and in what situations can offset punishment has yet to be investigated.

The medical literature also provides some data supporting the idea that fitting a regimen into a client's daily activities, or "tailoring" (as already mentioned), increases compliance. One effect of tailoring may be the reduction of undesirable disruptions in the patient's life and hence the reduction of potential negative consequences for complying (Fink, 1976; Haynes et al., 1976; Logan, Milne, Achber, Campbell, & Haynes, in press).

Proposition 10: The therapist should closely monitor compliance with as many sources as possible. In Chapter 2, monitoring was discussed as a way of measuring client progress. This proposition discusses situations where monitoring is used to strengthen compliance with homework assignments. Monitoring may include direct observation of the client's compliance behavior, or some indirect method of assessing the behavior. It may be carried out by the client (self-monitoring), by someone else in the client's environment who has the opportunity to observe compliance (or noncompliance) behavior, or both.

As noted in Chapter 1, monitoring is critical because of the "therapist absence" feature of this form of therapy. If the therapist cannot directly observe compliance, he or she must rely on some system of monitoring to determine that it has occurred and whether congratulations or further instructions are appropriate. Monitoring can also provide several direct benefits to the client. He or she can engage in self-reward when monitored data are good and will also be made more aware of the importance of the task being assigned.

One example of monitoring might occur in a smoking reduction program, where the assignment might be to reduce smoking by two cigarettes per day. Compliance could be self-monitored by having the client count the number of cigarettes smoked per day and might be co-monitored by having the client's spouse count the number of cigarettes remaining in the client's cigarette pack (assuming, of course, that the client was not smoking cigarettes other than his or her own).

In another monitoring situation, a parent could be assigned to increase the number of times he or she praises a child for appropriate behavior and to self-monitor progress. The assignment might be to have the parent count the number of positive statements made to the child during a particular time of day (e.g., 30 minutes twice a day). In addition, the parent might be asked to write down several examples of what he or she said to the child so the therapist could check the specificity of the parent's shaping statements. These data could be corroborated by a spouse or other family member who was recording the client's positive statements to the child during the same time.

As was seen in the preceding examples, monitoring does not have to be done only by the client. Family members, friends, or work associates can also monitor the client's compliance. Spouses, for example, can easily monitor eating behaviors during mealtimes or other appropriate periods when the spouse is present (such as during evening TV watching or social gatherings). If available to the therapist, trained observers sometimes may be placed in the client's environment as well. For example, a client who is a teacher may be monitored for classroom behavior by observers sitting in the back of the classroom. Finally, other methods discussed in Chapter 2 and in Gordis (1979) and Dunbar (1979), such as collecting data from permanent products or mechanical devices, may also be used to monitor compliance. As mentioned in our earlier discussions of monitoring, and for all monitoring techniques, our ethical stance is still for the client to be involved in the planning of any methods to monitor his or her behavior.

When monitoring for compliance is conducted by the client, several issues come up. One issue is that self-monitoring may be reactive — it may change behaviors being observed in a direction consistent with the therapeutic regimen (Nelson, 1977), although in some studies these effects have been transient or have not occurred at all (Mahoney, 1974; Mahoney et al., 1973; Stollak, 1967). Greiner and Karoly (1976), who also failed to find changes in their subjects' study behaviors due to self-monitoring alone, speculated that training in cognitive plan usage (Proposition 7) may increase the concreteness of goals, strengthen expectations (Proposition 4), and thereby enhance the effects of self-monitoring. Whether self-monitoring effects are in fact altered by changes in such goals and expectations has yet to be experimentally tested. Reactive effects can thus sometimes improve compliance; but it cannot be assumed that assignments given for periods when monitoring is not in effect will be complied with in the same way as when monitoring is in effect. The extent of the reactivity may also be affected by the valence of the behavior being monitored (Kanfer, 1970; Kazdin, 1974e; Nelson, Lipinski, & Black, 1976), by whether the behavior or its product is being monitored (e.g., eating behaviors versus weight, Romanczyk, 1974), or by the timing of the monitoring (Bellack, Rozensky, & Schwartz, 1974), among other factors. The therapist should consider these factors when deciding whether the goal is to increase or decrease the reactivity of self-monitoring.

Another issue to consider in using self-monitoring to improve compliance has to do with the accuracy of the information obtained. For example, it would certainly be undesirable if a therapist were reinforcing a client for desirable eating habits, as recorded on the client's self-monitoring sheet, if the client were not eating as indicated in the assignment. In this case, the client would be being reinforced for inaccurate recording and poor eating habits. Thus, it is important for the therapist to know how to determine and enhance the accuracy of the data received from the client. One way to promote data accuracy is to carefully teach clients how to record properly from the start. Also, the recommendations listed in the previous chapter by Barlow (Note 4) to enhance accuracy should be reviewed again for use in increasing accuracy of monitoring for compliance-enhancement purposes. One of the recommendations given is for the observer to be aware that accuracy will be checked. The only way this can occur, of course, is if more than one monitoring method (or person) is utilized. For this reason, this proposition recommends that monitoring should occur "with as many sources as possible."

Monitoring by others raises many of the same issues as self-monitoring. Monitoring by others may also be reactive, and could thus be utilized by the therapist to affect compliance in a desirable direction. Observers also need to be trained in accurate recording methods. Finally, the therapist needs to be aware of such factors as observer bias and drift, or changes in coding procedures (Wildman & Ericson, 1977).

As a final point, in working with the client or other persons to set up many of these compliance enhancers, such as monitoring (Proposition 10), reinforcement (Proposition 3), and cuing (Proposition 5), the therapist needs to be aware of the importance of viewing these activities as assignments themselves. Thus, if the therapist wishes compliance with such compliance-enhancement assignments as monitoring one's diet compliance, reinforcing oneself after completing an assignment, or putting up reminder notes after compliance on a refrigerator door, he or she should utilize this list of compliance-enhancement propositions to set up their implementation as well.

Empirical support for Proposition 10. Monitoring has been used extensively as a component of successful treatment programs in several studies in both behavior therapy and medicine. Books by Ciminero, Calhoun, and Adams (1977), Cone and Hawkins (1977), Haynes (1978), Haynes and Wilson (1979), and Keefe, Kopel, and Gordon (1978), as well as the journals *Behavioral Assessment* and the *Journal of Behavioral Assessment,* provide documentation of its use. For example, self-monitoring has been used in studies for medication taking (Carnahan & Nugent, 1975; Deberry, Jefferies, & Light, 1975; Epstein & Masek, 1978; Haynes et al., 1976; Moulding, 1961) and in obesity treatment programs (Bellack, 1976; Kingsley & Shapiro, 1977).

Several examples of monitoring by others to enhance compliance have also been reported in both the behavior therapy and medical literature. All of the nonobservational methods of assessment compliance in medicine (such as pill counts, prescription filling, blood and urinary levels and therapeutic outcomes) (Gordis, 1979) are examples of ways health care providers have monitored compliance. Clinician monitoring of blood pressure, for example, has been a part of some strategies to enhance compliance with antihypertension regimens (Logan et al., in press; McKenney, Slining, Henderson, Devins, & Barr, 1973; Takala, Niemela, Rosti, & Sivers, 1979). In addition, direct observation of desirable behaviors has been reported in the behavior therapy literature for eating (Epstein & Martin, 1977), drinking (Miller, 1978), and sexual behaviors (Zeiss, 1978), using colleagues, friends or relatives, and spouses, respectively. While many studies have incorporated monitoring into an intervention package or studied the effect of monitoring as an intervention itself, more research is needed on the implementation of monitoring to enhance compliance and the variables that influence the effects of monitoring on compliance.

Proposition 11: The therapist should use paradoxical strategies when necessary. All of the previous recommendations have been based on the assumption that the therapist and the client have clearly and openly shared all treatment goals and strategies for change. Although it would be unethical for a therapist to pursue treatment goals with which the client has not already agreed, he or she may, on occasion, resort to certain strategies for change that are not openly agreed upon. Most of these procedures may be labeled paradoxical and spring from the work of Haley (1963, 1973, 1976), Watzlawick (1974), and Johnson and Alevizos (Note 5). They use the client's uncooperative behaviors in such a way as to ultimately eliminate resistance and produce subsequent therapeutic results. When the therapist accepts the resistance, the client is caught in a position where resistance becomes cooperation.

These procedures should be used only as a "last resort." To date, little empirical evidence has been found to support their effectiveness, and they are extremely tricky and have the potential to be very harmful to clients. Judgments regarding when and with whom to use these procedures require long-term experience with clients and specific training in paradoxical procedures. In the absence of currently available data, therefore, these techniques should probably not be used with clients who have strong doubts as to their own abilities or are extremely depressed. They are also more indicated in situations where the client may have been reinforced for resistance (such as by an adolescent peer group) and where the therapist is reasonably assured that the client will not fail.

In using one of these procedures, a therapist may predict a negative reaction in such a way as to issue a challenge. For example, he or she might say, "I suspect you may very well find this homework too frustrating and difficult to accomplish." If the client is truly counter-controlling, such a challenge may stimulate the client's resistance so that he or she will complete the prescribed task in order "to show" the therapist. A recent case illustrates this point.

A 26-year-old outpatient male suffering from chronic pain was given the MMPI to take home and complete at his leisure. This homework was described as being very important and he was urged to complete the test and bring it back the next day. When he did not complete the test, the psychometrist called him and inquired why. The patient answered that he found the items confusing and wasn't sure how to answer them. He found countless problems with the test and delayed taking it despite several calls and pleas from the psychometrist. A psychologist was called in on the case to help solve the problem. He chose to take the paradoxical route. Calling the patient, he inquired about the test and accepted the fact that the patient had again not taken the test. After briefly hearing the patient's complaint he said the following: "I am not surprised you are having trouble with the test. I told the psychometrist that your lack of education would hamper your ability to complete it. I was sure you wouldn't be able to do it. I'll ask her to quit bugging you, since it isn't your fault." Having had his intelligence impuned, the client immediately got busy and finished the test. By accepting the client's resistance and issuing a challenge, the psychologist used the client's resistance to obtain compliance.

This technique has also worked well with adolescent clients, who frequently take a resistant stance. In one example, a 15-year-old girl who had previously been doing well at school began to get poor grades due to incomplete papers and assignments not turned in at school. She made excuses and complained that the work was just "too hard." An assessment showed that the attention she was receiving from her teachers, family, and peers for failure was much greater than that she received for successfully completing her homework. To interrupt this pattern of gaining attention for undesirable behavior, the therapist told her that she probably could not complete the homework, that it *was* probably too difficult, and that perhaps she should be asking her teachers for easier assignments. As in the previous case, she began to complete assignments "to show" the therapist and was able to again receive reinforcement for success at school rather than failure.

A modification of the paradoxical approach has been discussed by Johnson and Alevizos (Note 5). Their procedure requires the therapist to delay before prescribing the targeted therapeutic homework. This creates a mildly frustrating situation for the client, which is rationalized on the grounds that he or she is not yet ready to engage in such homework. For example, the sex therapist may restrain a couple from engaging in intercourse on the grounds that they would spoil the therapy. To increase the chances of the couple resisting the instructions, the therapist adds in no uncertain terms: "If you engage in sexual intercourse, I will be extremely displeased." The therapist then assigns a series of pleasant arousing sensual exercises such as sensate focus and mutual masturbation. If the couple proceeds to having sexual intercourse, they are distracted from their fear of failure by their concern over displeasing the therapist, and they often have highly pleasurable sex. If the intercourse fails, the failure may be discounted because it was predicted and is part of the normal course of events.

Of course, the recommendation to delay intercourse also serves other purposes. By delaying goal achievement, the therapist may enhance the goal's value. The next case illustrates this principle.

Roberta and Charles had been married nearly 20 years when suddenly Roberta began "changing." She began to demand changes within the marital contract, changes which were upsetting to Charles. In therapy, Roberta was very verbal and quickly began listing her demands and requests for change. Charles was angry and upset and said nothing. The more he was encouraged to talk, the less he participated.

A systematic homework assignment changed things dramatically. Roberta was asked to pinpoint all the things that Charles did that she wished him to change. Charles was told that he had to wait to voice his concerns until Roberta had listed her demands and work had begun on them. The next week it was obvious that Charles had resisted the therapist's suggestion that he not do anything. He came to therapy with a list of Roberta's problems, along with accompanying frequency counts. After that he opened up and talked freely.

It is clear that the client's resistance to the therapist's request not to respond resulted in the opposite: a willingness to get involved in therapy.

A final variation on the prediction and challenge theme involves predicting a relapse. Sometimes when a client is improving, particularly when he or she is improving very rapidly, the prediction of a relapse may be in order.

For years psychodynamically oriented therapists have chided their behavioral colleagues on the importance of a type of resistance that the analysts have called "the flight into health." Frequently, the client who is overcooperative and who appears to be recovering too rapidly will relapse and then express deep disappointment with treatment. In many cases such a setback may be enough to cause the patient to drop out of therapy. From a learning theory formulation, one can say that the client was on a continuous reinforcement schedule in which every homework assignment met with success. Thus, after some failure (withdrawal of reinforcement), the behavior quickly extinguished.

To prevent this occurrence, the therapist may choose to suggest that the client will probably relapse. There are two approaches. The therapist may say, "I want you to go back and feel as you did when you first came in with the problem, because I want you to see if there is anything that you wish to recover and salvage." Or the therapist might say, "I am very pleased with your rapid progress to date but I have found that most clients have a relapse about this time in treatment." When done effectively, the directive to relapse prevents a relapse. The therapist using this approach again puts the client in a therapeutic paradox. If the client resists the prediction and doesn't relapse, then everyone wins. If, on the other hand, a relapse does occur, the therapist has predicted it, eliminating or reducing the opportunity for the client to use it as an excuse to engage in nontherapeutic behaviors.

According to Haley (1973), acceptance of noncompliance is one important hallmark of paradoxical therapies that use prescribed outside activities. By accepting the client's uncooperative behaviors, the therapist reduces or eliminates their impact because giving permission brings the behavior under the control of the therapist, thereby cutting short its manipulative function. For example, after hearing that the client was unable to complete the systematic behavioral assignment, the therapist might say, "I am not surprised that you were unable to do the homework; everyone has limits, and this set of homework tasks was too difficult for you." By accepting the noncompliance, the therapist places the uncooperative client in a double bind. If the client chooses to resist the therapist, then he or she must engage in the homework assignment, that is, cooperate.

According to Haley (1973), counter-control or resistance is analogous to a river. If the therapist opposes the river by trying to block it, the river will merely go over and around him or her. However, if he or she accepts the force of the river and diverts it in a new direction, the force of the river will cut a new channel. This analogy may pose another rationale for giving the client a choice of a number of interventions to resist or reject. In this case, the therapist shifts the focus from whether the client might cooperate to how, what, or when he or she will act. The client is thus allowed to reject any number of therapeutic interventions before choosing one that "fits," without explicitly saying so. A case successfully treated by Erickson and reported by Haley (1973) is a good example of the procedure in action.

> A newly married couple came to therapy following their marriage because the wife had avoided having sexual intercourse. She reported intense anxiety at the thought of intercourse. To combat this, the therapist demanded that the client attempt intercourse within the next 7 days. Furthermore, the patient was strongly urged to complete the homework on Friday, the day before the next scheduled therapy session. At great length the therapist repeated that he preferred that it occur on Friday. This was repeated again and again to the point where the patient was becoming irritated. On Friday morning, the day after successful intercourse, the therapist was called by the husband, who conveyed to Erickson his wife's message: "It wasn't Friday." (p. 105)

By switching the issue away from *whether* the client would respond, the resistance was focused on *when* the homework would be completed.

Empirical Evidence for Proposition 11. As we have previously stated, there is little empirical evidence supporting the use of paradoxical strategies in the behavioral literature. However, one exception is a recent article by Ascher (1979), which involved the use of paradoxical intention in the treatment of urinary retention. In this particular study, five individuals were selected for paradoxical intention therapy who had previously tried and failed at a traditional behavioral regimen consisting of *in vivo* assignments, control of fluid intake, and systematic desensitization. The paradoxical intention procedure utilized by Ascher (1979) consisted of requesting that each client enter a bathroom in which he felt uncomfortable and engage in a number of activities that were commonly associated with urination. However, he was prohibited from actually urinating. For example, a male client was given the assignment to enter a men's room, walk to the urinal, unzip his fly, perform the appropriate manipulation and stand there as if to urinate, but under no circumstances was he to allow himself to pass urine. After a reasonable period of time, he was then instructed to readjust his anatomy, return his pants to the proper order, flush the urinal, wash his hands, and leave the bathroom. The assignments given the subjects in the ensuing 2 to 3 weeks consisted of very frequent opportunities to practice the paradoxical intention activity. They were never actually given the permission to urinate. Ascher (1979) assumed that when performance anxiety was sufficiently low and urgency to urinate was great, the clients would then violate the prohibition to urinate. Once clients reported the violation of the urinary prohibition they were instructed to inhibit the flow of urine for as long as possible each time they entered a restroom associated with anxiety. These instructions were continued for a period of 2 to 3 weeks, after which the program was discontinued. Ascher (1979) reports that all five subjects improved significantly within a 6-week program.

Other studies of this nature are largely lacking in the literature. However, the reader interested in paradoxical strategies can choose from a number of publications that focus primarily on paradoxical procedures. First and foremost among the contributions to paradoxical procedures are a number of books and articles by Jay Haley. His first book, *Strategies of Psychotherapy* (1963), remains a classic publication in the area of paradoxical strategy. Other books have followed and many address themselves to issues surrounding the use of paradoxical strategies to overcome patient resistance to change. For example, *Advanced Techniques of Hypnosis and Therapy: Selected Papers of Milton H. Erickson, M.D.* (1967) and *Uncommon Therapy: The Psychiatric Techniques of Milton H. Erickson, M.D.* (1973) both address themselves to issues involving paradoxical procedures. In addition an unpublished manuscript by Johnson and Alevizos (Note 5) contains a number of extremely useful observations regarding the use of paradoxical procedures in behavior therapy.

SUMMARY

The aim of this chapter is to describe compliance-enhancing tactics that the therapist could use in designing therapy and homework assignments. After a definition of compliance and some guidelines for predicting noncompliance, three types of reasons for noncompliance are explored, based on a model by Munjack and Ozieo (1978):

1. The client lacks the necessary skills or knowledge to complete some or all of the tasks in the assignment.

2. The client has cognitions that interfere with completion of the assignment.

3. The client's environment elicits noncompliance.

Recommendations for compliance enhancement are then suggested:

1. The therapist should be sure assignments contain specific detail regarding response and stimulus elements relevant to the desired behavior.

2. The therapist should give direct skill training when necessary.

3. Compliance should be reinforced.

4. The therapist should begin with small homework requests and gradually increase assignments.

5. The therapist should use cuing.

6. The therapist should have the client make a public commitment to comply.

7. The therapist should help the client develop a private commitment to comply.

8. The therapist should use cognitive rehearsal strategies to improve success with assignments.

9. The therapist should try to anticipate and reduce the negative effects of compliance.

10. The therapist should closely monitor compliance with as many sources as possible.

11. The therapist should use paradoxical strategies when necessary.

Each of these recommendations is considered separately, especially in regard to its use in designing homework or preparing the client for assignments, and supporting evidence is given for each.

This ends Section I. In the next section, Section II, 10 different problem areas are addressed in terms of how homework-based therapy has been used for each.

REFERENCE NOTES

1. Iwata, B.A., & Becksfort, S.M. *Behavioral approach to preventive dentistry: Contingent fee reductions.* Paper presented to the Annual

Conference of the American Psychological Association, Toronto, August 1978.

2. Brownell, K.D. *Partner's weight control manual.* Unpublished manuscript, Brown University, 1975.

3. Brigham, G., & Bushell, D. *Notes on autonomous environments: Student-selected versus teacher-selected rewards.* Unpublished manuscript, University of Kansas, 1972.

4. Barlow, D.H. *Self-report methods.* Paper presented at the High Blood Pressure Education Program Meeting, New Orleans, 1976.

5. Johnson, S.M., & Alevizos, P.N. *Strategic therapy: A systematic outline of procedures.* Paper presented at the Ninth Annual Conference of the Association for Advancement of Behavior Therapy, San Francisco, December 1975.

REFERENCES

Abernathy, J.D. The problem of non-compliance in long-term antihypertensive therapy. *Drugs,* 1976, *11,* 86-90.

Agras, W.S., Barlow, D.H., Chapin, H.N., Abel, G.C., & Leitenberg, H. Behavior modification of anorexia nervosa. *Archives of General Psychiatry,* 1974, *30,* 279-286.

Ajzen, I. Attitudinal messages: An investigation of the differential effects of persuasive communications on behavior. *Sociometry,* 1971, *34,* 263-280.

Ajzen, I., & Fishbein, M. The prediction of behavior from attitudinal and normative variables. *Journal of Experimental Social Psychology,* 1970, *6,* 466-487.

Alpert, J.J. Broken appointments. *Pediatrics,* 1964, *34,* 127-132.

Ascher, L.M. Paradoxical intention in the treatment of urinary retention. *Behaviour Research and Therapy,* 1979, *17,* 267-270.

Badgley, R.F., & Furnal, M.A. Appointment breaking in a pediatric clinic. *Yale Journal of Biology and Medicine,* 1961, *34,* 117-123.

Ballweg, J.A., & McCorquodale, D.W. Family planning method change and dropouts in the Phillippines. *Social Biology,* 1974, *21,* 88-95.

Bandura, A. *Principles of behavior modification.* New York: Holt, Rinehart & Winston, 1969.

Barkin, R.M., & Duncan, R. Broken appointments: Questions, not answers. *Pediatrics,* 1975, *55,* 747-748.

Beck, A. T. *Cognitive therapy and the emotional disorders.* New York: International Universities Press, 1976.

Becker, M.H., & Green, L.W. A family approach to compliance with medical treatment. *International Journal of Health Education,* 1975, *18,* 175-182.

Becker, M.H., & Maiman, L.A. Sociobehavioral determinants of compliance with health and medical care recommendations. *Medical Care,* 1975, *13,* 10-24.

Bellack, A.S. A comparison of self-reinforcement and self-monitoring in a weight reduction program. *Behavior Therapy,* 1976, *7,* 68-75.

Bellack, A.S., Rozensky, R., & Schwartz, J. A comparison of two forms of self-monitoring in a behavioral weight reduction program. *Behavior Therapy,* 1974, *5,* 523-530.

Blackwell, B. Treatment adherence: A contemporary overview. *Psychosomatics,* 1979, *20,* 27-35.

Bowen, R.G., Rich, R., & Schlatfeldt, R.M. Effects of organized instruction for patients with the diagnosis of diabetes mellitus. *Nursing Research,* 1961, *10,* 151-155.

Brownell, K.D., Heckerman, C.L., Westlake, R.J., Hayes, S.C., & Monti, P.M. The effects of couples training and partner cooperativeness in the behavioral treatment of obesity. *Behaviour Research and Therapy,* 1978, *16,* 323-333.

Brownlee, A. The family and health care: Explorations in cross-cultural settings. *Social Work in Health Care,* 1978, *4,* 179-198.

Caldwell, J.R., Cobb, S., Dowling, M.D., & DeJongh, D. The dropout problem in antihypertensive therapy. *Journal of Chronic Diseases,* 1970, *22,* 579-592.

Caplan, R.D., Robinson, S.A.R., French, J.R.P., Caldwell, J.R., & Shinn, M. *Adhering to medical regimen: Pilot experiments in patient education and social support.* Ann Arbor, Mich.: University of Michigan Press, 1976.

Carnahan, J.E., & Nugent, C.A. The effects of self-monitoring by patients on the control of hypertension. *The American Journal of Medical Sciences,* 1975, *269,* 69-73.

Cautela, J.R. Covert conditioning. In A. Jacobs and L.B. Sachs (Eds.), *The psychology of private events: Perspectives on covert response systems.* New York: Academic Press, 1971.

Cautela, J., Flannery, R., & Hanley, S. Covert modeling: An experimental test. *Behavior Therapy*, 1974, *5*, 494-502.

Christensen, A., Arkowitz, H., & Anderson, J. Practice dating as treatment for college dating inhibitions. *Behaviour Research and Therapy*, 1975, *13*, 321-331.

Christensen, D.B. Drug-taking compliance: A review and synthesis. *Health Services Research*, 1978, *13*, 171-187.

Ciminero, A.R., Calhoun, K.S., & Adams, H.E. *Handbook of behavioral assessment.* New York: John Wiley & Sons, 1977.

Cone, J.D., & Hawkins, R.P. *Behavioral assessment: New directions in clinical psychology.* New York: Brunner/Mazel, 1977.

Dapcich-Miura, E., & Hovell, M.F. Contingency management of adherence to a complex medical regimen in an elderly heart patient. *Behavior Therapy*, 1979, *10*, 193-210.

Davis, M.S. Variations in patients' compliance with doctors' advice: An empirical analysis of patterns of communication. *American Journal of Public Health*, 1968, *58*, 274-288.

Deberry, P., Jefferies, L.P., & Light, M.R. Teaching cardiac patients to manage medications. *American Journal of Nursing*, 1975, *75*, 2191-2193.

Doster, J.A. Effects of instructions, modeling, and role rehearsal on interview verbal behavior. *Journal of Consulting and Clinical Psychology*, 1972, *39*, 202-209.

Dunbar, J.M. Issues in assessment. In S.J. Cohen (Ed.), *New directions in patient compliance.* Lexington, Mass.: Lexington Books, 1979.

Dunbar, J.M., & Stunkard, A.J. Adherence to medical regimen. In R. Levy, B. Rifkind, B. Dennis, & N. Ernst (Eds.), *Nutrition lipids and coronary heart disease: A global view.* New York: Raven Press, 1979.

Earp, J.A., & Ory, M.G. The effects of social support and health professional home visits on patient adherence to hypertension regimens. *Preventive Medicine*, 1979, *8*, 155.

Ellis, A. *Reason and emotion in psychotherapy.* New York: Stewart, 1962.

Epstein, L.H., & Martin, J.E. Compliance and side effects of weight reduction groups. *Behavior Modification*, 1977, *1*, 551-558.

Epstein, L.H., & Masek, B.J. Behavioral control of medicine compliance. *Journal of Applied Behavior Analysis,* 1978, *11,* 1-9.

Erickson, M.H. *Advanced techniques of hypnosis and therapy: Selected papers of Milton H. Erickson, M.D.* (J. Haley, Ed.). New York: Grune & Stratton, 1967.

Eyberg, S.M., & Johnson, S.M. Multiple assessment of behavior modification with families: Effects of contingency contracting and order of treated problems. *Journal of Consulting and Clinical Psychology,* 1974, *42,* 594-606.

Fendrich, J.M. A study of the association among verbal attitudes, commitment, and overt behavior in different experimental situations. *Social Forces,* 1967, *45,* 347-355.

Fink, D.L. Tailoring the consensual regimen. In D.L. Sackett & R.B. Haynes (Eds.), *Compliance with therapeutic regimens.* Baltimore: Johns Hopkins University Press, 1976.

Flanders, J.P., & Thistlethwaite, D.L. Effects of informative and justificatory variables upon imitation. *Journal of Experimental Social Psychology,* 1970, *6,* 316-328.

Fordyce, W.E. Behavioral concepts in chronic pain and illness. In P.O. Davidson (Ed.), *The behavioral management of anxiety, depression, and pain.* New York: Brunner/Mazel, 1976.

Francis, V.F., Korsch, B.M., & Morris, M. Gaps in doctor-patient communication: Patients' response to medical advice. *New England Journal of Medicine,* 1969, *280,* 535-540.

Frankel, B.S., & Hovell, M.F. Health service appointment keeping. *Behavior Modification,* 1978, *2,* 435-464.

Freedman, J.L., & Fraser, S.C. Compliance without pressure: The foot-in-the-door technique. *Journal of Personality and Social Psychology,* 1966, *4,* 195-202.

Gates, S.J., & Colborn, D.K. Lowering appointment failures in a neighborhood health center. *Medical Care,* 1976, *14,* 263-267.

Gordis, L. Conceptual and methodologic problems in measuring patient compliance. In R.B. Haynes, D.W. Taylor, & D.L. Sackett (Eds.), *Compliance in health care.* Baltimore: Johns Hopkins University Press, 1979.

Greenwald, A.G. Effects of prior commitment on behavior change after a persuasive communication. *Public Opinion Quarterly,* 1965, *29,* 595-601.

Greiner, J.M., & Karoly, P. Effects of self-control training on study activity and academic performance: An analysis of self-monitoring, self-reward, and systematic-planning components. *Journal of Counseling Psychology,* 1976, *23,* 495-502.

Haley, J. *Strategies of psychotherapy.* New York: Grune & Stratton, 1963.

Haley, J. *Uncommon therapy: The psychiatric techniques of Milton H. Erickson, M.D.* New York: Norton, 1973.

Haley, J. *Problem-solving therapy.* San Francisco: Jossey-Bass, 1976.

Harfouche, J., Abi-Yaghi, M., Melidossian, A., & Azouri, L. Factors associated with broken appointments in an experimental family health center. *Tropical Doctor,* 1973, *3,* 128-133.

Harris, M.B., & Bruner, C.G. A comparison of a self-control and a contract procedure for weight control. *Behavior Research,* 1971, *9,* 347-354.

Hay, W., Hay, L., & Nelson, R.O. The adaptation of covert modeling procedures to the treatment of chronic alcoholism and obessive-compulsive behavior: Two case reports. *Behavior Therapy,* 1977, *8,* 70-76.

Haynes, R.B. A critical review of the determinants of compliance with therapeutic regimens. In D.L. Sackett & R.B. Haynes (Eds.), *Compliance with therapeutic regimens.* Baltimore: Johns Hopkins University Press, 1976.

Haynes, R.B., Sackett, D.L., Gibson, E.S., Taylor, D.W., Hackett, B.C., Roberts, R.S., & Johnson, A.L. Improvement of medication compliance in uncontrolled hypertension. *The Lancet,* 1976, *1,* 1265-1268.

Haynes, R.B., Taylor, D.W., & Sackett, D.L. *Compliance in health care.* Baltimore: Johns Hopkins University Press, 1979.

Haynes, S.N. *Principles of behavioral assessment.* New York: Gardner Press, 1978.

Haynes, S.N., & Wilson, C.C. *Behavioral assessment.* San Francisco: Jossey-Bass, 1979.

Israel, A.C., & Saccone, A.J. Follow-up effects of choice of mediator and target of reinforcement on weight loss. *Behavior Therapy,* 1979, *10,* 260-265.

Johnson, S.M. Self-observation as an agent of behavioral change. *Behavior Therapy,* 1971, *2,* 488-497.

Kanfer, F.H. Self-monitoring: Methodological limitations and clinical applications. *Journal of Consulting and Clinical Psychology,* 1970, *35,* 148-152.

Kanfer, F.H., & Grimm, L.G. Freedom of choice and behavioral change. *Journal of Consulting and Clinical Psychology,* 1978, *46,* 873-876.

Kanfer, F.H., & Karoly, P. Self-control: A behavioristic excursion into the lion's den. *Behavior Therapy,* 1972, *3,* 398-416.

Kanfer, F.H., Karoly, P., & Newman, A. Source of feedback, observational learning, and attitude change. *Journal of Personality and Social Psychology,* 1974, *29,* 30-38.

Kar, S.B. Community interventions in health and family planning programmes: A conceptual framework. *International Journal of Health Education,* 1977, *20,* 2-15.

Kazdin, A.E. Covert modeling and the reduction of avoidance behavior. *Journal of Abnormal Psychology,* 1973, *81,* 87-95.

Kazdin, A.E. Comparative effects of some variations of covert modeling. *Journal of Behavior Therapy and Experimental Psychiatry,* 1974, *5,* 225-231. (a)

Kazdin, A.E. Covert modeling, model similarity and reduction of avoidance behavior. *Behavior Therapy,* 1974, *5,* 325-340. (b)

Kazdin, A.E. The effect of model identity and fear-relevant similarity on covert modeling. *Behavior Therapy,* 1974, *5,* 624-635. (c)

Kazdin, A.E. Effects of covert modeling and model reinforcement on assertive behavior. *Journal of Abnormal Psychology,* 1974, *83,* 240-252. (d)

Kazdin, A.E. Reactive self-monitoring: The effects of response desirability, goal setting, and feedback. *Journal of Consulting and Clinical Psychology,* 1974, *42,* 704-716. (e)

Kazdin, A.E. Covert modeling, imagery assessment and assertive behavior. *Journal of Consulting and Clinical Psychology,* 1975, *43,* 716-724.

Kazdin, A.E. Assessment of imagery during covert modeling of assertive behavior. *Journal of Behavior Therapy and Experimental Psychiatry,* 1976, *7,* 213-219. (a)

Kazdin, A.E. Effects of covert modeling, multiple models, and model reinforcement on assertive behavior. *Behavior Therapy,* 1976, *7,* 211-222. (b)

Keefe, F.J., Kopel, S.A., & Gordon, S.B. *A practical guide to behavioral assessment.* New York: Springer, 1978.

Kidd, A.H., & Euphrat, J.L. Why prospective outpatients fail to make or keep appointments. *Journal of Clinical Psychology,* 1971, *27,* 394-395.

Kincey, J., Bradshaw, P., & Ley, P. Patients' satisfaction and reported acceptance of advice in general practice. *Journal of the Royal College of General Practitioners,* 1975, *25,* 558-566.

Kingsley, R.G., & Shapiro, J. A comparison of three behavioral programs for the control of obesity in children. *Behavior Therapy,* 1977, *8,* 30-36.

Kothandapani, V. Validation of feeling, belief, and intention to act as three components of attitude and their contribution to prediction of contraceptive behavior. *Journal of Personality and Social Psychology,* 1971, *19,* 321-333.

Krause, M.S. Comparative effects on continuance of four experimental intake procedures. *Social Casework,* 1966, *47,* 515-519.

Lazarus, A.A. *Multimodal behavior therapy.* New York: Springer, 1976.

Leitenberg, H. Feedback and therapist praise during treatment of phobia. *Journal of Consulting and Clinical Psychology,* 1975, *43,* 396-404.

Leon, G.R. Current dimensions in the treatment of obesity. *Psychological Bulletin,* 1976, *83,* 557-578.

Lepper, M.R. Dissonance, self-perception and honesty in children. *Journal of Personality and Social Psychology,* 1973, *25,* 65-74.

Leventhal, H. Fear communications in the acceptance of preventive health practices. In R.L. Rosnow & E.J. Robinson (Eds.), *Experiments in persuasion.* New York: Academic Press, 1967.

Levy, R.L. Relationship of an overt commitment to task compliance in behavior therapy. *Journal of Behavior Therapy and Experimental Psychiatry,* 1977, *8,* 25-29.

Levy, R.L., & Carter, R.D. Compliance with practitioner instigations. *Social Work,* 1976, *21,* 188-196.

Levy, R.L., & Claravall, V. Differential effects of a phone reminder on patients with long and short between-visit intervals. *Medical Care,* 1977, *15,* 435-438.

Levy, R.L., & Clark, H. The use of an overt commitment to enhance compliance: A cautionary note. *Journal of Behavior Therapy and Experimental Psychiatry,* 1980, *11,* 105-107.

Levy, R.L., Yamashita, D., & Pow, G. Relationship of an overt commitment to the frequency and speed of compliance with decision making. *Medical Care,* 1979, *17,* 281-284.

Lewis, S. A comparison of behavior therapy techniques in the reduction of fearful avoidance behavior. *Behavior Therapy,* 1974, *5,* 648-655.

Ley, P., Jain, V., & Skilbeck, C. A method for decreasing medication errors. *Psychiatry in Medicine,* 1976, *6,* 599-601.

Ley, P., Whitworth, M., Skilbeck, C., Woodward, R., Pinsent, R., Pike, L., Clarkson, M., & Clark, P. Improving doctor-patient communication in general practice. *Journal of the Royal College of General Practitioners,* 1976, *26,* 720-724.

Liebert, R.M., Hanratty, M., & Hill, J.H. Effects of role structure and training method on the adoption of a self-imposed standard. *Child Development,* 1969, *40,* 93-101.

Locke, E.A., Cartledge, H., & Koeppel, J. Motivational effects of knowledge of results: A goal-setting phenomenon. *Psychological Bulletin,* 1968, *70,* 478-485.

Logan, A.S., Milne, B.J., Achber, C., Campbell, W.P., & Haynes, R.B. Worksite treatment of hypertension by specially trained nurses: A controlled trial. *The Lancet,* in press.

Lovitt, T.C., & Curtiss, K. Academic response rate as a function of teacher- and self-imposed contingencies. *Journal of Applied Behavior Analysis,* 1969, *2,* 49-53.

Lowe, K., & Lutzker, J.R. Increasing compliance to a medical regimen with a juvenile diabetic. *Behavior Therapy,* 1979, *10,* 57-64.

Mahoney, M.J. Self-reward and self-monitoring techniques for weight control. *Behavior Therapy,* 1974, *5,* 48-57.

Mahoney, M.J. Cognitive therapy research: A question of questions. *Cognitive Therapy and Research,* 1977, *1,* 5-16.

Mahoney, M.J., & Mahoney, J. Treatment of obesity: A clinical exploration. In B.T. Williams, S. Martin, & J.P. Foreyt (Eds.), *Obesity.* New York: Brunner/Mazel, 1976.

Mahoney, M.J., Moura, N.G., & Wade, T.C. Relative efficacy of self-reward, self-punishment, and self-monitoring techniques for weight loss. *Journal of Consulting and Clinical Psychology,* 1973, *40,* 404-407.

Maiman, L.A., & Becker, M.H. The health belief model: Origins and correlates in psychological theory. *Health Education Monographs,* 1974, *2,* 455-469.

Maiman, L.A., Becker, M.H., Kirscht, J.P., Haefner, D.P., & Drachman, R.H. Scales for measuring health belief dimensions: A test of predictive value, internal consistency, and relationships among beliefs. *Health Education Monographs,* 1977, *5,* 215-230.

Malahy, B. The effects of instruction and labeling on the number of medication errors made by patients at home. *American Journal of Hospital Pharmacy,* 1966, *23,* 283-292.

Mann, R.A. The behavior-therapeutic use of contingency contracting to control an adult behavior problem: Weight control. *Journal of Applied Behavior Analysis,* 1972, *5,* 99-109.

Mazzulo, S.M., Lasagna, L., & Griner, P.F. Variations in interpretation of prescription assignments. *Journal of the American Medical Association,* 1974, *227,* 929-931.

McFall, R.M., & Marston, A.R. An experimental investigation of behavior rehearsal in assertive training. *Journal of Abnormal Psychology,* 1970, *76,* 295-303.

McKenney, J.M., Slining, J.M., Henderson, H.R., Devins, D., & Barr, M. The effect of clinical pharmacy services on patients with essential hypertension. *Circulation,* 1973, *48,* 1104-1111.

Meichenbaum, D.H. *Cognitive-behavior modification: An integrative approach.* New York: Plenum, 1977.

Miller, W.R. Behavioral treatment of problem drinkers: A comparative outcome study of three controlled drinking therapies. *Journal of Consulting and Clinical Psychology,* 1978, *46,* 74-86.

Moulding, T. Preliminary study of the pill calendar as a method of improving self-administration of drugs. *American Review of Respiratory Disease,* 1961, *84,* 284-287.

Munjack, D.J., & Ozieo, R.J. Resistance in the behavioral treatment of sexual dysfunction. *Journal of Sex and Marital Therapy,* 1978, *4,* 122-138.

Nazarian, L.F., Machuber, J., Charney, E., & Coulter, M.D. Effect of a mailed appointment reminder on appointment keeping. *Pediatrics,* 1974, *53,* 349-351.

Nelson, R.O. Methodological issues in assessment via self-monitoring. In J.D. Cone & R.P. Hawkins (Eds.), *Behavioral assessment: New directions in clinical psychology.* New York: Brunner/Mazel, 1977.

Nelson, R.O., Lipinski, D.P., & Black, J.L. The relative reactivity of external observations and self-monitoring. *Behavior Therapy,* 1976, *7,* 314-321.

Nesse, M., & Nelson, R.O. Variations of covert modeling on cigarette smoking. *Cognitive Therapy and Research,* 1977, *1,* 343-354.

Nessman, D.G., Carnahan, J.E., & Nugent, C.A. Improving compliance: Patient operated hypertension groups. *Archives of Internal Medicine,* in press.

Ostrom, T.M. The relationship between the affective, behavioral and cognitive components of attitude. *Journal of Experimental Social Psychology,* 1969, *5,* 12-30.

Patterson, G.R., & Gullion, M.E. *Living with children.* Champaign, Ill.: Research Press, 1968.

Pendleton, L.R., Shelton, J.L., & Wilson, S.E. Social interaction training using systematic homework. *The Personnel and Guidance Journal,* 1976, *54,* 484-491.

Phillips, R. Self-administered systematic desensitization. *Journal of Consulting and Clinical Psychology,* 1966, *18,* 491-501.

Rappaport, J., Gross, T., & Lepper, C. Modeling, sensitivity training and instruction. *Journal of Consulting and Clinical Psychology,* 1973, *40,* 99-107.

Reiss, W., Piotrowski, W., & Bailey, J.S. Behavioral community psychology: Encouraging low-income parents to seek dental care for their children. *Journal of Applied Behavior Analysis,* 1976, *9,* 387-397.

Romanczyk, R.G. Self-monitoring in the treatment of obesity: Parameters of reactivity. *Behavior Therapy,* 1974, *5,* 531-540.

Rosenstock, I.M. Why people use health services. *Milbank Memorial Fund Quarterly,* 1966, *44,* 94-124.

Saccone, A.J., & Israel, A.C. Effects of experimenter versus significant other-controlled reinforcement and choice of target behaviors on weight loss. *Behavior Therapy,* 1978, *9,* 271-278.

Sackett, D.L., Haynes, R.B., Gibson, E.S., Hackett, B.C., Taylor, D.W., Roberts, R.S., & Johnson, A.L. Randomized clinical trial of strategies for improving medication compliance in primary hypertension. *The Lancet,* 1975, *1,* 1205-1207.

Schulman, B. Active patient orientation and outcomes in hypertensive treatment. *Medical Care,* 1979, *17,* 267-280.

Shepard, D.S., & Moseley, T.A. Mailed vs. telephoned appointment reminders to reduce broken appointments in a hospital outpatient department. *Medical Care,* 1976, *14,* 268-273.

Steckel, S.B., & Swain, M.A. Contracting with patients to improve compliance. *Hospitals,* 1977, *51* (23), 81-84.

Stokols, D. The reduction of cardiovascular risk: An application of social learning perspectives. In A.J. Enelow & J.B. Henderson (Eds.), *Applying behavioral science to cardiovascular risk.* Dallas: American Heart Association, 1975.

Stollak, G.E. Weight loss under different experimental conditions. *Psychotherapy: Theory, Research and Practice,* 1967, *4,* 61-64.

Stuart, R.B., & Davis, B. *Slim chance in a fat world.* Champaign, Ill.: Research Press, 1972.

Suinn, R.M. Behavior rehearsal for ski racers. *Behavior Therapy,* 1972, *3,* 519-520. (a)

Suinn, R.M. Removing emotional obstacles to learning and performance by visuo-motor behavior rehearsal. *Behavior Therapy,* 1972, *3,* 308-310. (b)

Suinn, R.M. Behavioral methods at the Winter Olympic Games. *Behavior Therapy,* 1977, *8,* 283-284.

Svarstad, B. Physician-patient communication and patient conformity with medical advice. In D. Mechanic (Ed.), *The growth of bureaucratic medicine.* New York: John Wiley & Sons, 1976.

Takala, J., Niemela, N., Rosti, J., & Sivers, K. Improving compliance with therapeutic regimens in hypertensive patients in a community health centre. *Circulation,* 1979, *59,* 540-543.

Thomas, E.J., & Carter, R.D. Instigative modification with a multi-problem family. *Social Casework,* 1971, *52,* 444-455.

Turk, D. Cognitive behavioral techniques in the management of pain. In J.P. Foreyt & D.P. Rathgen (Eds.), *Cognitive behavior therapy.* New York: Plenum, 1977.

Watzlawick, P.A. A structured family interview. *Family Process,* 1974, *5,* 256-271.

Wicker, A.M. An examination of "other variables" explanation of attitude-behavior inconsistency. *Journal of Personality and Social Psychology,* 1971, *19,* 18-31.

Wildman, B.G., & Ericson, M.T. Methodological problems in behavioral observation. In J.D. Cone & R.P. Hawkins (Eds.), *Behavioral assessment: New directions in clinical psychology.* New York: Brunner/Mazel, 1977.

Wilson, G.T., & Brownell, K.D. Behavior therapy for obesity including family members in the treatment process. *Behavior Therapy,* 1978, *9,* 943-945.

Wilson, G.T., & Evans, I.M. The therapist-client relationship in behavior therapy. In A.S. Gurman & A.M. Razin (Eds.), *The therapist's contribution to effective psychotherapy: An empirical approach.* Elmsford, N.Y.: Pergamon Press, 1972.

Wurtele, S.K., Galanos, A.N., & Roberts, M.C. Increasing return compliance in a tuberculosis detection drive. *Journal of Behavioral Medicine,* 1980, *3,* 311-318.

Zeiss, R.A. Self-directed treatment for premature ejaculation. *Journal of Consulting and Clinical Psychology,* 1978, *46,* 1234-1241.

Zifferblatt, S. *Improving study and homework behaviors.* Champaign, Ill.: Research Press, 1970.

Zitter, R.E., & Freemouw, W.J. Individual vs. partner consequation for weight loss. *Behavior Therapy,* 1978, *9,* 808-813.

SECTION II

This section contains descriptions of 10 problem-specific treatment programs. In each chapter, emphasis is given to homework-based treatment and the specific homework assignments that are appropriate for the problems discussed. It is presumed that the reader has clinical experience and familiarity with most or all of the treatment approaches mentioned in this section. Therefore the overviews of the problems and treatments presented here are only intended to provide the context in which homework assignments are given, not to provide a comprehensive treatment text. Each chapter focuses primarily on homework assignments and also includes some compliance-enhancement techniques that have been found to be particularly useful in treating clients in the problem area discussed. The assignments in each homework-based treatment section provide examples of how homework is systematically integrated into therapy. While the specific assignments used by the reader may vary with varying treatment approaches, these writers provide their own examples within the general format we are advocating. The compliance-enhancement procedures in the following chapters represent many specific adaptations of the propositions discussed in Chapter 3.

CHAPTER 4

Anxiety

Jerry L. Deffenbacher
Department of Psychology
Colorado State University

OVERVIEW OF ANXIETY

Anxiety and fear are pervasive problems, so much so that the 20th century has sometimes been called the "Age of Anxiety." Nearly everyone's life is punctuated with moments of tension and stress, but for some the experience of anxiety is much more frequent and chronic. This degree of anxiety in our society is reflected in the fact that Valium and Librium are two of the most frequently prescribed drugs.

Despite its pervasive presence, anxiety has been difficult to define. One useful approach is to view it as an inferential construct (Lang, 1969; Suinn, 1977) that is derived from data from one or more response domains. If derived from the *affective-physiological* domain, anxiety is characterized by feelings of apprehension, dread, and tension and is often accompanied by increased autonomic arousal, such as increased heart rate. Anxiety from the *cognitive* domain may be inferred from overt verbal communications ("I'm really uptight") or by covert image and verbal patterns that tend to be overgeneralized and distorted ("I know I'm going to fail; she'll laugh at me, and I just can't stand the thought of that"). The third area is the *somatic-behavioral* domain. Here anxiety is reflected in phenomena such as tremors, speech dysfluencies, disrupted performance, and avoidance behavior. Furthermore, not all the response components just mentioned may be present at once (Lang, 1969). An individual may report considerable anxiety (cognitive), experience heightened autonomic arousal (affective-physiological), and yet demonstrate approach behavior toward anxiety-arousing stimuli (Leitenberg, Agras, Butz, & Wincze, 1971).

Anxiety has many causes. In some cases, people become anxious because of skill or information deficits (Bandura, 1969). If they do not have the requisite skills for a situation, such as social skills, they are likely to perform poorly, experience the consequent social punishers, and then become anxious whenever similar circumstances arise. If they have informational deficits, they may have the requisite skills but may not know what behavior is appropriate for the situation. Feeling anxious when not knowing the proper etiquette for an important social event is an example. Anxiety may also be precipitated by mediational cognitions such as attributions, self-evaluative statements, and other forms of self-talk (Girodo, 1976). For example, if a person labels a situation as "awful," regardless of its actual stimulus properties, it will probably make the person anxious whenever he or she thinks about or approaches it. Anxiety also may result from classical conditioning (Solomon, 1964). Neutral cues that are paired contiguously with aversive unconditioned stimuli and unconditioned response sequences can come to elicit all or part of the autonomic arousal elicited originally by the unconditioned stimuli. Fear of dogs stemming from actually being bitten is an example of such classically conditioned fear. Anxieties may also be acquired vicariously (Bandura, 1969); here the anxiety is learned simply by observing the consequences to others. Fear of dogs based on observing someone else being bitten is an example of a vicariously conditioned fear.

Regardless of how anxiety is acquired or prompted, it appears to persist because of avoidance and escape behaviors. When anxiety is aroused, it has aversive cue properties. Because of its aversiveness, individuals work to reduce it and to prevent its further arousal. This reduction of aversiveness strengthens and maintains the avoidance and escape behaviors through negative reinforcement. Thus, regardless of its source, anxiety appears to be maintained by operant conditioning.

The terms anxiety and fear have so far been used interchangeably. A relative distinction, however, can be made. People who have fears are able to specify the stimulus conditions that elicit the tensional state. Anxiety typically is used in reference to more general terms such as "trait anxiety," "free-floating anxiety," or "anxiety neurosis," where the cue conditions are so diffuse or so numerous that individuals are unable to specify them.

It is also useful to note that cues that elicit tension may be either internal or external. External stressors involve learned or real threats (tests, speeches, or social interactions) that are outside the individual. Internal stimuli may be specific thoughts or images. These internal stressors may produce cognitive or affective-physiological feedback loops. For example, individuals may begin to experience an increase in autonomic arousal, and by focusing their attention upon it, may then become further aroused. Or, as they pay attention to the arousal, they may think, "I can't cope," which leads to further arousal and performance deterioration.

HOMEWORK-BASED TREATMENT

Overview of Treatment

Relaxation as self-control (RSC) (Deffenbacher, 1976; Deffenbacher & Snyder, 1976) was developed in the early 1970s to overcome the lack of generalized effects found for some traditional behavior approaches to anxiety reduction. Several procedures effectively break the relationship between anxiety responses and external cues; for example, desensitization counterconditions relaxation to these cues, and flooding extinguishes the stimulus-response relationship. Clients receiving such treatment experience relief from their presenting phobia (Paul, 1969; Rimm & Masters, 1974), but learn little about how to generalize and cope with other anxieties or stressors. RSC was developed to help clients handle not only the presenting anxiety, but also other present and future stressors.

Because RSC was developed to specifically teach self-managed relaxation coping skills with which to lower physiological-affective arousal, it is most relevant to the treatment of phobic, general anxiety, and psychophysiological disorders where autonomic-affective overreactivity is a key feature. RSC is less useful in cases where anxiety stems primarily from cognitive distortion or behavioral skill deficit. Even here, however, RSC may prove useful, since it has been shown to reduce worry, the cognitive component of test anxiety (Deffenbacher, Mathis, & Michaels, 1979; Snyder & Deffenbacher, 1977); furthermore, relaxation coping skills could be a beneficial addition to an individual with a skill deficit that is contributing to anxiety. Thus, RSC is most useful as a primary treatment when anxiety is inferred primarily from the affective-physiological response domain or as an element of a comprehensive, multimodal treatment plan where anxiety is inferred from other response domains. Since it trains generalized coping skills, it is particularly appropriate for clients with multiple phobias or generalized sources of stress. It has also been used on a case basis with both anger arousal and agitation. To date, however, it has been employed primarily with outpatient, nonpsychotic late adolescents and adults.

RSC has reduced anxiety in a variety of populations. In two studies (Deffenbacher, 1976; Deffenbacher & Rivera, 1976), it effectively reduced debilitating anxiety in black women who had failed the Clerk Typist I portion of the state civil service exam and were in danger of losing their jobs. Anxiety assessments taken before and after the practice exams revealed significant reductions of debilitating anxiety, lower state anxiety before retaking the test, and improvements in facilitating test anxiety. The women made fewer errors on practice exams, and upon retaking the civil service exam, they all passed the Clerk Typist II test, which was a more difficult exam than the one they had failed. Follow-up revealed continued vocational development and anecdotal reports of generalized anxiety reduction.

RSC is also effective in reducing anxiety in college students. Deffenbacher (1976) reported reductions of debilitating test anxiety and preexam anxiety ratings along with improved facilitating test anxiety and grade-point averages. Several other studies have found similar reductions in debilitating test anxiety and improvements in facilitating test anxiety (Deffenbacher et al., 1979; Deffenbacher & Snyder, 1976; Snyder & Deffenbacher, 1977). Although no performance differences were found on a stressful anagrams task (Snyder & Deffenbacher, 1977), subjects receiving RSC training were less worried and anxious, found the situation less aversive, and perceived themselves and their abilities more favorably than the controls. In another stressful analogue testing (Deffenbacher et al., 1979), RSC subjects reported significantly less worry, emotionality, and state test anxiety than controls. Although no performance differences were found in the analogue situation, the RSC subjects had better introductory psychology grades than did the no-treatment expectancy controls. Follow-up a year after the initial follow-up (Deffenbacher & Michaels, 1980) showed that the RSC subjects continued to report less debilitating test anxiety than controls. Finally, Deffenbacher and Payne (1977) found that RSC led to reduction of fear of negative social evaluation, increases in assertiveness, and reduced communication apprehension in student teachers.

RSC has reduced generalized anxiety as scored on measures such as the Fear Inventory, Trait Anxiety Inventory, and IPAT Anxiety Scale (Deffenbacher et al., 1979; Deffenbacher & Snyder, 1976; Snyder & Deffenbacher, 1977). Six-week follow-ups (Deffenbacher et al., 1979) and one-year follow-ups (Deffenbacher & Michaels, 1980) revealed that these nontargeted anxiety reductions were maintained.

Three studies (Deffenbacher et al., 1979; Deffenbacher & Payne, 1977; Snyder & Deffenbacher, 1977) have compared RSC to a self-control variant of desensitization. In all studies, RSC has done as well as desensitization in reducing targeted and nontargeted anxieties, and studies with follow-up (Deffenbacher et al., 1979; Deffenbacher & Michaels, 1980) suggest equal and in some cases slightly superior maintenance of nontargeted anxiety reduction.

To summarize, RSC appears to reliably reduce targeted or presenting anxieties, lead to generalized anxiety reduction, maintain targeted and nontargeted anxiety reduction, and compare favorably to desensitization on targeted and nontargeted anxiety reduction.

The RSC model assumes that four conditions are necessary for developing relaxation as a self-managed coping skill: individuals must be skilled at detecting the internal cues associated with the presence and buildup of tension; they must develop a basic relaxation response; they must become capable of self-inducing relaxation quickly for *in vivo* application; and they must learn to chain those skills together and practice them extensively to insure the reliability of those skills for application in the face of stress. Practice of the "discrimination-of-anxiety-application-of-relaxation" sequence provides individuals with self-directed methods of preventing or reducing anxiety. The coping skills are not tied to specific anxiety-arousing situations because the cues for application come from within the individual, and these internal cues comprise the one set of cue conditions that cuts across anxiety-arousing situations for the individual.

Mastery of RSC generally takes from five to eight sessions after the initial assessment processes. Before starting RSC, the therapist gives the client an extensive self-control rationale following the model of Goldfried (1971). Training in RSC proceeds by four phases.

1. *Discrimination training* teaches clients to become aware of and sensitive to anxiety and associated response-produced cues, especially physiological cues that covary with the onset of anxiety. Discrimination training is outlined in the first two sessions and reviewed in subsequent sessions.

2. *Relaxation training* follows standard progressive relaxation procedures but also includes cue-produced relaxation, in which clients covertly say the word "relax" before releasing each muscle group. Tensing and releasing the muscles is completed in the first two sessions, and relaxation without tension is generally introduced in the third session.

3. *Application training* introduces methods of accelerating and deepening relaxation for *in vivo* application. Procedures include cue-produced relaxation, deep chest and stomach breathing, breath tracing, a three-breath technique, individually tailored tension-release exercises for problem areas and larger muscle units, and combinations of these (see

Deffenbacher & Snyder, 1976, for further details). Two or three of these applied relaxation skills are introduced and practiced in the second through fourth sessions. Each new skill is added to the relaxation homework so that clients practice them for a number of trials at the end of each relaxation practice session at home. Typically between the fourth and fifth sessions clients coordinate the best procedures into a written set of relaxation instructions with which to cue their applied relaxation for use in therapeutic training tasks and *in vivo* application.

4. *Guided practice* gives clients practice in coupling the discrimination and application skills under circumstances of increasing stress. Within treatment clients first apply relaxation sets during differential relaxation, for example, while walking, sitting, or standing. In subsequent sessions, they apply relaxation procedures during simulated stressful situations, for example, during a mock interview or while taking a test.

Homework Assignments

Homework is an integral part of RSC. Various homework activities as they relate to specific steps of RSC will be described now.

Assessment. The first homework assignment given to clients follows the initial assessment interview. It introduces the client to self-monitoring and provides the therapist with additional information about the problem.

> **Assignment:** After the initial assessment interview(s), begin self-monitoring your affective state. Three times per day (morning, afternoon, and evening), attend to and record the following: the date and time of observation, the precipitating event (situation), and your emotional state (feelings). Record this data on a homework sheet laid out in the following manner (Stress Log 1):
>
> *Date/Time*   *Situation*   *Feelings*

As with most homework involving recording, these homework sheets should be dropped off the day before the next therapy session. This practice gives the therapist time to review the material and decide how to integrate the data into the next session.

The decision to have self-monitoring occur at least once in the morning, afternoon, and evening is the result of several practical compromises. Originally clients were asked to monitor and record more frequently, for example, every hour and then every 2 hours. This practice, however, seemed to be so aversive that clients tended not to record at all. The present method appears to have reduced aversiveness and increased compliance, while at the same time providing a reasonable time sampling of client affect over the course of the day.

This initial self-monitoring serves several important functions. First, it signals the importance and use of homework in therapy. It also introduces clients to self-monitoring behavior. For many persons, systematic self-observation is a new, and often difficult, behavior; however, learning it is critical to the practice of RSC, since the application of relaxation coping skills is based upon the awareness of the response-produced cues of anxiety. Thus, this initial self-monitoring assignment is the first step to shaping *in vivo* tracking of the internal cues of anxiety. Furthermore, self-monitoring can greatly facilitate diagnosis and case conceptualization. The client may have been using words such as "tense" and "uptight" to refer to anger and frustration, while the therapist may have thought they referred to anxiety. Data from self-monitoring could greatly clarify these and other misunderstandings. Finally, self-monitoring may lead to the identification of problem areas not discussed in the assessment interview. For example, considerable stress might surface around the management of children, which was not originally identified as problematic. In all, self-monitoring homework provides the interviewer with leads from which to develop a more detailed picture of the presenting problem.

Discrimination training. In subsequent sessions self-monitoring is further refined and shaped to train clients to become aware of their specific internal cues of anxiety arousal. Clients develop this awareness by tracking areas of tension during relaxation training and by keeping a stress log. The log involves having clients monitor their state anxiety level at least three times a day, then giving this experience a subjective units of disturbance (SUDS) value (Wolpe, 1969), and finally recording this and the internal cues of anxiety.

Assignment: Between the first and second RSC sessions, self-monitor your reactions and also rate the intensity of your affective state on a 0 to 100 scale, where 0 represents the absence of tension and 100 represents maximal tension.

This data provides both therapist and clients with estimates of the magnitude of anxiety reactions, and in some cases the internal rating of stress alone will serve as the cue to relax. Thus although clients may not be able to identify specific anxiety-related cues, they may be able to reliably rate the experience and to intervene when tension rises to a certain level.

Assignment: Between the second and third session, begin to record the physical cues of tension.

The stress log (Stress Log 2) by then looks like the following:

Date/Time   Situation   Feelings   Tension Level (0-100)   Physical Cues

Clients continue to record in such a manner until they begin actually applying relaxation *in vivo* for tension control. This refined and continued tracking may not only facilitate awareness of anxiety arousal, but may also help to pinpoint other problem situations.

Relaxation training. Progressive relaxation exercises within the first and second sessions are supplemented by home practice.

Assignment: Set aside approximately 30 minutes when you can be unhurried and uninterrupted, and practice the relaxation exercises. Practice at least 5 out of the next 7 days, daily if possible.

Clients are given a 2-page relaxation handout to facilitate this practice. The first page describes how to set up home practice, and the second lists the muscle groups in order, along with the means of tensing them.

Assignment: Record home practice in a relaxation log in which you record the date and time of practice, body areas that were easily relaxed, body areas with tension, and tension level before and after practice.

The relaxation log looks like the following:

Date/Time	*Body Areas Easily Relaxed*	*Body Areas with Tension*	*Tension Level (0-100)*	
			Before	*After*

This log provides the therapist with information on the amount of tension reduction that is attributable to relaxation practice and also the bodily areas that may need individual attention. In addition, monitoring of before and after practice tension levels can help clients who have difficulty seeing changes that are not immediate and dramatic.

Beginning with the third or fourth session, relaxation practice shifts to relaxation without the muscle tension procedures. Clients continue to record their relaxation practice on the same form. Like the stress logs, relaxation logs are turned in before the next session.

The importance of relaxation practice is described in terms of skill development. Relaxation is a skill like reading or riding a bike; clients will only become skillful if they practice. The self-control aspect, that is, that clients come to have the skills under their own control, is also emphasized. Clients are told that with practice and subsequent application, they will acquire their own repertoire of coping skills with which to reduce stress. Use of relaxation tapes is discouraged because it may foster a dependency on resources other than the client's own abilities. Our experience is that, with few exceptions, clients develop the skills in roughly the same amount of time on their own as they do with tapes. They develop a greater sense of self-efficacy and also avoid the problem of weaning themselves from the tapes.

Application training. Relaxation procedures for use in stressful situations are taught next.

Assignment: As the various methods of applying relaxation *in vivo* are introduced, add them to the home practice and record them on the relaxation log.

These records are discussed in the next session. When clients have developed proficiency with the new methods — usually about the end of the fourth session — they select the procedures that work best for them and develop a set of written self-instructions with which to initiate the procedures *in vivo*.

Assignment: Construct instructions between sessions and turn them in before the next session. After these are explored and honed, rewrite the final version between sessions.

Guided practice. As clients gain proficiency in applying relaxation within sessions, application is gradually shifted to the external world. This shift follows three steps. First, after about the third or fourth session, the following assignment is given:

Assignment: Practice relaxation in situations that involve no tension, for example, waiting for a class to begin or walking to work.

The following second assignment is made a session or two later.

Assignment: Begin applying relaxation in mildly to moderately tension-arousing situations, for example, when studying a couple of days before an anxiety-causing test or practicing a speech to be given in a few days.

Finally, after clients have demonstrated good control within sessions, the third assignment is given:

Assignment: Apply relaxation coping skills across the full range of life events, including very stressful situations. Monitor "early warning" cues and relax away felt tension.

Clients contract for at least one applied relaxation effort before the next session.

Assignment: Record all attempts to apply relaxation in a third stress log format (Stress Log 3):

Date/Time	Situation	Physical Cues	Tension Level (0-100)	
			Before	After

This homework is turned in before the next session and is discussed in terms of methods of relaxation attempted, ways of tuning the procedures for greater effect, and reinforcement of success. In addition to providing corrective feedback for changes in procedure, this log provides a progress report of intervention effectiveness. It supplies data for determining when clients are consistently controlling stress and are ready for termination.

COMPLIANCE ENHANCEMENT PROCEDURES

Training in RSC embodies a number of principles and procedures designed to facilitate homework compliance. Several of these are outlined in this section.

Active Client and Therapist Participation

Clients are encouraged to see stress as a normal part of living but also as something over which they can learn to exercise control, if they practice. Thus from the start they receive a positive set that stresses the necessity for active homework.

A common problem, however, is that therapists often do not take seriously their own injunctions about the importance of homework. They may excuse lack of compliance or simply pay little or no attention to homework. To do this is to signal that homework is not really all that important. It is no wonder that clients quickly imitate therapist behavior and fail to attend to assignments. In RSC the importance of homework is continually underscored by having clients drop off homework the day before therapy. The therapist reviews the homework before the next session and makes clear reference to it. This practice stresses the importance and the collaborative nature of homework, since both the clients and the therapist must do it to continue therapy.

Nonpunitive Therapist Behavior

Clients are not blamed or made to feel guilty for their anxiety reactions. They are helped to see that anxiety is a normal function of their learning histories and not some sort of personal inadequacy or personality defect. Failure to comply with homework is treated in the same way. Since many anxious clients are sensitive to social rejection, they may become anxious about the therapist's reaction to failure and may even avoid the therapist and drop out of treatment. Therapists should therefore minimize criticism regarding failure to comply.

One approach is always "blaming the first mistake on the therapist." The first lack of compliance is accepted and clarified straightforwardly and suitable homework is given to replace the original assignment. The therapist thus assumes that the client had good intentions. The therapist also makes the benign assumption (overlooked by some) that the client failed to comply because he or she did not understand either the nature of the assignment or the way to perform it. Handling the problem in this manner communicates acceptance to clients and decreases the chances of anxiety interfering with therapy. At the same time, it allows homework to be emphasized by being described more clearly and concretely.

Should problems in compliance persist, therapists may want to apply contingency procedures. Even here, blame and negative labeling should be minimized, for the reasons noted previously. One type of contingency system is positive reinforcement for completion of homework. For example, clients might make television time contingent upon relaxation practice. Another approach is to make therapy time contingent upon compliance. With this method, clients may be asked to practice relaxation or record stress a given number of times before scheduling the next appointment. A third approach is the use of positive punishment techniques such as a penalty deposit system. Students who are very apprehensive about orals for the master's degree might be asked to deposit specific amounts of money, which are to be sent to their "least favorite charity" if they do not attend mock orals in which guided practice can take place. If such a procedure is employed, it is important for the therapists to emphasize that they are only serving as mediators in helping clients execute contracts with themselves and are not personally punishing the clients for failure to comply.

Therapists also should be alert to the possibility of clients construing things in counterproductive ways, without blaming them when it happens. For example, it is not uncommon for clients to interpret relaxation practice as a direct means of reducing anxiety. Consequently they do not practice at home, stating that they were not anxious and therefore had no need to practice. If this happens, they should be reminded that the goal of relaxation practice is to develop skill, not to alleviate anxiety directly. Analogies to the learning involved in other complex skills, such as driving a car or playing basketball, may also clarify this point. Pointing out the inefficiency of the full progressive relaxation procedures may help because clients see they will not always have time to go through the whole procedure to manage tension. Should the problem continue, however, it is suggested that contingency procedures be instituted.

Graduated Task Difficulty

The coping skills of anxious clients are often minimal, leaving them with few resources with which to handle failure and setbacks. Every effort, therefore, should be made to minimize failure and maximize success. This is done most easily by making therapeutic steps within both treatment sessions and homework small and progressive. Clients move to a more complex or difficult step when they have demonstrated success at the previous step. The homework for RSC is built around this principle. For example, initial self-monitoring involves recording only the date, time of day, the affective state, and the precipitating event. Ratings of response magnitude and the covarying physiological cues are added after clients successfully complete the less complex self-monitoring task. *In vivo* practice is begun only after clients have demonstrated self-control within sessions, and then the homework is graduated from situations arousing no anxiety to moderately tension-producing situations and finally to the most stressful circumstances. Movement to the next step is based on the data collected during the *in vivo* tryouts.

Concrete Assignments and Homework Supports

Compliance appears to be facilitated by clearly defined, concrete assignments (Shelton & Ackerman, 1974), and assignments in RSC tend to be very concrete and specific. For example, clients are to set aside 30 minutes in 5 of the next 7 days and practice tensing and releasing each muscle group once in the order demonstrated in therapy. They are to observe their affective state during three specified times and record the observation in their stress logs. They contract to apply their relaxation skills in at least one specific situation before the next session during the latter portion of guided practice. This experience too is recorded in the stress log. Thus, as much as possible, clients know specifically and concretely what they are to do in their homework.

Compliance seems to be aided by clearly communicated and understood instructions. In this respect it is often helpful to ask clients to paraphrase their understanding of the assignment. This allows the therapist to check client understanding and provide corrective feedback before the assignment has been undertaken. It may also be helpful to write down the specific nature of the homework and to give this to clients to take with them. Carbon paper or similar duplication procedures provide records for clients and therapist alike.

Compliance also seems to be enhanced through the use of various response induction aids, supports, and prompts. The use of handouts describing how to implement homework, such as relaxation handouts, and specific recording forms and procedures, such as various stress and relaxation logs, seems to minimize confusion and facilitate actual tryout in the home setting. Phone calls can also provide support and prompting. The progress of a very anxious client can be checked by phone between sessions. Success can be reinforced, and problems can be resolved over the phone. Specific therapist-client contracts for given behavior help the client engage in homework. The RSC program has several such contracts, for example, turning in assignments the day before the next session and contracting for at least one *in vivo* tryout before the next session during guided practice.

Maintenance

Some clients develop good coping skills but 6 months later are experiencing high levels of stress. They have stopped using the very skills that once reduced the stress. Clients need to be told that coping is a lifelong process. Life will continue to stress them, and they will need to continue to apply their coping skills to manage it. Continued coping will make coping easier, but not unnecessary. Providing clients with this general orientation seems to help maintain attention to continued practice and reduce problems of relapse.

Several other strategies may be employed to strengthen maintenance. First the latter sessions of treatment may be spaced at greater intervals, such as every 2 or 3 weeks. This practice gives clients greater experience in applying coping skills between sessions yet still maintains therapeutic contact for needed assistance. Then periodic follow-up or booster sessions, perhaps every 10 or 12 weeks, may be planned. This practice too keeps client attention focused upon further development and practice of coping skills especially since they must be discussed in a few weeks. If no further sessions are planned, clients can continue to self-monitor and report to the therapist by phone or mail. They may also develop schedules of self-reinforcement for continued practice and coping. Finally, in cases where many individuals go through the same treatment, they may stay in touch with each other and form an informal support group. All of these tend to keep attention upon continued work at a time when skills should be consolidated further but the tendency to stop using them is high because stress may be relatively low.

ILLUSTRATIVE CASE

The following section will describe briefly the application of RSC in the cases of two test-anxious college students (Deffenbacher,1976).

Pretreatment assessment interviews with two male juniors suggested long histories of moderate to severe test anxiety, average to above average intellectual ability, and no other evidence of severe psychopathology. The students were treated together and were seen in five weekly sessions, each lasting approximately 45 minutes. In session 1 the self-control rationale of RSC was introduced, the initial steps of discrimination training were outlined, and progressive relaxation training was begun. Homework involved monitoring their anxiety level three times per day, recording the level of anxiety and the cues associated with its buildup, and practicing relaxation daily. In sessions 2 and 3 progressive relaxation training was continued, moving to relaxation without tension in both the sessions and the intersession homework. Applied relaxation skills were introduced in the sessions and added to the homework between sessions. Discrimination training continued as before, with clients additionally pegging the lowest SUDS level that represented a significant level of personal distress (30 for one client and 50 for the other). Tension at or above this level was to be the cue for relaxation coping skills in sessions 4 and 5 and homework between sessions. In addition, between sessions 3 and 4 clients selected the most effective applied relaxation procedures and coordinated them into a written self-instructional statement to facilitate their cuing.

In sessions 4 and 5 clients practiced becoming aware of tension and applying relaxation coping skills under conditions of evaluative stress. They worked on both old academic tests and subtests of the Differential Aptitude Test in a small classroom where the therapist attempted to replicate evaluative cues present during exams, such as announcing time on the board. During the tests the clients monitored their anxiety level and employed their relaxation skills to relax away tension. If they were unable to relax away tension, testing was stopped, problems were discussed, and they returned immediately to testing for further practice. Between sessions clients practiced applying relaxation coping skills whenever anxiety was experienced and recorded these self-control attempts in their logs. After the fifth session, clients were contacted by phone at 1-week, 2-week, and 4-week follow-ups, where practice of relaxation coping skills was discussed and reinforced. Clients reported reductions of both test and general anxiety and use of relaxation coping skills in other situations, such as when angry or going to sleep. Grades also improved, with one client raising his grades to a 3.00 from 2.16 and 2.00 the two terms before treatment and with the other client raising his grades to a 3.40 from 2.71 and 2.80 pretreatment levels.

SUMMARY

Anxiety has always been a difficult problem to define and explain. In this chapter it is viewed as an inferential construct derived from data from one or more of the following response domains: the affective-physiological domain, the cognitive domain, and the somatic-behavioral domain. It can be caused by a number of things — skill or information deficits, negative thoughts, classical conditioning, or learning through observation — and it persists due to operant conditioning of avoidance behaviors. Anxiety differs from fear in that fear is a result of specific stimulus conditions, whereas anxiety has more diffuse cues. There are both internal and external stressors that may cue anxiety.

Relaxation as self-control (RSC) is the treatment for anxiety discussed here. It has an advantage over other treatments in that it is generalizable to stressors other than the ones targeted in treatment. Because it was developed to lower physiological-affective arousal, RSC is best used with disorders caused by autonomic-affective overreactivity or as part of a multimodal plan for other sources of anxiety. Several studies have shown that RSC reliably reduces targeted anxieties and general anxiety, maintains that reduction, and compares favorably to desensitization in its results.

The RSC model lists four conditions for the development of relaxation as a self-managed coping skill: skill in detecting internal cues of tension; acquisition of a basic relaxation response; ability to self-induce relaxation quickly for *in vivo* use; and chaining of the first three plus practice to insure the reliable use of the procedure. Training proceeds through four phases corresponding to the four conditions: Phase 1 is discrimination training, Phase 2 is relaxation training, Phase 3 is application training, and Phase 4 is guided practice. Homework assignments in assessment and all four phases are described.

Compliance enhancement procedures incorporated in the treatment program are then outlined. Active client and therapist participation in therapy is encouraged, and the therapist is counseled to not blame the clients for any failures in therapy. Assignments are kept small, with gradually increasing difficulty, to maximize the clients' success, and are expressed as clearly and concretely as possible. Aids, supports, and prompts for homework are utilized. Finally, maintenance procedures are suggested for use after the initial program.

The discussion of RSC ends with a case study of the application of RSC to two test-anxious college students. Their treatment resulted in reduction of anxiety and an improvement in grades for both of them.

REFERENCES

Bandura, A. *Principles of behavior modification.* New York: Holt Rinehart & Winston, 1969.

Deffenbacher, J.L. Relaxation *in vivo* in the treatment of test anxiety. *Journal of Behavior Therapy and Experimental Psychiatry,* 1976, 7, 289-292.

Deffenbacher, J.L., Mathis, J., & Michaels, A.C. Two self-control procedures in the reduction of targeted and nontargeted anxieties. *Journal of Counseling Psychology,* 1979, *26,* 120-127.

Deffenbacher, J.L., & Michaels, A.C. Two self-control procedures in the reduction of targeted and nontargeted anxieties — A year later. *Journal of Counseling Psychology,* 1980, *27,* 9-15.

Deffenbacher, J.L., & Payne, D.M.J. Two procedures for relaxation as self-control in the treatment of communication apprehension. *Journal of Counseling Psychology,* 1977, *24,* 255-258.

Deffenbacher, J.L., & Rivera, N. A behavioral self-control treatment of test anxiety in minority populations: Some cases and issues. *Psychological Reports,* 1976, *39,* 1188-1190.

Deffenbacher, J.L., & Snyder, A.L. Relaxation as self-control in the treatment of test and other anxieties. *Psychological Reports,* 1976, *39,* 379-385.

Girodo, M. Self-talk: Mechanism in anxiety and stress management. In I. Sarason & C. Spielberger (Eds.), *Stress and anxiety, Volume IV.* Washington, D.C.: Hemisphere, 1976.

Goldfried, M.R. Systematic desensitization as training in self-control. *Journal of Consulting and Clinical Psychology,* 1971, *37,* 228-235.

Lang, P.J. The mechanics of desensitization and the laboratory study of human fear. In C.M. Franks (Ed.), *Behavior therapy: Appraisal and status.* New York: McGraw-Hill, 1969.

Leitenberg, H., Agras, W.S., Butz, R., & Wincze, J.P. Relationship between heart rate and behavioral change during the treatment of phobias. *Journal of Abnormal Psychology,* 1971, *78,* 59-68.

Paul, G.L. Outcome of systematic desensitization: II. Controlled investigations of individual treatment, technique variations, and current status. In C.M. Franks (Ed.), *Behavior therapy: Appraisal and status.* New York: McGraw-Hill, 1969.

Rimm, D.C., & Masters, J.C. *Behavior therapy: Techniques and empirical findings.* New York: Academic Press, 1974.

Shelton, J.L., & Ackerman, J.M. *Homework in counseling and psychotherapy.* Springfield, Ill.: Charles C. Thomas, 1974.

Snyder, A.L., & Deffenbacher, J.L. Comparison of relaxation as self-control and systematic desensitization in the treatment of test anxiety. *Journal of Consulting and Clinical Psychology,* 1977, *45,* 1202-1203.

Solomon, R. Punishment. *American Psychologist,* 1964, *19,* 239-253.

Suinn, R.M. Treatment of phobias. In G.A. Harris (Ed.), *The group treatment of human problems.* New York: Grune & Stratton, 1977.

Wolpe, J. *The practice of behavior therapy.* Elmsford, N.Y.: Pergamon Press, 1969.

CHAPTER 5

Depression

Anthony Biglan
Behavior Change Center and Oregon Research Institute
David R. Campbell
Behavior Change Center and Sacred Heart Medical Center

OVERVIEW OF DEPRESSION

Depression is perhaps the single most common clinical problem to be encountered among adult outpatients (Levitt & Lubin, 1975; Lehmann, 1977). However, considerable controversy still exists on what criteria should be used for diagnosis (Rehm, 1977). One of the more widely accepted approaches was proposed by Feighner, Robins, Guze, Woodruff, Winokur, and Munoz (1972). They suggested that a person be diagnosed as depressed if he or she exhibits a dysphoric mood and at least five of the following symptoms: (1) poor appetite or weight loss; (2) difficulty sleeping, including insomnia or hypersomnia; (3) loss of energy, such as fatigue or tiredness; (4) agitation or retardation; (5) loss of interest in usual activities or decrease in sexual drive; (6) feelings of self-reproach or guilt; (7) complaints of or actually diminished ability to think or concentrate; and (8) recurrent thoughts of death or suicide. In addition, the person must have "no preexisting psychiatric conditions such as schizophrenia, anxiety neurosis, etc."

Disagreement exists about whether all of the problems just described result from a single source, such as a biochemical deficit

(Akiskal & McKinney, 1973). However, even if this cluster of events does not constitute a unitary phenomenon, diagnostic criteria such as those proposed by Feighner et al. (1972) are useful in that they allow one to assess whether the clients being treated are similar to subjects in depression treatment research.

In light of the wide range of events that may indicate depression, it is not surprising that the specific problems of depressed clients are quite diverse. Table 5.1, which is drawn from the work of McLean (1976a, (1976b), Craighead (1980), and Liberman (1980), presents a list of the most common problems reported by depressed persons.

Table 5.1

Independent and Dependent Variables in Depression
Treatment Research*

INDEPENDENT VARIABLES	DEPENDENT VARIABLES
SETTING CONDITIONS	OVERT BEHAVIOR
Arrangements for Treatment Delivery	*Nonsocial*
Group Treatment	Inactivity
Timing of Sessions	Insomnia
Money Deposits	Suicidal Behavior
Charges for Treatment	*Social*
Therapist Characteristics	Low Rate or Range of Interactions
Intake and Assessment Procedures	Avoidance of Others
Extent and Content of Assessment	Skill Deficits
Goal Setting	Conflict with Others
	Sexual Inactivity
MAJOR TREATMENT COMPONENTS	*Verbal*
Modification of Activities	Complaints (including questionnaire
Self-Monitoring of Activity and Mood	responses)
Planning Small Increases in Activities	
Instructions	COVERT BEHAVIOR
Rewards for Activities	*Feelings*
Modification of Social Behavior	Anxiety
Social Skill Interventions (assertive	Dysphoria
responses)	Fatigue
Covert and overt modeling;	*Verbal Cognitive Events*
instruction; social reinforcement;	Worry
coaching; behavior rehearsal; biblio-	Indecisiveness
therapy; token reinforcement	Negative Self-Talk
Increasing Social Activity	Suicidal Thoughts
Same as for increasing activities	*Somatic Events*
Marital Interventions	Weight Loss
Feedback about interpersonal be-	Headaches
havior; contracting with spouse;	Pain
communications training	Gastrointestinal Problems
	Dizziness

*Reprinted by permission from A. Biglan and M. Dow. Toward a second generation model: A problem-specific approach. In L. P. Rehm (Ed.), *Behavior therapy for depression: Present status and future directions*. New York: Academic Press, 1981.

Table 5.1   *(Continued)*

INDEPENDENT VARIABLES	DEPENDENT VARIABLES
Modification of Verbal Cognitive Events Suppression of Negative Self-Talk Self-monitoring; thought stopping; flooding; punishment; systematic desensitization; paradoxical intention; delay between thoughts and overt behavior; extinction; geographical control (thinking restricted to certain places); temporal control (thinking restricted to certain times) Analysis of Thought Content Self-monitoring; identifying themes or content; distancing thoughts by labeling them as hypotheses; evaluating evidence for thoughts, then implications if true; identifying other ways to look at them; testing validity of thoughts or beliefs; bibliotherapy; writing and saying rational refutations of thoughts *Anxiety Treatment* Systematic Desensitization Flooding Relaxation Training with Coping Skill Instructions *Insomnia Treatment* Relaxation Training Stimulus Control Procedures	

Etiology

Although there is evidence of genetic factors in some types of depression (Winokur, 1971), knowledge about the etiology of the typical unipolar depression seen in outpatient settings is limited. Among the causative factors suggested are biochemical deficits (Akiskal & McKinney, 1973), stressful events (McLean, 1976a), the absence of effective self-control procedures (Rehm, 1977; Kanfer & Hagerman, 1980), problematic cognitions (Beck, 1967), learned helplessness (Seligman, 1980), and a low rate of reinforcement (Lewinsohn, Biglan, & Zeiss, 1976). Obviously, these factors are not mutually exclusive.

Several variables are strongly associated with depression. A high incidence of depression exists among certain groups of patients with chronic disease. According to MMPI criteria (Mlott & Allain, 1974), the typical male hemodialysis patient is depressed. Chronic back pain patients (Beals & Hickman, 1972), facial pain patients (Raft, Toomey, & Gregg, 1979), and pulmonary insufficiency patients (Agle, Baum,

Chester, & Wendt, 1973) present similar significant elevations on the MMPI. Data also suggest that the spouses of seriously brain-injured persons are often clinically depressed.

The etiology of depression is not necessarily relevant to its treatment, however. Although biochemical deficits may produce depression, psychological interventions may still provide the most effective treatment. Conversely, although stressful life events may produce depression, pharmacological interventions could prove to be the best treatment.

Problem Conceptualization

Dysphoria. Dysphoria is central to both common language descriptions of depression and clinical criteria for depression. Feeling down, blue, sad, and despondent are just a few of the many ways we have to describe this event. The richness of descriptive language available to us suggests the prevalence of this human condition. Clinical specifications of depression such as those of Feighner et al. (1972) include dysphoria as an essential criterion, and questionnaires such as the Beck Depression Inventory contain questions about sadness, pessimism, self-dislike, guilt, and self-accusation. The primary goal of treatment in depression is usually alleviating dysphoria.

The problems of assessing the occurrence of dysphoria are similar to those for assessing pain: no completely reliable and valid criterion exists. Therapists are dependent upon a person's verbal report and such nonverbal behavior as frowning or hesitant speech. As with pain, clients appear to vary in the private events they learn to label as depressing (Skinner, 1945). Some label events as depressing that others would call anxiety-producing.

Emotions have generally been viewed as respondents rather than operants (Skinner, 1953). Lewinsohn (1974) has suggested that the experience of dysphoria is an unconditioned response to conditions of a low rate of reinforcement. Perhaps for this reason, most behavioral treatments do not attempt to directly modify the dysphoric mood, but focus on changing other aspects of depression, such as rate of activity, in the hope that such changes will improve the mood (Lewinsohn, 1974).

We are inclined to view dysphoria as an operant and to attempt to directly modify its occurrence by changing the contingencies of reinforcement. This view is based on the evidence from biofeedback research that private events (Weiss & Engel, 1975) and such observable "signs" of dysphoria as crying (Reisinger, 1972) can be reinforced, as well as from the results of our own work with clients. For some people, especially the more chronically depressed, dysphoria seems to be reinforced in a number of subtle ways. Some people stay in bed or "rest" when feeling depressed. Others sit down, drink coffee, and smoke.

Marital problems. Several studies implicate problematic marital relations as a significant source of depression (Coleman & Miller, 1975; Weiss & Birchler, 1978; Weissman & Paykel, 1974). Evidence suggests that this association is more prominent among males (Johnson & Lobitz, 1974; Weiss & Aved, 1978).

Cognitions. A common characteristic of clinically depressed clients is a high rate of negative self-talk (Beck, 1972). The content and pattern of negative self-talk is perhaps unique for each person, but the thoughts are frequent, unpleasant, and associated with feelings of dysphoria. Clients will usually readily assent to "reducing worrying" as a treatment goal. Self-depreciation, self-blame, somatic preoccupation, and indecision may best be categorized as problematic worry.

Anxiety. Anxiety is frequently a problem among clinically depressed individuals (Biglan & Dow, 1980) but has been overlooked in discussions of treatment. In one group of 19 depressed clients, 8 identified recurrent anxiety as a problem for which they wanted help.

Activities. Depressed individuals report fewer pleasant activities (Lewinsohn & Graf, 1973; Lewinsohn & Libet, 1972; Lewinsohn & MacPhillamy, 1974; MacPhillamy & Lewinsohn, 1974) and indicate experiencing more unpleasant events (Grosscup & Lewinsohn, 1980) than nondepressed individuals. Although the value of increasing pleasant activities for improving dysphoria has yet to be established (Blaney, 1980), many depressed individuals request help in increasing recreational and work activities.

Social skills. Although social behavior deficits have been identified in some studies of depressed individuals (Libet & Lewinsohn, 1973; Libet, Lewinsohn, & Javorek, Note 1) we are far from a complete understanding of the social behavior problems of the depressed. Evidence exists that depressed individuals report being less assertive (Sanchez, 1978), less comfortable around others, and less skilled (Youngren & Lewinsohn, 1980) than nondepressed subjects. Direct observations of their behavior, however, have not always confirmed these reports (Sanchez, 1978; Youngren & Lewinsohn, 1980). For these reasons, it is important that the therapist resist making too many assumptions about the social skill deficits of the depressed individual.

Additional factors. Assessment for depression should probably include questions directed toward a person's use of alcohol and other drugs, since such usage could be a complicating factor, if not a primary problem itself. Financial problems often require discussion and problem solving. It is also useful to ask how long the person has been depressed, because treatment strategies would probably differ greatly for a person who reports a depression lasting 1 week as opposed to someone who has been depressed for more than 1 year. Since many depressed persons express thoughts of suicide, procedures for managing clients who are judged significantly suicidal need to be specified. The reader is referred to Schneidman (1975) as a resource for guidelines to this issue.

HOMEWORK-BASED TREATMENT

Overview of Treatment

A problem-specific model. Our approach to treating depression involves pinpointing the specific problems that the client is having and then intervening on each of them. Such a problem-specific model has been recommended in one form or another by McLean (1976b), Biglan and Dow (1980), and Liberman (1980). Interventions on each problem can be assigned priority according to client choice, evidence for the efficacy of each intervention, and consideration of the cost-effectiveness and risks of the interventions (Liberman, 1980).

Some evidence exists that treatment programs designed along these lines are more effective than alternative procedures. McLean and Hakstian (1979) found that their behavior therapy treatment program was more effective than the use of drugs, placebos, or psychotherapy. Similarly, Biglan, Craker, and Dow (Note 2) found that a problem-specific treatment approach was more effective in treating depressed clients than a self-monitoring-only control condition. Although not conclusive, these results suggest the efficacy of a problem-specific approach.

Biglan and Dow (1980) have summarized the interventions that characterize behaviorally oriented depression treatment programs. A list of these appeared in Table 5.1.

The role of medication. The efficacy of lithium in treating bipolar affective disorders is reasonably well established (Schou, 1974). However, those affected by bipolar affective disorders constitute a fairly small proportion of all depressed persons (Weissman & Paykel, 1974). A moderate proportion of unipolar depressed clients have been shown to respond to tricyclic antidepressive medication. Unfortunately, only a few studies have been able to predict a client's response to medication (Donnelly, Murphy, Waldman, & Goodwin, 1979). Liberman (1980) suggests providing pharmacological interventions before using behavioral interventions. Clients unresponsive to medication would then be treated using behavioral techniques. Sometimes medication will remediate some of the problems of depression, such as inactivity and dysphoria, but additional problems remain that require behavioral interventions. Thus a combination of pharmacological and behavioral treatment may be appropriate.

Homework Assignments

Assessment. In our initial consultation with a client we develop a tentative list of treatment goals. It is emphasized that the client must decide which aspects of his or her behavior he or she wants to change. If the client is depressed, he or she is asked about each of the typical problem areas described at the beginning of this chapter. At the end of this session four alternative courses of action are suggested: (1) start on treatment immediately, (2) go home and think about it, (3) go to another agency, or (4) decline treatment.

When and if treatment begins, the first assignments are designed to elaborate upon the information the client has provided in the initial consultation and to help him or her mobilize support from family and friends. It is important that these assignments be easy since depressed clients already have a low estimate of their abilities. We ask the client to stop us if we give him or her more than he or she can do. After the assignments have been described, we ask again if the client is sure that he or she can do everything that has been worked out.

Assignment: Self-monitor one or two problems of most concern.

Since giving the client choices among procedures may enhance their efficacy, the client is given as much latitude as possible in choosing the specific format for recording, the frequency of recording, and the amount of detail to produce. Examples of two forms are presented in Figure 5.1. The first of these is simply a calendar in which the client can write in the days of the week at the top and the date in the upper right-hand corner of each box. The actual size of this form is 8½ x 11. The boxes are large enough to write the number of times specific events have occurred (for example, pleasant activities) or brief notes about target events. The lower form allows the person to indicate the time at which target events occur so that their relationship to time of day can be assessed. If social interactions are relevant, the form presented in Figure 5.2 is recommended because it prompts the person to analyze how he or she might have responded differently in the interaction (Column 4). Where possible, we specify positive events to be tracked; this procedure prompts the client to attend to these events and may increase their rate of occurrence (Nelson, 1977).

Assignment: Complete the mood-monitoring questionnaire(s).

Figure 5.1   Recording forms for self-monitoring of events

Monday	Tuesday	Wednesday	Thursday	Friday	Saturday	Sunday
☐	☐	☐	☐	☐	☐	☐
☐	☐	☐	☐	☐	☐	☐
☐	☐	☐	☐	☐	☐	☐
☐	☐	☐	☐	☐	☐	☐
☐	☐	☐	☐	☐	☐	☐

Initials:_____   Rating: 1 = _____ 10 = _____
Dates: From_____ to _____

	Monday	Tuesday	Wednesday	Thursday	Friday	Saturday	Sunday
6 am							
7 am							
8 am							
9 am							
10 am							
11 am							
12 am							
1 pm							
2 pm							
3 pm							
4 pm							
5 pm							
6 pm							
7 pm							

Figure 5.1 *(Continued)*

	Monday	Tuesday	Wednesday	Thursday	Friday	Saturday	Sunday
8 pm							
9 pm							
10 pm							
11 pm							
12 pm							
1 am							
2 am							

Figure 5.2   Social interaction recording form

1 Date	2 Brief Description of Situation	3 How You Reacted (said, did, felt)	4 A Better Reaction Would Have Been	5 Dates When You Imagined the Better Reaction

Behavioral treatment of depression usually includes some means of monitoring mood. Such procedures might include repeated administration of standard brief questionnaires such as the Self-Rating Depression Scale (Zung, 1965), the Beck Depression Inventory (Beck & Beamesderfer, 1974), or the Depression Adjective Checklist (DACL-A; Lubin, 1965).

Assignment: Complete the packet of questionnaires provided before the second session.

Listed next are the questionnaires we use. Each provides a brief measure of a problem area common among depressed individuals. Such questionnaires also allow assessment of treatment outcome.

Beck Depression Inventory (Beck & Beamesderfer, 1974)

State-Trait Anxiety Inventory (Spielberger, Gorsuch, & Lushene, 1970)

Fear Inventory (Wolpe & Lang, 1964)

Social Avoidance and Distress (Watson & Friend, 1969)

Assignment: Self-monitor your mood during specific activities.

None of the measures just mentioned provides a direct report of the specific occurrences of dysphoric mood and the events accompanying it. Therefore, we have found it useful to have the client keep track of what he or she is doing and note his or her mood during different activities. A 1- to 10-point scale with agreed-upon anchors (1 = depressed, 10 = happy; 1 = feeling blue, 10 = feeling normal) is used. This procedure helps to pinpoint the events associated with dysphoria and to evaluate the effects of various interventions. In particular, it provides information about the factors that may be reinforcing depression.

Assignment: Talk to family members and friends about the treatment plan.

This assignment could mobilize support for the client's effort at changing behavior. If his or her depressed behavior is aversive to others, the announcement that he or she will try to change could alter the stimulus value of the client and might prompt some positive reinforcement. Even when marital difficulties are not present, the spouse should attend at least some sessions. A specific assignment might be to ask the spouse if he or she would be willing to come to one session. Finally, the client is asked to consider taking antidepressive medication. If the client agrees, he or she is requested to make an appointment with his or her physician, or a physician is recommended if he or she has none.

Modification of dysphoria. These assignments are meant to modify dysphoria directly. Often it is useful to intervene directly on dysphoria by helping the person change the contingencies for feeling depressed. It is helpful to reduce possible reinforcers such as cigarette smoking, coffee drinking, and rest when self-monitoring data suggest that a client is doing these contingent upon dysphoria. It is also useful to suggest response costs such as completing avoided tasks or mildly aversive activities contingent upon dysphoria. Sometimes a client is asked to make a list of such activities so that they are visible and available.

> **Assignment:**   If you feel depressed for more than 5 minutes, begin working on a task from your list. During that time don't smoke cigarettes or drink coffee until your mood has improved.

Housecleaning and related activities are relevant because they are usually readily available. A person may take some time to develop consistent responses to dysphoria, and it may be necessary to shape the use of these strategies by, for example, having the person use them only in the evening at first. Although following through with such recommendations might not immediately improve the client's mood, at least he or she can feel good about getting something done that had been put off.

Identification of target activities. Many different methods have been used to increase activity (Biglan & Dow, 1980). Existing evidence suggests that it may be best to identify activities that the client wants to increase and to minimize the extent to which the client perceives that the therapist is responsible for changes in activity (Hammen, Rook, & Harris, Note 3).

The client is asked to identify the most pressing work activities that he or she needs to do and the pleasant activities that he or she is most interested in trying. If the client has difficulty thinking of pleasant activities, he or she is asked to tell the therapist about things that seemed enjoyable before the depression began.

> **Assignment:**   Ask family or friends for suggestions of pleasant activities.

If the client is married, it is suggested that the spouse come to the next session to discuss what pleasant activities could be tried.

> **Assignment:**   Complete Pleasant Events Schedule.

The client may also be offered a copy of the Pleasant Events Schedule (MacPhillamy & Lewinsohn, Note 4) if additional prompts to identify pleasant activities appear to be needed. We place particular emphasis on identifying social activities since they are frequently associated with mood (Youngren & Lewinsohn, 1980).

Assignment of specific activities. As specific pleasant activities are identified, small steps the person can take to do the activity are enumerated.

> **Assignment:**   If you are interested in pottery, call the local community college to inquire about classes.

Because client choice among treatments may enhance treatment efficacy (Kanfer & Grimm, 1978), the therapist discusses and lists a number of possible small steps and activities with the client.

Assignment: Do a portion of the things discussed in therapy. For example: In the next week do three of the following: call a friend; go to a movie; go out to dinner with your family; read a news magazine; have coffee with an old friend; look into getting some new golf clubs.

Clients should be prepared for some failure. At this stage failures to engage in assigned activities or to enjoy them are diagnostic data. They provide more information about the obstacles to pleasant activity and lead to further problem solving.

Facilitation of increased activity. A number of assignments may be useful for facilitating the client's engagement in pleasant activities. *Goal clarification* can help the client sort out which activities are important to him or her.

Assignment: Read the book *How to Get Control of Your Time and Your Life* (Lakein, 1973).

The person identifies goals and sets priorities among them for each of the following time frames: (1) his or her lifetime, (2) the next 5 years, (3) if he or she had 6 months to live. We have the client *literally follow* these instructions and bring the goal list to the next session. This goal clarification sometimes helps a client establish priorities among work and recreational activities. Moreover, by identifying long- and short-range goals, the client can identify meaningful activities that otherwise might not be obvious to him or her.

Training in time management skills. These skills may be necessary if a person is going to get needed tasks done and also find time for pleasant activities.

Assignment: Make "To Do" lists each day and cross off completed activities.

In subsequent sessions, "To Do" lists are reviewed and, if needed, suggestions such as the following are made:

1. Put nothing on your list that takes more than 15 minutes to do (SMALL STEPS!).

2. Don't put more things on today's "To Do" list than you got done yesterday.

3. Always include a pleasant activity on your "To Do" list.

4. Review your list of life goals before making your "To Do" list.

Training in social skill. Few studies have systematically assessed whether social skill training is an effective treatment for depression (Blaney, 1980). It may be effective in modifying social behavior and may also improve other aspects of depression (Hersen & Bellack, 1976; Hersen, Eisler, & Miller, 1973; Wells, Hersen, Bellack, & Himmelhoch, Note 5). The most salient features of social skill training include pinpointing the problematic social situations, identifying appropriate social responses, and increasing the frequency of those responses in the targeted situations through self-monitoring, overt and covert modeling, and behavior rehearsal (Biglan & Dow, 1980).

Chapter 12 of this volume presents a detailed discussion of the modification of one of the most common social behavior problems: nonassertiveness. The ideas presented in that chapter provide a useful guide for treating other social behavior problems, and we recommend that it be used in working with depressed individuals who have difficulties in interpersonal relations.

Assignment: Monitor yourself to pinpoint the specific situations that are difficult and to identify more effective and satisfying ways to behave in those situations.

The skill practice assignments described in Chapter 12 are suitable for treating the assertiveness problems of the depressed. Other skills that may be relevant are increasing the talking rate (Robinson & Lewinsohn, 1973) and decreasing depressive talk. Depressive talk probably achieves short-range reinforcement, such as sympathy, but has long-range negative consequences, such as turning off friends and relatives.

It should be remembered, however, that evidence for what constitutes a skilled social response in a given situation is quite limited. Perhaps the best guide to the appropriateness of social behavior is the client's own judgment. It is the client, after all, who is in the situation and must live with the consequences of new social behavior. If the client is uncomfortable with a new behavior, he or she is likely to discontinue practice, making generalization to problem situations unlikely.

Marital assignments. Specific procedures for marital treatment are presented by Jacobson in Chapter 6 of this book. They are quite relevant to the problems encountered in treating a married, depressed client.

Whether or not marital therapy is begun, a spouse can help by agreeing to do the following assignment.

Assignment: Engage in pleasant activities with your partner, prompting him or her to engage in nondepressive behavior and tackling problems that both of you are concerned with, such as arranging a budget or taking a class on child management.

An example of partner assignments that we have used in depression treatment is as follows:

Assignment: During a quiet time together that has minimal inter-
                    ruptions, plan some recreational experiences with
                    just the two of you or the entire family. Follow
                    through on at least one experience you plan.

Modification of verbal cognitive events. The first step in modifying verbal cognitive events is obtaining a record of such events.

Assignment: Monitor all negative thoughts, recording them in the
                    manner agreed upon.

The client's tracking of negative thoughts should make him or her more aware of those thoughts. Such awareness is an initial step in developing responses to control or terminate the negative thoughts. Self-monitoring also helps the client evaluate the effectiveness of the intervention. Since improvements in the ability to control or terminate negative thoughts may be very small at first, unless the client is aware of these improvements, he or she may be disinclined to continue procedures that are, in fact, working.

It is important to choose a self-monitoring technique that does not increase the frequency of the problematic thought. The best approach may be to provide alternative techniques and let the person choose the one he or she feels most comfortable with. The client should be warned that self-monitoring negative thoughts may lead to an increase in their frequency, and a contingency plan for this event should be made. For example, the client may terminate self-monitoring until the next session if the frequency of the thoughts increases, or he or she may switch to a different monitoring technique.

Thought-suppressing treatments. These are designed to help the person stop negative or unpleasant thoughts without analyzing their content. Treatments include thought stopping (Campbell, 1973; Rosen & Schnapp, 1974; Wolpe, 1958), flooding (Boulougouris & Bassiakos, 1973; Hackmann & McLean, 1975), punishment with electric shock (Kenny, Solyom, & Solyom, 1973), snapping a rubber band at the wrist (Mahoney, 1971), mildly aversive activities (Steinbock, 1976), paradoxical intention, where the client tries to dwell on the thoughts when they occur (Solyom, Garza-Perez, Ledwidge, & Solyom, 1972), delay between thoughts and overt behavior (Meyer, 1973), restricting the thoughts to one place, such as a particular chair (McLean, 1976b), postponing thought until fixed, regular time periods, such as the last 5 minutes of each half hour (McLean, 1976b), extinction (Hallam, 1974), and systematic desensitization (Gentry, 1970). An additional treatment for troublesome thoughts that we have used involves instructing the client to do something when the thoughts occur. Paying bills when worried about overdue payments and outlining steps for working on an avoided major project are examples of ways to take action.

None of these procedures have been validated in well-controlled research. In most case reports it is not clear whether the subjects were depressed or simply bothered by obsessional thoughts. In the case of thought stopping, a controlled study failed to show that the procedure was more effective than a presumably ineffective procedure where subjects practiced stopping thoughts of an image of a blank television screen (Stern, Lipsedge, & Marks, 1973). Thus, in attempting to reduce worry, it may be necessary to try a number of procedures before an effective one is found, and in some cases an effective intervention may not be found.

In practice, we ask clients what they have already tried and what results they have had. We then describe additional techniques that seem palatable and let the client choose the specific one he or she wants to try first. Often the thoughts occur in a limited number of situations, such as lying in bed or watching television.

Assignment: Leave the situation in which you are worrying and do not return until the thoughts cease.

If the thoughts have involved unfinished tasks, we suggest that they work on those tasks until the thoughts cease. Other suggestions might include sitting and doing nothing in the garage or bathroom until the thoughts cease or doing some mildly aversive housework or yardwork. The former procedure may produce an initial increase in rumination, but has led to improvement for some clients.

Since there is no clear evidence that any of these alternative activities are necessary, we let the client decide whether or not he or she wants the alternative tasks to be part of his or her worry-control program. However, we strive to have this decision made in the session so that the precise steps to be followed can be specified in writing.

If the negative thoughts do not appear to be under any situational control, the client is given a choice between punishment and postponement techniques. Punishment of thoughts might involve the following assignments:

Assignment: Do aversive tasks, such as washing dishes, when you worry.

Assignment: Wear a rubber band around the wrist and snap it whenever the unpleasant thoughts occur.

The postponement technique (McLean, 1976b) involves the person doing whatever he or she can to suppress the thought for a brief period of time but being allowed to think about the topic for a fixed period later on.

> **Assignment:** Avoid a worry as best you can for the first 55 minutes of each hour, but allow yourself to worry for the last 5 minutes.

The length of time to postpone the thought depends on the client's estimate of how well he or she can suppress the thought and how often the thought appears (McLean, Note 6). If the negative thoughts occur in many different situations, the following assignment can be given:

> **Assignment:** If you worry during the first 25 minutes of every half hour, do whatever you can to postpone worrying until the last 5 minutes of the half hour. You might try any of the following to help you suppress the worry: snap yourself with a rubber band, do housework, or take a walk around the block.

In subsequent sessions the client's self-monitoring records are reviewed and the client is asked for detailed descriptions of what he or she has done to suppress his or her worry. Reports of compliance with the treatment program and reports of success are reinforced. If the worries have gotten worse or are not improving, modifications are suggested, such as varying the techniques the client is using, substituting different techniques, switching to content-oriented treatments, or abandoning the focus on dealing with negative verbal-cognitive events (that is, switching to other goals).

Content-oriented treatments. These approaches focus on teaching the client to examine the validity of what he or she is saying and to think in new and less distressing ways (Hollon & Beck, in press). The therapist attempts to prompt the client to "distance" the thoughts, that is, to think of them as hypotheses, not as facts. The client is prompted through discussion with the therapist to examine the evidence for the thoughts, to consider how the thoughts are making him or her upset, and to examine other ways of thinking about the topic. These procedures have been included as a component of a number of depression treatment programs. In general, the total program, of which this was only a part, has been found to produce significantly greater improvement in questionnaire measures of depression than comparison conditions (Blaney, 1980). However, the specific impact of the content-oriented component on worry has not been evaluated.

The treatment begins with a dialogue that is guided by two questions: What is your evidence that the things you think are accurate? What other ways could you think about this situation? The therapist asks each of these questions explicitly and when necessary suggests relevant answers. Arguments with the client are avoided; if a client doesn't agree with suggested answers to these questions, the therapist simply moves to a different area of discussion. The client is encouraged to answer these questions in his or her own words. The dialogue ends with an assignment to analyze additional negative thoughts each day in the same manner.

Assignment: Each day, pick the worry that has occurred most frequently or has been most upsetting. For that worry, answer in writing the following questions: What is your evidence? What other ways could you think about it?

In subsequent sessions the therapist reviews this assignment in detail. The client is often asked to read his or her own responses as a way of prompting him or her to respond in more constructive ways to negative thoughts. Client efforts should be reinforced by praising, paraphrasing, and careful listening on the part of the therapist.

In some instances, this assignment is sufficient to prompt clients to analyze their negative thoughts when they occur. However, if such generalization does not occur spontaneously, an assignment can be given to complete such an analysis for each occurrence of a particular worry or unpleasant thought.

Assignment: Each time you find yourself thinking "I will never get better," take at least 2 minutes to answer the two basic questions about the thought. Note each time you were successful.

Treatment of anxiety. The anxiety reduction procedures outlined by Deffenbacher in Chapter 4 of this book provide an excellent guide for the treatment of depressed clients who suffer from anxiety. Our own procedures are strikingly similar to the ones described by Deffenbacher.

In treating the anxiety of depressed clients, we especially look for fears that may be interfering with the person's activity. Since an essential element in the treatment of specific fears involves getting the person to approach the feared object, an anxiety treatment program is quite compatible with assignments to increase activities.

Treatment of insomnia. Two nonpharmacological procedures appear to be effective in treating sleep-onset insomnia.

Assignment: After relaxation training, relax at the hour of sleep.

Assignment: Practice "stimulus control" by getting out of bed whenever you do not fall asleep within an agreed-upon number of minutes. Return to bed only when you feel sleepy and keep getting up when you do not fall asleep. (A prohibition against sleeping during the day is also an effective element of this procedure [Tokarz & Lawrence, Note 7]).

These procedures appear to be effective when used in combination (Woolfolk, Carr-Kaffashan, & McNulty, 1976), even in a self-administered format (Alperson & Biglan, 1979). Either procedure may be preferable to pharmacological treatments which can, in the long run, exacerbate sleep difficulties (Bootzin & Nicassio, 1978).

The efficacy of these procedures for treating early morning awakening has not been systematically evaluated. We have used the combined relaxation-stimulus control treatment in treating three people for early morning awakening. All clients reported initial success, although follow-up data were not obtained. Norton and DeLuca (1979) reported that stimulus control procedures were effective in reducing the incidence of early morning awakening in a 22-year-old male.

Assignment: Practice relaxation whenever you are unable to sleep.

If the person is not receiving relaxation training or if this intervention is not successful, we use a brief set of instructions on meditational relaxation and stimulus-control procedures. The meditative form of relaxation was devised by Benson (Benson, Beary, & Carol, 1974). For a 5- to 10-minute period the person says the word "one" each time he or she exhales.

Assignment: Practice meditational relaxation with stimulus-control procedures.

When early morning awakening is a problem, these instructions are supplemented with the following assignment.

Assignment: Practice meditational relaxation with stimulus control. Get out of bed if falling back to sleep does not occur within 10 minutes. Relax while lying in bed.

COMPLIANCE ENHANCEMENT PROCEDURES

Statement of Expectations

Our procedures for introducing clients to treatment have been influenced considerably by the United States Department of Health, Education, and Welfare's guidelines on the Protection of Human Subjects (1971). We believe that the principle of informed consent is not only ethically and legally wise, but enhances the probability that the client will comply with assignments. Evidence, while sparse, does appear supportive of such an approach (see Kanfer & Grimm, 1978).

In our initial consultation, we have the client read a statement of our general methods of working with the client (see Figure 5.3). The first 15 or 20 minutes of the consultation is spent going over these procedures to answer any questions that the client has and to help insure that the client is clear about how we will proceed. The client is told that he or she will not have to make any decisions during the session.

Figure 5.3   Handout of procedures used at the Behavior Change Center

PROGRAMS
AT THE
BEHAVIOR CHANGE CENTER

We want you to understand how we work at the Behavior Change Center. Here we describe the type of assistance you can expect from us, what we will ask you to do, and other things you should know before deciding to begin a program at the Center. Please read what follows carefully. Feel free to ask questions about anything that is not clear to you. Then sign one copy of the booklet on the back page for us. One copy is for you to keep.

Some Standard Procedures

You will meet regularly with one of the three behavior therapists on our staff. They are Dr. Anthony Biglan, Dr. David Campbell, and Dr. Nancy Hawkins. Each is a licensed psychologist with experience as a behavior therapist. If you prefer, and when it is possible for us to arrange them, group sessions will be available.

During your first one or two sessions, we will help you to *set your goals for behavior change*. In other words, *we will help you to describe how you would like to think, feel, and act differently*. If you want help in dealing with your child's behavior, we will assist you in defining how you want your child to think, feel, or act differently. For example, suppose your children often upset you by fighting. You, your children, and your therapist might settle on a number of goals such as:

1. Susan and Joe play cooperatively (without fighting) for half an hour at a time.
2. Susan and Joe share their toys.
3. Mom and Dad play with Susan and Joe for at least 15 minutes a day.

As another example, suppose you are frequently bothered by anxiety when you talk to someone of the opposite sex. You and your therapist might set as the goal: "Be able to talk to a man (or woman) for 15 minutes and remain comfortable." By establishing goals at the beginning, you make it more likely that you will achieve the changes you want, quickly and efficiently.

We want you to establish *your goals* rather than rely on us to pick goals for you. When you discuss your goals with your therapist, be sure to directly state what changes you would like to see. By being clear about what you want, you will more likely be satisfied with the outcome of our work with you.

At each session you and your therapist will agree on *between-session assignments*. Your therapist will make suggestions for things you can do to achieve your goals. You and your therapist will work out specific details for those assignments. For example, your therapist might teach you how to get relaxed and suggest that you practice relaxation twice each day. As another example, if you were trying to toilet train your child, your therapist might show you how to teach your child to go into the bathroom without fussing and ask you to follow the same procedures at home. By agreeing on between-session assignments, we make it more likely that you will reach your goals in a comfortable and efficient manner.

Fees

The fee for services at the Behavior Change Center is $11 for each 15 minute unit of service. We will make every effort to keep both the number of visits and the amount of time you spend in each session to a minimum. Some ways we do this are by giving you things you can do on your own such as keeping track of your behavior or practicing

Figure 5.3   *(Continued)*

relaxation, and by carefully preparing an "agenda" in advance of each session. In addition, we try to develop the most efficient behavior change procedures. In general, the number of sessions you require at the Center and the length of each session will depend on the type of problem you are working on, the amount of between-session effort you put into the programs we develop, and the complexity of your problems.

The Importance of Research

The behavior change strategies we use are based on the best available research evidence. In other words, we develop our programs by carefully considering what we and others in the field have found to be the most effective and economical ways of achieving changes in behavior. Of course, knowledge about how to effectively help people change their behavior is still quite limited. For this reason, we try to get a good deal of accurate information about the effects of our programs whenever we work with a client.

We will ask you to keep track of the behaviors you are trying to change and, possibly, to keep track of other people's behavior (if they agree to it). In this way we will be able to evaluate whether the recommendations we make to you are helpful, and can identify changes in your programs that are needed. Moreover, the information you provide to us helps us measure the effectiveness of our programs. We regularly review the results of our work with people who have particular problems and discuss among ourselves how we might further improve the effectiveness and efficiency of those programs. In doing so, we make it more likely that we can develop better services as time goes by.

From time to time we may write descriptions of our programs and present data about their effects to other professionals. By doing this we believe that we can contribute to the development of our field. Naturally, in presenting descriptions of programs or results, we will not identify anyone we have worked with by name.

Risks and Likely Benefits of Your Participation

Naturally, we will need to know a lot about you. So, there is a risk that your privacy could be invaded if information about you were not kept confidential. Be assured that we keep all information about our clients in strict confidence. We do not discuss cases except as part of our case planning and outcome evaluation. Everyone who works at the Behavior Change Center is aware of the importance of confidentiality. No information about you, or our work with you, is released to anyone unless you authorize us to do so in writing.

You should also know that even with the most effective programs, some people occasionally get worse. For example, it is possible that keeping track of your behavior could lead to increases in behaviors you are trying to reduce. Similarly, from time to time, a program which is intended to produce improvements in your child's behavior may lead to temporary worsening of problem behaviors. We have done everything possible to reduce these risks to a minimum. If problems such as these arise, be sure to bring them to the attention of your therapist. He or she will make changes in the programs you have worked out in order to deal with such problems.

I have read and understand the description of the Behavior Change procedures printed in this booklet.

Signature _____

Witness _____

Date _____

Choice of Goals

We indicate both verbally and in writing that we will help the person clarify goals for treatment but that we will not tell him or her what those goals should be. We assume that the client would not have come if he or she did not have some things he or she wanted to change, and that the client is most likely to follow through on assignments that focus on what he or she is most concerned about. We will sometimes suggest goals that the client had not considered if available research or our experience with other clients indicates that they may be relevant. For example, a client might not recognize that increasing his or her activity could be beneficial in helping him or her to feel better and worry less. We might therefore describe how such a goal could be relevant to treatment. However, if the client is disinterested in such a goal, we defer to his or her wishes.

Between-Session Assignments

It is made explicit that we only *suggest* assignments. If a client refuses to try an assignment, we respect that stance. In this way, we minimize arguments, increase our own comfort, and maximize the likelihood that the client will complete assignments.

A between-session assignment specifies what the client agrees to do between one session and the next. The therapist usually suggests something that is likely to help the client toward a goal. Therapist and client decide on a specific assignment acceptable to the client and write it down as explicitly as possible. The therapist keeps a carbon copy of these assignments to enhance the client's commitment and to guide preparation for the subsequent session.

Money Deposit

The money deposit form that we use is presented in Figure 5.4. The deposit calls for the person to put up an amount of money that he or she "wouldn't want to lose." Failure to do an assignment that he or she has agreed to do results in him or her losing half of the deposit, which must be redeposited in order to keep the balance the same. At the end of treatment, or if the client terminates for any reason, deposited money is returned. Naturally, we attempt to design assignments so clients are likely to succeed. If compliance problems appear to have been caused by poorly designed assignments, no money is forfeited.

When a client puts up $50 or $100, having to demand that he or she forfeit half of it can make the therapist quite uncomfortable. At times we have asked a client to deposit *less* money than he or she has proposed because we feared that we would be unwilling to follow through on fining. However, since it would destroy the effect of the deposit and would even be unethical if we failed to follow through, we always demand forfeiture for gross failure to complete assignments. With failure to do one or two things on a list of five or six assignments, we warn the client and put a dollar sign next to the statement of that assignment for the next time (if the assignment isn't altered). The dollar sign will remind both of us that this is a second chance, and we indicate that we have never backed away from following through on fining a person who failed to do such an assignment.

Figure 5.4 Money deposit form

APPOINTMENTS AT THE BEHAVIOR CHANGE CENTER
AND
DEPOSIT FOR BETWEEN SESSION ASSIGNMENTS

A basic principle of the Behavior Change Center is that you must be actively involved in your own treatment in order to change your behavior. First, you must keep your scheduled appointments. Second, it is essential that you understand and agree to all between-session assignments that you work out with your therapist. Finally, it is essential that you *actually carry out those assignments.*

You are requested to cancel appointments at least 24 hours in advance. Otherwise, you will be charged for one unit of service, or $11.

We require clients to make a money deposit. *This involves putting up an amount of money that you would not want to lose.* This can be any amount as long as you would be sorry to lose it. The deposit is for *completing all between-session assignments that you agree to.* We have found that money deposits make it much more likely that our clients will be actively involved in their behavior change programs and successful in achieving their goals. If you fail to complete agreed-upon assignments, you will lose half of your deposit and you will be asked to deposit that amount to continue your program.

Any money you lose is donated to the United Way.

(Return this portion to the Behavior Change Center.)

I have read and understand the procedures regarding appointments and the deposit for between-session assignments at the Behavior Change Center. I understand that if I cancel an appointment with less than 24 hours notice, I will be charged for one unit of service ($11). I understand that if I fail to complete the between-session assignments that my therapist and I work out, I will forfeit *one-half* of the deposit and will have to redeposit that amount in order to continue in the program. I agree to deposit the amount of $_____.

Signature _____

Witness _____

Date _____

Review of Assignments

Each assignment is reviewed at the following session. We ask the client to keep records that elaborate upon areas where they have been successful and problems they have been having so that we can suggest modifications of assignments.

If the client has failed to do any of the assignments (a rare event), we drastically reduce the number of assignments and collect the money deposit. Such noncompliance usually leads us to completely review the assumptions under which we have been operating. We go back over the goals and ask the client if each is still a goal. We ask the client if there is some way that we are behaving that creates problems and if he or she has doubts about the general approach we are taking.

Admittedly, such failure is not a good prognostic sign. Our impression is that people who have a history of failure in completing other tasks and who are vague and unsure about their goals for treatment are usually those who fail to complete assignments.

Failure to complete one or two assignments is dealt with by gently prompting the client to be explicit about precisely what he or she did and did not do. This gives us an opportunity to praise partial completion while at the same time making noncompletion aversive and helping us to pinpoint the obstacles to completion. The specific assignment may be revised, withdrawn, or simply reiterated, according to the client's wishes, our judgment of how important the assignment is for goal achievement, and whether a revised version is likely to be adhered to.

Contingencies for Assignment Completion

We think about assignment completion in terms of the contingencies governing this behavior. The money provides one obvious contingency — monetary loss as a punishment for noncompletion. But more subtle contingencies are also involved — even with the deposit. Our explanation of the deposit in the first session, prior to discussion of the client's goals, suggests that we will take any failures to comply very seriously. Our discussion in the first session of how we develop and specify (in writing) between-session assignments further establishes the failure to complete assignments as a conditioned aversive event. In that session, we also indicate that the "most important issue" is to follow through on assignments. This serves to establish the completion of assignments as a reinforcer.

Our "collaborative set" is also relevant. We tell our clients that they don't have to do any assignment unless they think it will help. (For example, "Unlike homework assignments in school, you can negotiate what you are going to do between our sessions.") This technique probably has two effects. First, it enhances the clients' own attribution that they "really" want to do what they are agreeing to do. Second, if arguing with the therapist is reinforcing — which sometimes seems to be the case for depressed individuals — it reduces the opportunity since we simply won't argue.

Small steps are also critical. By giving assignments that our experience suggests can be readily completed, we increase the probability that they will be done and that the client will be reinforced for his or her efforts. We also limit the number of assignments the person takes on.

The most relevant contingency, however, involves the success of the assignment. Doing things that "work" is reinforcing. Trying a pleasant activity that turns out to be enjoyable reinforces the behavior of trying pleasant activities.

Finally, the detailed review of assignments provides social reinforcement for compliance with assignments and mild punishment for failure to comply. The punishment is in the form of "having to tell the therapist you didn't do something." However, we do not criticize clients for failure to complete assignments. Rather, we avoid arguments by suggesting that there must have been something wrong with the assignment and then modify it in light of the problems discussed.

ILLUSTRATIVE CASE

Ms. L. was a 35-year-old white bank teller. She was divorced from her husband of 10 years for a year before treatment. She had no children. At the time treatment began she was living in a one-bedroom apartment.

Goals

In the initial consultation, Ms. L. and her therapist identified the following treatment goals:

1. Worrying about herself less frequently
2. Becoming more active socially
3. Having more positive interactions with coworkers
4. Being unhappy less often

The goals were established in response to Ms. L.'s complaints that she spent a good deal of time alone worrying about whether she would ever feel better. She had few positive interactions with coworkers but quite often got into arguments with two of the other tellers she worked with. She also had several arguments with her supervisor. In the third treatment session another goal was added:

5. Learning to relax

This goal was added because we found that Ms. L. was experiencing anxiety, particularly in social situations.

Session 1

At the initial consultation, Ms. L. decided she wanted to get started right away. We therefore developed the following assignments:

1. Complete the questionnaires for next time.
2. Note pleasant and unpleasant social interactions that you have by writing brief descriptions of them each evening on the social

interaction sheets; if you can think of a better way that you might have reacted in the situation, note that too.

Session 2

In this session we briefly reviewed the questionnaires we had given. However, detailed scoring and feedback from the questionnaires were deferred to the third session since it takes time to score them.

Much of the time in Session 2 was taken with Ms. L. describing her positive and negative interactions with others. Ms. L. had recorded only two positive interactions (brief conversations such as passing the time of day and work discussions did not have to be monitored). Both of these interactions had been initiated by someone else. There had been five negative interactions, which turned out to be either direct or indirect results of critical statements that Ms. L. had made to coworkers. In one instance she criticized a coworker for the way she had recorded a debit and was told to "shut up and mind your own business!" In another instance she felt she was ignored by a coworker when she said good morning. She believed this was due to the fact that she had criticized the worker's manner of speech on the previous day.

On the basis of our analysis, we suggested that it would be useful for Ms. L. to initiate some positive conversations with these coworkers. Since she felt she could do this and was able to describe what she might say to one coworker, we dispensed with modeling and roleplaying in the session. Her assignments relevant to her social interactions at work were as follows:

1. Continue to keep track of your positive and negative social interactions.

2. Each day initiate one positive conversation with at least one coworker; be sure to note this on your records.

3. For each negative conversation that you have, describe a better reaction.

Further discussion revealed that Ms. L. had several old friends whom she had not seen in some time. We therefore added the following social interaction assignment:

4. Call one of the friends we discussed and arrange to get together with her.

We then turned our attention to her worry and her unhappiness. Since the worry and unhappiness seemed to occur together and to be most intense and frequent when she was home alone, she was given the following assignment:

5. Each evening plan one brief pleasant activity and one brief household chore that you could do that evening.

This assignment was given because it appeared that much of the worry and depression functioned to keep Ms. L. from taking action — she was "too worried and depressed to do anything."

6. If you worry or feel depressed for more than about 5 minutes, get up (she was usually sitting watching television when these events occurred) and do one of the following:
   a. Iron
   b. Wash dishes
   c. Take a walk around the block
   d. Call a friend

The activities were chosen simply because Ms. L. was willing to do them and they seemed likely to be incompatible with worry and dysphoria.

Session 3

Session 3 began with a review of progress on previous assignments. Ms. L. had had some successes with initiating positive interactions with her coworkers; however, she said that sometimes she was unsure what to say when someone else initiated a conversation with her. In addition, she found that she would become anxious at these times. We congratulated her on the successes and had her describe them in greater detail. We then developed the following additional assignments:

1. Continue to keep track of positive and negative social activities.

2. Each evening write brief descriptions of better reactions you could have had in negative social situations.

3. Initiate one conversation with each of the two "problem" coworkers each day.

4. Begin daily practice of relaxation and note your practice on the record you have.

Relaxation instructions were provided via tape-recorded instructions. They involved progressive muscular relaxation (Bernstein & Borkovec, 1973). She was asked to note when she practiced and to rate the degree of relaxation she achieved on a 10-point scale.

Our review of her progress on the worry and depression control strategies revealed that she had seldom followed through in engaging in any of the incompatible activities. We asked her if she felt the proposed program didn't make sense to her or if it was just a matter of getting her to follow through. She said that she felt that she should try to get herself to follow through for one more week. We agreed to this and wrote the assignments out as follows:

$6. Continue to plan one household chore and one pleasant activity each evening; do this just after you get home.

$7. If you worry or feel depressed for more than 5 minutes, get up and do one of the activities we agreed to.

The dollar signs indicated that Ms. L.'s failure to follow through with these assignments would cost her half of her money deposit. While it is true that we could have fined her in this session, she had complied in part with the assignments and it seemed wiser to give her another opportunity. We explained to her that we could have fined her but didn't, and that we would put dollar signs next to those assignments. We then added that we "never back away from fining a person who fails to do something that has a dollar sign in front of it."

Session 4

We first reviewed her progress. Ms. L. reported some positive conversations with the problematic coworkers. She said she was beginning to feel more comfortable with them and less critical toward them. We simply kept her going with the following:

1. Continue to note positive and negative interactions: note better reactions for negative interactions; imagine an interaction that is likely to come up the next day.

We had forgotten to suggest an assignment involving social activities outside work, but Ms. L. had kept at it. We simply noted her plans for the coming week:

2. Get together with Charlene to make reservations for cross-country skiing.

Noting this as an assignment would help us to remember to ask about it in the fifth session.

Ms. L. reported that she was getting relaxed in her practice sessions. We gave her instructions for developing a briefer form of relaxation and asked her to begin checking her tension four or five times a day and to relax for 1 minute at each of these times.

3. Continue daily relaxation practice: use the tape only if needed; at the end of your practice, take 15 deep breaths and say "relax" as you exhale and let your muscles go.

4. Do four or five tension checks each day.

Ms. L. had begun planning chores and pleasant activities each evening. She felt it was helping her to be less depressed. We simply reiterated this assignment:

5. Continue your planning for the evening.

She had also followed through on the response cost for worry and depression, so we reiterated:

6. Continue your activities when depressed or worried.

Session 5

This session involved a brief review of all her assignments. She was doing well on most of them so we simply reiterated most assignments. Ms. L. had had some discomfort talking to a man she met at work, and she was interested in him, so we suggested the following:

1. If you see John, do a tension check. Relax!

2. Each evening practice what you'd like to say to him in your imagination.

Session 6

Ms. L. seemed to be doing well. We discussed the factors that seemed to have led to her getting depressed, and we talked about how she could use the same skills she had been using if trouble developed. For each thing she had been doing we suggested that she could maintain her gains by slowly backing away from record keeping. Since her finances were limited, she was interested in keeping the cost of treatment low. We therefore set up an appointment for a month later to review how she was doing. We suggested she call us if there were any problems.

Session 7

Things were still going well. We discussed one argument she had had with a coworker. Instead of being cold and argumentative, Ms. L. went to the other person and said that she didn't want to fight. It turned out that her coworker was glad to settle the argument.

We again reviewed the factors that seemed to have led to her depression and talked about how she could use the skills we had taught her to deal with future problems. Finally, we gave Ms. L. our questionnaires to complete and mail to us.

SUMMARY

Although depression is one of the most common clinical problems, there is no agreement on the criteria for diagnosis or the cause of the disorder. One of the more widely accepted approaches to diagnosis is that of Feighner et al. (1972). It suggests that depression is present if the client exhibits a dysphoric mood, has no preexisting psychiatric conditions, and displays at least five of these symptoms: poor appetite or weight loss, difficulty sleeping, loss of energy, loss of interest in usual activities or sex, feelings of reproach or guilt, a perceived inability to think or concentrate, and recurrent thoughts of death or suicide. The specific problems of depressed people are often quite diverse. Many possible causative factors have been named, such as biochemical deficits, stressful events, lack of effective self-control procedures, problematic cognitions, learned helplessness, and a low rate of reinforcement, as well as certain chronic medical problems. However, depression can be effectively treated without knowledge of its etiology.

Areas of concern to the therapist in assessing depression are dysphoria, marital problems, negative cognitions, anxiety, lack of pleasant activities, and social skill deficits. Assessment should also include investigation of alcohol or drug use, financial problems, the length of the depression, and the possibility of suicide.

The treatment described here is problem-specific, involving intervention on each problem separately. Medication may be tried, and sometimes a combination of drug treatment and behavioral therapy works well. Homework assignments are discussed for the following areas of treatment: assessment; direct modification of dysphoria; identification and assignment of specific activities, and facilitation of an increased activity level; training in time management skills; training in social skills; marital assignments; modification of verbal cognitive events; and treatment of anxiety and insomnia.

Various compliance enhancement procedures incorporated in the treatment program are highlighted. The responsibilities of clients are made clear before treatment begins, so there is no misunderstanding. Goals are chosen jointly by client and therapist, as are between-session assignments. Clients are required to deposit an agreed-upon amount of money at the beginning of therapy, which may be forfeited in part if homework assignments are not carried out. The therapist carefully reviews each assignment during the scheduled session, and clients who have not complied are questioned as to the reasons for failure. The assignment may then be revised, withdrawn, or reassigned, according to the judgments of the client and therapist. From the beginning of the program, it is made clear that homework is important, that the therapist will keep track of whether or not it has been done, and that assignments will be made only with the client's consent. Assignment steps are kept small to increase the probability of successful completion, and that experience of success will also reinforce compliance. Having to report assignment results to the therapist may also act as a mild social reinforcer for compliance and a punishment for noncompliance.

The chapter concludes with an illustrative case study of a divorced woman who had become depressed. A combination of assignments aimed at having her change negative social behaviors, worry less, become more active socially, engage in more activities (especially when depressed), and relax systematically helped to get rid of the depression.

REFERENCE NOTES

1. Libet, J.M., Lewinsohn, P.M., & Javorek, F.J. *The construct of social skill: An empirical study of several behavioral measures on temporal stability, internal structure, validity and situational generalizability.* Mimeo, University of Oregon, 1973.

2. Biglan, A., Craker, D., & Dow, M. *A problem-specific approach to the treatment of depression.* Unpublished manuscript, University of Oregon, 1978.

3. Hammen, C.L., Rook, L.S., & Harris, G. *Effects of activities and attributions on depressed mood.* Unpublished manuscript, University of California, Los Angeles, 1977.

4. MacPhillamy, D.J., & Lewinsohn, P.M. *The pleasant events schedule.* Mimeo, University of Oregon, 1971.

5. Wells, K.C., Hersen, M., Bellack, A.S., & Himmelhoch, J. *Social skills training for unipolar depressive females.* Paper presented at the meeting of the Association for Advancement of Behavior Therapy, Atlanta, December 1977.

6. McLean, P.D. Personal communication, 1978.

7. Tokarz, T.P., & Lawrence, P.S. *An analysis of temporal and stimulus factors in the treatment of insomnia.* Paper presented at the Association for Advancement of Behavior Therapy Convention, Chicago, November 1974.

REFERENCES

Agle, D.P., Baum, G.L., Chester, E.H., & Wendt, M. Multidiscipline treatment of chronic pulmonary insufficiency. 1. Psychologic aspects of rehabilitation. *Psychosomatic Medicine,* 1973, *35,* 41-49.

Akiskal, H.S., & McKinney, W.T., Jr. Depressive disorders: Toward a unified hypothesis. *Science,* 1973, *182,* 20-29.

2

Alperson, J., & Biglan, A. Self-administered treatment of sleep onset insomnia and the importance of age. *Behavior Therapy*, 1979, *10*, 347-356.

Beals, R.K., & Hickman, N.W. Industrial injuries of the back and extremities. *Journal of Bone and Joint Surgery*, 1972, *54-A*, 1593-1611.

Beck, A.T. *Depression: Clinical, experimental, and theoretical aspects.* Philadelphia: University of Pennsylvania Press, 1967.

Beck, A.T. *Depression: Causes and treatment.* Philadelphia: University of Pennsylvania Press, 1972.

Beck, A.T., & Beamesderfer, A. Assessment of depression: The depression inventory. In P. Pichot (Ed.), *Modern problems in pharmocopsychiatry* (Vol. 7). Basel, Switzerland: Karger, 1974.

Benson, H., Beary, J., & Carol, M. The relaxation response. *Psychiatry*, 1974, *37*, 37-45.

Bernstein, D.A., & Borkovec, T.D. *Progressive relaxation training: A manual for the helping professions.* Champaign, Ill.: Research Press, 1973.

Biglan, A., & Dow, M. Toward a "second generation" model of depression treatment: A problem-specific approach. In L.P. Rehm (Ed.), *Behavior therapy for depression: Present status and future directions.* New York: Academic Press, 1981.

Blaney, P.H. Cognitive and behavioral therapy of depression: A review of their effectiveness. In L.P. Rehm (Ed.), *Behavior therapy for depression: Present status and future directions.* New York: Academic Press, 1981.

Bootzin, R.R., & Nicassio, P.M. Behavioral treatments for insomnia. In M. Hersen, R.M. Eisler, & P.M. Miller (Eds.), *Progress in behavior modification* (Vol. 6). New York: Academic Press, 1978.

Boulougouris, J.C., & Bassiakos, L. Prolonged flooding cases with obsessive-compulsive neurosis. *Behaviour Research and Therapy*, 1973, *11*, 227-231.

Campbell, L.M. A variation of thought stopping in a twelve-year-old boy: A case report. *Journal of Behavior Therapy and Experimental Psychiatry*, 1973, *4*, 69-70.

Coleman, R.E., & Miller, A.G. The relationship between depression and marital maladjustment in a clinic population: A multitrait-multimethod study. *Journal of Consulting and Clinical Psychology,* 1975, *43,* 647-651.

Craighead, W.E. Issues resulting from treatment studies. In L.P. Rehm (Ed.), *Behavior therapy for depression: Present status and future directions.* New York: Academic Press, 1981.

Donnelly, E.F., Murphy, D.L., Waldman, I.N., & Goodwin, F.K. Prediction of antidepressant responses to imipramine. *Neuropsychobiology,* 1979, *5,* 94-101.

Feighner, J.P., Robins, E., Guze, S.B., Woodruff, R.A., Jr., Winokur, G., & Munoz, R. Diagnostic criteria for use in psychiatric research. *Archives of General Psychiatry,* 1972, *26,* 57-63.

Gentry, W. *In vivo* desensitization of an obsessive cancer fear. *Journal of Behavior Therapy and Experimental Psychiatry,* 1970, *1,* 315-318.

Grosscup, S.J., & Lewinsohn, P.M. Pleasant and unpleasant events, and mood. *Journal of Clinical Psychology,* 1980, *36,* 252-254.

Hackmann, A., & McLean, C. A comparison of flooding and thought stopping in the treatment of obsessional neurosis. *Behaviour Research and Therapy,* 1975, *13,* 263-269.

Hallam, R.S. Extinction of ruminations: A case study. *Behavior Therapy,* 1974, *5,* 565-568.

Hersen, M., & Bellack, A.S. Social skills training for chronic psychiatric patients: Rationale, research findings, and future directions. *Comprehensive Psychiatry,* 1976, *17,* 559-580.

Hersen, M., Eisler, R.M., & Miller, P.M. Development of assertive responses: Clinical, measurement and research considerations. *Behaviour Research and Therapy,* 1973, *11,* 505-521.

Hollon, S.D., & Beck, A.T. Cognitive therapy of depression. In P.C. Kendall & S.D. Hollon (Eds.), *Cognitive-behavioral interventions: Theory, research, and procedures.* New York: Academic Press, in press.

Johnson, S.M., & Lobitz, G.K. The personal and marital readjustment of parents as related to observed child deviance and parenting behaviors. *Journal of Abnormal Child Psychology,* 1974, *2,* 193-207.

Kanfer, F.H., & Grimm, L.G. Freedom of choice and behavioral change. *Journal of Consulting and Clinical Psychology,* 1978, *46,* 873-878.

Kanfer, F.H., & Hagerman, S. The role of self-regulation in depression. In L.P. Rehm (Ed.), *Behavior therapy for depression: Present status and future directions.* New York: Academic Press, 1981.

Kenny, F.T., Solyom, L., & Solyom, C. Faradic disruption of obsessive neurosis. *Behavior Therapy,* 1973, *4,* 448-457.

Lakein, A. *How to get control of your time and your life.* New York: New American Library, 1973.

Lehmann, H.E. Depression: Somatic treatment methods, complications, failures. In G. Usdin (Ed.), *Depression: Clinical, biological, and psychological perspectives.* New York: Brunner/Mazel, 1977.

Levitt, E.E., & Lubin, B. *Depression: Concepts, controversies, and some new facts.* New York: Springer, 1975.

Lewinsohn, P.M. Clinical and theoretical aspects of depression. In K.S. Calhoun, H.E. Adams, & K.M. Mitchell (Eds.), *Innovative treatment methods in psychopathology.* New York: John Wiley & Sons, 1974.

Lewinsohn, P.M., Biglan, A., & Zeiss, A.S. Behavioral treatment of depression. In P.O. Davidson (Ed.), *The behavioral management of anxiety, depression, and pain.* New York: Brunner/Mazel, 1976.

Lewinsohn, P.M., & Graf, M. Pleasant activities and depression. *Journal of Consulting and Clinical Psychology,* 1973, *41,* 261-268.

Lewinsohn, P.M., & Libet, J.M. Pleasant events, activity schedules, and depression. *Journal of Abnormal Psychology,* 1972, *79,* 291-295.

Lewinsohn, P.M., & MacPhillamy, D.J. The relationship between age and engagement in pleasant activities. *Journal of Gerontology,* 1974, *29,* 290-294.

Liberman, R.P. A model for individualizing treatment strategies. In L.P. Rehm (Ed.), *Behavior therapy for depression: Present status and future directions.* New York: Academic Press, 1981.

Libet, J.M., & Lewinsohn, P.M. Concept of social skill with special reference to the behavior of depressed persons. *Journal of Consulting and Clinical Psychology,* 1973, *40,* 304-312.

Lubin, B. Adjective checklists for the measurement of depression. *Archives of General Psychiatry,* 1965, *12,* 57-62.

MacPhillamy, D.J., & Lewinsohn, P.M. Depression as a function of levels of desired and obtained pleasure. *Journal of Abnormal Psychology,* 1974, *83,* 651-657.

Mahoney, M.J. The self-management of covert behavior: A case study. *Behavior Therapy,* 1971, *2,* 575-578.

McLean, P.D. Depression as a specific response to stress. In C.D. Spielberger & I.G. Sarason (Eds.), *Stress and anxiety.* New York: John Wiley & Sons, 1976. (a)

McLean, P.D. Therapeutic decision-making in the behavioral treatment of depression. In P.O. Davidson (Ed.), *Behavioral management of anxiety, depression, and pain.* New York: Brunner/Mazel, 1976. (b)

McLean, P.D., & Hakstian, A.R. Clinical depression: Comparative efficacy of outpatient treatments. *Journal of Consulting and Clinical Psychology,* 1979, *47,* 818-836.

Meyer, R.G. Delay therapy: Two case reports. *Behavior Therapy,* 1973, *4,* 709-711.

Mlott, S.R., & Allain, A. Personality correlates of renal dialysis patients and their spouses. *Southern Medical Journal,* 1974, *67,* 941-944.

Nelson, R.O. Methodological issues in assessment via self-monitoring. In J.D. Cone & R.P. Hawkins (Eds.), *Behavioral assessment: New directions in clinical psychology.* New York: Brunner/Mazel, 1977.

Norton, G.R., & DeLuca, R.V. The use of stimulus control procedures to eliminate persistent nocturnal awakenings. *Journal of Behavior Therapy and Experimental Psychiatry,* 1979, *10,* 65-68.

Raft, D., Toomey, T., & Gregg, J. Behavior modification and haloparidol in chronic facial pain. *Southern Medical Journal,* 1979, *72,* 155-159.

Rehm, L.P. A self-control model of depression. *Behavior Therapy,* 1977, *8,* 787-804.

Reisinger, J.J. The treatment of "anxiety depression" via positive reinforcement and response cost. *Journal of Applied Behavior Analysis,* 1972, *5,* 125-130.

Robinson, J.C., & Lewinsohn, P.M. Experimental analysis of a technique based on the Premack principle changing verbal behavior of depressed individuals. *Psychological Reports,* 1973, *32,* 199-210.

Rosen, R.C., & Schnapp, B.J. The use of a specific behavioral technique (thought stopping) in the context of conjoint couples therapy: A case report. *Behavior Therapy,* 1974, *5,* 261-264.

Sanchez, V.C. *Assertion training: Effectiveness in the treatment of depression.* Unpublished doctoral dissertation, University of Oregon, 1978.

Schneidman, E.S. Suicide. In A.M. Freedman, H.I. Kaplan, & B.J. Sadock (Eds.), *Comprehensive textbook of psychiatry* (2nd ed.). Baltimore: Williams & Wilkins, 1975.

Schou, M. Lithium prophylaxis in recurrent endogenous affective disorders: Debate, development, and documentation. In N.S. Kline (Ed.), *Factors in depression.* New York: Raven Press, 1974.

Seligman, M.E.P. A learned helplessness point of view. In L.P. Rehm (Ed.), *Behavior therapy for depression: Present status and future directions.* New York: Academic Press, 1981.

Skinner, B.F. The operational analysis of psychological terms. *Psychological Review,* 1945, *52,* 270-277.

Skinner, B.F. *Science and human behavior.* New York: Macmillan, 1953.

Solyom, L., Garza-Perez, J., Ledwidge, B., & Solyom, C. Paradoxical intention in the treatment of obsessive thoughts: A pilot study. *Comprehensive Psychiatry,* 1972, *13,* 291-297.

Spielberger, C., Gorsuch, R., & Lushene, R. *Test manual for the State Trait Anxiety Inventory.* Palo Alto, Calif.: Consulting Psychologists Press, 1970.

Steinbock, E. A. *Live versus tape recorded versus written manual versus minimal treatment relaxation instructions: A comparison of methods.* Unpublished master's thesis, University of Oregon, 1976.

Stern, R.S., Lipsedge, M.S., & Marks, I.M. Obsessive ruminations: A controlled trial of thought-stopping technique. *Behaviour Research and Therapy,* 1973, *11,* 659-662.

United States Department of Health, Education, and Welfare. *Institutional guide to DHEW policy on protection of human subjects.* DHEW publication No. (NIH) 72-102. Washington, D.C.: U.S. Government Printing Office, 1971.

Watson, D., & Friend, R. Measurement of social evaluation anxiety. *Journal of Consulting and Clinical Psychology,* 1969, *33,* 448-457.

Weiss, R.L., & Aved, B.M. Marital satisfaction and depression as predictors of physical health status. *Journal of Consulting and Clinical Psychology,* 1978, *46,* 1379-1384.

Weiss, R.L., & Birchler, G.R. Adults with marital dysfunction. In M. Hersen & A.S. Bellack (Eds.), *Behavior therapy in the psychiatric setting.* Baltimore: Williams & Wilkins, 1978.

Weiss, T., & Engel, B. Operant conditioning of heart rate in patients with premature ventricular contractions. In R.C. Katz & S. Zlutnick

(Eds.), *Behavior therapy and health care: Principles and applications.* Elmsford, N.Y.: Pergamon Press, 1975.

Weissman, M.M., & Paykel, E.S. *The depressed woman: A study of social relationships.* Chicago: University of Chicago Press, 1974.

Winokur, G. The genetics of manic-depressive illness. In R.R. Fieve (Ed.), *Depression in the 1970's.* Amsterdam: Excerpta Medica Foundation, 1971.

Wolpe, J. *Psychotherapy by reciprocal inhibition.* Stanford: Stanford University Press, 1958.

Wolpe, J., & Lang, P.J. A fear survey schedule for use in behavior therapy. *Behaviour Research and Therapy,* 1964, *2,* 27-30.

Woolfolk, R.L., Carr-Kaffashan, L., & McNulty, T.F. Meditation training as a treatment for insomnia. *Behavior Therapy,* 1976, *7,* 359-365.

Youngren, M.S., & Lewinsohn, P.M. The functional relationship between depression and problematic interpersonal behavior. *Journal of Abnormal Psychology,* 1980, *89,* 333-341.

Zung, W.W.K. A self-rating depression scale. *Archives of General Psychiatry,* 1965, *12,* 63-70.

CHAPTER 6

Marital Problems

Neil S. Jacobson
   Department of Psychology
   University of Washington

OVERVIEW OF MARITAL PROBLEMS

Behavioral marital therapy (BMT) can be defined in many ways (Azrin, Naster, & Jones, 1973; Jacobson & Margolin, 1979; Jacobson & Martin, 1976; Patterson, Weiss, & Hops, 1976; Stuart, 1969, 1976; Weiss, Hops, & Patterson, 1973), and to elaborate on the various treatment techniques and theoretical underpinnings of the BMT movement is far beyond the scope of this chapter (see Gottman, 1979; Jacobson, 1979; Jacobson, 1981; Jacobson, Elwood, & Dallas, in press; Jacobson & Margolin, 1979; Jacobson & Martin, 1976; O'Leary & Turkewitz, 1978, for reviews of theoretical underpinnings, assessment techniques, clinical innovations, and empirical contributions). Most of the studies mentioned share the bottomline assumption that BMT is instigative (Kanfer & Phillips, 1970), that is, that it instructs couples to enact certain behaviors in their natural environment. Consistent with the behavior therapy tradition, generalization to the natural environment is not left to chance (Baer, Wolf, & Risley, 1968). Therefore, homework assignments play a major role in therapy.

The present chapter is based on several assumptions. First, it assumes that couples generally enter marital therapy with the genuine desire to improve their relationship. When they have other goals, such as divorce, the strategies outlined in this chapter are inappropriate. Occasionally, one spouse has a "hidden agenda," for example, a covert goal of divorce, and may be using marital therapy to demonstrate to the spouse that the marriage is hopeless. Or one partner may simply want a history of marital therapy to be "on the record" so that the courts will be satisfied that the couple has tried to salvage the relationship. But these cases are exceptional. It is generally the case that couples can be taken at their word, that is, that they are entering therapy to improve their marriage.

Second, it is assumed that, given the commitment to the goals of an improved relationship, any resistance by clients is due to the short-term costs of compliance. Spouses may resist a therapist's directive for many reasons, most of which relate to the aversiveness of the task itself: they may view the request as unfair because the problem really lies with their partner's behavior, not their own; they may find the task difficult, tedious, or unpleasant in some other way; or they may be deficient in the skills needed to fulfill the assignment. This is not to say that spouses never resist because they oppose the goals of therapy or because they oppose any attempts at external control. But given their stated agreement to the treatment goals, these other possibilities should be explored first, and in the vast majority of cases, interventions that are directed at overcoming barriers presumably created by task aversiveness are sufficient. These interventions involve the generally direct instructional strategies outlined in this chapter.

The dilemma facing the marital therapist is strikingly similar to that for treating individuals with self-control deficiencies (cf. Rachlin, 1974). Alcoholics consume alcohol excessively, despite its punishing effects, because the short-term reinforcers are more salient. The therapist's task in such cases is twofold: he or she must help make the long-term punishing contingencies sufficiently salient that they supersede the short-term contingencies and must help the client find reinforcers to replace those obtainable through alcohol ingestion. Similarly, the marital therapist is faced with two spouses who are behaving in a way that detracts from a satisfying relationship. Often the changes demanded of each spouse in marital therapy are costly, and these costs, because of their immediacy, are more salient than the distant and uncertain reinforcers inherent in an improved relationship. The therapist's task is to increase the salience of the long-term contingencies and to replace the reinforcing effects derived from current, dysfunctional behavior with new immediate reinforcers for more positive behaviors.

HOMEWORK-BASED TREATMENT

Overview of Treatment

During the pretreatment assessment, couples are asked to complete various self-report questionnaires and also to collect baseline data on the frequencies of rewarding and punishing behaviors that occur in the home (Jacobson et al., in press; Jacobson & Margolin, 1979; Weiss & Margolin, 1977). Once treatment commences, homework is integral to both the instigative, behavior-change intervention strategies and also to the more skill-oriented, process-training intervention strategies. When the focus is on prompting more positive behavior, couples are asked to continue to collect data in the home and to engage in various practices involving pinpointing, monitoring, and implementing behavior changes. When the focus is on communication or problem-solving training, couples are asked to practice the new skills at home.

Content-oriented and process-oriented BMT can also be dichotomized as behavior exchange versus communication training (O'Leary & Turkewitz, 1978; Weiss & Birchler, 1978). Behavior exchange encompasses a variety of procedures, all of which focus on behavior change in the marriage. Communication training usually tackles behavior change only indirectly, if at all. Instead, the assumption is that the specific behavioral problems in the marriage result, at least in part, from ineffective communication. Moreover, the communication skills acquired in therapy are presumed to serve a preventative function; if and when new marital problems develop, it is hoped that couples will use the skills previously acquired in therapy to deal with them effectively.

Both behavior exchange and process interventions use homework. Behavior exchange homework assignments are directed toward the instigation of behavior changes in the natural environment, and communication training homework assignments require couples to practice the skills developed during the therapy sessions.

Homework Assignments

Assessment. There are generally two kinds of assignments presented to couples during a typical behavioral assessment of marital dysfunction. First, in addition to the clinical interview and the direct observation of marital interaction, couples are asked to complete a variety of self-report questionnaires.

Assignment: Complete the pretreatment questionnaires.

Numerous instruments can be utilized for assessment purposes (Jacobson & Margolin, 1979; Jacobson et al., in press; Weiss & Margolin,

1977). Such questionnaires provide a wealth of information, including a pinpointing of each spouse's target complaints, an enumeration of strengths and positive aspects of the relationship, statements from each spouse regarding his or her perceptions of how decisions are made and how authority is distributed across the various tasks required by marriage, lists of common interests, and steps taken by each spouse to dissolve the relationship.

Second, in a typical behavioral assessment of a dysfunctional marriage, couples are asked to collect data in the home. This extremely important task provides invaluable assessment information and also serves as a springboard for subsequent clinical interventions. The most commonly used version of this assignment provides couples with an extensive checklist to be completed each evening.

Assignment: Each of you should complete a Spouse Observation Checklist and daily satisfaction rating each evening.

In the widely used Spouse Observation Checklist (SOC) developed by the Oregon Marital Studies Program, couples are presented with a comprehensive checklist consisting of approximately 400 items that survey the various aspects of married life. In the version currently used by the Oregon Marital Studies Program, the items are divided into 12 major categories: Companionship, Affection, Consideration, Sex, Communication, Coupling Activities, Childcare and Parenting, Household Responsibilities, Financial Decision-making, Employment-Education, Personal Habits and Appearance, and Self and Spouse Independence. Items in each major category are further subdivided into the subcategories "Pleases" and "Displeases," depending on the impact that each item has on the spouses. In one revision of the SOC (Jacobson, Waldron, & Moore, 1980), the same items are grouped into four major categories: Companionship Activities, Interactive Events, Physical Affection, and Instrumental Behaviors.

Data collection by spouses in the home provides a wealth of information, most of which is inaccessible by other means. First, a baseline is provided for the frequencies of target behaviors. This baseline exists as a desirable alternative to simply asking spouses how often various rewarding and punishing behaviors occur, since husbands and wives, particularly those who are distressed, are not objective commentators on the day-to-day events of their marriage (Robinson & Price, 1980). Not only does this baseline aid in specifying treatment goals, but it also provides the basis for evaluating the effects of therapeutic interventions.

Second, if spouses are recording both the frequency of various behaviors and the subjective impact of these behaviors on themselves, therapists are liberated from the often treacherous task of inferring which behaviors are reinforcing and which are punishing. Since couples are highly idiosyncratic in their preferences (Jacobson et al., 1980), this information is essential.

Third, the degree of *reciprocity*, that is, the extent to which spouses tend to reciprocate rewarding and punishing behavior, can often be inferred from the ongoing collection of such data (Gottman, 1979; Gottman, Markman, & Notarius, 1977; Gottman, Notarius, Markman, Bank, Yoppi, & Rubin, 1976; Jacobson & Martin, 1976; Patterson & Reid, 1970). If frequencies of reinforcing behavior delivered by husbands and wives are uncorrelated across days, therapy may require a focus on instructing couples to provide reinforcing consequences for desirable behavior delivered by the partner. On the other hand, when negative behavior is highly reciprocal, the therapeutic task may consist of helping spouses interrupt escalating chains of coercive behavior by finding other responses to punishing overtures.

Fourth, by adding an additional element to the assignment, the therapist can gather information on the most important reinforcers and punishers in the relationship. The addition consists of asking couples to give each day a global rating based on the overall level of relationship satisfaction for that day (Wills, Weiss, & Patterson, 1974). For example, a 7-point scale might be used, where "4" constitutes an "average" day, "7" a "perfect" day, and "1" is equivalent to "the pits." These ratings are given as an adjunct to the behavioral data. It then becomes possible to correlate the frequencies of various response classes with these daily satisfaction ratings (DSR), and it is reasonable to suppose that events positively correlated with DSR are reinforcers, while those inversely associated with DSR are punishers. Although this method of identifying reinforcers and punishers is imprecise and open to numerous criticisms (Christensen & Nies, 1980; Jacobson, 1979; Jacobson et al., in press; Jacobson & Moore, in press), it is far superior to simply asking spouses what they like and dislike if the goal is to find out which spouse-provided behaviors are of functional significance in the relationship.

Fifth, data collection can be examined for the degree of consensus between husband and wife. Do spouses agree on what has occurred on a particular day? In what areas do their perceptions diverge? A lack of consensus suggests that at least one spouse, and perhaps both, are not perceiving reality accurately. Given the startling lack of consensus found in recent studies (Christensen & Nies, 1980; Jacobson & Moore, in press), it may be that for many couples altering perceptual processes will be at least as important as modifying behavior.

Assignments focused on behavior exchange. Instigation of behavior change in the natural environment of a distressed couple can take many forms, and assignments should be structured according to the idiosyncracies of particular couples. Jacobson (1981) and Jacobson and Margolin (1979) structure the behavior exchange format so that homework tasks become gradually more demanding over time. Since behavior changes are often both difficult and costly, spouses must not be overwhelmed with tasks that may exceed their current capabilities. Couples should also be allowed a maximum amount of flexibility and freedom of choice at all times. The ultimate goal is to actively involve spouses in a sustained effort to improve their relationship. Particularly during the early stages of therapy, what is important is not so much what each spouse does, but that he or she does something. (For alternative ways to structure homework tasks, the reader is referred to Azrin et al., 1973; Weiss, 1975; O'Leary & Turkewitz, 1978; Stuart, 1976; Weiss & Birchler, 1978; Weiss et al., 1973.)

The initial homework assignments presented here seek to develop spouses' abilities to be behavior analysts of their own relationship. A first step in this process will often include a request that they simply look over the data collected by the partner each night.

Assignment: Study your spouse's SOC data.

Each spouse is recording daily frequencies of various behaviors, along with a DSR. By studying the partner's checklist, each spouse will learn which behaviors have a functional impact on the other's subjective satisfaction. For example, one client noticed that on most days when his partner's DSR was low, he had provided very little in the way of affectionate behavior. This apparent association between affection from him and satisfaction from her identified the former as a *possible* determinant of the latter.

Each spouse is expected to discuss his or her hypotheses during the next treatment session. The question is best phrased as follows: "What behaviors on my part are most predictive of my spouse's daily satisfaction?" The next assignment involves testing those hypotheses at home. If a spouse has correctly identified the important determinants of his or her partner's satisfaction, then increasing the frequency of those behaviors presumed to be directly associated with DSR (or decreasing the frequency of those behaviors presumed to vary inversely with DSR) should result in increased satisfaction for the partner.

The next phase of behavior-exchange assignments evolves from exchanges that occur during the treatment session. Instead of each spouse privately forming and testing hypotheses on how to increase the partner's satisfaction, the receiver's input is incorporated into the procedure. Now, each partner is urged to indicate additional behavior changes which would lead to his or her own increased satisfaction. Upon hearing these suggestions, in each case the partner retains the option of declining as long as he or she agrees to do something. The focus is initially on minor issues, and the demands on each spouse are again instigated with a maximum of flexibility: neither is obligated to change any particular behavior, but each is obligated to select at least some behavior from the pool of requests.

Assignment: Implement the behavior changes agreed upon during the treatment sessions.

The salience of behavior changes negotiated during the treatment sessions gradually escalates. The ability of spouses to implement these changes gives evidence as to whether the demands placed on them are excessive. Each therapy session begins with a discussion of the past week, focusing on the couple's success (or lack thereof) in producing the agreed-upon changes in the natural environment. When changes are agreed to but not implemented, there are but a limited number of potential explanations: a lapse in memory; a skill deficit precluding implementation; a situational constraint such as a physical illness; or an excessively costly change for one or both spouses, one which never should have been agreed to. When the requisite behavior changes do not occur, whatever steps may be necessary to insure success in implementing them are undertaken.

Although this has been little more than a summary showing how homework assignments are incorporated into a behavior exchange program, the important themes should be apparent. Homework is used both to implement the changes to which spouses commit themselves during the treatment sessions, and to document the success of therapy. Homework assignments are not merely a means to an end; in fact, they often comprise the very changes that couples seek when they enter therapy for marital problems.

Assignments during communication and problem-solving training. Training in communications skills differs from behavior exchange formats primarily in its emphasis on skill acquisition. Problem-solving and communication training with couples have been described elsewhere (Gottman, Notarius, Gonso, & Markman, 1976; Jacobson, 1977a, 1977b; Jacobson & Margolin, 1979; Margolin & Weiss, 1978; O'Leary & Turkewitz, 1978). The focus here will be on the structure and function of homework assignments connected with such training.

The essential homework assignment connected with communication training is practicing communication skills that have been developed during treatment sessions.

Assignment: Practice the communications skills developed during the treatment session.

Thus, the relationship between homework assignments and treatment sessions is different than in behavior exchange approaches. With communication training, homework assignments are designed to promote generalization of positive communication into the couple's everyday interactional domain. This generalization cannot be left to chance. As I have argued elsewhere (Jacobson, 1977b; Jacobson & Margolin, 1979), couples can be deceptively competent in their manifest communication during treatment sessions without practicing such behaviors at home. Homework assignments are designed to establish discriminative stimuli for desirable communication in the natural environment and to gradually fade out these cues so that the couple can function autonomously by the time therapy is over. The principle of assigning progressively more difficult tasks is utilized here, just as it is in the assignment of behavior exchange tasks.

Problem-solving training exemplifies how the assignment of homework tasks is interwoven with skills taught during treatment sessions (Jacobson, 1977a, 1977b, 1981; Jacobson & Margolin, 1979). Before direct training begins, couples are given a manual to read (Jacobson & Margolin, 1979).

Assignment: Read the manual.

Then, as skills are demonstrated and rehearsed during treatment sessions, they are assigned as homework tasks. *A couple will never be asked to engage in a task at home until they have demonstrated their competence at the same task during the therapy session.* Although this practice does not eliminate the possibility of an unsuccessful effort at home, it greatly reduces its likelihood.

An additional safeguard against a negative experience during homework practice attempts is to maximize the similarities between the treatment environment and the natural environment, especially during the early stages of training.

Assignment: Practice newly learned problem-solving skills, following the rules and structure set during the treatment session.

Assignment: Record all home practice sessions on tape.

Similarity is created by teaching couples that a set of rules structure the practice sessions at home in ways similar to the structure provided by the therapist during the treatment sessions. For example, practice sessions are to be held at a predetermined time on a predetermined day, and never spontaneously convened to deal with immediate problems. Thus, couples are discouraged from attempting to solve problems "at the scene of the crime," a practice that is seldom productive from the standpoint of conflict resolution. Instead, their discussions can be dispassionate, since by the time of the next scheduled practice session, they have some "emotional distance" from the problem. Rules also dictate a protocol for taking turns speaking, responding appropriately and inappropriately, and the like. To facilitate compliance with these rules, couples are given cassette tapes and tape recorders to tape all home practice sessions. This practice has proved to be a very useful way of extending the therapist's influence into the natural environment.

Even though communication training emphasizes direct instruction during the treatment session itself and is therefore inherently less instigative than the behavior exchange approach, the therapist must pay attention to the couple's efforts to implement their newly acquired skills at home. Thus, the beginning of each communication training session should be devoted to a discussion of the efforts that were made at home since the previous session. This can be done either by replaying the tapes of the homework sessions or by simply discussing the home practice attempts. A great deal of troubleshooting goes on during this phase of the treatment session. Attempts are made to pinpoint where the problems occurred, and at times the couple will roleplay the events of the practice session until the exercise is mastered.

Gradually, as the communication skills are mastered, the homework assignments are altered to decrease the similarities between the therapy environment and the natural environment. By the time the couple terminates, they should be communicating effectively at home without the need for the discriminative stimuli mentioned above.

Assignment: Practice your problem-solving and communication skills at home. Conduct your own therapy session in lieu of an office visit.

The final homework assignment has the couple conducting their own therapy session at home (see Jacobson & Margolin, 1979). Here they survey the past week, pinpointing both positive and negative exchanges. They also monitor previous behavior change agreements to make sure that they are being upheld. Finally, any new problems that have emerged result in a problem-solving session. If the couple can integrate this weekly session into their normal routine and if the session can be conducted successfully, the necessary conditions for the maintenance of positive changes have been satisfied. The spouses have now learned to monitor their own progress and to use what they have learned in therapy to counter any reversion to destructive pretherapy interaction patterns.

COMPLIANCE ENHANCEMENT PROCEDURES

It is a rather obvious fact that homework assignments are useless unless the clients comply with them. Despite the self-evident nature of this statement, very little attention has been given to the technology of compliance in the behavior therapy literature, and, of more immediate relevance to this chapter, in the behavioral marital therapy literature. Nevertheless, therapists continually express frustration regarding the difficulties of inducing client compliance.

Psychoanalytic theorists (Ables & Brandsma, 1977; Sager, 1976) and systems theorists (Haley, 1963; Sluzki, 1978; Steinglass, 1978) share fundamentally different assumptions regarding compliance. Both assume that spouses enter therapy at best ambivalent, and at worst opposed, to changes in their relationship. Among psychoanalytic theorists, this resistance is hypothesized to be based on a collusive bond between the spouses by which each has agreed to protect the other from anxiety resulting from the surfacing of unconscious conflicts (Dicks, 1967). The agreement itself is presumed to be unconscious, but because of it, clients will stubbornly cling to dysfunctional interaction patterns that keep them both at a safe distance from a more pernicious enemy, the anxiety stemming from still unresolved intrapsychic conflicts. Systems theorists, such as Haley (1963), invoke the concept of homeostasis as a characteristic of all "systems," of which the marital dyad is but one example. It is believed to be a characteristic of all systems that any external attempt to change the basic structure of a system will be resisted.

Proponents of the notion of unconscious resistance differ among themselves as to the best strategies for scaling this therapeutic hurdle. Some advocate an insight-oriented approach, in which spouses are made aware of both the collusive bonds that shackle them and their historical antecedents (Dicks, 1967). Others advocate paradoxical intervention, in which clients are induced to behave differently through instructions to continue their dysfunctional behavior.

To a behavior therapist the concept "unconscious resistance" is unsatisfactory, both as an explanatory concept and in its clinical ramifications (see discussion in Jacobson, 1981; Jacobson & Margolin, 1979; Jacobson & Weiss, 1978). Both psychoanalytic and systems theorists infer the existence of unconscious resistance on the basis of spouses' manifest resistance to therapists' directives. However, the concept of resistance is then used to explain the very behaviors from which its existence was inferred. From a logical standpoint, resistant behavior is clearly insufficient grounds for inferring an unconsciously motivated deficit that pits spouses against their own conscious goals. One might argue that certain clinical strategies are dictated by the existence of unconscious resistance and that the utility of the concept is justified by the efficiency of these clinical strategies in overcoming resistant behavior. But there is no evidence that either psychoanalytic or systems strategies for overcoming marital resistance are successful. Since the higher-order inference involving the positing of an unconscious mechanism is considerably less parsimonious than the social learning hypothesis, the burden of proof is on advocates of the unconscious construct to demonstrate that their clinical strategies are more effective than those following from an environmentally based model.

The accumulating body of clinical and experimental evidence demonstrating that couples do quite often follow instructions without resisting argues against the "unconscious resistance" notion. Moreover, as Jacobson and Margolin (1979) pointed out, a bias on the part of the therapist can act as a self-fulfilling prophecy: the expectation of resistance can create resistance. At least for the present, our clients will be better served by giving them the benefit of the doubt and by using direct strategies to induce compliance with our directives.

In marital therapy, *compliance can generally be insured by direct instructional interventions that capitalize on social influence processes that have been well documented in both social psychological and clinical literature.* Compliance is prompted by a presentation that is forcefully persuasive and that underscores the importance of the task. Thus, it might be said that compliance can be brought under stimulus control. In addition, compliance can be reinforced and noncompliance can be punished in various ways. The following paragraphs specify some of the more successful strategies.

Stimulus Control Strategies

Tendencies toward noncompliance can be short-circuited if, when the assignment is presented to the client, the message contains certain essential components.

Emphasize the task's importance. The therapist must emphasize that the agenda for subsequent sessions depends upon compliance with the homework assignment. The first of the following presentations de-emphasizes the importance of the task, whereas the second properly emphasizes the task's importance:

Message 1
I would like you to complete this checklist each evening, if at all possible. The checklist requires that you begin to record some of the events that take place between the two of you every day. This will help us understand the patterns of inter- action and exchanges that go on at home. You will be doing this from now until the end of therapy, if we should decide to pursue that. I would like you to try as hard as you can to complete this task.

Message 2
Now I'm going to assign a task which may be *the most important task which you will do from now until the end of therapy.* As part of our evaluation procedure, you will begin to record some of the events that take place between the two of you every day. *This will give us some information that we can't get in any other way,* namely, the patterns of interaction and exchanges that go on at home. You will be doing this from now until the end of therapy, if we should decide to pursue that. *So, later we will be using this information to begin working on some of the problems. We'll look at it every week and see how we're doing. So, we'll be making a lot of use of this information, and I find that it functions like a seeing eye dog for me. I am blind without it. So, it is neces- sary that you do the work every day, and do it carefully.*
(Jacobson & Margolin, 1979, p. 127, italics added.)

The italicized portions of the second presentation emphasize critical components of the message, all of which are lacking in the first presentation. First, the importance of the task is made explicit. Second, it is directly stated that, in addition to being important, the information cannot be acquired in any other way. Third, some of the uses of the checklist are enumerated so that clients understand the rationale for the task. Fourth, it is clear from the second message that, in the therapist's expert opinion, progress will be greatly impeded by noncompliance. Indeed, it is suggested that the therapist will be ineffective without the information provided by the checklist. Fifth, the tentativeness in the first message ("if at all possible..."; "try as hard as you can...") is eliminated, and instead the clients are told that the task *must* be completed carefully and on a daily basis.

Beyond the obvious impact of a therapist emphasizing, in a clear and unambiguous manner, that a task is essential, the message circum- vents a major source of noncompliance. Once the task is made synonymous with therapeutic progress, noncompliance becomes a tacit admission that progress is undesirable to the noncompliant spouse. Resisting the task becomes tantamount to admitting that the client is not interested in therapy. It is impossible for the client to assert that "I want the relationship to improve, but I did not do the assignment." Although many clients may be ambivalent about the desirability of relationship changes, few are willing to behave in a way that would so blatantly cast doubt on their motivation. Thus, once couples enter the clinical arena, even their competitiveness and power struggles work in favor of compliance. Neither spouse wants to be the one to be blamed for treatment failure, since each wants to feel that his or her partner is in the wrong.

Exaggerate the task's aversiveness. Since one antecedent of noncompliance is that a homework task is more difficult or tedious than the client had foreseen, overstating or exaggerating task aversiveness will cause the client to experience the task as being more pleasant than anticipated. Although there is a mild risk that this tactic will boomerang, and that the emphasis on task aversiveness will become a self-fulfilling prophecy, in practice this result seldom occurs.

When introducing the SOC, it is prudent to give the following warning: "You are not going to enjoy doing this. At first it will be difficult. Then, once you get the hang of it, you are likely to find it boring." In fact, many couples are pleasantly surprised to find that the task is both easier and more interesting than the warning suggested.

Anticipate excuses. The likelihood of compliance is enhanced by incorporating potential obstacles into the initial instructions. In introducing the SOC, I have often told couples that "I know you are both busy, but you must complete the assignment however hectic your schedules might be on a particular day. This must become a priority, not something to do only when time allows." Although lack of time is by far the most common excuse for noncompliance, it is by no means the only one. The validity of any excuse can be undercut and disqualified if it can be anticipated and then labeled as "no excuse" before it is invoked.

Gain the clients' commitment. In our contract-oriented culture, a written commitment would be even more desirable. We use a general treatment contract that both therapist and clients sign at the beginning of therapy and in which clients agree to complete all homework tasks.

Maximize client choice. Since clients often react adversely to the perception of being controlled or "told what to do," compliance is more likely if spouses have the freedom to choose among various options or to participate in formulating their own tasks. Even if their reluctance to being "told what to do" is interpreted more parsimoniously as an attempt to avoid excessively costly behavior changes (Jacobson, 1981;

Jacobson & Margolin, 1979), it still behooves marital therapists to use client input in their assignment of tasks.

As mentioned earlier, as an initial statement of their commitment to therapy, I often ask couples to increase the behaviors that each thinks would increase the other's satisfaction (Jacobson, 1981). However, rather than asking each spouse what he or she wants from the other or having the therapist assign specific behavior changes, each spouse decides for him or herself exactly what changes will be implemented. The directive is that they each demonstrate their good faith; how they obey that directive is up to them. Later, once the relationship has begun to improve, the directives will be more demanding; but even then, spouses always retain the privilege of choosing among various behavior change options. Only in rare circumstances are specific requests made and then clients are free to decline these requests, although it often becomes their responsibility to offer alternatives.

Consequences for Noncompliance

Interrupt therapy. If the therapist alters the plan for the treatment session whenever the client does not comply, he or she makes clear how compliance functions in therapy and tells the client that failure to comply with homework assignments delays treatment progress. Altering the planned agenda is not to be undertaken punitively but simply to show that "business as usual" is not viable when the homework assignment has not been completed. The session that would normally be consumed by the pursuance of treatment goals should then be devoted to the question, "What can we do about this very serious problem?" Reasons for the failure in compliance should be explored, and whatever steps are needed to insure completion of the assignment should be undertaken.

Revise the assignment. Whenever possible, the therapist should see the compliance problem as a sign that the demands created by the assignment were excessive. Even though clients usually choose whether or not to comply with a homework assignment, it is often useful to refer to their failure in terms that imply that their noncompliance was involuntary. For example, when a husband reported that he did not spend 30 minutes each morning talking to his wife over breakfast, as he had agreed, the therapist responded, "I should never have let you agree to that. In retrospect, it is obvious to me that you weren't ready to give up that time. You still need to distance yourself from her in the morning." Another example involves a wife who failed to respond positively to her husband's affectionate overtures. The therapist responded as follows: "Right now you are still incapable of giving to him in that way. You are afraid to let go of that freedom to be physically unresponsive." After relabeling the assignment as excessively difficult, the task then becomes one of finding an assignment that is less demanding, more within the current capabilities of the clients.

This allows for a more benign, less discouraging interpretation of the problem. Even if such an interpretation turns out to be invalid, it can often foster subsequent compliance. Spouses often rebel against the inference that they are "incapable" of carrying out assignments, particularly when it is implied that the incapability implies an inability to "give." Paradoxically, spouses often respond to such a reframing by a renewed determination to disprove the therapist's unfavorable assessment of their capabilities. Furthermore, if the assignment immediately following an episode of noncompliance is significantly beneath the couple's capabilities, spouses will often exceed the requirements of the assignment. This transformation in turn often sets a precedent for future compliance.

Prompt with evening phone calls. During the first week or two following the original assignment asking couples to collect data in the home, use brief evening phone calls to insure compliance. The caller (usually a research assistant) simply collects summaries of the data. Since the telephone calls are gradually faded as compliance becomes assured, their termination negatively reinforces compliance. These phone calls dispel any doubts, if such doubts still exist, as to the importance of the data collection assignment. They also act as prompts. In the event that the data collection has not occurred on a particular evening, the caller simply responds, "It is very important that you complete the checklist every evening."

Reinforcement for Compliance

In addition to the negative consequences already mentioned as responses to noncompliance, it is essential that couples be effectively reinforced for successful completion of the assignments. The most powerful reinforcer of all—an improved relationship between partners—is not completely under the therapist's control, although its likelihood is considerably greater if homework prescriptions are regularly followed. For instance, if spouses learn to talk more precisely about their feelings as to how housework should be divided, they are more likely to reach compromises that will satisfy both of them. Or a wife who agrees to not criticize her husband when he is late for engagements may be gratified to find that he tries harder to be on time.

Short of guaranteeing an improved relationship, the material generated by the homework assignments should be used extensively in the therapy sessions, and the way it is used should be clear to the clients.

For example, each week the data that couples collect in the home should be plotted, and on the basis of this data an ongoing analysis of the relationship should be presented week-by-week during the therapy sessions. An assignment should never be given unless the material generated by it plays an important role in subsequent therapy sessions. The therapist should repeat him or herself whenever necessary in order that clients understand exactly how the material is used and why it is necessary to therapy.

ILLUSTRATIVE CASE

Ron and Harriet were in their late 30s. They had been married for 13 years and had two teenaged daughters, the oldest of whom had a history of anorexia nervosa. They both had high school educations. Ron was an extremely compulsive, industrious man who had advanced to a position of some responsibility as an administrator at a large state university. He was a strict disciplinarian with his children and a conservative thinker on most moral and political issues, and he had a difficult time either enjoying himself or acting spontaneously. Harriet was a quiet, passive, mildly depressed woman who had become increasingly discontented and rebellious in regard to her role in their highly traditional marriage. Other complaints spanned a wide spectrum of relationship areas, including his insistence on hegemony in financial matters, his attempts to rely exclusively on an aversive control system in his relationship with his children, and her pervasive aversion to his sexual and affectionate overtures.

Treatment with this couple focused on problem-solving training. Both partners were highly motivated to improve their relationship, and for the most part they worked diligently. The wife was desperate, because although she felt that she no longer loved her husband, she wanted to continue the relationship if at all possible "for the sake of the children." The husband insisted that he still loved his wife and was willing to do anything to keep her in the marriage.

The first step with this couple, after a thorough evaluation (cf. Jacobson et al., in press; Jacobson & Margolin, 1979), was to have them read a treatment manual describing problem-solving training. Then Ron and Harriet were taught to apply these principles to their target problems one by one. Homework played a major role, perhaps more so than is usually the case when the primary treatment emphasis in on problem-solving training. This is because they mastered the skills quickly and easily and because they were able to deal effectively with many of their presenting problems by conducting problem-solving sessions at home. These sessions were recorded on cassettes. The treatment sessions served primarily to provide feedback on home problem-solving sessions and to monitor the effectiveness and durability of the change agreements produced by the sessions.

The couple improved markedly during the course of therapy, and the improvements continued after therapy sessions were terminated. They continued to have weekly therapy sessions on their own, where they assessed the state of their marriage, reviewed the current status of their change agreements, and solved problems regarding any new issues that had arisen. Homework had played a pivotal role in the treatment of this couple, and lent confidence to the hope that they could serve as their own therapists in the future.

SUMMARY

Although there are many approaches to behavioral marital therapy (BMT), most of them are instigative to assure that generalization of skills from therapy to the natural environment takes place. The approaches described in this chapter are based on the assumptions that couples who enter therapy have a genuine desire to improve their relationship and that resistance to the therapist's directives is primarily due to the short-term costs of compliance.

Two main types of BMT are content-oriented and process-oriented therapy, which are also referred to as behavior exchange and communication training. Behavior exchange focuses on changing behaviors in the marriage, while communication training aims to foster effective communication skills between marriage partners. Both types of therapy use homework. Examples of assignments for assessment, behavior exchange, and communication training are discussed.

Stimulus control strategies, consequences for noncompliance, and reinforcement for compliance are covered under compliance enhancement procedures. Some of the stimulus control strategies are placing emphasis on the task's importance; exaggerating the task's aversiveness; anticipating excuses; gaining the clients' commitment; and maximizing the clients' choice of tasks. Consequences for noncompliance can be interrupting therapy to deal with resistance, revising the assignment, and prompting with evening phone calls. Compliance is reinforced by showing progress in therapy by plotting data collected weekly, giving relevant assignments that are subsequently discussed in sessions, and insuring that clients know what they are to do and why.

The final section is a description of a case study of a couple, Ron and Harriet, who are trying to save a failing marriage. After receiving communication training, they are able to successfully handle their problems by holding weekly therapy sessions on their own.

REFERENCES

Ables, B.S., & Brandsma, J.M. *Therapy for couples.* San Francisco: Jossey-Bass, 1977.

Azrin, N.H., Naster, B.J., & Jones, R. Reciprocity counseling: A rapid learning-based procedure for marital counseling. *Behaviour Research and Therapy,* 1973, *11,* 365-382.

Baer, D.M., Wolfe, M.M., & Risley, T.R. Some current dimensions of applied behavior analysis. *Journal of Applied Behavior Analysis,* 1968, *1,* 91-97.

Christensen, A., & Nies, D.L. The spouse observation checklist: Empirical analysis and critique. *American Journal of Family Therapy,* 1980, *8,* 69-79.

Dicks, H. *Marital tensions.* New York: Basic Books, 1967.

Gottman, J.M. *Marital interaction.* New York: Academic Press, 1979.

Gottman, J.M., Markman, H., & Notarius, C. The topography of marital conflict: Sequential analysis of verbal and nonverbal behavior. *Journal of Marriage and the Family,* 1977, *39,* 461-477.

Gottman, J.M., Notarius, C., Gonso, J., & Markman, H. *A couple's guide to communication.* Champaign, Ill.: Research Press, 1976.

Gottman, J.M., Notarius, C., Markman, H., Bank, S., Yoppi, B., & Rubin, M.E. Behavior exchange theory and marital decision making. *Journal of Personality and Social Psychology,* 1976, *34,* 14-23.

Haley, J. Marriage therapy. *Archives of General Psychiatry,* 1963, *8,* 213-234.

Jacobson, N.S. Training couples to solve their marital problems: A behavioral approach to relationship discord. Part I: Problem-solving skills. *International Journal of Family Counseling,* 1977, *5* (1), 22-31. (a)

Jacobson, N.S. Training couples to solve their marital problems: A behavioral approach to relationship discord. Part II: Intervention strategies. *International Journal of Family Counseling,* 1977, *5* (2), 20-28. (b)

Jacobson, N.S. Behavioral treatments for marital discord: A critical appraisal. In M. Hersen, R.M. Eisler, & P.M. Miller (Eds.), *Progress in behavior modification* (Vol. 8). New York: Academic Press, 1979.

Jacobson, N.S. Behavioral marital therapy. In A.S. Gurman & D.P. Kniskern (Eds.), *Handbook of family therapy.* New York: Brunner/ Mazel, 1981.

Jacobson, N.S., Elwood, R., & Dallas, M. Behavioral assessment of marital dysfunction. In D.H. Barlow (Ed.), *Behavioral assessment of adult disorders.* New York: Guilford, in press.

Jacobson, N.S., & Margolin, G. *Marital therapy: Strategies based on social learning and behavior exchange principles.* New York: Brunner/ Mazel, 1979.

Jacobson, N.S., & Martin, B. Behavioral marriage therapy: Current status. *Psychological Bulletin,* 1976, *83,* 540-556.

Jacobson, N.S., & Moore, D. Spouses as observers of the events in their relationship. *Journal of Consulting and Clinical Psychology,* in press.

Jacobson, N.S., Waldron, H., & Moore, D. Toward a behavioral profile of marital distress. *Journal of Consulting and Clinical Psychology,* 1980, *48,* 696-703.

Jacobson, N.S., & Weiss, R.L. Behavioral marriage therapy: The contents of Gurman et al. may be hazardous to our health. *Family Process,* 1978, *17,* 149-64.

Kanfer, F.H., & Phillips, J.S. *Learning foundations of behavior therapy.* New York: John Wiley & Sons, 1970.

Margolin, G., & Weiss, R.L. Comparative evaluation of therapeutic components associated with behavioral marital treatment. *Journal of Consulting and Clinical Psychology,* 1978, *46,* 1476-1486.

O'Leary, K.D., & Turkewitz, H. Marital therapy from a behavioral perspective. In T.J. Paolino, Jr., & B.S. McCrady (Eds.), *Marriage and marital therapy: Psychoanalytic, behavioral, and systems theory perspectives.* New York: Brunner/Mazel, 1978.

Patterson, G.R., & Reid, J.B. Reciprocity and coercion: Two facets of social systems. In C. Neurunger & J.L. Michael (Eds.), *Behavior modification in clinical psychology.* New York: Appleton-Century-Crofts, 1970.

Patterson, G.R., Weiss, R.L., & Hops, H. Training of marital skills: Some problems and concepts. In H. Leitenberg (Ed.), *Handbook of behavior modification.* New York: Appleton-Century-Crofts, 1976.

Rachlin, H. Self-control. *Behaviorism,* 1974, *2,* 94-127.

Robinson, E.A., & Price, M.G. Pleasurable behavior in marital interaction: An observational study. *Journal of Consulting and Clinical Psychology,* 1980, *48,* 30-38.

Sager, C. *Marriage contracts and couple therapy: Hidden forces in intimate relationships.* New York: Brunner/Mazel, 1976.

Sluzki, C. Marital therapy from a systems theory perspective. In T.J. Paolino, Jr., & B.S. McCrady (Eds.), *Marriage and marital therapy: Psychoanalytic, behavioral, and systems theory perspectives.* New York: Brunner/Mazel, 1978.

Steinglass, P. The conceptualization of marriage from a systems theory perspective. In T.J. Paolino, Jr., & B.S. McCrady (Eds.), *Marriage and marital therapy: Psychoanalytic, behavioral, and systems theory perspectives.* New York: Brunner/Mazel, 1978.

Stuart, R.B. Operant interpersonal treatment for marital discord. *Journal of Consulting and Clinical Psychology,* 1969, *33,* 675-682.

Stuart, R.B. An operant interpersonal program for couples. In D.H.L. Olson (Ed.), *Treating relationships.* Lake Mills, Iowa: Graphic, 1976.

Weiss, R.L. Contracts, cognition, and change: A behavioral approach to marriage therapy. *The Counseling Psychologist,* 1975, *5*(3), 15-26.

Weiss, R.L., & Birchler, G.R. Adults with marital dysfunction. In M. Hersen & A.S. Bellack (Eds.), *Behavior therapy in the psychiatric setting.* Baltimore: Williams & Wilkins, 1978.

Weiss, R.L., Hops, H., & Patterson, G.R. A framework for conceptualizing marital conflict, a technology for altering it, some data for evaluating it. In L.A. Hamerlynck, L.C. Handy, & E.J. Mash (Eds.), *Behavior change: Methodology, concepts, and practice.* Champaign, Ill.: Research Press, 1973.

Weiss, R.L., & Margolin, G. Marital conflict and accord. In A.R. Ciminero, K.S. Calhoun, & H.E. Adams (Eds.), *Handbook for behavioral assessment.* New York: John Wiley & Sons, 1977.

Wills, T.A., Weiss, R.L., & Patterson, G.R. A behavioral analysis of the determinants of marital satisfaction. *Journal of Consulting and Clinical Psychology,* 1974, *42,* 802-811.

CHAPTER 7

Addictive Behaviors

Judith R. Gordon
Department of Psychology
University of Washington

G. Alan Marlatt
Department of Psychology
University of Washington

OVERVIEW OF ADDICTIVE BEHAVIORS

Addictive behaviors are notoriously resistant to modification, and recidivism rates among individuals who have successfully completed treatment are discouragingly high. Common lore and empirical data alike indicate that relapse is at least as critical a problem as the initial induction of positive behavior changes, if not more so. In a classic study comparing treated heroin addicts, alcoholics, and habitual smokers, Hunt, Barnett, and Branch (1971) found relapse to be the norm rather than the exception and relapse curves to be very similar across addictions: by 90 days after treatment, approximately 66 percent of the subjects in all categories had relapsed, with the majority of relapses occurring in the first month following treatment. Despite continuing and extensive efforts at developing more effective treatment techniques, the instability of treatment outcomes continues to plague addicted individuals, treatment providers, researchers, and theoreticians.

The field of addictions is currently dominated by two viewpoints that differ on theoretical grounds and approaches to treatment. The traditional view, or disease model, of addiction is that the addictive substance activates a basic underlying disease process that is chronic, permanently incurable, and probably genetic in origin. Exposure to the drug is presumed to stimulate intense physiological cravings and uncontrollable urges that lead to loss of control over the consummatory behavior; this inexorable cycle can be controlled only by avoiding ingestion of the drug. In this framework relapse is viewed as a behavioral manifestation of the reemergence of the disease in the form of urges, which again cause a loss of control. Thus the primary intervention focus is on cessation, and the addict is seen as a victim of a disease that at best he or she can only hope to keep in remission.

An alternate view that has received increasing attention in recent years is the social-learning model, which is derived from principles of learning theory, cognitive psychology, and experimental social psychology. In this view, addictive behaviors are seen as overlearned, maladaptive habit patterns whose acquisition and maintenance can be explained by principles of classical and operant conditioning and social learning. This model can accommodate a range of physiological factors, such as genetic predisposition, biochemical mechanisms, and pharmacological reinforcers, but psychosocial factors are held to play the primary role in mediating the addictive behavior. The major treatment focus is on implementing cognitive-behavioral interventions that will help the addicted individual deautomatize the problem behavior and acquire alternative positive responses. Until recently, relapse was seen as an extinction or decay over time of the new, less well-established, positive responses that were acquired as substitutes for the old, habitual, problem responses. This conceptualization led to the development of broad spectrum or multimodal treatment packages with a "more is better" philosophy. The programs attempt to enhance and stabilize long-term maintenance of positive change by introducing more techniques aimed both at inducing cessation of the target behavior and at developing responses incompatible with the original ones. Thus although relapse is a more legitimate treatment concern than it is in the disease model, maintenance is still addressed by attempting to strengthen and reinforce the initial change strategies.

A new trend within the social-learning framework is an increasing emphasis on relapse itself, including attempts to investigate it as a separate phenomenon as well as using it as an important focus of treatment intervention. Treatment applications derived from this perspective are of two types: strategies for anticipating and preventing relapse and for coping with relapses that do occur may be added to existing packages, or they may be integrated within them, providing a maximum amount of flexibility. The critical ingredient is the underlying philosophy that the induction and maintenance of positive behavior change must be supported and reinforced by active efforts toward preventing relapse (Marlatt, 1978; Marlatt & Gordon, 1980).

Our research on the relapse phenomenon across addictive behaviors appears to support the social-learning model of addictions in general, as well as the argument for a relapse prevention approach. In the relapses we investigated, situational determinants played a key role, suggesting that addicted individuals might benefit from training in coping with situational factors associated with relapse. For example, in a situational analysis of relapses reported by 137 treated alcoholics, smokers, and heroin addicts, only 4 percent of all relapses were associated with craving for the substance. In contrast, 76 percent of the relapses were associated with negative emotional states (37 percent), social pressure (24 percent), and interpersonal conflict (15 percent) (Marlatt & Gordon, 1980). In a more extensive study comparing relapses reported by 327 subjects who had been treated for alcoholism, smoking, heroin addiction, compulsive gambling, or weight reduction, 72 percent of all relapses were associated with the same factors: negative emotional states (30 percent), social pressure (27 percent), and interpersonal conflict (15 percent) (Cummings, Gordon, & Marlatt, 1980). These data are congruent with the social-learning conceptualization of addiction, according to which addictive behaviors are learned maladaptive behaviors that are initially acquired through a combination of pharmacological and psychosocial reinforcers, become overlearned and automated through repetition, and are maintained as habitual responses associated with coping with a wide variety of situations. What once were voluntary behaviors become maladaptive responses because of negative physiological, psychological, or social consequences and lack of flexibility or appropriateness due to a constricted response set. The similarity of temporal and situational relapse patterns for behaviors that do not involve an addictive substance, such as gambling or compulsive eating, further supports the argument that psychosocial factors are more significant determinants of relapse than pharmacological or biochemical ones.

In addition to our view that there is solid empirical evidence to support the social-learning model, we have also come to believe that the clinician's decision to use either the disease or the social-learning model will have a significant effect on the client's attitudes, beliefs, and expectations regarding the problem behavior, and that treatment outcomes may be affected as much by these factors as by the specific techniques used in treatment. A corollary to the belief that a behavior is a symptom of a disease or genetic weakness is that the individual has no control over it. This corollary appears to be borne out by the observation that addicted individuals report feeling out of control of their behavior.

The conclusion is then that any contact with the substance or performance of the behavior will inevitably lead to total loss of control. We have postulated, however, that the so-called loss of control phenomenon may be due to expectancy or self-fulfilling prophecy and may not be a symptom of disease (see Marlatt, 1978, for a full discussion of the loss of control phenomenon, and Marlatt & Rohsenow, 1980, for a review of the role of expectancies in alcohol use). Some evidence also exists that the self-attribution of addiction in smokers, for example, may provide a justification for continuing to smoke even when health risks are acknowledged (Eiser, Sutton, & Wober, 1978).

Most individuals who view themselves as addicted believe that control is something one either has or lacks, so if they are not in control 100 percent of the time they believe they are addicted and have no control at all; this belief then gives rise to the self-fulfilling prophecy that one slip inevitably leads to a full-blown relapse. We would argue that the human condition and the realities of the world are such that total control is unattainable and that the expectation of it is therefore maladaptive. A more adaptive conceptualization is that control lies along a continuum, and can be operationally defined as being the result of acquiring and implementing enough strategies to tip the balance in the direction of *sufficient* control.

Because the individual needs to learn many coping strategies and use them in the natural environment, homework-based treatment is especially appropriate. It gives the client an opportunity to practice each strategy repeatedly with guidance until it can successfully be used by him or her in everyday situations.

HOMEWORK-BASED TREATMENT

Overview of Treatment

Goals. Our major treatment goals are to modify the client's maladaptive belief system, to replace it with a more balanced set of expectations, and then to teach the client more effective coping skills. "Being in control" is defined as having enough awareness of the situation (its antecedents and the consequences of various responses) and possessing sufficient coping skills to make adaptive choices enough of the time to maintain a sense of choice and self-efficacy, or the expectation of being able to perform effectively in specific situations (Bandura, 1977). Greater balance between those times when the individual can and cannot maintain control insures greater stability, more ease in regaining equilibrium, and less susceptibility to overreacting to slips and thereby giving up any further attempts at self-control. We prefer to designate the problem behavior as excessive rather than addictive to express this concept of balance.

Consistent with the goals of a more balanced set of expectations about control and better coping skills, our basic therapeutic thrust is toward prevention of relapse. In our view the issue of maintenance is not separate from induction of change but is rather a reflection of the reality that individuals need to anticipate and be prepared for coping with situations that will challenge their control. The treatment described in this chapter is derived from a relapse prevention model based on our research on determinants of relapse (Marlatt & Gordon, 1980). By orienting treatment around the problem of relapse from the start, we hope to prepare individuals to deal with the inevitable threats to the maintenance of positive changes more systematically and effectively.

The relapse prevention model. We define relapse as any violation of a self-imposed rule regarding a consummatory behavior, whether the rule involves abstinence or controlled use. According to our conceptualization, the determinants of whether or not an individual will relapse are as follows. First, the individual encounters a "high-risk situation"— an environmental occurrence, an interpersonal interaction, or an affective, cognitive, or physiological internal state to which he or she has typically responded in the past by performing the problem behavior. If the individual is able to execute an alternate coping response, he or she should experience an increased sense of self-efficacy, that is, the expectation that he or she will continue to be able to cope effectively with the situation in the future (Bandura, 1977), and this perception of personal control will decrease the probability of relapse in the future.

If the individual is unable to perform an alternate coping response, either because of a skill deficit or because of an inability to utilize the skill (for example, anxiety may block performance), he or she will have a decreased sense of self-efficacy, control, and power. In addition, he or she will probably believe that the old habitual response will give an increased sense of power ("If only I had a cigarette I could cope" or "A drink would relax me so I could handle this"). Indulgence in the behavior will be reinforcing both because of familiarity and the effects of the substance used. We have postulated a cognitive-affective reaction to the first slip that further increases the probability of relapse: the abstinence violation effect, or AVE (Marlatt, 1978). According to the AVE, the individual experiences cognitive dissonance as a result of the discrepancy between the self-imposed rule and the actual behavior, and to reduce the dissonance concludes that he or she is weak and incapable of controlling his or her behavior. This cognitive response provides a rationalization for dropping the rule and discontinuing attempts to regain control. The associated affective response is guilt resulting from the self-attribution that the individual's inability to cope was due to personal failure (lack of will power) rather than lack of coping skills to deal with the particular situation.

The following chart (see Table 7.1) indicates interventions that can be employed both to decrease the probability of relapses and to control the magnitude of any that do occur. The treatment plan described in the next section will illustrate the application of some of these interventions; for more detailed discussion, the reader is referred to our other work (Cummings et al., 1980; Marlatt, 1979; Marlatt & Gordon, 1980).

Table 7.1

Relapse Prevention Intervention Strategies

1. *High-Risk Situations*
   Variety of assessment procedures to identify individual high-risk situations

2. *Coping Responses*
   Assessment of availability of alternative coping responses

   Skill training if deficits exist

   Stress management and relaxation skills

3. *Self-Efficacy Enhancement*
   Analysis of beliefs and expectations

   Training in awareness of self-statements, attributions, and performance assessment

   Global lifestyle interventions to increase general sense of control and manage stress—for example, "positive addictions"

   Coping imagery and guided fantasy

4. *Use of Substance*
   Training in moderate or controlled-use skills if abstinence is not the goal

   Education about substance effects

5. *Abstinence Violation Effect*
   Cognitive restructuring

   Self-control interventions

   Relapse rehearsal

6. *Individualized Relapse Prevention Plan*
   Training in decision-making and problem-solving

   Construction of individual "road map" to predict problem situations and plan advance strategies for coping

   Identification of potential traps and pitfalls

   Use of reminder cards—what to do if a slip occurs

Overview of treatment plan. Our treatment plan follows a self-control model in which client and therapist work together as colleagues engaged in problem solving and skill training. The client learns to employ a variety of cognitive-behavioral strategies to implement positive behavior change within a framework of preventing and coping with slips. Maintenance is therefore addressed and dealt with from the very beginning and not added on as a later stage of treatment. Belief systems and expectations are viewed as a primary focus for intervention, since the goal is not only to improve the client's performance, but also to develop the client's sense of self-efficacy with regard to the problem behavior.

We assume that the reader is familiar with the principles of cognitive behavior modification, and we will not discuss them in detail. Rather than addressing addictive behaviors one by one, we will use the modification of smoking and drinking behaviors to illustrate the application of our model. Clearly the sequencing and selection of strategies will vary as a function of individual differences and the particular target behavior. It should also be noted that the components of the relapse prevention model are still in the process of being empirically tested, and we expect to make further changes and refinements. Thus the current outline is intended to provide guidelines only, and we encourage others to apply them with flexibility and creativity.

The goals of treatment are as follows. First, treatment should deautomatize the problem behavior, which by the time the client seeks treatment is routinized, overlearned, and enacted with little sense of real choice or control. Second, treatment should expand the client's available response repertoire so that more adaptive responses can be generated in situations previously eliciting the problem response. Third, it should increase the client's degree and perception of control by (a) helping him or her identify high-risk situations in which control is likely to be threatened and develop specific strategies either to avoid or cope with those situations or regain control if he or she loses it, and (b) focusing on lifestyle management to increase a global sense of control and well-being.

The first two sessions are usually devoted to establishing a working relationship, presenting the treatment rationale, assessing the history of the problem behavior and current usage patterns, and enhancing motivation. In addition to gathering information, we communicate our basic philosophy that with appropriate information and skills clients can learn to exert more influence over their responses, instead of maintaining a reactive, passive, victimized stance. The third or fourth session marks the quit or change date, depending on when sufficient assessment and baseline data have been collected. The next six or so sessions focus on training in coping with immediate problematic situations, general lifestyle management, and relapse prevention. At least three follow-up sessions are scheduled on a fading basis or as the client needs them, and arrangements are made to maintain contact and collect progress reports for at least a year.

The next section describes sessions and homework assignments in the treatment of problem drinking and habitual smoking. Differences in the treatment of the two behaviors will be indicated where applicable.

Homework Assignments

Session 1. In this session we gather a history of the problem behavior, including onset, duration, attempts to stop, and consequences the person is suffering in terms of health, work, relationships, and self-image. We discuss our perspective on the problem and attempt to determine how amenable the client is to this approach. Because our treatment requires active collaboration on the part of the client, it may be appropriate to refer dependent or poorly motivated individuals to other treatment plans that require less individualized self-control—Alcoholics Anonymous and SmokEnders are good examples.

> **Assignment:** Complete two brief autobiographies, one of yourself as a smoker (or problem drinker) now, and one of yourself as a nonsmoker (or controlled drinker) as you imagine you will be.

The form we use for smokers is shown in Figure 7.1 as an example. The purpose of this task is to help the client and therapist become aware of both the function the behavior has played up to now and the positive and negative consequences anticipated by the client as a result of modifying the behavior. (The issue of appropriate treatment goals, though critical, is beyond the scope of this chapter, but our approach is geared toward helping the person achieve a greater sense of actual and perceived control, whether the goal is abstinence or moderation.) The task also serves as a means of beginning to identify the situations, thoughts, or feelings that are likely to be high risks for relapse.

Figure 7.1   Autobiographical form for smokers

I. Autobiography of a Smoker

Write a brief history of yourself as a smoker, including any experiences, images, and feelings related to your smoking that have particular meaning for you. You may want to note how or why you began smoking, important people in your life who smoked, or the role smoking has played in your life. Be as loose and unchronological as you like; the goal is to capture your image of yourself as a smoker with its unique mixture of positive and negative qualities and associations.

II. Autobiography of a Nonsmoker

Write a brief description of your life as a nonsmoker, as you anticipate it to be. Include your reasons for stopping, projected details of your lifestyle without cigarettes, and the benefits and advantages you enjoy from not smoking. Also list any problem situations or difficulties you think you may encounter as a result of this change, and reflect on how you have made the transition easier for yourself and how the pressure did ease up over time. Visualize yourself without cigarettes as clearly as you can. Imagine both how you feel physically and your attitude and feelings about yourself now that you've stopped smoking.

Assignment: Record for 2 weeks the following information each time the problem behavior occurs:

Time	Situation	Mood or Feelings	Amount Consumed	Satisfaction Rating (on a scale of 1-10)

In assigning this task we are not as concerned with reliability of data collection as we are with (1) increasing awareness, and (2) determining antecedents of the behavior so we can begin to anticipate high-risk situations and explore specific alternatives. (Obviously, if treatment is being conducted as part of a research project, the reliability of the data is a much more critical issue.) We present this rationale to the client and explain that incomplete or inaccurate self-monitoring resulting from guilt or denial will greatly detract from the benefits of the task. In our experience clients find this very liberating and are able to develop the stance of a detached observer and colleague.

If it is essential that the client refrain from engaging in the behavior from the very beginning, other means must be employed to gather the same information.

Assignment (problem drinkers): Complete one of the following therapist-administered interviews: the Drinking Profile (Marlatt, 1976) or the Situational Competency Test (Chaney, O'Leary, & Marlatt, 1978).

Assignment: At the end of the first week, just prior to the second session, draw a histogram illustrating the response patterns based on the satisfaction rating data collected during the week.

The satisfaction rating is the subjective rating given by the client to indicate the degree of satisfaction experienced while consuming the problem substance in that particular instance, where *1* is the lowest possible rating and *10* is the highest possible rating. The categories along the abscissa in the histogram are selected to represent the 5 to 10 situations most typically associated with the behavior. For the drinker, for example, these might include after work, after a fight with my partner, after being unassertive in an interpersonal interaction. The smoker might include after meals, when working, during phone conversations, when I am bored or angry, when relaxing. The height of each bar is determined by the average satisfaction rating reported for all episodes occurring in that category. These data summarize the information about which situations are most likely to produce strong urges. The average amount consumed (or smoked) per day is also computed by the client before the second session.

Session 2. Homework from the previous week is discussed and analyzed, and a list of high-risk situations is generated from the data. The therapist can then begin to explore the client's existing repertoire of alternative coping responses to determine whether skill deficits exist. During this session we teach a mental relaxation technique and ask the client to practice it twice a day, 15 to 20 minutes each time. The rationale is that since addictive behaviors are frequently attempts to cope with stress, relaxation is a good alternate response. Further, because undertaking any behavior change is stressful, it is important to actively reduce stress levels during this time.

Assignment: Complete identical self-monitoring task for the second week.

This assignment may be necessary in the treatment of problem drinkers, since not all the typical situations associated with drinking may have arisen during the first week. With smokers, a week is usually sufficient for this assignment.

Assignment (smokers):   Smoke in an altered way and continue to self-monitor.

A technique that promotes nicotine fading, which may be helpful for heavy smokers, is to ask them to stop smoking in the situations receiving the highest satisfaction ratings the previous week and to smoke only in the situations that were least satisfying. We ask light to moderate smokers to eliminate smoking in the most satisfying situations but to employ a satiation technique by smoking double amounts in the least satisfying situations (see Best & Bloch, 1980, for a review of this technique). In both cases smokers must begin practicing alternative behaviors in those situations when smoking is prohibited to get a sense of which urges are strongest.

Session 3. At this point we believe that whether the goal is abstinence or moderation, it is essential that the client abstain from the problem behavior for at least 2 weeks to determine the client's coping repertoire and to evaluate the intensity of situational and emotional factors associated with urges. We inform clients about this abstinence period at the beginning of treatment, presenting it as an integral, unnegotiable part of the program. Drinkers usually find they can stop drinking for 2 weeks, discovery of which enhances their sense of control and motivates them to continue working. Any "failures" or slips are treated as opportunities to identify coping deficits in order to prevent future relapses.

Assignment: Announce your commitment to change to at least two significant others and enlist their support.

Assignment: Reward yourself in some way at the end of each week of abstinence.

In each session from this point on, we ask clients to anticipate any high-risk situations that may arise during the coming week so that we can plan and rehearse strategies.

Assignment: Practice coping responses in place of the target behavior and report each situation as follows:

Time	Situation	Mood or Feelings	Alternative Used	Satisfaction Rating (1-10)

Session 4. In this session we review the week's experiences and assignments, focusing on strong urge situations and modeling and rehearsing appropriate responses where necessary. We also discuss self-efficacy and the abstinence violation effect, notions that are easily understood now that the client is in the active phase of behavior change. If the client has successfully coped and avoided the target response, we discuss the importance of incorporating this success into a set of expectations of continuing to be able to respond adaptively, emphasizing that each situation thus dealt with should be used as evidence for developing an increasingly broad sense of self-efficacy. Too often clients and therapists make the mistake of focusing exclusively on failures, fears, and deficits, rather than on accomplishments.

If the client has experienced a slip, or if we discuss what would have happened if a slip had occurred, we describe the difference between a slip and a relapse, how the AVE operates to increase the chance of relapse, and associated cognitive-behavioral strategies for coping with the AVE. We also, at this time, provide information about drug effects, describing how the pharmacological action of the substance used may enhance the erroneous belief that the person is empowered by the drug.

Assignment: Write coping instructions on index or wallet-sized cards and use in the event of a slip.

For example, the Oregon Smoking Control Program distributes wallet-sized cards to smoking clients with the following instructions (adapted from Marlatt & Gordon, 1980):

Directions: Please carry this card with you at all times. In the event that you smoke a cigarette, take this card out *immediately,* read it, and follow the instructions.

A slip is not all that unusual. It does not mean that you have

failed or that you have lost control over your behavior. You
will probably feel guilty about what you have done, and will
blame yourself for having slipped. This feeling is to be expected; it is part of what we call the Abstinence Violation
Effect.

There is no reason why you have to give in to this feeling
and continue to smoke. The feeling will pass in time. Look
upon the slip as a learning experience. What were the elements of the high-risk situation that led to the slip? What
coping response could you have used to get around the situation?...Just because you slipped once does not mean you are a
failure, that you have no will power, that you are a hopeless
addict. Look upon the slip as a single independent event,
something that can be avoided in the future with an alternative coping response.

Assignment: Continue to monitor urges and alternatives used,
following the same format as the previous week.

Assignment: Predict any thoughts, rationalizations, or apparently irrelevant decisions (AIDs; see Marlatt & Gordon,
1980, for full description) that might set the scene
for a relapse.

For example, a smoking client may use temporary weight gain to
rationalize resumption of smoking. Or a drinking client may set the stage
for relapse by deciding that now that he or she is in control, liquor should
be kept in the house in case guests drop by, creating a temptation that
may be too strong to resist. (The latter is an example of an AID: a
behavior that appears to be unrelated to the target response but that in
fact significantly increases the probability that the individual will engage
in it.) For each example the client must think of an antidote, either
through specific action or self-statements, to this potential threat. The
following form is used:

Challenge to Control   *Prevention*
(Thought, Rationalization, or AID)   *Strategy*

Session 5. At this time the therapist may begin to train problem
drinkers who wish to learn controlled drinking skills in a variety of
techniques, including estimation of blood alcohol levels, timing and
spacing of drinks, assertive responses to social pressure situations, and
other coping strategies. (For more detailed descriptions of treatment
techniques, the reader is referred to Marlatt, 1979, and Miller & Muñoz,

1976.) As soon as clients are engaged in the active treatment phase, in which they are practicing the goal they have selected, each successive session should troubleshoot specific high-risk situations to strengthen clients against relapse. Although some clients are resistant to the notion that they might relapse, fearing that even thinking about the possibility will increase its likelihood, we liken relapse prevention to a fire drill, saying essentially that forewarned is forearmed. We sometimes show the relapse curves for alcohol, smoking, and heroin published by Hunt, Barnett, and Branch (1971), or share findings from our research on determinants of relapse.

Assignment (for each week):   Continue to monitor strong urges and alternatives.

Assignment (for each week):   Predict upcoming high-risk situations and plan and implement alternative responses.

During this session, or at an earlier session if we feel the client is ready to begin examining a new component of the change program, we also introduce the concept of lifestyle management. We have been using the concept of a "want-should ratio" (Marlatt & Gordon, 1980) to express the notion that excessive indulgence in any consummatory behavior is often an attempt to compensate for a sense of deprivation caused by a state of imbalance between obligations and rewards in the individual's life. Many of our clients are "workaholics" who spend most of their time engaging in obligatory activities (shoulds) and seldom allow themselves time for activities that are solely self-rewarding (wants). Our hypothesis is that a lifestyle in which wants and shoulds are more balanced will lead to a greater sense of satisfaction, personal control, and self-efficacy. Addictive behaviors, which trade short-term payoffs against harmful long-term effects, should become easier to control if the individual has a chance to engage in a positive indulgence on a frequent (preferably daily) basis.

The prior function of the addictive behavior as a way of treating or indulging oneself amidst a daily routine of obligations is usually crystal clear to the client and provides strong motivation for experimenting with some major changes in daily lifestyle balance.

Assignment: Monitor all activities for at least two normal weekdays and one typical weekend, as follows:

Time	Activity	Mood or Feeling	Want-Should Rating
			(1 = total want
			9 = total should
			5 = equal mix)

Assignment: Upon completion of the previous task, begin to set aside at least 1 half hour per day for "self-time."

This "self-time" can be spent in any activity as long as it meets the requirements for positive addictions stated by Glasser (1976); essentially, clients must engage in a solitary, noncompetitive activity that is not subject to self-evaluation, for example, meditation, physical exercise, a hobby, or playing or listening to music. The time is to be blocked out beforehand like any other appointment.

Session 6. This session covers more troubleshooting, practice in adaptive responses to problematic situations, and a review of the client's progress, including positive addictions, urges, and any slips.

Assignment: Continue to monitor urges and alternatives and engage in self-time each day.

Assignment: Draw a "road map" to illustrate your individualized plan for relapse prevention.

The map can be as straightforward or as creative as the client wishes. The goal is to include, either in list or picture form, all major high-risk situations of which the client is aware, based on all of the work that has been done up to this point, including situations, thoughts, and feelings. Next to each the client is to indicate one or more coping responses, again representing them either pictorially or in words.

Session 7. Homework from the previous week is gone over, and the therapist acts as consultant on the road map. At this time we recommend a relapse rehearsal. The client selects a very high-risk situation and describes it in detail to the therapist, who then runs through it as a guided fantasy in which the client imagines being in the situation and engaging in the problem behavior. The client is then asked to imagine as vividly as possible all the thoughts and feelings that arise in reaction to this slip, and finally to imagine coping successfully with the AVE by stopping the behavior and reinstating the desired responses. The therapist may wish to conduct some of this session *in vivo* or with the forbidden substance in the room.

Assignment: For the next few sessions, continue lifestyle management interventions and anticipate and prepare responses for high-risk situations.

Once sessions are being faded out, arrangements should be made for reporting in by phone or mail during the intervals between sessions. It is important that these reports also be made on a fading schedule, so that the client has an increasing sense of control without therapist support.

COMPLIANCE ENHANCEMENT
PROCEDURES

To enhance compliance, we rely on a range of approaches and specific techniques. First, we very deliberately create a certain therapeutic set; second we use a variety of specific procedures to enhance compliance; and third, we communicate our philosophy of self-control and self-management.

Creating a Therapeutic Set

In the first session it is emphasized that the therapist and client are colleagues in a problem-solving endeavor. This attitude fosters detachment from guilt and self-blame, increases curiosity and motivation, and facilitates the development of the client's self-image as a scientist, a maintenance person, and an active participant in the learning process.

Using Compliance Enhancement Procedures

In initial phases of treatment, contingency contracting for rewards is used. For example, money saved from not purchasing cigarettes or drinks can be spent on positive rewards. To enhance the perception of control and to reduce stress, positive addictions (hobbies, exercise, music) are encouraged as substitute indulgences.

Public commitment through announcements to significant others and enlisting of their support often helps. The application of treatment in a group format may also provide social support and peer pressure, in addition to minimizing the role of the therapist in effecting change.

Clients are encouraged to create images for themselves that will strengthen their active involvement and weaken tendencies toward passivity, self-pity, or guilt. One of the most effective ones is that of the Warrior described in Castaneda's books (Castaneda, 1968, 1972). The Warrior sees life as a series of challenges or opportunities and tries to be aware and prepared at all times, in contrast with the victim, who has little sense of control and tends to attribute positive events to luck and negative ones to fate.

Communicating a Philosophy of Self-Management

Throughout therapy a positive approach to mistakes is taught, modeled, and rehearsed so that they will be seen not as failures but as opportunities for furthering self-understanding, learning, and improved performance. Finally, and perhaps most important, slips in compliance can be treated in much the same way as relapses in general. One instance of noncompliance need not be interpreted as grounds for total withdrawal from the change program. Rather, the instance can be examined to find out what happened at the time to create the slip. No matter what happens, no matter what slip occurs, the goal is always the same: to prevent the next one from occurring. Client and therapist can examine the situational determinants, identify the attributions and expectancies, and plan the next step.

ILLUSTRATIVE CASE

Mary was a 32-year-old executive who came in for treatment, saying she thought she was an alcoholic. She had a demanding, challenging job which she handled very conscientiously. While her husband Don was supportive of her career, he felt it was important that evenings be spent in shared activities. They had had several arguments recently because Mary was drinking before coming home and had been hiding liquor around the house. Don was threatening to leave if she did not stop drinking altogether, and Mary also was feeling alarmed by her behavior. Mary was seen over a 3-month period, with follow-up contact over the following year.

Mary's first week's assignment was to complete an autobiography of the history and development of her drinking problem—her parents' drinking behavior, her first drinking experience and first "drunk," the role of drinking in her adult life, her self-image, problems associated with drinking, and her attempts to control her drinking. She also self-monitored her drinking for 2 weeks, noting the exact amounts of alcohol consumed each day, the time, and the antecedents and consequences. The Drinking Profile (Marlatt, 1976) was administered to her during the second session.

At the third session, the following patterns were identified. Mary would start work at 8:30, typically had a rushed business lunch, and often would not leave work until 6:00, by which time she was tense and wound up. Because she knew Don did not approve of her drinking, she had begun to pick up a pint of vodka after work and would drink half of it during the 20-minute drive home so that she could get relaxed for the evening. She had also begun stashing liquor away in the house just in case she wanted a drink. She realized that drinking while driving was dangerous, that she was drinking too much too quickly, and that she was feeling very guilty and out of control. Her husband's anger seemed to increase her urges to drink.

Mary agreed to abstain from any drinking during the third and fourth weeks of treatment. During this period it became apparent that drinking was her only means for reducing the tension that built up during the day and also represented the one indulgence she allowed herself in a daily routine of obligations to external job demands and commitments to her husband and friends. A plan to modify her general lifestyle was worked out that included alternative ways of relaxing and indulging that were not destructive.

Mary joined a local health club and began going for a swim and a sauna every morning on the way to work. She also set aside 2 days a week to have lunch alone or with a friend. She learned a meditation technique which she began using at the end of the day after getting home from work. She negotiated with Don to spend one evening a week doing separate activities so that she could resume her old hobby of painting.

Mary also decided that she wanted to continue drinking in a moderate way and that Don's support was essential so that she could drink openly. Don attended the sixth session with Mary, the treatment plan was explained to him, his feelings and concerns were explored, and he agreed to support Mary in her efforts to alter her lifestyle as well as to be more accepting of her drinking.

During the next few sessions Mary learned a number of controlled drinking techniques, including setting limits for herself and pacing her drinking by alternating liquor with soft drinks, and developed strategies for dealing with high-risk situations, which for her were primarily the buildup of tension at work and feelings of guilt or anger toward Don. She learned to become more aware of these situations as they were developing and began to practice more direct ways of communicating with Don. She also was instructed to use any urges to return to old drinking patterns as cues to pay attention to situational factors and use alternative responses rather than to interpret them as signs that she was an alcoholic.

The final two sessions were spent planning and rehearsing what to do if a relapse occurred. Strategies included slowing herself down, cognitive restructuring to deal with the abstinence violation effect, a decision-making exercise to review the consequences and relative merits of drinking according to both old and new patterns, analysis of the situation that led to the relapse, problem solving to come up with a better coping response to use next time, and the possibility of scheduling a booster session with her therapist.

At the final follow-up a year later, Mary reported that she was feeling better about herself and more in control, was drinking moderately on social occasions, and was communicating better with Don. She had had a couple of slips but had managed to retrieve the situation, in one case by being more assertive with a superior, and in the other by simply deciding that she could accept some mistakes on her part without having to punish herself by continuing the mistake.

Mary was an ideal client—motivated, bright, and already

possessing many basic life skills. We are finding, however, that even those clients who do not begin treatment was as many strengths can develop them fairly rapidly if they receive support for relinquishing the helpless victim role. The support of significant others in the treatment of these clients is particularly important and should not be overlooked by the therapist.

SUMMARY

In the treatment of addictions, the prevention of relapse is as important as the initial success of therapy. The two dominant viewpoints in this area, the medical model and the social-learning model, view relapse in different ways. In the medical model, which presumes that the addictive substance activates an underlying disease process, relapse is due to the reemergence of the disease. However, in the social-learning model, which views addiction as an overlearned, maladaptive pattern of behavior, relapse is the extinction or decay of new, less-established responses in favor of old ones. The treatment described in this chapter focuses on relapse as seen through the social-learning model. Throughout it is assumed that there is empirical evidence for the validity of that model, and that the clinician's decision to use one or the other model of addictive behavior will significantly affect the client's attitudes, beliefs, and expectations, and the outcome of treatment.

The major goals of treatment are to supplant the client's maladaptive belief system with a more balanced set of expectations and to teach the client more effective coping skills. All treatment is oriented around relapse, here defined as any violation of a self-imposed rule on consumption of an addictive substance, whether the rule involves abstinence or controlled use. A relapse model is postulated: a client encounters a high-risk situation, in which he or she either performs a coping response or fails to because of skill deficiency or inability; if the client fails, he or she is reinforced by the familiar effects of the substance and, due to the abstinence violation effect (AVE) caused by the cognitive dissonance between the rule and its violation, develops feelings of weakness and guilt.

Treatment aims at developing self-control in the client, with the client and therapist working together at problem solving and skill training. A variety of cognitive-behavioral strategies are taught to de-automatize the behavior, expand the client's repertoire of coping skills, and help him or her identify high-risk situations and learn how to avoid or cope with them, while developing a healthier lifestyle. During the first two sessions the client and therapist establish a working relationship and exchange information. The third or fourth session is the time that the client actually quits using the addictive substance for 2 weeks.

(Controlled use may begin after the 2 weeks, if desired.) Then the next six sessions focus on coping with problems, managing a new lifestyle, and preventing relapse. Three follow-up sessions are scheduled on a fading basis or as the client needs them, and contact is kept with the client for at least a year. Examples of homework assignments for the follow-up sessions are given.

Many different compliance enhancement procedures are incorporated in this treatment. It is emphasized that therapy is a problem-solving task shared by client and therapist. Contingency contracting, enlisting the help of others and making public commitments, and creating strong self-images all act to support compliance. Finally, mistakes or failures are not punished, but are treated as opportunities for further explorations of high-risk situations that can be anticipated and planned for.

The case of Mary, a woman executive with a drinking problem, illustrates the application of this treatment. Since her drinking was mainly the result of tension at work and guilt or anger toward her husband, she first modified her lifestyle to allow for more relaxing activities and learned how to communicate more directly with her husband. Her husband's aid was enlisted in supporting her attempts to drink only in moderation, and Mary was taught controlled drinking techniques. She also learned problem-solving and cognitive strategies to use in case of relapse. A year later Mary felt more in control of herself, was able to drink moderately, and communicated better with her husband, despite a few relapses during that time.

REFERENCES

Bandura, A. Self-efficacy: Toward a unifying theory of behavioral change. *Psychological Review,* 1977, *84,* 191-215.

Best, J.A., & Bloch, M. Compliance in the control of smoking. In R.B. Haynes, D.W. Taylor, & D.L. Sackett (Eds.), *Compliance with therapeutic and prevention regimens.* Baltimore: Johns Hopkins University Press, 1980.

Castaneda, C. *The teachings of Don Juan: A Yaqui way of knowledge.* New York: Ballantine Books, 1968.

Castaneda, C. *Journey to Ixtlan: The lessons of Don Juan.* New York: Simon & Schuster, 1972.

Chaney, E.F., O'Leary, M.R., & Marlatt, G.A. Skill training with alcoholics. *Journal of Consulting and Clinical Psychology,* 1978, *46,* 1092-1104.

Cummings, C., Gordon, J.R., & Marlatt, G.A. Relapse: Strategies of prevention and prediction. In W.R. Miller (Ed.), *The addictive behaviors: Treatment of alcoholism, drug abuse, smoking, and obesity.* Oxford, England: Pergamon Press, 1980.

Eiser, J.R., Sutton, S.R., & Wober, M. "Consonant" and "dissonant" smokers and the self-attribution of addiction. *Addictive Behaviors,* 1978, *3,* 99-106.

Glasser, W. *Positive addictions.* New York: Harper & Row, 1976.

Hunt, W.A., Barnett, L.W., & Branch, L.G. Relapse rates in addiction programs. *Journal of Clinical Psychology,* 1971, *27,* 455-456.

Marlatt, G.A. The drinking profile: A questionnaire for the behavioral assessment of alcoholism. In E.J. Mash & L.G. Terdal (Eds.), *Behavior therapy assessment: Diagnosis, design, and evaluation.* New York: Springer, 1976.

Marlatt, G.A. Craving for alcohol, loss of control, and relapse: A cognitive-behavioral analysis. In P.E. Nathan, G.A. Marlatt, & T. Löberg (Eds.), *Alcoholism: New directions in behavioral research and treatment.* New York: Plenum, 1978.

Marlatt, G.A. Alcohol use and problem drinking: A cognitive-behavioral analysis. In P.C. Kendall & S.P. Hollon (Eds.), *Cognitive-behavioral interventions: Theory, research, and procedures.* New York: Academic Press, 1979.

Marlatt, G.A., & Gordon, J.R. Determinants of relapse: Implications for the maintenance of behavior change. In P. Davidson & S. Davidson (Eds.), *Behavioral medicine: Changing health lifestyles.* New York: Brunner/Mazel, 1980.

Marlatt, G.A., & Rohsenow, D.J. Cognitive processes in alcohol use: Expectancy and the balanced placebo design. In N.K. Mello (Ed.), *Advances in substance abuse: Behavioral and biological research.* Greenwich, Conn.: JAI Press, 1980.

Miller, W.R., & Muñoz, R.F. *How to control your drinking.* Englewood Cliffs, N.J.: Prentice-Hall, 1976.

CHAPTER 8

Obesity

David R. Campbell
Sacred Heart Medical Center and Behavior Change Center

Chuck Bender*
Sacred Heart Medical Center

Norma Bennett
Sacred Heart Medical Center

Joann Donnelly
Sacred Heart Medical Center

OVERVIEW OF OBESITY

Definition

Although obesity is often cited as a problem that lends itself to objective, reliable assessment, it has nevertheless proven to be difficult to define (Stunkard, 1975). The traditionally used Metropolitan Life Insurance Standards, which take into account sex, age, and body type, present problems of validity, especially in relation to body type. For example, according to those criteria, a stocky, muscular athlete could readily be classified obese even with a normal percentage of body fat. Some researchers such as Stuart (1971) have suggested that the percentage of body fat is a more accurate measure of obesity. Although skinfold calipers are most frequently used for evaluating percentage of body fat, this criterion also presents problems, especially with increasingly obese people. The water displacement method, clearly the

---

*The last three authors are listed alphabetically; their contributions were equal.

most reliable means of assessing body fat, is costly, impractical, and generally unavailable.

A useful treatment-focused definition of obesity is simply the discrepancy between a person's present and desired weight. This definition assumes the involvement of the allegedly obese person in defining his or her treatment goals and allows weight-control programs to be assessed according to the percentage of goals attained by the people seeking such services. This definition too presents problems in that people may have unrealistic weight goals (albeit surprisingly few do, from our experience) and after initial treatment, their desired weight might change. Nevertheless, the advantages of having clients define their goals, as opposed to having their goals defined by external and too often arbitrary standards, outweighs the disadvantages. Wooley, Wooley, and Dyrenforth (1979) argue rather persuasively for such an involvement.

Etiology

The history of research on obesity abounds with searches for an all-encompassing cause. Thyroids were once popular but have since fallen into disfavor. The search for unconscious mechanisms motivated earlier psychodynamic endeavors. Past and current popular diets often rely upon simplistic etiologies and interventions. More recently, investigators are inclined toward multicausal factors and have directed their questions toward relationships among the variables and toward the implications for treatment (Bray, 1976). A brief discussion of the most important of these variables follows.

Genetics and somatotypes. Neel (1962) argues that there is evolutionary survival value in the ability to store fat and that those who are capable of storing fat are more likely to survive periods of famine. Montague (1966) suggests that obesity is partly a function of body types originally selected by climate. Another viewpoint which favors genetic influences has been advanced by Mayer (1965) who reports an 80 percent incidence of obesity when both parents are obese, 40 percent when one parent is obese, and 10 percent if neither parent is obese. However, as Stunkard (1975) notes, it is most difficult to separate genetic influence from family social learning and socioeconomic factors that could readily account for such correlations. It would seem prudent to continue evaluating this potential, because if such factors are identified, they could provide useful consumer information and suggest different intervention strategies.

Childhood onset. Childhood obesity shows a strong tendency to persist (Brownell & Stunkard, 1978b). For instance, Abraham and Nordsieck (1960) report that 86 percent of males who were obese as adolescents were obese as adults, as compared with 42 percent who were normal weight as adolescents; the discrepancy is even greater for females. Evidence also exists that childhood obesity contributes to the development of an increased number of adipose cells (hyperplasia) and that dieting reduces the size but not the number of those cells (Bray, 1976; Stricker, 1978). Although this factor has been suggested to increase the difficulty of weight loss, there are no data to support differential response to behavioral treatment based on this distinction (Wilson, in press). Work by Björntorp (1976) suggests that the presence of hyperplasia may have treatment implications. Wooley et al. (1979) propose alternative therapies based upon the hyperplasia-hypertrophia distinction. Thus it appears that evidence exists to support increased intractability associated with childhood obesity, as well as treatment implications that may relate to hyperplasic and hypertrophic obesity.

Metabolic differences. Evidence for significant metabolic differences among people has been increasing. One report suggests that differences of 400 to 500 calories burned per day in resting metabolism may be common (Warwick, Toft, & Garrow, 1978). Obese and normal people may also differ in the extent of thermogenesis, with the specific effect that after overeating, people of normal weight burn significantly more calories than obese people because of energy dissipation from metabolizing food (Miller, Mumford, & Stock, 1967). Evidence also suggests that during fasting or low-calorie dieting regimens, obese men burn fewer calories during both resting and moderate exercise than normal men (Drenick & Dennin, 1973).

Socioeconomic and cultural factors. Sociologists and anthropologists have ably documented the effects of socioeconomic and cultural factors on the incidence of obesity, with data suggesting significant variation within and across cultures (Bray, 1976). In the United States, women with lower socioeconomic status appear to be especially vulnerable (Stunkard, 1968), but men from a similar socioeconomic status appear to have a lower incidence of obesity because they tend to work in highly active jobs.

Decreased activity stands as a most prominent factor contributing to our current obesity problem. Data suggest that since 1900 we are consuming significantly fewer and less nutritional calories (United States Senate Select Committee on Nutrition and Human Needs, 1977). The relationship between inactivity and obesity may be especially important for women (Chirico & Stunkard, 1960). The nutritionist Jean Mayer (1968) argues that inactivity is the single most important factor explaining the gradually increasing obesity in our culture. Furthermore, decreased activity may promote increased eating, whereas increased activity may help control eating (Mayer, Roy, & Mitra, 1956).

Since 1900, U.S. citizens have experienced dramatic shifts in their eating habits (United States Senate Select Committee, 1977). We now consume significantly more fat, refined sugar, and salt, and significantly fewer complex carbohydrates, fresh fruits, and vegetables; resultant declines in vitamins and minerals have also been noted (United States Senate Select Committee, 1977).

Many societal contingencies support these changes in our nutritional and activity habits. They include the ready availability of fast foods and snacks of lower nutritional value, advertising that promotes consuming such foods (fresh fruits and vegetables are rarely advertised on TV) and a gradual yet significant increase in the tendency to eat out. Decreased activity is promoted by overreliance on the automobile, a host of labor-saving devices, and a shift toward more sedentary jobs.

Food as an operant. A classic study by Neuringer (1969) suggests that it is not necessary to deprive animals of food before they will try to obtain it, suggesting that further inquiry about the operant parameters of food may be productive, especially given the increased access to food in our society. Withdrawing food that has previously been eaten contingent upon negative moods would theoretically lead to an initial increase in such moods and account for some negative reactions to dieting and subsequent overeating.

Iatrogenic effects of dieting. Wooley et al. (1979) have argued convincingly that for some obese people, dieting exacerbates previously existing metabolic dysfunctions and lowers the obese person's maintenance caloric requirement. Caloric restriction, especially if severe, results in decreased basal metabolism, apparently a starvation reflex that has survival benefits during times of famine; with some obese people the effect may increase after each diet and continue well after a fast or diet is terminated (Garrow, 1974; Wooley et al., 1979). Bray (1976) suggests that because of that effect, it is unlikely that obese people will lose more weight by reducing caloric intake by more than 800 calories per day. In addition, it appears that dieting results in a rebound effect when such "restrained" persons return to eating, with the result that reentry eating "primes the pump" and leads to additional eating (Herman & Mack, 1975; see Coates, 1977, for further discussion). This idea may help explain an earlier finding, that obese people buy more food after eating (they are much more likely to be dieting and "restrained" eaters), whereas people of normal weight buy less (Nisbett & Kanouse, 1969). It also appears that after severe dieting, the capacity for fat storage is significantly increased, which may have important implications with respect to enhanced medical risk (Tepperman & Tepperman, 1964).

Finally, Wooley et al. (1979) summarized data suggesting that there is little evidence that obese people eat more than people of normal weight, which in itself raises questions about the historical emphasis upon dieting for weight control.

Obese eating style. Behavioral interventions for obesity have been predicated upon assumed differences between normal-weight and obese eaters. Reviews of empirical data suggest few, if any, consistent differences except that the obese seem more responsive to palatable food (Stunkard & Kaplan, 1977; Wooley & Wooley, 1975; Wooley et al., 1979). There is also some indication that obese people chew less and spend less time chewing (Adams, Ferguson, Stunkard, & Agras, 1978; Gaul, Craighead, & Mahoney, 1975; Hill & McCutcheon, 1975; Marston, London, Cohen, & Cooper, 1977) and that they may tend to leave less food on their plates than normal-weight people (Krassner, Brownell, & Stunkard, 1979; Marston et al., 1977). Thus there is some basis for behavioral strategies directed toward developing "permanent" behaviors, such as chewing more slowly, leaving food on one's plate, increasing the cost of access to tasty, high-calorie food, and increasing the ease of access to tasty, low-calorie food. Clearly dramatic differences in eating style do not exist. It may be that some of the differences summarized by Schachter (1968) are partially due to the increased likelihood that obese people are "restrained" eaters. The value of teaching the behavioral strategies to obese people remains an empirical question.

Current Treatment

"Most obese persons will not stay in treatment for obesity. Of those who stay in treatment, most will not lose weight and of those who lose weight, most will regain it" (Stunkard, 1958). With few exceptions, Stunkard's often quoted statement continues to stand as an uncomfortably candid appraisal of current obesity treatment. Diverse programs continue to promote rapid weight loss, despite evidence suggesting that rapid weight loss leads to consequent weight gain and increased health risk. And despite a remarkably ineffectual history, pharmacological interventions continue to be used. Thermogenic drugs may hold promise (Evans & Miller, 1978), and thyroid medication may be helpful for some people experiencing negative metabolic reaction while dieting (Bray, 1976; Drenick, 1975). Procedures such as wiring a person's mouth shut (the ultimate in response prevention, at least for solid food) appear to be on the wane, but diets, the backbone of most weight-control efforts, continue to multiply. Hypnosis is often cited as a viable treatment, and at least one report suggests significant results from a treatment program combining hypnosis and behavioral strategies (Kline, 1976); however, data from controlled investigations are noticeably lacking.

Surgery. One surgical intervention is the small bowel bypass, which appears to be the only effective treatment for morbid obesity at this time (Bray, 1976; Itallie & Burton, 1979). This procedure is clearly associated with risks including death. Some evidence suggests that the risks are being reduced with improved surgical procedures and postsurgery management; there is also some indication that bypass surgery is associated with less psychological dysphoria than most other weight control procedures (Bray, 1976; Itallie & Burton, 1979). At least one writer has suggested that the weight loss effects of bypass surgery are caused by attempts to avoid the increased discomfort associated with eating and drinking after surgery (Pilkington, 1976). However, more recent research suggests that the results cannot be explained by attempts to avert diarrhea, nausea, decreased appetite, liver disease, and other bypass surgery consequences (Robinson, Folstein, & McHugh, 1979). For those people with medical problems exacerbated by morbid obesity (usually defined as 100 or more pounds overweight or 200 percent or more of desirable weight as defined by Metropolitan Life Insurance Standards), bypass surgery provides a means of losing and maintaining the loss of clinically significant amounts of weight. The risks and benefits involved present a difficult decision for people considering undergoing this procedure.

Fasting. Long-term fasting clearly promotes significant weight loss. However, such procedures are associated with both negative psychological effects during the later stages of treatment and with rapid weight gain after treatment (Bray, 1976; Stunkard & Rush, 1974). Brief fasting appears to be relatively well tolerated, and associated with surprisingly few dysphoric reactions (Stunkard & Rush, 1974). The possibility of combining short-term fasting procedures with instruction in behavioral strategies including exercise would appear to have some potential in obesity treatment.

Behavioral approaches. Stuart (1967, 1971) demonstrated the potential for the behavioral approach in individual work with six people; his work produced a mean weight loss of 28 pounds, a result that has yet to be replicated. Lublin and Kirkish (Note 1) recently reported data suggesting a mean weight loss of 36 pounds, with a mean loss of 29 pounds at a 30-month follow-up; however, these promising results are compromised by the limited percentage of people they were able to contact. The Dietary Rehabilitation Clinic at Duke Medical School reports significant weight loss, such that 53 percent of their patients lost

20 or more pounds and 23 percent lost 40 or more pounds (Musante, 1976). This intensive day treatment approach can be criticized because of a lack of follow-up, with the reasonable suspicion that rebound effects occurred because of the high degree of program control.

Most behavioral approaches report modest results — generally mean losses of 6 to 15 pounds — with much variation among clinical populations (students to clinically experienced obese), dropout rates (and whether or not such data are included), and therapist experience (which appears to be a relevant factor; see Jeffrey, Wing, & Stunkard, 1978), to name a few. Furthermore, mean weight loss does not capture the picture accurately because individual weight loss is so varied. Thus behavioral treatment of obesity is associated with modest weight loss and apparently fewer negative psychological effects (Bray, 1976; Brightwell & Sloan, 1977; Stunkard, 1975, 1978). It does not appear to be associated with better maintenance, as was previously hoped (Brightwell & Sloan, 1977; Stunkard & Penick, 1979).

There is some indication that group treatment is more effective than individual procedures. However, this is not a consistent finding, especially since two of the best reports of weight loss use individual approaches. Group procedures are a more efficient way to provide services and are significantly less expensive to consumers.

As suggested by a follow-up of Mahoney's (1974) original study of this issue (Stunkard & Penick, 1979), it is not clear that weight loss in behavioral programs is due to habit change (Brownell & Stunkard, 1978a) or that reinforcing habit change is more effective than reinforcing weight loss in maintaining weight loss. As Wilson (in press) has suggested, behavioral treatment of obesity began with too much hope, and the treatment paradigm became fixed prematurely.

Activity change. Increased activity remains the single modality most frequently mentioned and least frequently investigated as a procedure for weight control. Carefully supervised activity increases are associated with few negative effects and generally positive emotional benefits (as opposed to dieting). Increased activity is associated with better appetite control and direct alteration of several health risk factors (Dahlkoetter, Callahan, & Linton, 1979; Lewis, Haskell, Wood, Manogian, Bailey, & Pereira, 1976). At least two reports suggest that relatively simple activity change systems, such as walking or use of the aerobic point system, can be taught and maintained for 1 year (Keefe, Note 2; Wysocki, Hall, Iwata, & Riordan, 1979). One investigation suggests that weight loss with a pure activity approach is quite compatible with behavioral approaches (Lewis et al., 1976). More importantly, at least two studies report that the addition of exercise to behavioral procedures produced results similar to those of behavioral procedures alone at the end of treatment but significant differences favoring exercise at follow-up (Harris & Hallbauer, 1973; Stalanos, Johnson, & Christ, 1978). A recent and well-controlled study reports that exercise and behavioral approaches combined resulted in better results, both at the termination of treatment and at follow-up, with continuation of weight loss after termination (Dahlkoetter et al., 1979).

Implications for obesity treatment. It has been argued that obesity is the result of rather diverse etiologies, that treatment results thus far have been modest, and that there appear to be social and individual risks associated with obesity treatment. Given these assumptions, several clinical implications follow.

It appears important to develop procedures that maximize clients' understanding of treatment and its expected results. Once in treatment, they should be involved in establishing their own weight loss and related goals, which might well include learning to maintain their present weight, or simply feeling comfortable and able to deal with the consequences of being overweight (Wooley et al., 1979). It is quite realistic and desirable to provide services to clients who wish to learn how to eat more nutritionally and to increase their activity while maintaining a current weight that is overweight by standard criteria.

It also seems relevant to develop ongoing evaluations of clients' goal achievement and the potential negative effects of treatment. A 1-year follow-up would seem minimal and desirable. Goal attainment scaling may lend itself to assessing such client-centered treatment outcomes. It requires the client to identify a long-range goal or ideal outcome and the small steps it will take to reach that outcome. Each small step is chosen to build upon the previous one, creating a scale of levels of attainment that can be used for measuring client progress.

A greater emphasis on individualizing treatment procedures seems warranted. A review of our own clients' records shows a great variation between the bingers, late-night eaters, people who eat snacks, people who seem quite inactive, people who eat in response to negative moods or events, and people who can only lose when they reduce eating to semistarvation levels of caloric intake. These remain rough categories at this point, but it does seem clear that with such diverse etiologies and presenting data, a focus upon particular eating and activity patterns seems well justified (Wilson, 1976; Wilson, in press), with single subject design providing a means for analysis (Wilson, 1978).

Obesity treatment should probably be presented within the overall perspective of risk factors. Bray (1976) proposes that treatment for individuals who are less than 30 pounds overweight should have minimal treatment risk because that degree of overweight is associated with

w that slowing the rate of eating takes advantage of
& Wooley, 1975), that strategy is also included. We
or salad first, eating fruit to take the edge off hunger,
meals, planning interruptions, counting bites, putting
tween bites, and finishing last in social situations.
bout nutrition is presented throughout the program.
ed toward limiting the amounts of fat, sugar, and
d. Weighing and measuring food are stressed and
are presented. Students are taught to read and use
ation on food labels and to reduce the calories in
meals.

ments

are integral to each class session. A typical group
ader initiating a discussion about the past week's
class ends with students developing their assignments

Figure 8.3   Pocket food diary

FOOD DIARY

Date:_____

	Type of food

Daily Calorie Summary

Noon	PM	Total Exchange	Calories
			Total

minimal health risk (see Mahan, 1979, for further discussion). Other writers (Mahoney, Rogers, Straw, & Mahoney, in press) criticize the emphasis on weight loss, suggesting that more attention should be given to factors directly related to health. It is easy to conceive of a person losing statistically significant but clinically insignificant amounts of weight while increasing consumption of sodium and saturated fat and thereby actually increasing the potential for medical problems. If we professionals assist in such endeavors, we are readily contributing to the long history of iatrogenic treatment effects.

It is increasingly important to acknowledge and support other helpful agents, including physicians and self-help groups like Weight Watchers and TOPS (Take Off Pounds Sensibly). The approaches used by these groups can be useful, and such groups may have available more natural support and maintenance systems than brief behavioral treatment. Encouraging clients to use such approaches is most defensible.

Since the incidence of obesity seems much greater in lower socioeconomic groups, finding relevant cost-effective interventions is important. Some indication exists that behavioral approaches have such benefits (Dahms, Molitch, Bray, Greenway, Atkinson, & Hamilton, 1978). Group procedures do have the benefit of lower cost to consumers. There is also some evidence that minimal contact can be as effective as more intensive contact (Dilley, Balch, & Balch, 1979), an issue of economical importance to most consumers.

In the final analysis, persons involved with providing obesity treatment should at least strive to do no harm, a point well discussed by Fullarton (1978) in a fine review of social aspects of obesity treatment.

HOMEWORK-BASED TREATMENT

Overview of Treatment

The program description that follows is based on behavioral strategies conducted in a group context. Therapeutic homework assignments emphasizing self-control play a major role in this approach. Treatment conducted in a group is preferred because it is deemed the most efficient method. The approach described in this chapter can be used with individuals as well.

Initially, before treatment begins, it is worthwhile to meet with students individually to begin assessment and prepare them for the classes. Clients read and sign both an informed consent form (Figure 8.1) and a consent for follow-up and scientific presentation (Figure 8.2). A refundable deposit is required, and refunds are contingent upon both attendance and assignment completion. Clients are encouraged to modify assignments to enhance the likelihood of success. Special notebooks can be provided to organize handouts, assignments, and progress, along with pocket-sized food diaries for ease of recording.

Figure 8.1   Informed consent form

INFORMED CONSENT
GROUP WEIGHT CONTROL PROGRAM

Treatment for obesity is controversial. There are many programs and approaches available. There is little evidence to support the long term effectiveness of these various approaches. The weight control program you are currently enrolled in attempts to combine several different approaches that have demonstrated some effectiveness. However, *there is no guarantee that this program will be effective for you, especially on a long term basis.*

This group program for weight control will demand your time and energy. You have been provided with a program description for details and you are requested to read this and a description of the bonus refund system. Your signing the *Consent for Scientific Presentation* is completely optional; if you decline to sign this form, this will not change your chance to participate in the weight control program or the treatment you will receive while in the program.

I understand that current medical opinion suggests that weight loss should not be attempted during pregnancy. Sacred Heart's Weight Control program provides sound nutritional information which may be helpful in avoiding excess weight gain during pregnancy, but is not designed to monitor this or other specific aspects of pregnancy.

I have read the program description and the bonus refund system. I understand that this program, as with many weight programs, may not be successful on a long term basis. I understand that I may withdraw at any time; however, I will be refunded only whatever part of the bonus refund I have earned. I understand that my signing the *Consent for Scientific Presentation* is optional.

Signature _____

Witness _____

Date _____

Figure 8.2   Consent form for scientific presentation

CONSENT FOR SCIENTIFIC PRESENTATION

I agree to allow data (information) from my participation in the Group Weight Control Program to be used for scientific presentation. I understand that such presentations might include either oral presentations during meetings of professional associations or groups or written publication in professional journals.

In so allowing, I understand that this data will be presented primarily in a group form and that whatever individual presentation occurs will be done in a manner that does not specifically identify me by using my real name, occupation, or address, but that my age, sex, and weight may be presented. In addition, I agree to being contacted 1 year and 5 years after completing this program; this contact will be for the purpose of determining how successful I have been in maintaining weight loss which will help in evaluating this weight loss program.

Signature _____

Witness _____

Date _____

Because obesity mana[...] that professionals broaden [...] and advanced classes. T[...] approximately 10 weeks. [...] advanced classes as curren[...] Basic Class, focuses on nu[...] weight control. The second [...] directed toward lifestyle ch[...] Cognitive interventions can [...]

Self-observation throu[...] of the Basic Class. Previou[...] modest treatment in itself [...] (Bellack, Rozensky, & Sch[...] Green (1978) suggests that t[...] begin by suggesting that cl[...] gradually teach clients the [...] general. We have developed [...] clients review their own re[...] goals based upon identifie[...] collected, reviewed, and [...] presents a pocket-sized foo[...] month's recording, using [...] methods. Food exchanges a[...] simplify calorie counting. [...] system because it is relative[...] home. The food diary has su[...] successes. With the diary [...] changes and food thoughts c[...]

Initial behavioral strat[...] that lead to problematic e[...] include keeping problem foo[...] cupboards, serving from the[...] with other stimuli such as T[...] focused on eating at home; h[...] driving home by interesting r[...] stimuli in one's work envirc[...] experiment and then choose[...] permanently. We also sugges[...] fresh fruit visible and availa[...] reminders on the refrigerator[...] fading), shopping lists, and m[...]

We suggest procedures [...] food, such as recording befor[...] the house and making it diffic[...]

Since data sh[...] satiation (Wooley [...] suggest serving soup[...] conversing during [...] one's fork down be[...]

Information [...] Assignments direct[...] meat are presente[...] relevant exercises [...] nutritional inform[...] favorite recipes and[...]

Homework Assign[...]

Assignments [...] begins with the l[...] assignments. The [...]

Day:_____

Time	Amoun[...]

Exchange Group	AM
Milk	
A veg.	
B veg.	
Fruit	
Bread	
Meat	
Fat	
Free foods	
Misc.	

Figure 8.3 *(Continued)*

	Weekly Summary	Weight:
	Calories eaten	Activity
Monday		
Tuesday		
Wednesday		
Thursday		
Friday		
Saturday		
Sunday		
Total		

Daily caloric needs at present weight = _____ (a)
Weekly caloric needs . . . . (a × 7 days) = _____ (b)
Weekly caloric intake . . . . = _____ (c)
+ or - weekly calories (b - c) . . . . = _____

Success:

Goals for Next Week	Plan

for the next week. The assignment sheet is duplicated on NCR paper so that both leader and student have a copy. Although assignments are proposed by the leader, students are encouraged to modify the proposed assignments so that they are agreeing to something they can accomplish. The leader reviews individuals' assignments, offers suggestions, and cosigns the assignment sheet.

Discussions center on last week's assignment and lead naturally to assignments for the coming week. Nonpunitive quizzes help insure that students understand presentations and homework assignments.

During the presentations it is important to teach students how to readily calculate calories in most eating situations. It is also necessary to provide a supportive structure for students to develop desired eating and nutritional habits and activity changes. It is helpful to proceed gradually and attempt to insure success at each step before proceeding to a more difficult task. A sample of the type of assignments made in each session is now presented.

Basic Class. Information on nutrition and behavior change is presented. Students learn to monitor their eating behavior, identify problems, and establish behavioral goals.

Initial individual session. Individual appointments are scheduled approximately 1 week before the initial group meeting. New students are introduced to the group leader, who conducts the individual interviews. During this session, student expectations about the class are elicited and clarified. Procedural details such as the handling of absences and the bonus refund system (Figure 8.4) are covered. Students turn in signed copies of the Informed Consent and optional Consent for Scientific Presentation forms. A history of prior dieting attempts and other relevant information is obtained, with students readily discussing their previous efforts and inability to keep weight off. Skinfold and current

Figure 8.4   Bonus refund form

BONUS REFUND SYSTEM

What is the Bonus Refund?

A central part of Sacred Heart's Weight Control Program is the Bonus Refund System. This system will require you to make a $50 deposit in addition to the course fee of $80. Thus, of the total initial payment ($130), you can earn back up to $50 for completing assignments between sessions and for completing the entire program.

Only the money you have earned will be refunded; this means that if you drop out of the program you will lost all the bonus refund other than what you have already earned. The only exception to this would involve your moving out of the Eugene-Springfield area during the program; if this occurs, you will be refunded what you have earned and the amount of money left that is possible to earn.

How Much Are the Assignments Worth?

The amount of money you can earn back will vary. After the initial "honeymoon stage" when motivation is high, weight control becomes more difficult; therefore assignments near the end of the program will be worth more money. At this time the most incentive is built into the program.

Specifically, assignments and completion are worth the following:

Based on nine assignments and two follow-up sessions:

Assignments 1, 2, 3, 4, 5, 6, 7	$ 2 =	$14
Assignments 8, 9	5 =	10
6-month follow-up	10 =	10
12-month follow-up	16 =	16
	Potential Bonus Refund =	$50

You will be penalized one-half of the individual assignment deposit for not completing one part (task) of the assignment. You will be penalized all of the individual assignment deposit for not completing two or more parts of the assignment.

If you miss a session without notifying Hospital Education prior to your appointment, you will automatically lose the bonus refund for that session. If you notify Hospital Education ahead of time and bring in the assignment to the next session, you will receive credit for what you have completed. Money earned is refunded twice during the program, after Session 10 and after the 12-month follow-up appointment.

I have read and understand the above.

Signature _____

Witness _____

Date _____

weight measurements are obtained at this session. The following assignment is then given:

Assignment: Begin recording food without counting calories (see Figure 8.5).

Figure 8.5   Sample food diary: No calorie count

TIME	FOOD EATEN			SOCIAL	WHERE
	Amount	Type of Food		Alone? With Whom?	Home, Work, Restaurant, Recreation
8:30	2 slices 1 bowl 2 cups	buttered toast cornflakes & milk black coffee		alone	home
10:30	3 1 cup	peanut butter cookies coffee		alone	home
12:30	1 2 1 glass (10 oz)	tuna sandwich dill pickles 2% milk		with Joyce	restaurant

Session 1. The class, which is limited to 12 students, begins with a warm-up exercise that ends in everyone knowing one another by first name. Group members share what they hope to learn and change, and leaders promote the idea that everyone is there for a common struggle by providing guidelines for constructive participation. Next the initial food diary assignment is reviewed. Students generally report that the initial recording resulted in decreased food consumption (even though it was suggested to continue eating normally during this initial recording). Since they also report that remembering to record food is a frequent problem, information about accurate recording of food is presented. Self-observation is presented as an initial step toward change, and pinpointing problems and changing problems into behavioral goals are suggested as following steps. This assignment is then given:

Assignment: Complete an eating habit questionnaire, begin to measure food at home, and pinpoint at least four problematic patterns.

Session 2. This session begins with an exercise such as "reintroduce yourself and describe at least two noneating-related activities you enjoy." During the assignment review noncooks in the group usually report that estimating portion size is difficult because of limited previous experience with weights and measurements. Students are taught to calculate their caloric requirements according to a nomogram procedure which considers individual variables such as age, height, current weight, sex, and activity (Bray, 1976). Exercises focusing on fat as a food are presented; group members consistently express surprise at the number of calories fats contribute to daily meals and snacks. The following task is part of the weekly assignment.

Assignment: Add the recording of fats as a food exchange; look for goals related to reducing fat consumption.

Session 3. This and subsequent classes begin with a review of last session's assignments. The presentation introduces students to meat exchanges, which usually provoke much surprise about the number of calories contained in various meats. Because many students have already reduced their food intake, we experience some problems making assignments and exercises relevant to their typical eating patterns. Here is a sample assignment:

Assignment: Add meat exchanges to the food diary recordings; bring in a food label with nutritional information to the next class; and if fat intake appears excessive, limit fat to _____ exchanges on _____ days.

Students are introduced to signal (stimulus) control (see Figure 8.6). In addition, they are encouraged to begin working on one goal they have identified by changing a signal relevant to that goal. We use a "goal

Figure 8.6   Signal control form

SIGNAL CONTROL

Controlling signals involves two strategies: (a) reducing problem food signals and (b) increasing positive food signals. Below are some examples of eating signal changes to consider. The chart may help you practice controlling one specific signal and watching your progress over time.

Eating Signal Changes

Positive Eating Signals

Good food in sight
Good food attractive
Signs/charts on refrigerator, cupboards
Other _____

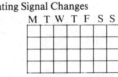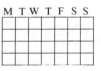

Decrease Signals that Lead to Eating

Designated eating places for problem food
Eating and talking only
Problem food out of sight
Problem food out of house
Problem food hard to reach
Other _____

minimal health risk (see Mahan, 1979, for further discussion). Other writers (Mahoney, Rogers, Straw, & Mahoney, in press) criticize the emphasis on weight loss, suggesting that more attention should be given to factors directly related to health. It is easy to conceive of a person losing statistically significant but clinically insignificant amounts of weight while increasing consumption of sodium and saturated fat and thereby actually increasing the potential for medical problems. If we professionals assist in such endeavors, we are readily contributing to the long history of iatrogenic treatment effects.

It is increasingly important to acknowledge and support other helpful agents, including physicians and self-help groups like Weight Watchers and TOPS (Take Off Pounds Sensibly). The approaches used by these groups can be useful, and such groups may have available more natural support and maintenance systems than brief behavioral treatment. Encouraging clients to use such approaches is most defensible.

Since the incidence of obesity seems much greater in lower socioeconomic groups, finding relevant cost-effective interventions is important. Some indication exists that behavioral approaches have such benefits (Dahms, Molitch, Bray, Greenway, Atkinson, & Hamilton, 1978). Group procedures do have the benefit of lower cost to consumers. There is also some evidence that minimal contact can be as effective as more intensive contact (Dilley, Balch, & Balch, 1979), an issue of economical importance to most consumers.

In the final analysis, persons involved with providing obesity treatment should at least strive to do no harm, a point well discussed by Fullarton (1978) in a fine review of social aspects of obesity treatment.

HOMEWORK-BASED TREATMENT

Overview of Treatment

The program description that follows is based on behavioral strategies conducted in a group context. Therapeutic homework assignments emphasizing self-control play a major role in this approach. Treatment conducted in a group is preferred because it is deemed the most efficient method. The approach described in this chapter can be used with individuals as well.

Initially, before treatment begins, it is worthwhile to meet with students individually to begin assessment and prepare them for the classes. Clients read and sign both an informed consent form (Figure 8.1) and a consent for follow-up and scientific presentation (Figure 8.2). A refundable deposit is required, and refunds are contingent upon both attendance and assignment completion. Clients are encouraged to modify assignments to enhance the likelihood of success. Special notebooks can be provided to organize handouts, assignments, and progress, along with pocket-sized food diaries for ease of recording.

Figure 8.1   Informed consent form

INFORMED CONSENT
GROUP WEIGHT CONTROL PROGRAM

Treatment for obesity is controversial. There are many programs and approaches available. There is little evidence to support the long term effectiveness of these various approaches. The weight control program you are currently enrolled in attempts to combine several different approaches that have demonstrated some effectiveness. However, *there is no guarantee that this program will be effective for you, especially on a long term basis.*

This group program for weight control will demand your time and energy. You have been provided with a program description for details and you are requested to read this and a description of the bonus refund system. Your signing the *Consent for Scientific Presentation* is completely optional; if you decline to sign this form, this will not change your chance to participate in the weight control program or the treatment you will receive while in the program.

I understand that current medical opinion suggests that weight loss should not be attempted during pregnancy. Sacred Heart's Weight Control program provides sound nutritional information which may be helpful in avoiding excess weight gain during pregnancy, but is not designed to monitor this or other specific aspects of pregnancy.

I have read the program description and the bonus refund system. I understand that this program, as with many weight programs, may not be successful on a long term basis. I understand that I may withdraw at any time; however, I will be refunded only whatever part of the bonus refund I have earned. I understand that my signing the *Consent for Scientific Presentation* is optional.

Signature _____

Witness _____

Date _____

Figure 8.2   Consent form for scientific presentation

CONSENT FOR SCIENTIFIC PRESENTATION

I agree to allow data (information) from my participation in the Group Weight Control Program to be used for scientific presentation. I understand that such presentations might include either oral presentations during meetings of professional associations or groups or written publication in professional journals.

In so allowing, I understand that this data will be presented primarily in a group form and that whatever individual presentation occurs will be done in a manner that does not specifically identify me by using my real name, occupation, or address, but that my age, sex, and weight may be presented. In addition, I agree to being contacted 1 year and 5 years after completing this program; this contact will be for the purpose of determining how successful I have been in maintaining weight loss which will help in evaluating this weight loss program.

Signature _____

Witness _____

Date _____

Because obesity management is a lengthy procedure, it is suggested that professionals broaden their program to include a series of beginning and advanced classes. The classes can be spaced to occur over approximately 10 weeks. What follows is an example of beginning and advanced classes as currently conducted by the authors. The initial, or Basic Class, focuses on nutritional change and behavioral strategies for weight control. The second class, open to graduates of the Basic Class, is directed toward lifestyle change, with an emphasis on increasing activity. Cognitive interventions can be introduced during advanced classes.

Self-observation through the use of a food diary is a central aspect of the Basic Class. Previous research suggests that this is an effective, modest treatment in itself, especially if people record before eating (Bellack, Rozensky, & Schwartz, 1974), although more recent work by Green (1978) suggests that this practice may increase noncompliance. We begin by suggesting that clients record after eating, and we attempt to gradually teach clients the utility of recording and planning ahead in general. We have developed initial self-monitoring assignments that have clients review their own records to identify problems and to develop goals based upon identified problems. Food diaries are consistently collected, reviewed, and commented on by instructors. Figure 8.3 presents a pocket-sized food diary that has sufficient room to allow 1 month's recording, using either standard longhand or food-exchange methods. Food exchanges are a way of categorizing foods into groups to simplify calorie counting. We strive to teach people the food-exchange system because it is relatively easy and applicable to eating away from home. The food diary has sufficient space for recording weekly goals and successes. With the diary developed for ease in recording, activity changes and food thoughts can also be recorded.

Initial behavioral strategies are directed toward reducing stimuli that lead to problematic eating. Frequent suggestions by instructors include keeping problem food in covered containers in the refrigerator or cupboards, serving from the stove, and restricting the pairing of food with other stimuli such as TV and reading. Most of these strategies are focused on eating at home; however, we also suggest approaches such as driving home by interesting routes that avoid bakeries and reducing food stimuli in one's work environment. We encourage students to initially experiment and then choose goals that they feel they can stick with permanently. We also suggest developing positive signals, such as having fresh fruit visible and available (response ease), and using aids such as reminders on the refrigerator (with routine changes to counter stimulus fading), shopping lists, and menus.

We suggest procedures that increase the response cost of obtaining food, such as recording before eating, and keeping problem food out of the house and making it difficult to reach or prepare.

Since data show that slowing the rate of eating takes advantage of satiation (Wooley & Wooley, 1975), that strategy is also included. We suggest serving soup or salad first, eating fruit to take the edge off hunger, conversing during meals, planning interruptions, counting bites, putting one's fork down between bites, and finishing last in social situations.

Information about nutrition is presented throughout the program. Assignments directed toward limiting the amounts of fat, sugar, and meat are presented. Weighing and measuring food are stressed and relevant exercises are presented. Students are taught to read and use nutritional information on food labels and to reduce the calories in favorite recipes and meals.

Homework Assignments

Assignments are integral to each class session. A typical group begins with the leader initiating a discussion about the past week's assignments. The class ends with students developing their assignments

Figure 8.3   Pocket food diary

Day:_____   Date:_____   FOOD DIARY

Time	Amount	Type of food

Daily Calorie Summary

Exchange Group	AM	Noon	PM	Total Exchange	Calories
Milk					
A veg.					
B veg.					
Fruit					
Bread					
Meat					
Fat					
Free foods					
Misc.					
						Total

Figure 8.3   *(Continued)*

	Weekly Summary	Weight:
	Calories eaten	Activity
Monday		
Tuesday		
Wednesday		
Thursday		
Friday		
Saturday		
Sunday		
Total		

Daily caloric needs at present weight = _____ (a)
Weekly caloric needs . . . . (a × 7 days) = _____ (b)
Weekly caloric intake . . . . = _____ (c)
+ or - weekly calories (b - c). . . . . = _____

Success:

Goals for Next Week	Plan

for the next week. The assignment sheet is duplicated on NCR paper so that both leader and student have a copy. Although assignments are proposed by the leader, students are encouraged to modify the proposed assignments so that they are agreeing to something they can accomplish. The leader reviews individuals' assignments, offers suggestions, and cosigns the assignment sheet.

Discussions center on last week's assignment and lead naturally to assignments for the coming week. Nonpunitive quizzes help insure that students understand presentations and homework assignments.

During the presentations it is important to teach students how to readily calculate calories in most eating situations. It is also necessary to provide a supportive structure for students to develop desired eating and nutritional habits and activity changes. It is helpful to proceed gradually and attempt to insure success at each step before proceeding to a more difficult task. A sample of the type of assignments made in each session is now presented.

Basic Class. Information on nutrition and behavior change is presented. Students learn to monitor their eating behavior, identify problems, and establish behavioral goals.

Initial individual session. Individual appointments are scheduled approximately 1 week before the initial group meeting. New students are introduced to the group leader, who conducts the individual interviews. During this session, student expectations about the class are elicited and clarified. Procedural details such as the handling of absences and the bonus refund system (Figure 8.4) are covered. Students turn in signed copies of the Informed Consent and optional Consent for Scientific Presentation forms. A history of prior dieting attempts and other relevant information is obtained, with students readily discussing their previous efforts and inability to keep weight off. Skinfold and current

Figure 8.4   Bonus refund form

BONUS REFUND SYSTEM

What is the Bonus Refund?

A central part of Sacred Heart's Weight Control Program is the Bonus Refund System. This system will require you to make a $50 deposit in addition to the course fee of $80. Thus, of the total initial payment ($130), you can earn back up to $50 for completing assignments between sessions and for completing the entire program.

Only the money you have earned will be refunded; this means that if you drop out of the program you will lost all the bonus refund other than what you have already earned. The only exception to this would involve your moving out of the Eugene-Springfield area during the program; if this occurs, you will be refunded what you have earned and the amount of money left that is possible to earn.

How Much Are the Assignments Worth?

The amount of money you can earn back will vary. After the initial "honeymoon stage" when motivation is high, weight control becomes more difficult; therefore assignments near the end of the program will be worth more money. At this time the most incentive is built into the program.

Specifically, assignments and completion are worth the following:

Based on nine assignments and two follow-up sessions:

Assignments 1, 2, 3, 4, 5, 6, 7	$ 2 =	$14
Assignments 8, 9	5 =	10
6-month follow-up	10 =	10
12-month follow-up	16 =	16
	Potential Bonus Refund =	$50

You will be penalized one-half of the individual assignment deposit for not completing one part (task) of the assignment. You will be penalized all of the individual assignment deposit for not completing two or more parts of the assignment.

If you miss a session without notifying Hospital Education prior to your appointment, you will automatically lose the bonus refund for that session. If you notify Hospital Education ahead of time and bring in the assignment to the next session, you will receive credit for what you have completed. Money earned is refunded twice during the program, after Session 10 and after the 12-month follow-up appointment.

I have read and understand the above.

Signature _____

Witness _____

Date _____

weight measurements are obtained at this session. The following assignment is then given:

Assignment: Begin recording food without counting calories (see Figure 8.5).

Figure 8.5   Sample food diary: No calorie count

TIME	FOOD EATEN			SOCIAL	WHERE
	Amount	Type of Food		Alone? With Whom?	Home, Work, Restaurant, Recreation
8:30	2 slices 1 bowl 2 cups	buttered toast cornflakes & milk black coffee		alone	home
10:30	3 1 cup	peanut butter cookies coffee		alone	home
12:30	1 2 1 glass (10 oz)	tuna sandwich dill pickles 2% milk		with Joyce	restaurant

Session 1. The class, which is limited to 12 students, begins with a warm-up exercise that ends in everyone knowing one another by first name. Group members share what they hope to learn and change, and leaders promote the idea that everyone is there for a common struggle by providing guidelines for constructive participation. Next the initial food diary assignment is reviewed. Students generally report that the initial recording resulted in decreased food consumption (even though it was suggested to continue eating normally during this initial recording). Since they also report that remembering to record food is a frequent problem, information about accurate recording of food is presented. Self-observation is presented as an initial step toward change, and pinpointing problems and changing problems into behavioral goals are suggested as following steps. This assignment is then given:

Assignment: Complete an eating habit questionnaire, begin to measure food at home, and pinpoint at least four problematic patterns.

Session 2. This session begins with an exercise such as "reintroduce yourself and describe at least two noneating-related activities you enjoy." During the assignment review noncooks in the group usually report that estimating portion size is difficult because of limited previous experience with weights and measurements. Students are taught to calculate their caloric requirements according to a nomogram procedure which considers individual variables such as age, height, current weight, sex, and activity (Bray, 1976). Exercises focusing on fat as a food are presented; group members consistently express surprise at the number of calories fats contribute to daily meals and snacks. The following task is part of the weekly assignment.

Assignment: Add the recording of fats as a food exchange; look for goals related to reducing fat consumption.

Session 3. This and subsequent classes begin with a review of last session's assignments. The presentation introduces students to meat exchanges, which usually provoke much surprise about the number of calories contained in various meats. Because many students have already reduced their food intake, we experience some problems making assignments and exercises relevant to their typical eating patterns. Here is a sample assignment:

Assignment: Add meat exchanges to the food diary recordings; bring in a food label with nutritional information to the next class; and if fat intake appears excessive, limit fat to _____ exchanges on _____ days.

Students are introduced to signal (stimulus) control (see Figure 8.6). In addition, they are encouraged to begin working on one goal they have identified by changing a signal relevant to that goal. We use a "goal

Figure 8.6   Signal control form

SIGNAL CONTROL

Controlling signals involves two strategies: (a) reducing problem food signals and (b) increasing positive food signals. Below are some examples of eating signal changes to consider. The chart may help you practice controlling one specific signal and watching your progress over time.

Eating Signal Changes

Positive Eating Signals	M T W T F S S	M T W T F S S
Good food in sight		
Good food attractive		
Signs/charts on refrigerator, cupboards		
Other _____		

Decrease Signals that Lead to Eating	M T W T F S S	M T W T F S S
Designated eating places for problem food		
Eating and talking only		
Problem food out of sight		
Problem food out of house		
Problem food hard to reach		
Other _____		

Figure 8.6 *(Continued)*

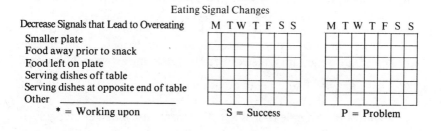

Eating Signal Changes

Decrease Signals that Lead to Overeating	M T W T F S S	M T W T F S S
Smaller plate		
Food away prior to snack		
Food left on plate		
Serving dishes off table		
Serving dishes at opposite end of table		
Other _____		

* = Working upon   S = Success   P = Problem

organizer'' (Figure 8.7) to help focus students' efforts in working on identified problematic patterns throughout the Basic and Advanced Classes. Handouts describing how to use the goal organizer are provided; students usually need several sessions to learn to use this device.

Figure 8.7   Sample goal organizing form

GOAL ORGANIZER

Pinpointed Problem
(What you hope to change)
Inactivity during problem snack time (4:00-5:30 pm)

Long-Range Goal
(What you would like to see happen)
Enjoy routine snack (less than 200 calories)
Use time more constructively: Accomplish tasks
Work on hobbies (develop)
Walk 3/wk
Swim 2/wk

Strategies for Change
Strategy *Increase Activity from 4:00-5:30 pm*
Weekly Steps

1. *Make "To Do" List*
   once/wk and post on   **First Month**
   refrigerator (x) | |x| | | | | | |x| | | | | | | | | | | | | | | |x| | | | |

                                              First Month
2. *Walk (w) 3/wk* |w| |w| | | | |w| |w| |w| | | |w| |w|w| | | |w| |w| |w|w| |

                                              Second Month
3. *Walk (w) 3/wk*
   Swim (s) 1/wk |w| |w|s| |w| | |w|w|s| |w| | |w| |w| |w| | |w|w| |s| |w| |

                                              Third Month
4. *Walk 3/wk*
   Swim 2/wk |w| |w|s| |s| | |w| |w|s|w|s| | |w| |s|w| |w| |w|w| |s| |s|w|

Session 4. By the fourth class session, members are generally feeling more comfortable in the group and readily sharing experiences and discoveries. Nutritional labels are discussed, and students are generally pleased that they have already acquired skills in understanding and using such information. The importance of attending to behavioral change, not immediate weight loss, is stressed. The following assignment is given:

Assignment: Add bread exchanges to the food diary (Figure 8.8).

Figure 8.8   Sample food diary: Fat, meat, and bread exchanges

TIME	FOOD EATEN			SOCIAL	WHERE
	Amount	Type of Food	Fat, Meat, & Bread Exchanges	Alone? With Whom?	Home, Work, Restaurant, Recreation
8:30	2 slices 4 tsp 3/4 cup 1 tbsp 1/2 cup 2 cups	toast butter cornflakes sugar 2% milk black coffee	2 bread 4 fat 1 bread	alone	kitchen
10:30	3 1 cup	peanut butter cookies black coffee		alone	living room
12:30	2 slices 1/4 cup 1 tbsp 1 leaf 1 tbsp 2 10 oz	bread tuna mayonnaise lettuce celery dill pickles 2% milk	2 bread 1 meat 3 fat	with Joyce	restaurant

Total
7 fat units @ 45 calories   = 315 calories
5 bread units @ 68 calories = 340 calories
1 meat unit @ 73 calories   = 73 calories

Total calories from Fat,
  Bread, & Meat units   = 728 calories

Session 5. At this class session, members are introduced to the complete exchange list, which includes fruits, vegetables, and dairy products. A new food diary form to assist in recording exchanges is reviewed; students are now ready to record exchanges for all foods (Figure 8.9). Students are favorably responsive to the new recording form because food can be recorded more quickly, and the form allows them to readily identify problematic eating groups.

Assignment: Keep a complete exchange food diary and place limits upon food groups as desired.

Figure 8.9   Sample food diary: Total calories using complete exchange list

TIME	FOOD EATEN		Meat	Fat	Bread	Fruit	A Veg.	B Veg.	2% Milk	Misc.	Calorie Chart	
	Amount	Type of Food										
2:00	1 piece	apple pie									351	
	1 cup	black coffee										
5:30	1/2 cup	peanuts									452	
	12 oz	Diet Pepsi—free										
6:00	6 pieces	fried shrimp	3	6	1							
	1/2 large	baked potato			1							
	2 tbsp	sour cream		1								
	1/2 cup	peas						1				
	1 tsp	margarine		1								
	2 slices	tomato					1					
	1 small	dinner roll			1							
	1 tsp	margarine		1								
9:00	3	peanut butter cookies									165	(55x3)
	1 cup	apple juice				3						
			3	9	3	3	1	1			968	
			x73	x45	x68	x40	x 0	x36	x125			

219 + 135 + 204 + 120 + 0 + 36 + 0   + 968 = 1682

Session 6. By this session most group members can estimate calories in most eating situations. The following assignments are therefore given:

Assignment: Begin to record total calories consumed on a daily basis.

Assignment: Write away for nutritional information about a favorite food.

Nonpunitive quizzes are used to prompt review of materials and help leaders evaluate their instruction. The importance of calories derived from alcohol is presented and discussed, and a sample letter requesting nutritional information from a major company is provided. Students are introduced to response slowing and strategies for delaying and preventing eating urges.

Session 7. Students are introduced to several different topics, including fast-food snacks and quick ways to determine calories in favorite recipes. Leaders present a number of snacks, and students estimate the calories they contain. The final shortcut food diary is introduced (Figure 8.10). This session includes the following assignments:

Figure 8.10   Sample shortcut food diary

Time	Amount	Type of Food
8:30	1/2 cup 1/2 cup 1 slice 1 tsp 8 oz	granola 2% milk toast margarine orange juice
10:30	3 1 cup	peanut butter cookies black coffee
12:30	1 whole 3 oz 1 oz 1 tbsp 10 oz	hamburger bun hamburger patty cheese mayonnaise, lettuce, dill pickle 2% milk
2:00	1 piece	apple pie, black coffee
5:30	1/2 cup 12 oz	peanuts Diet Pepsi
6:00	6 pieces 2 tbsp 1/2 cup 1 small	fried shrimp, 1/2 large bk potato sour cream peas w/1 tsp margarine, 2 slices tomato dinner roll, 1 tsp. marg.
9:00	3 1 cup	peanut butter cookies apple juice

Daily Calorie Summary

Exchange Group	AM	Noon	PM	Total Exchange		Calories
2% Milk	1/2	1-1/4		1-3/4	1-3/4 x 125	219
A veg.			/	1	1 x 0	0
B veg.			/	1	1 x 36	36
Fruit	//		///	5	5 x 40	200
Bread	///	//	///	8	8 x 68	544
Meat		////	///	7	7 x 73	511
Fat	///	///	++++ ////	15	15 x 45	675
Free foods	1 cup bl. coffee	lettuce dill pickle	Diet Pepsi			0
Misc. pb cookies	3		3	6	chart 6 x 55	330
Apple pie		1 piece	1 piece		chart 1 x 351	351
Peanuts		1/2 cup	1/2 cup		from chart	452
					Total	3318

Assignment: Continue to calculate total calories using the short-cut diary, and plan five personally acceptable snacks under 150 calories.

Assignment: Complete reducing calories in a favorite recipe.

Assignment: Calculate the calories saved over 1 year from one small habit change.

Session 8. A film "For Tomorrow We Shall Diet" is shown to add variety to the presentations and to demonstrate students' awareness of their own increased knowledge about nutrition and weight control. Planning for holidays is introduced and discussed as a general topic; more time is devoted to this issue when both Thanksgiving and Christmas are approaching. Students are introduced to the general importance of activity in weight control and to the use of activity as an alternative to eating. They are also given the pocket-sized food diary for ongoing recording and planning.

Assignment: Continue to record and plan food intake in pocket diary.

Session 9. Lifestyle change as a general framework for weight control is introduced, and activity change is further discussed. Students report their progress on their behavioral change goals. At this point group members express concerns about the sessions nearing an end; therefore, details about the follow-up (Advanced Class) are provided. The group begins generating some of its own support, as is demonstrated by members sharing phone numbers and transportation. Subtle changes, such as increased use of the stairs in reaching class, are often noted by students. The following task is part of the assignment given:

Assignment: Complete course evaluations by the next session.

Session 10. The last session concludes with a round-robin status report in which members are encouraged to describe both their current situation and future plans for weight control. The problem of maintaining change is discussed in detail. Students are provided with additional pocket-sized food diaries.

Assignment: Arrange 6- and 12-month follow-up procedures with group leaders and complete postcards to be mailed as reminders before the group follow-up sessions.

Advanced Class. Activity change is currently receiving greater attention. Suggestions include both subtle changes, such as standing rather than sitting while talking on the phone and taking the stairs rather than the elevator, and more intensive commitments, such as beginning a walking program, joining a cardiovascular fitness program, and signing up for a community-based exercise program. Physician referral is required for this class because of the emphasis upon activity changes. Procedures for effectively initiating and hopefully maintaining activity changes are becoming increasingly available. Obese people, especially those quite overweight, often express considerable discomfort with public activity; we therefore attempt an approach of gradual exposure utilizing group support.

The manner in which individuals talk to themselves about food and related private events is also receiving increasing recognition. General strategies for change include (a) response cost and response prevention procedures for negative food thoughts, such as postponing urges with a timer, doing an activity before following through with an eating urge, and (b) turning food urges into occasions for problem analysis, problem solving, and constructive planning. Eating in response to negative moods and related events poses an interesting arena for intervention, especially given the potential power of food as a reinforcer.

Eating occasions involving family and friends, restaurants, vacations, and holidays present a number of complex problems. Little research has been directed toward evaluating relevant interventions, but a strong case for the importance of further work has been presented by Wilson (in press) and others. Involving spouses and friends in one's program presents a number of possibilities, with mixed results thus far. This could be a ripe area for assertiveness training and for helping people prepare specific responses for problem situations they have already encountered or anticipate encountering (see Chapter 12).

The emphasis in the initial Advanced Class is upon activity change, with additional time built in for nutritional topics. The goal organizer and pocket food diary provide a means of continuing to follow changes that students are working on.

Session 1. Because students are drawn from several different Basic Classes and are not necessarily acquainted, this class begins with a group introduction similar to that used in the Basic Class. Students summarize their current weight control efforts. A more detailed presentation on activity ensues. The following assignments are then given:

Assignment: Wear comfortable clothing and shoes for the next classes.

Assignment: Continue to work on already developed changes and record detailed activity for an agreed-upon number of days.

Session 2. This class, as with most of the subsequent classes, begins with a small group warm-up. In this session members are asked to pair off and discuss one activity they found enjoyable this past week. Assignments are debriefed as they were with the Basic Class.

Assignment: Graph weight loss using the system presented in this session.

The general benefits of and strategies for walking are discussed, and members are paired off for a brief walk. Aerobic activity is presented for discussion, and relevant assignments given.

Assignment: Take a brief and pleasurable walk.

Assignment: Continue to use the pocket food diary, noting any changes in activity.

Sessions 3-10. The next seven classes target upon three general areas for activity change: (a) walking, (b) a major activity commitment, and (c) subtle activity change. Eating and nutritional habit changes continue to be monitored.

Assignment: Develop contracts that include commitments to gradually increase walking.

A forum during each subsequent class session is provided for students to report new "discoveries." These discoveries might include ways to build in walking, such as taking a leisurely walk to the grocery store at least once a week.

Assignment: Find ways to make walking more intrinsically reinforcing, such as taking different routes, finding a walking partner, looking for interesting hikes, and taking the family dog along (who may also need exercise).

Developing a major activity change is initiated with several group fantasy exercises, such as "take a few quiet minutes to remember an activity you once found enjoyable during childhood or as an adult; remember what made that activity enjoyable for you." Group members then share their experiences in small groups and return to the larger group. The following assignments are given:

Assignment: List two or three activities for further exploration and present these to the group at the next class.

Assignment: Check out, borrow, or buy a book or other material related to one of those activities; again, share what you have found with other class members.

Assignment: Gather information about how to pursue a desired activity. This might include phoning for specific information about a class or the cost of a spa membership and other relevant information, going to the local "Y" to acquire brochures, or talking with friends who are already involved with the relevant activity.

Assignment: Make a commitment, such as signing up for a class or developing a verbal agreement with a friend, relative, or classmate to begin a regular activity program.

Since some students state that they do not have enough time for such changes, a brief time management package is presented. Leaders also press for some type of commitment by saying something like the following: "O.K., sounds like it would be difficult to swim four times a week, so what might you consider doing that you could complete in a briefer amount of time?"

Subtle activity change is promoted through the use of handouts describing possibilities (Figure 8.11). Students are assisted in developing such habit changes by using the goal organizer. A system for keeping track of activity changes on a calendar is presented, along with the following assignments:

Figure 8.11   Activity change recording form

SUBTLE ACTIVITY CHANGES

Increasing Activity at Home
  Walk to store
  Do activity while watching TV
  Use TV commercials as activity signals
  User smaller wastebaskets
  Use manual can opener
  Stand during phone conversation
  Use most distant phone
  Use most distant bathroom
  Increase housework, yard work
  Use manual toothbrush
  Develop activity room
  Other _____
  Other _____

M T W T F S S   M T W T F S S

Assignment: Keep track of activity increases in your food diaries, your weight graph, or calendars.

Assignment: Begin developing activities for one problematic eating time.

COMPLIANCE ENHANCEMENT PROCEDURES

Most of our clients begin their initial class session reasonably eager to begin working on weight control. Prior payment probably contributes to selection factors and results in more motivated clients. We have found that meeting individually with clients before their initial group participation is helpful both in developing an initial relationship and in clarifying expectations. Both during this initial meeting and during class sessions, it seems important to anticipate questions and have reasonable answers prepared. Many of our clients know something about weight control, and it is not unusual to be "checked out" by them.

Maintaining compliance, the target of most of our efforts, has been difficult; problems usually begin at about the fifth or sixth session. We continue to use several procedures to enhance compliance. We require a refundable deposit with refunds contingent upon both attendance and assignment completion, and we encourage students to change proposed assignments whenever possible so that they are within their capabilities (Hagen, Foreyt, & Durham, 1976). As class sessions progress, students assume greater responsibility for developing their own assignments. We also attempt to promote a supportive group environment by suggesting relevant group rules, modeling helpful behavior, and developing both small-group and all-class exercises that increase students' participation. We explicitly encourage students to attend class with a partner, since we have been impressed with the results such partners have had in sticking with weight control. Throughout the program, we reiterate certain ideas: that change is usually quite gradual, that it will take time to develop new habits, and that people should become their own experts in weight control. We suggest that problems are to be expected and that learning to handle them, as opposed to temporarily avoiding them, is most important.

We have changed several aspects of our program that we felt exacerbated compliance problems. When we began our classes, we tried to present nearly all information and skills relevant to weight control. However, we found that too many students misunderstood the presentations and that we could not adequately monitor students' progress. We now present fewer topics and follow them throughout the program. A second major change is that we no longer offer booster sessions. Our initial classes met for twenty sessions spread out over a year, gradually fading out to a monthly booster basis. We also offered a second-year class that met monthly for booster sessions. However, we found that consistent with recent research (Ashby & Wilson, 1977; Beneke & Paulsen, 1979; Kingsley & Wilson, 1977) neither of these booster approaches worked well. Our current focus is therefore on providing ongoing active treatment and encouraging students to continue their efforts with programs such as Weight Watchers if they have had prior success with such endeavors.

We have found several other factors generally important for promoting compliance. When possible, it is useful to predict possible problems; for instance, if a person has cut back calories to a fairly low level with a resulting weight loss and a holiday is approaching, we can predict that the scales will show several pounds of weight gain even if the person increases eating only modestly. We have also found that some students state goals too generally, thereby inhibiting themselves from taking initial steps toward a goal; with this problem brief individual tutoring before or after a class session has been of benefit. People who focus on activity increases for weight control may be discouraged by results shown on the scale; for these people we have found feedback about skinfold changes useful. Finally, it is our impression that alcohol use is underrecorded in food diaries; however, we are unsure about how to encourage better accuracy in recording this food.

Maintaining compliance for more obese people and for people who have lost to their desired levels are clearly the important issues. Most of what has been published under the rubric of compliance is misleading: most clients do not achieve their desired goal, and the time framework in such studies is spuriously short, usually less than a year. Even relatively brief follow-ups readily show different results at different data collection points (Wollersheim, 1977). Perhaps the best we can do at this time is to preserve an empirical stance by placing an emphasis on following students, clients, and patients over time, evaluating more carefully the longer-term impact of our treatments, and modifying our programs according to both current literature and our own data.

ILLUSTRATIVE CASE

Initial Individual Session

Jane, married with several children, is in her 30s and works full time, in addition to being a mother and a housewife. She was somewhat skeptical at her initial session. She had been on many different diets and through several programs with success in losing as much as 20 pounds, but she had always gained the weight back within a year. She now weighed her maximum and hoped to lose at least 60 pounds. She requested a diet, and the class instructor used this request as a basis for clarifying the nature of our program. Although Jane had read materials describing the program in detail, many features were still unclear to her. This individual session ended with her being more enthusiastic about taking the class. She seemed interested but somewhat puzzled by the "simple" initial assignment of recording her food without attempting to change her eating habits.

Session 1. Jane reported success in following through with the initial assignment, except she reported that it was difficult to remember everything she ate. Class members readily agreed that this was a problem, and the leader suggested several ways to make recording easier. Jane also reported happily that recording made it difficult to eat as much. She stated that she had the most difficulty remembering to record snacks and that snacking might be a significant problem for her.

Session 2. Jane reported that she identified several problematic patterns. It seemed that one especially difficult time was right after returning home from work, when she felt tired and hungry. She generally began preparing dinner soon after arriving home. She found that this time was especially problematic for snacking and that she nibbled while preparing dinner.

Session 3. Jane reported being especially surprised at the amount of fat in her diet, and she decided there were relevant changes to work upon in this area, particularly the amount of margarine she used on bread, potatoes, and similar foods. She reported that she was gradually improving in recording food before eating and felt that this practice would be especially useful in learning to control snacking. She felt that some type of a planned snack right after work might help; class members suggested several possibilities.

Session 4. Jane reported problems finding and following through with planned snacks. After a brief class discussion, the group leader suggested a program that included gradually learning to eat more fruit, since Jane had previously found fruit to be a satisfying food and it would be easy to have available. She reported that she was continuing to progress, but she also seemed a little discouraged that she had only lost 4 pounds so far.

Session 5. Jane reported that planned snacking worked better this time, but that she also felt that some type of activity after work would be beneficial. She stated that she would like to begin by either taking a brief walk or completing a task around the house upon arriving home from work. She also hoped to reward her activity with a planned snack while preparing dinner.

Session 6. Jane reported problems continuing to record all of her food, but stated that she wanted to continue. This was discussed briefly in class, with several other members acknowledging similar problems. The instructor attempted without success to more clearly pinpoint the difficulty, so she simply noted that the class was moving toward an easier system for recording. The instructor also suggested a 1- or 2-day break from recording after complete recording on the other days.

Session 7. Jane reported that the past week proceeded more smoothly, and she participated in this class session quite constructively. She especially seemed to enjoy the class presentation on snacks and reported having identified several snacks that she would try. She reported success in cutting back the amount of margarine on bread, potatoes, and vegetables.

Session 8. Jane continued to follow through with recording and reported that the briefer recording system really helped. She had now lost 8 pounds. She seemed especially interested in today's activity presentation and felt this would be an important area for her to change.

Session 9. Jane reported that she enjoyed using the pocket diary. She began to express concerns about the class ending, and the entire class participated in this discussion. She had become friends with another person in class; they discussed either signing up for an exercise class or joining a local spa.

Session 10. Jane decided to join a spa with her friend and to go there at least 3 days a week after work. Her husband and family were agreeable and willing to both help with food preparation at home and go out for dinner once a week. She had now lost 11 pounds and hoped that she would be able to continue on her own. She felt that she had success-fully reduced her use of margarine and other fats and had made good progress with her snacking problem. She took some pocket food diaries home and stated that she might well return for the Advanced Class.

Six-month-follow-up. Jane had now lost about 10 pounds. She reported that she had problems with backsliding, especially when her friend was ill and she temporarily quit going to the spa. She apparently had tried several brief fasts in the past month. She reported thinking more seriously about taking the Advanced Class in the fall.

SUMMARY

Obesity is difficult to define; one treatment-focused definition might be simply the difference between a person's present and desired weight. Many etiologies have been suggested for adult obesity, such as genetics, childhood obesity, metabolic differences, socioeconomic and cultural factors, the operant effects of food, iatrogenic effects of dieting, and eating styles.

Many types of treatment are presently applied to obesity. They range from medical interventions to fasting, behavioral approaches, and activity change. However, all have shown only modest results, and some have social and health risks involved. Therefore, procedures should be developed that maximize client understanding and participation in treatment. Ongoing evaluation of goals and negative effects should be included. Individualized treatment procedures seem necessary, and client risk should be taken into account. Helpful agents, such as doctors or weight-loss groups, should be utilized in treatment, and interventions should be kept as cost-effective as possible.

The program described here is based on behavioral group therapy. Before treatment, the clients and therapist meet to begin assessment and prepare for classes. Both a basic program and an advanced one are offered. The basic program begins with self-observation through the use of a food diary. Diary entries are reviewed by clients to identify problems and develop goals. Strategies for reducing stimuli that trigger eating are explained, and procedures to increase the response cost of eating are also suggested. Another possible strategy offered is slowing the rate of eating to take advantage of satiation. Information about nutrition is provided throughout the classes. Homework assignments, which are integral to each class session, are discussed in detail.

An advanced program might cover topics such as activity change, additional methods for dealing with eating urges, and special problem situations such as vacations. The class described places emphasis on activity change, with some additional time for nutritional topics. Homework for this set of classes is also discussed.

Initial compliance is secured by the clients' own enthusiasm, a required payment before classes start, and an individual meeting prior to group participation. Maintenance of compliance is difficult to achieve, but a refundable deposit with refunds contingent upon compliance, client involvement in formulating assignments, and a supportive group environment seem to help. During the program it is reiterated that new habits take time to develop and that people are encouraged to become their own weight control experts. Some aspects of the program that used to exacerbate noncompliance which have been changed were presenting too much information all at once and providing booster sessions. Several factors promote noncompliance: high-risk situations (e.g., holidays), which can be anticipated by the therapist; vague statement of goals, which requires the therapist to tutor the client in setting goals; lack of reduction in weight shown by those who focus upon activity increases, who may be helped by feedback from skinfold changes instead of weight; and underrecording of alcohol in food diaries.

The illustrative case study ending this chapter provides a look at how one client went through the basic program. Jane learned to record her food intake, modify the types of food she ate, and participate in more physical activity. At the follow-up, she had lost 10 pounds, but had had trouble with backsliding and planned to attend the advanced classes.

REFERENCE NOTES

1. Lublin, I., & Kirkish, P. *An original behavior modification program for weight reduction: Minimal intervention and permanent habit change.* Presented at the 10th Annual Meeting, Southern California Conference on Behavior Modification, Los Angeles, February 1978.

2. Keefe, F.J. *The life fitness program: A behavioral approach to making exercise a habit.* Paper presented at the Annual Meeting of the Association for Advancement of Behavior Therapy, Chicago, November 1978.

REFERENCES

Abraham, S., & Nordsieck, M. Relationship of excess weight in children and adults. *Public Health Reports,* 1960, *75,* 263-273.

Adams, N., Ferguson, J., Stunkard, A.J., & Agras, W.S. The eating behavior of obese and nonobese women. *Behaviour Research and Therapy,* 1978, *16,* 225-233.

Ashby, W.A., & Wilson, G.T. Behavior therapy for obesity: Booster sessions and long term maintenance of weight loss. *Behaviour Research and Therapy,* 1977, *15,* 451-463.

Bellack, A.S., Rozensky, R., & Schwartz, J. A comparison of two forms of self-monitoring in a behavioral weight reduction program. *Behavior Therapy,* 1974, *5,* 523-530.

Beneke, W.M., & Paulsen, B.K. Long-term efficacy of a behavior modification weight loss program: A comparison of two followup maintenance strategies. *Behavior Therapy,* 1979, *10,* 8-13.

Björntorp, P. Exercise in the treatment of obesity. *Clinics in Endocrinology and Metabolism,* 1976, *5,* 431-453.

Bray, G.A. *The obese patient.* Philadelphia: W.B. Saunders, 1976.

Brightwell, D.R., & Sloan, C.L. Long-term results of behavior therapy for obesity. *Behavior Therapy,* 1977, *8,* 898-905.

Brownell, K.D., & Stunkard, A.J. Behavior therapy and behavior change: Uncertainties in programs for weight control. *Behaviour Research and Therapy,* 1978, *16,* 301. (a)

Brownell, K.D., & Stunkard, A.J. Behavioral treatment of obesity in children. *American Journal of Diseases of Children,* 1978, *132,* 403-412. (b)

Chirico, A.M., & Stunkard, A.J. Physical activity and human obesity. *New England Journal of Medicine,* 1960, *263,* 935-946.

Coates, T.J. Theory, research and practice in treating obesity: Are they really all the same? *Addictive Behaviors,* 1977, *2,* 95-103.

Dahlkoetter, J., Callahan, E.J., & Linton, J. Obesity and the unbalanced energy equation: Exercise versus eating habit change. *Journal of Consulting and Clinical Psychology,* 1979, *47,* 898-905.

Dahms, W.T., Molitch, M.E., Bray, G.A., Greenway, F.L., Atkinson, R.L., & Hamilton, K. Treatment of obesity: Cost-benefit assessment of behavioral therapy, placebo, and two anorectic drugs. *The American Journal of Clinical Nutrition,* 1978, *31,* 774-778.

Dilley, D., Balch, P., & Balch, K. A comparison of strategies for behavioral obesity treatment. *Journal of Behavior Therapy and Experimental Psychiatry,* 1979, *10,* 193-197.

Drenick, E.J. Exogenous thyroid hormones to accelerate weight loss. *Obesity/Baritric Medicine,* 1975, *4,* 244-250.

Drenick, E.J., & Dennin, H.F. Energy expenditure in fasting obese men. *Journal of Laboratory and Clinical Medicine,* 1973, *81,* 421-430.

Evans, E.E., & Miller, D.S. Slimming aids. *Journal of Human Nutrition,* 1978, *32,* 433-438.

Fullarton, J.E. Obesity: A new social policy perspective. *International Journal of Obesity,* 1978, *2,* 267-285.

Garrow, J. *Energy balance and obesity in man.* New York: American Elsevier, 1974.

Gaul, D.J., Craighead, W.E., & Mahoney, M.J. Relationship between eating rates and obesity. *Journal of Consulting and Clinical Psychology,* 1975, *43,* 123-125.

Green, L. The temporal and stimulus dimensions of self-monitoring in the behavioral treatment of obesity. *Behavior Therapy,* 1978, *9,* 328-341.

Hagen, R.L., Foreyt, J.P., & Durham, T.W. The dropout problem: Reducing attrition in obesity research. *Behavior Therapy,* 1976, *7,* 463-471.

Harris, M.B., & Hallbauer, E.S. Self-directed weight control through eating and exercise. *Behaviour Research and Therapy*, 1973, *11*, 523-529.

Herman, C.P., & Mack, D. Restrained and unrestrained eating. *Journal of Personality*, 1975, *43*, 646-660.

Hill, S.W., & McCutcheon, N.B. Eating responses of obese and non-obese humans during dinner meals. *Psychosomatic Medicine*, 1975, *37*, 395-401.

Itallie, T.B., & Burton, B.T. National Institutes of Health Consensus Development Conference on Surgical Treatment of Morbid Obesity. *Annals of Surgery*, 1979, *189*, 455-457.

Jeffrey, R.W., Wing, R.R., & Stunkard, A.J. Behavioral treatment of obesity: The state of the art 1976. *Behavior Therapy*, 1978, *9*, 189-199.

Kingsley, R.G., & Wilson, G.T. Behavior therapy for obesity: A comparative investigation of long-term efficacy. *Journal of Consulting and Clinical Psychology*, 1977, *45*, 288-298.

Kline, M.V. Group hypnotherapy in the treatment of obesity. In M.V. Kline, L. Coleman, & E. Wick (Eds.), *Obesity: Etiology, treatment, and measurement.* Springfield, Ill.: Charles C. Thomas, 1976.

Krassner, H.A., Brownell, K.D., & Stunkard, A.J. Cleaning the plate: Food left over by overweight and normal weight persons. *Behaviour Research and Therapy*, 1979, *17*, 155-156.

Lewis, S., Haskell, W.L., Wood, P.D., Manogian, N., Bailey, J.E., & Pereira, M. Effects of physical activity on weight reduction in obese middle-aged women. *The American Journal of Clinical Nutrition*, 1976, *29*, 151-156.

Mahan, L.K. A sensible approach to the obese patient. *Nursing Clinics of North America*, 1979, *14*, 229-243.

Mahoney, B.K., Rogers, T., Straw, M.K., & Mahoney, M.J. *Human obesity: Assessment and treatment.* Englewood Cliffs, N.J.: Prentice-Hall, in press.

Mahoney, M.J. Self-reward and self-monitoring techniques for weight control. *Behavior Therapy*, 1974, *5*, 48-57.

Marston, A.R., London, P., Cohen, N., & Cooper, L.M. In vivo observation of the eating behavior of obese and nonobese subjects. *Journal of Consulting and Clinical Psychology*, 1977, *45*, 335-336.

Mayer, J. Genetic factors in obesity. *Annals* (New York Academy of Science), 1965, *131*, 412-421.

Mayer, J. *Overweight: Causes, cost, and control.* Englewood Cliffs, N.J.: Prentice-Hall, 1968.

Mayer, J., Roy, P., & Mitra, K.P. Relation between caloric intake, body weight and physical work: Studies in an industrial male population in West Bengal. *American Journal of Clinical Nutrition,* 1956, *4,* 169-175.

Miller, D.S., Mumford, P., & Stock, M.J. Gluttony: Thermogenesis in overeating man. *American Journal of Clinical Nutrition,* 1967, *20,* 1223-1229.

Montague, A. Obesity and the evolution of man. *Journal of the American Medical Association,* 1966, *195,* 105-107.

Musante, G.J. The dietary rehabilitation clinic: Evaluative report of a behavioral and dietary treatment of obesity. *Behavior Therapy,* 1976, *7,* 198-204.

Neel, J.F. Diabetes mallitus: A "thrifty" genotype rendered detrimental by "progress?" *American Journal of Human Genetics,* 1962, *14,* 353-362.

Neuringer, A.J. Animals respond for food in the presence of free food. *Science,* 1969, *166,* 399-401.

Nisbett, R.E., & Kanouse, D.E. Obesity, food deprivation, and super-market shopping behavior. *Journal of Personality and Social Psychology,* 1969, *12,* 289-294.

Pilkington, T.R. Obesity. *Journal of Biosocial Science,* 1976, *8,* 201-204.

Robinson, R.G., Folstein, M.F., & McHugh, P.R. Reduced caloric intake following small bowel bypass surgery: A systematic study of possible causes. *Psychological Medicine,* 1979, *9,* 37-53.

Schachter, S. Obesity and eating. *Science,* 1968, *161,* 751-756.

Stalanos, P.M., Johnson, W.G., & Christ, M. Behavior modification for obesity: The evaluation of exercise, contingency management, and program adherence. *Journal of Consulting and Clinical Psychology,* 1978, *46,* 463-469.

Stricker, E.M. Hyperphagia. *The New England Journal of Medicine,* 1978, *298,* 1010-1013.

Stuart, R.B. Behavior control of overeating. *Behaviour Research and Therapy,* 1967, *5,* 357-365.

Stuart, R.B. A three-dimensional program for the treatment of obesity. *Behaviour Research and Therapy,* 1971, *9,* 177-186.

Stunkard, A.J. The management of obesity. *New York Journal of Medicine,* 1958, *58,* 79-87.

Stunkard, A.J. Environment and obesity: Recent advances in our understanding of regulation of food intake in man. *Federation Proceedings,* 1968, *6,* 1367-1373.

Stunkard, A.J. Obesity. In S. Arieti (Ed.), *American handbook of psychiatry* (Vol. 4). New York: Basic Books, 1975.

Stunkard, A.J. Behavioral treatment of obesity: The current status. *International Journal of Obesity,* 1978, *2,* 237-248.

Stunkard, A.J., & Kaplan, P. Eating in public places: A review of reports of the direct observation of eating behavior. *International Journal of Obesity,* 1977, *1,* 89-101.

Stunkard, A.J., & Penick, S.B. Behavior modification in the treatment of obesity. *Archives of General Psychiatry,* 1979, *36,* 801-806.

Stunkard, A.J., & Rush, J. Dieting and depression reexamined. *Annals of Internal Medicine,* 1974, *81,* 526-533.

Tepperman, H., & Tepperman, J. Adaptive hyperlipogenesis. *Federation Proceedings,* 1964, *23,* 73-75.

United States Senate Select Committee on Nutrition and Human Needs. *Eating in America: Dietary goals for the United States.* Cambridge, Mass.: MIT Press, 1977.

Warwick, P., Toft, R., & Garrow, J. Individual differences in energy expenditure. In G.A. Bray (Ed.), *Recent advances in obesity research* (Vol. 2). London: Newman, 1978.

Wilson, G.T. Obesity, binge eating, and behavior therapy: Some clinical observations. *Behavior Therapy,* 1976, *7,* 700-701.

Wilson, G.T. Methodological considerations in treatment outcome research on obesity. *Journal of Consulting and Clinical Psychology,* 1978, *46,* 687-702.

Wilson, G.T. Behavior therapy and the treatment of obesity. In W.R. Miller (Ed.), *Addictive disorders.* Elmsford, N.Y.: Pergamon Press, in press.

Wollersheim, J.P. Follow-up of behavioral group therapy for obesity. *Behavior Therapy,* 1977, *8,* 996-998.

Wooley, O.W., & Wooley, S.C. The experimental psychology of obesity. In T. Silverstone & J. Fincham (Eds.), *Obesity: Pathogenesis and management.* Lancaster, England: Medical and Technical Publishing, 1975.

Wooley, S.C., Wooley, O.W., & Dyrenforth, S.R. Theoretical, practical and social issues in behavioral treatments of obesity. *Journal of Applied Behavior Analysis,* 1979, *12,* 3-25.

Wysocki, T., Hall, G., Iwata, B.A., & Riordan, M. Behavioral management of exercise: Contracting for aerobic points. *Journal of Applied Behavior Analysis,* 1979, *12,* 55-64.

CHAPTER 9

Chronic Operant Pain*

Jo Ann Brockway
Department of Rehabilitation Medicine
University of Washington School of Medicine

Jeffrey C. Steger
Department of Rehabilitation Medicine
University of Washington School of Medicine

OVERVIEW OF CHRONIC OPERANT PAIN

Pain is a multifaceted and complex phenomenon that affects millions of people each year. It is one of the most pervasive complaints of consumers in the health care system and one of the most common disabling conditions. Its annual economic cost has been estimated to be between 40 and 50 billion dollars (Bonica, 1979). As Weisenberg (1977) observes, pain is "the basis of a multimillion-dollar drug industry that promises relief to the thousands who are guided by the societal norm in which ills are dealt with by popping the right pill" (p. 1008).

Although pain may be one of the most common problems of persons seeking health care, it is by no means a well-defined disorder. Melzack (1973) notes that "pain has obvious sensory qualities, but it also

*The authors wish to acknowledge the contribution made by Wilbert E. Fordyce, Ph. D., in developing the concept of and a treatment approach to chronic operant pain. The conceptual framework and much of the treatment strategies presented in this chapter are based on his work.

The preparation of this manuscript was supported in part by Research and Training Center Grant #16-P-56818/0 from the Rehabilitation Services Administration.

has emotional and motivational properties. It is usually caused by intense, noxious stimulation, yet it sometimes occurs spontaneously without apparent cause. It normally signals physical injury, but it sometimes fails to occur even when extensive areas of the body have been seriously injured; at other times it persists after all the injured tissues have been healed and becomes a crippling problem that requires urgent, radical treatment" (p. 11). Liebeskind and Paul (1977) have further stated, "Pain means many different things, and the variables which correlate with, inhibit or enhance one kind of pain, and the neural mechanisms which underlie it, may not be associated with or influence other kinds. Thus, one must distinguish between the normal perception of noxious stimuli and pain of pathological origin, and between pathological pain and chronic, intractable pain conditions" (pp. 41-42).

The distinction between acute pain of pathological origin and chronic, intractable pain is crucial to any discussion of treatment. Acute pain, such as that from appendicitis or a recently broken leg or sprained back, most often serves as a warning signal that damage to body tissue is occurring or impending. Acute pain generally requires medical attention to identify and treat the organic pathology. When treatment is successful, the pain is alleviated.

The picture of chronic pain, however, is quite different. In chronic pain problems the painful sensation does not necessarily reflect an underlying pathological condition or the presence or threat of tissue damage, though, as in chronic arthritis or cancer, it of course may. Most often chronic pain results from a complex interaction involving the history of the pathological condition, the iatrogenic effects of various treatment attempts, the environmental consequences of the original condition, and a host of psychological, emotional, and cognitive factors.

Chronic pain occurs when diagnostic procedures and treatments fail to resolve the acute pain problem. As the pain problem persists, the patient's lifestyle changes. In the acute pain situation, a temporary disruption in the individual's activities may occur; chronicity allows for these disruptions to become systematic changes in the habit patterns of the patient and his or her family. The patient may not have worked for several years, and family members may have taken over a number of his or her household responsibilities. His or her skills may have also diminished. If the patient has not worked for several years, he or she may not have kept up with job-related skills or with advances in his or her field. Conversational skills may have become focused rather narrowly on pain and health-related topics. Finally, his or her behavioral repertoire may become restricted as he or she discontinues social and recreational activities. In short, when pain becomes chronic, many aspects of the individual's lifestyle are likely to undergo change.

The present chapter is concerned with chronic pain rather than acute pain. Specifically, it focuses on the use of homework assignments in the treatment of chronic operant pain, that is, the chronic pain problem for which probable reinforcers can be specified.

The concept of chronic operant pain, developed by Fordyce and his associates (Fordyce, 1979; Fordyce, Fowler, & deLateur, 1968; Fordyce, Fowler, Lehmann, & deLateur, 1968), is based on the notion that pain is behavior. Since one cannot see the transmission of nerve impulses from sensory receptors to the brain, the health care professional (or family or friends) knows that the patient is experiencing pain only when he or she exhibits certain behaviors. These behaviors may be verbal messages such as complaints, requests for medication, or moans or sighs, or nonverbal behaviors such as taking medication, limping, grimacing, massaging part of the body, or lying in bed. If such behaviors do not occur, a clinical pain problem does not exist.

If pain is behavior, then, like any other behavior, it can be modified by its consequences. Chronic operant pain is acquired much as are many other behaviors — through the systematic occurrence of behavior-consequence sequences (Fordyce, 1976). These sequences may be caused by direct or indirect reinforcement of pain behaviors, as well as by punishment or simple nonreinforcement of nonpain, or well, behaviors by the individual's environment.

Direct reinforcement of pain behavior may occur when the behavior is followed by a positive outcome, such as attention from a normally inattentive spouse, expressions of sympathy from friends, or helpful behavior from children or spouse that does not typically otherwise occur. Medications may also be potent reinforcers, since those that are prescribed for pain relief often also alleviate anxiety or produce a general overall pleasurable feeling. To the individual, these pleasurable effects become pain-contingent.

Pain behaviors may be reinforced indirectly by the avoidance of unpleasant activity. For a worker who is injured after having been promoted to a supervisory position in which he or she feels unable to perform adequately, pain may be reinforced by time off from work, which allows the avoidance of a stressful situation. For older people who have experienced a decline in intellectual abilities, pain may provide a time out from activities that are likely to reveal, to themselves or others, their intellectual deficits.

Finally, well behaviors may go unreinforced or may be punished. Family members may scold the person to "take it easy" or "lie down and rest" when he or she attempts to engage in well behavior. The person who has been on bed rest or limited activity and is somewhat deconditioned may attempt to engage in rather strenuous activity and then experience discomfort. Thus activity, or well behavior, is followed by pain, or punishment.

It often appears that persons who suffer from chronic operant pain are caught in a cycle where activity leads to increased pain, which is followed by rest, which leads to decrease in pain, which is followed by activity, and so on, *ad infinitum,* so that activity is continually punished and inactivity is continually reinforced. The person therefore does less and less, resulting in further physical deconditioning and increased discomfort when activity is attempted.

HOMEWORK-BASED TREATMENT

Overview of Treatment

The patient with chronic operant pain most often presents multiple problem areas, including medication abuse, excessive exhibition of pain behaviors, physical deconditioning, a decreased range and amount of functional activities, and vocational impairment. Thus the treatment of chronic operant pain frequently necessitates a well-coordinated multidisciplinary program typically involving medication reduction, nonreinforcement of pain behavior, reinforcement of well behavior, physical reconditioning, generalization of improved strength and endurance to functional activities, patient and family behavior training, and vocational evaluation and training. A brief review of each of these components follows. The reader who desires a more thorough discussion of the treatment approach should consult Fordyce (1976).

Medication reduction is usually accomplished with the pain cocktail (Fordyce, 1976; Halpern, 1973). During the evaluation period, a medication-usage baseline is established. The patient may take as much medication (within limits of safe medical prudence) as he or she requests. The types and amounts taken are recorded. When treatment begins, medications are given in liquid form and consist of active ingredients combined with a taste-masking vehicle such as cherry syrup. The type and concentration of active ingredients in the cocktail is determined by the baseline medication usage. The pain cocktail is administered on a strict time-contingent basis, for example, every 4 hours. This practice breaks up the relationship between pain behavior (requesting and taking medication) and positive reinforcement (pleasurable effects of medication), since time rather than expressions of pain determine when medication will be received. However, the 24-hour level of ingested analgesic remains the same, yielding an overall pain medication management strategy of equivalent strength.

Nonreinforcement of pain behavior and reinforcement of well behavior are practiced by all members of the treatment team. Staff members allow for nonreinforcement by responding neutrally to pain behavior, such as by dropping eye contact, changing the subject, or simply making no social response. Social reinforcement is provided for well behaviors such as socially appropriate conversation, exercises, or productive activity. In an inpatient treatment program, passes off the ward can be made contingent on the successful completion of prescribed exercises and activities and are generally designed to be consistent with the patients' endurance levels as exhibited during therapies.

Physical reconditioning is accomplished using an exercise and activity program. First, baseline levels of various exercises and activities for each individual's specific pain problem are chosen. The patient is told to do as many of each exercise as he or she can before pain, fatigue, or weakness makes him or her want to stop. Daily quotas are then set for each exercise, beginning at a level that is less than what the patient has done and increasing gradually to a level compatible with the individual's age and physical condition. The patient monitors his or her progress by keeping records of exercises and activities done. As the patient's strength and endurance increase, more functional activities such as social and recreational activities or household chores are systematically introduced into the treatment program, often through homework assignments.

Patient and family behavior training are also important aspects of treatment that utilize homework assignments. Spouses and family members are taught to recognize and avoid reinforcing pain behaviors and to reinforce well behaviors. Patients are often taught biofeedback or other relaxation techniques to control tension-related discomfort. Depending on the patient's needs, assertion training, social-skills training, weight control, marital communication and problem solving, or parenting skills may be incorporated into the treatment program.

Vocational evaluation and training are often included in the treatment program. When a sufficient level of strength and endurance is reached, the patient may begin a job station where he or she performs work in a job-like setting. The patient may be evaluated for general work skills, such as punctuality, or for his or her ability to perform a specific job skill, such as clerical work or electronics assembly. The amount of time and responsibility given to the patient on the job station are increased systematically over the course of treatment.

Homework Assignments

Homework plays an important and crucial role in all phases of treatment. It is used to assist in the assessment of the patient's pain problem, monitor patient progress, aid in the generalization of improved strength and endurance to functional activities, enhance specific skills of the patient and family, and improve maintenance of treatment gains.

Assessment. Homework is used in the initial evaluation* of the patient's pain problem to help determine whether there appears to be an operant component to the pain and to assess the patient's baseline level of functioning. Before the patient is seen for evaluation, he or she is sent activity diaries (as shown in Figure 9.1) to complete and return.

Assignment: Complete a diary page each day, filling it in a little bit at a time several times a day. Indicate what major activity you engaged in for each hour block of time in a 24-hour day in each of three categories — sitting, standing or walking, and reclining. Record each episode of medication usage, including what medication was taken and in what amounts. Record hourly pain levels using a scale of 0 to 10, where 0 indicates no pain and 10 indicates unbearable pain.

These diaries are to be completed for a 2-week period and mailed in when completed. The evaluation is scheduled when the diaries are received.

The activity diaries provide information on the relationships between activity, rest, and pain, and the time patterns of pain fluctuation and medication usage. Such information suggests hypotheses about the nature of the patient's pain problem that may be further pursued in the evaluation interviews. For example, the patient who reports taking narcotics or other types of medications with roughly consistent time intervals between doses may be addicted or habituated to that medication. In such a case, the issue of medication usage warrants careful exploration. Activity diaries also provide information about the patient's baseline levels of functioning, for example, what proportion of the patient's time is spent sitting, standing or walking, and reclining. The patient who spends a near-normal amount of time in productive activities may have little to gain from an operant treatment program that emphasizes a systematic, gradual increase in activities.

Monitoring of progress. Once the treatment program has begun, the patient monitors his or her progress by keeping graphs of his or her prescribed exercises and activities (Figure 9.2). The patient may keep a graph of the number of laps walked, the number of miles ridden on a stationary bicycle, the number of rows completed on a weaving project, or the number of pounds lost.

---

*"Initial evaluation" here refers to the initial evaluation made by the behavioral therapist to assess the extent to which pain behaviors are reinforced by the environment. A thorough medical evaluation of the pain problem is typically completed before or in conjunction with the behavioral evaluation. The information from the medical and behavioral evaluation is pooled to determine whether the patient appears to be a good candidate for an operant approach to treatment.

Figure 9.1   Sample activity diary

Day: _____ *Thursday* _____   Date: _____ *4/18/81* _____

	SITTING		WALKING		RECLINING		MEDICATIONS		PAIN LEVEL
	Major Activity	Time (min)	Major Activity	Time (min)	Major Activity	Time (min)	Amt.	Type	
12-1 am					Reading	60	100 mg	Darvocet-N	7
1-2 am					Reading	60	300 mg	Noludar 300	7
2-3 am	Reading	30			Rest/ Sleep	30			6
3-4 am					Rest/ Sleep	60			7
4-5 am	Rest	15			Rest/ Sleep	45	100 mg	Darvocet-N	7
5-6 am					Sleep	60			
6-7 am					Sleep	60			
7-8 am					Sleep	60			
8-9 am					Sleep	60			
9-10 am	Reading	45	Grooming	15			100 mg	Darvocet-N	7
10-11 am	Rest	60					10 mg	Flexeril	8
11-12 am	Reading	60							8
12-1 pm					Rest	60	200 mg	Darvocet-N	9
1-2 pm					Rest	60			9
2-3 pm	TV	60					8 mg	Periactin	8
3-4 pm	TV	60					100 mg	Darvocet-N	8
4-5 pm	Rest	15	Grooming	30	Rest	15			9
5-6 pm			Doctor's Appt.	60			100 mg	Demerol IM (in office)	9
6-7 pm	Riding/ Dinner	60							3
7-8 pm	Dinner/ TV	60					10 mg	Flexeril	2
8-9 pm	TV/ Sleep	60					8 mg	Periactin	4
9-10 pm	TV	60							4
10-11 pm			Grooming	15	Playing cards	45	300 mg 100 mg	Noludar 300 Darvocet-N	5
11-12 pm					Playing cards	60			4

Total Hours   Sitting = 9:45   Walking = 2:00   Reclining = 12:15
(Hours Sitting + Hours Walking + Hours Reclining = 24 Hours)

Assignment: Keep a record of the amount of each prescribed exercise or activity performed by recording it on the appropriate graph (Figure 9.2).

Assignment: Record the data on the graph at appropriate intervals that are specific to the exercise or activity;* keep the

Figure 9.2   Sample exercise graph

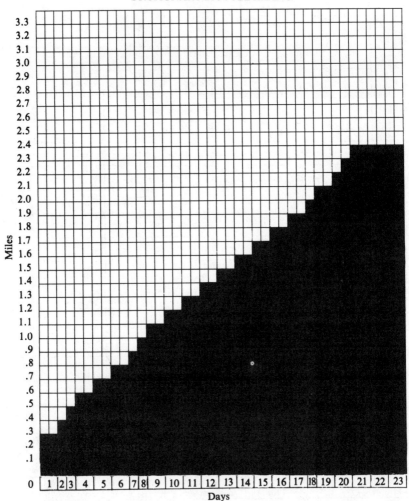

STATIONARY BICYCLE RIDING

Miles

Days

*For example, weight is recorded twice a week if the patient is instructed to weigh twice weekly, and miles ridden on the bicycle are recorded twice daily if the patient rides the bicycle twice a day.

graphs in a notebook provided by the therapist and carry them at all times to all assigned treatment activities.

Feedback from the graphs clearly shows the patient's gains. He or she is also given verbal reinforcement by the therapist and other members of the treatment team who view and comment on the graphs. The graphs provide feedback not only to the patient but to the entire team.

Activity diaries are also used throughout the treatment program to monitor progress and to provide feedback to the patient. They are essentially the same as those used in assessing the pain problem (shown in Figure 9.1), except that the patient does not record hourly pain levels. The instructions are essentially the same except that the diaries are delivered to the therapist weekly. The therapist then constructs a graph showing the average number of hours per day the patient spent sitting, standing or walking, and reclining for that week and discusses the graph with the patient. (An example is shown in Figure 9.3.)

Generalization to functional activities. One of the primary aims of treatment is to allow patients to engage in an increased range and level of

Figure 9.3   Sample graph of uptime, sitting, standing, and reclining

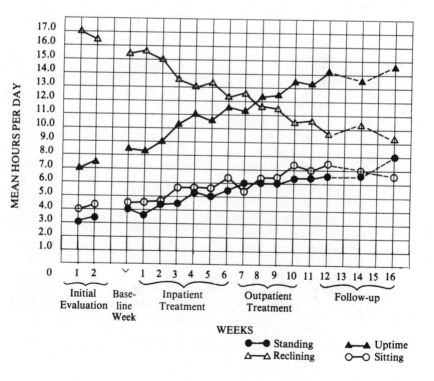

functional activities. Thus an important component of treatment is the use of homework assignments that facilitate the resumption of any number of social activities, avocational pursuits, or household chores. Such assignments may be given to be completed in the inpatient setting, on a pass out of the hospital, or in an outpatient program and are directed towards the goals of each particular patient. The patient's spouse or another family member may also be given an assignment if the goal involves the spouse or family. It is essential that all assignments be within the patient's strength and endurance capabilities. Appropriate breaks or changes in type of activity should be planned as well to facilitate endurance.

The patient who wishes to resume the household responsibility of vacuuming the floors may be given an activity assignment to vacuum a specific area of floor space at home once he or she has reached a point in increased strength and endurance that would permit him or her to accomplish that activity, *and* once he or she has performed that or a functionally similar activity using proper body mechanics and techniques in the structured occupational therapy situation. The homework assignment may then be carefully planned between patient and therapist, including appropriate breaks in the activity. Following is one example:

Assignment: Vacuum only the living room and dining room at home on Saturday afternoon without moving any heavy furniture; take a 15-minute sit-down break before and after doing the vacuuming.

The following recording assignment is then added:

Assignment: Record the activity and breaks in the activity diary.

As usual, the diary is to be brought to the next therapy session, at which time the success of the assignment is discussed. The therapist reviews the record with the patient and provides social reinforcement for having accomplished the assignment.

It is frequently necessary to use a series of graded activity assignments. A second assignment might therefore add the kitchen and hallway to be vacuumed along with the living and dining rooms, with two bedrooms added for the third assignment.

As another example, the patient and spouse who wish to resume playing tennis together might be given a series of assignments to play increasing amounts of tennis at regular intervals.

Assignment: Play tennis twice a week, beginning with a 20-minute session, and increasing by 10 minutes a session until a 60-minute session is reached.

Assignment: Record each session in your activity diary.

The therapist then provides social reinforcement for the increasing well behavior. In addition, the spouse will be programmed to provide feedback to the patient regarding enjoyment of the activity. Presumably, playing tennis will be enjoyable to the patient and thus be reinforcing in and of itself.

Enhancement of specific skills. The acquisition and enhancement of specific skills by the patient and family members is a vital part of the treatment program and typically involves the use of homework assignments. The specific skills to be acquired or enhanced depend upon the skill deficits of each particular patient or family. Very often spouses and other family members consistently, and frequently unknowingly, provide reinforcement for pain behaviors. In such cases the spouse (or family member) is instructed in the identification and nonreinforcement of pain behaviors and is given assignments to practice these skills outside of the treatment session. The spouse may then be given the following assignments:

Assignment: Identify and count the patient's pain behaviors over two 20-minute intervals, once on the ward and once off the ward.

Assignment: Record the number of pain behaviors observed.

The spouse is to bring the record of pain behaviors observed to the next therapy session. The next assignment may be as follows:

Assignment: Identify the patient's pain behaviors and also what you (the spouse) do or say when such pain behaviors occur.

This assignment could be done over a pass with the patient and/or during telephone calls.

Assignment: Record the pain behavior that occurred and your (the spouse's) response to it. Bring this information to the next session.

When this step is accomplished, the spouse will be taught how to respond in a neutral, nonreinforcing manner to the patient's pain behaviors. Such responses may be modeled by the therapist and practiced by the spouse in the therapy session. The following homework assignments may then be given.

Assignment: Note the occurrence of pain behavior and respond to it in a nonreinforcing manner, as practiced in the therapy session.

Assignment: Record occurrence of pain behavior and your response to it and bring information to the next session.

This assignment may be given repeatedly throughout treatment to improve and maintain the skill of not reinforcing pain behavior.

Development and enhancement of relaxation skills are often an important part of the patient's treatment program. Relaxation may be taught using biofeedback or other relaxation training methods. The patient first receives an explanation of the treatment rationale and techniques. Treatment sessions are scheduled from one to four times weekly. A client receiving biofeedback for general stress management may be given the following assignments:

Assignment: Practice the biofeedback techniques for 20 minutes twice a day.

Assignment: Record the number of minutes of practice and when practice occurred, and record hourly stress levels on a 0 to 10 scale.

These data are brought to the next treatment session for discussion with the therapist.

As the patient improves in his or her tension-reduction skills, he or she may be loaned equipment for use in the specific situations in which the tension occurs. In each case the patient is assigned the following:

Assignment: Use the portable equipment to practice tension reduction each time the tension-producing situation occurs.

Assignment: Record when the tension-producing situation occurred and the stress levels before and after you use the tension-reduction techniques; bring these data in at the next session to be reviewed with the therapist.

The use of homework appears to enhance results in biofeedback training. Steger and Harper (1980) compared two groups of subjects receiving biofeedback or relaxation tapes for treatment of tension headache. In general, both groups learned equal amounts of muscle tension reduction. However, those in the "high" compliance group regarding homework assignments showed greater clinical improvement in terms of subjective headache pain than did those who demonstrated less than 50 percent adherence to the exercise assignments.

Maintenance of treatment gains. An attempt is made to maximize the maintenance of gains made during treatment by using homework assignments directed towards establishing nonpain habits in the home environment. One technique used is a type of "inoculation" against pain behavior in situations where that behavior was previously exhibited. Although the spouse and close family members are involved in treatment, obviously not everyone who is aware of the patient's pain problem can be involved in the treatment. The patient must therefore learn how to respond to friends, coworkers, and other well-wishers who ask, "How do you feel?" or, "Did they fix (help) your back?" The patient is asked how he or she would respond to such questions, and possible response alternatives are discussed. Roleplaying may be used to enable the patient to rehearse appropriate responses. A related assignment is given:

> **Assignment:** Get involved in a situation, such as a social gathering, where questions regarding pain are likely to be encountered. Respond appropriately to such inquiries and note what others say regarding health or pain and your responses.

> **Assignment:** Record those examples and bring them into the next therapy session for discussion with the therapist.

Another type of homework assignment frequently given involves activity planning. Often when a patient with chronic pain "feels well," he or she engages in an activity that is beyond his or her capacity, and then "pays for it" with increased pain. The patient must therefore learn to schedule activities more appropriately within his or her limitations and avoid activities that are not within those limitations. Guidelines for scheduling activities are discussed in the therapy sessions, and early in the program passes off the ward are planned jointly by the patient and therapist. The following assignments are then given:

> **Assignment:** Follow the guidelines for scheduled activities.

> **Assignment:** Plan the pass schedule in detail, specifying what activities, at what times and length, are to be done.

> **Assignment:** Write down the schedule and bring it into the therapy session so that it may be reviewed with the therapist before the pass.

If necessary, changes are made in the schedule to render it more compatible with the patient's capabilities. The following assignment is also given:

> **Assignment:** During the pass, continue to record activities in the activity diary.

These records are discussed in the next therapy session following the pass. Such homework assignments continue throughout the inpatient program and into the outpatient phase.

When the patient begins the outpatient phase of the program, particularly as the hospital-based portion of treatment is decreased and more outside activities are assigned, he or she will be given homework of longer duration. An example is the following:

Assignment: Make and record a schedule of activities for several days or a week at a time for review with the therapist.

COMPLIANCE ENHANCEMENT PROCEDURES

Several procedures for enhancing patient compliance with the pain treatment program have evolved over time and have become standard programmed steps for virtually every patient. Many of these techniques were initially incorporated into the treatment program on an empirical basis, that is, because they "worked." As the follow-up discussion will show, however, most of the techniques related nicely to one or more of the propositions presented in Chapter 3.

The first step in enhancing compliance is providing an explanation of the treatment rationale. The patient and spouse or other family member are given a careful explanation of the treatment rationale, including an explanation of pain as behavior, how pain behavior can be learned, and the difference between acute and chronic pain. This explanation is made both before and after the patient is admitted for treatment, but before treatment begins. The patient is also given a written handout which explains the rationale and treatment.

Repetition of the rationale is considered necessary because for most patients and their families the notion of pain as a behavior is unfamiliar. Many accept that pain is either "real" (that is, caused by underlying physiological pathology) or "all in your head" (that is, caused by underlying psychological pathology). Patients may have been told that their pain is not real, a suggestion which often serves only to reinforce their search for a medical or physiological cure. It is therefore necessary to carefully explain the treatment rationale so that the patient and his or her family understand that the concept of learned pain is congruent with the notion that pain is quite real. This understanding aids in enlisting compliance with the treatment program in two ways. It helps build a good relationship between the therapist and the patient and family members, and it provides a framework within which the treatment program, including systematic behavioral assignments, can be presented.

A behavioral contract is the second step in enhancing compliance. This contract lists the main elements of the program — use of the pain cocktail, nonreinforcement of pain behavior, exercise quotas, record-keeping responsibilities, and the rationale for each. A copy is given to each patient and is reviewed in detail in a conference involving the patient, the spouse, and members of the treatment team. Each separate item in the proposal is discussed. Thus, the patient and his or her family know what treatment will entail. They then take time to discuss the program among themselves and to make an informed and (hopefully) carefully considered decision about proceeding with treatment. Thus the patient who decides to proceed makes an overt commitment to the treatment program, including the completion of homework assignments.

Compliance-contingent reinforcers are used as a third method for increasing adherence to the program. Reinforcers such as passes off the ward can be contingent upon the patient's having completed his or her quotas. Completion of assignments is monitored by each team member in his or her treatment area. Thus, the entire team is observing the patient's compliance and progress and the feedback from numerous sources effectively enhances follow-through. Passes may also be made contingent upon the patient and his or her family having adequately completed relevant homework assignments. For example, appropriate scheduling of pass activities may be a prerequisite for receiving a pass. Such contingency arrangements, when used as part of treatment, must be explained to the patient *before* treatment begins. It is also extremely important that the therapist review completed assignments with the patient and provide feedback regarding progress. In addition, the therapist should collect activity diaries each week, keep a graph of mean daily uptime, sitting time, etc., and review these data each week with the patient. When homework assignments are reinforced in these ways, we have found that compliance is rarely a problem.

The fourth step in enhancing compliance involves therapist specification of treatment tasks. Assignments such as making a weekend pass activity schedule should be preceded by therapist instructions regarding specific strategies for scheduling pass activities. Assignments involving observation and recording of pain behaviors can be modeled by the therapist and practiced by the spouse as a prelude to actually attempting the task. Homework assignments should also specify how much the patient is to do. The patient may be instructed, for example, to practice relaxation for 20 minutes two times a day, to mow only the front lawn, or to play six holes of golf.

It should be noted that although the above-mentioned techniques for enhancing compliance are those most regularly used in the pain treatment program, they are by no means the only methods used. Other techniques, such as skill training or cognitive rehearsal, are also used when appropriate to improve compliance with homework assignments and ultimately to augment success in the treatment program.

ILLUSTRATIVE CASE

Mr. R. was a 45-year-old married man with chronic low back and right leg pain of 3 years' duration. He had been employed cleaning machinery in a recycling plant and had caught his leg in a piece of machinery, sustaining a back sprain and an ankle fracture that required surgery. After the surgery he developed an infection in his leg that caused swelling and pain. After 3 months he returned to work for 15 days, during which time he sustained a double hernia that necessitated surgical repair. He did not return to work, and since that time had gained 75 pounds. Preevaluation activity diaries completed by Mr. R. indicated that he spent about 18 hours a day reclining, less than 2 hours a day standing, and about 4 hours a day sitting. Medication intake was moderate.

The initial evaluation disclosed that at the time of injury Mr. R. had been married for 3 months to his second wife, a nurse 18 years his senior. He had been divorced from his first wife following a "nervous breakdown" that had resulted in a year-long psychiatric hospitalization some 7 years previously. Before his breakdown Mr. R. had had a good employment record. He began working at the age of 14, had worked steadily, and had held two jobs throughout much of his first marriage. When he met his second wife, however, he was "down and out." He stated that he was depressed, drank too much, and was unemployed. He credited his second wife with "picking me up by my bootstraps" and "putting me on my feet." She helped him overcome his depression, decrease his use of alcohol, and find employment.

The behavioral evaluation suggested that there were likely reinforcers for Mr. R's pain behavior. After his leg become infected, Ms. R. quit her job to take care of him. She was very sympathic and nurturing, asked him frequently how he felt, waited on him, and discouraged his attempts at activity. He continued to do minor repairs and cosmetic modifications to their home and also took care of the plants. Ms. R. indicated that she enjoyed his being home all the time and their being able to spend so much time together.

It was decided to admit Mr. R. to the Operant Program. Baseline activities showed that he had decreased strength and endurance and was generally physically deconditioned. He could sit or stand for only 20 to 30 minutes at a time. A treatment program was designed and reviewed with Mr. and Ms. R. and the treatment team. Mr. and Ms. R. agreed to the program. Mr. R.'s goals for treatment included being able to sit for 2 hours at a time, stand for up to 4 hours so he could go shopping with his wife, walk 2 miles, squat and bend, lift 25 pounds, and lose 50 pounds.

Specific aspects of the program included physical reconditioning, weight reduction, vocational exploration, and skill training for Ms. R. in both identifying and neutrally responding to pain behaviors and in positively reinforcing rather than discouraging well behaviors. Homework assignments were used in all of these. As Mr. R. progressed, he also began a job station to generalize increased strength and endurance to more functional activities. Passes out of the hospital were contingent on his fullfilling his treatment quotas. Specific homework assignments designed to increase his participation in household chores and recreational activities during his passes were given. Over time he was able to resume several activities in which he had previously engaged, including cooking, yardwork, shopping with his wife, and fishing. A return-to-work program was laid out with Mr. R. which included a gradual increase from part-time to full-time employment over 2 months.

SUMMARY

Pain can be either acute or chronic. Acute pain usually is of pathological origin, while chronic pain may or may not indicate illness or tissue damage. Chronic operant pain, the subject of this chapter, often disrupts the patient's normal activities and home life. Such pain is seen here as a behavior, which can be acquired and modified like other behaviors. There may be direct reinforcers for pain, such as sympathy or medication, or indirect reinforcers, such as avoidance of aversive activity. Well behaviors may even be punished by family members. The patient suffering from chronic pain may also get caught in a cycle of activity leading to pain, which causes the person to become inactive and so relieve the pain, which in turn allows increased activity again resulting in pain, so that activity is punished and inactivity reinforced.

Because patients often have multiple problems, treatment may include medication reduction, nonreinforcement of pain behavior, reinforcement of well behavior, physical reconditioning, generalization of improved physical condition to functional activities, patient and family behavior training, and vocational evaluation and training. Homework plays an important part in treatment, especially in the areas of assessment, monitoring of progress, generalization of improvements in strength and endurance to functional activities, enhancement of specific skills of the patient and family, and maintenance of treatment gains. Sample assignments are provided and explained.

Four main steps to enhance compliance are taken in this program. First, the treatment rationale is carefully explained to the patient and family members. Since many of them believe that pain is either exclusively mental or physical, the concept of learned pain needs to be clarified. Providing this understanding helps in building a good relationship between the therapist and the patient and family members, and it provides a general framework within which the program can be presented. A behavioral contract is the second step in enhancing compliance. Through the contract all the elements of the program are made clear, and the patient makes an overt commitment to comply. The third step is the use of compliance-contingent reinforcers. For this to be effective, the patient must understand the contingency prior to treatment, assignments must be reviewed by the therapist after completion, and progress records must be kept and shown to the patient. The final step is therapist specification of assignments. Other techniques such as skill training or cognitive rehearsal may also be added.

Mr. R., a 45-year-old man with chronic back and leg pain, is the subject of the illustrative case. He had been injured in accidents at work, and was being reinforced by his wife for remaining incapacitated. His treatment included physical reconditioning, weight reduction, vocational exploration, and, later, generalization of his increased strength and endurance to functional activities. His wife also received skill training in responding neutrally to pain behaviors and reinforcing well behaviors. Over time Mr. R. was able to resume several normal activities and finally return to full-time work.

REFERENCES

Bonica, J.J. Important clinical aspects of acute and chronic pain. In R.F. Beers, Jr., & E.G. Bassett (Eds.), *Mechanisms of pain and analgesic compounds.* New York: Raven Press, 1979.

Fordyce, W.E. *Behavioral methods for chronic pain and illness.* St. Louis: C.V. Mosby, 1976.

Fordyce, W.E. An operant conditioning method for managing chronic pain. *Postgraduate Medicine,* 1973, *53,* 123-128.

Fordyce, W.E., Fowler, R.S., & deLateur, B.J. An application of behavior modification technique to a problem of chronic pain. *Behaviour Research and Therapy,* 1968, *6,* 105-107.

Fordyce, W.E., Fowler, R.S., Lehmann, J.F., & deLateur, B.J. Some implications of learning in problems of chronic pain. *Journal of Chronic Diseases,* 1968, *21,* 179-190.

Halpern, L.M. Analgesics and other drugs for relief of pain. *Postgraduate Medicine,* 1973, *53,* 91-100.

Liebeskind, J.C., & Paul, L.A. Psychological and physiological mechanisms of pain. *Annual Review of Psychology,* 1977, *28,* 41-60.

Melzack, R. *The puzzle of pain.* New York: Harper & Row, 1973.

Steger, J.C., & Harper, R.G. EMG biofeedback versus self-monitored relaxation in the treatment of tension headaches. *Headache,* 1980, *20,* 137-142.

Weisenberg, M. Pain and pain control. *Psychological Bulletin,* 1977, *84,* 1008-1044.

CHAPTER 10

Sexual Dysfunction

John L. Shelton
Department of Rehabilitation Medicine
University of Washington School of Medicine

OVERVIEW OF SEXUAL DYSFUNCTION

Highly noted experts such as Masters and Johnson (1966, 1970), Annon (1974, 1975a), and Heiman, LoPiccolo, and LoPiccolo (1976) have all indicated that dysfunction of the human sexual response is extremely common. Although precise numbers are difficult to obtain, many researchers agree that about 15 percent of all women have never experienced an orgasm (Hunt, 1974), a percentage that has remained essentially unchanged since the Kinsey report 20 years earlier (Kinsey, Pomeroy, Martin, & Gebhard, 1953). In addition, it is generally concluded that about 50 percent of all couples involved in an intimate, long-standing sexual relationship experience sexual difficulties (Robinson, 1974).

Until recently, sexual dysfunctions were accepted as symptomatic of "deep-seated" personality disturbances that reflected the impact of instinctual drives, developmental changes, and critical early childhood experiences. This theoretical viewpoint asserted that sexual dysfunctions could be treated only by individual insight-oriented psychotherapy requiring "an appointment several times a week for a minimum of eight months" (Bergler, 1947).

Treatment prospects based on this theoretical stance were meager. For example, Coleman (1964) stated that it "may be difficult or impossible to modify frigidity once it is well established." Other writers such as Hastings (1967) reported virtually no success with such problems as erectile failure and premature ejaculation. However, beginning in the early 1970s, this negative outlook changed dramatically.

The emergence of an alternative approach to the treatment of sexual dysfunction was highlighted by the landmark publication of Masters and Johnson's *Human Sexual Inadequacy* (1970). These authors described an approach involving brief, time-limited directive counseling aimed at behavior change rather than attainment of insight and resolution of intrapsychic conflicts. Before Masters and Johnson's (1970) publication, a number of behaviorally oriented researchers had begun treating sexual dysfunctions with behavioral methods (Lazarus, 1963; Wolpe, 1958), but it was the former publication by Masters and Johnson that captured the public interest in the "new sex therapy."

The theoretical background supporting the effectiveness of behaviorally oriented treatments for sexual dysfunction is based on the assumption that human sexual behaviors are primarily the result of learning. This particular assumption has been suggested repeatedly over the past 25 years by a number of writers. Ford and Beach (1948), Kinsey, Pomeroy, Martin, and Gebhard (1953), Michelmore (1964), and Ullmann and Krasner (1967) have all voiced this viewpoint. However, it has been only recently that this position has gained empirical support. Researchers such as Annon (1973), LoPiccolo and Lobitz (1972), LoPiccolo, Stewart, and Watkins (1972), Marquis (1970), and Razani (1972) have all conducted research that supports the hypothesis that sexual dysfunction is a result of learning. The essence of this viewpoint is that there are no separate principles that explain deviant and normal sexual behavior. All sexual behaviors are learned through the same means. This argument does not preclude the impact of biological variables on sexual responses; it merely argues that the form and direction of the human sexual response may be attributed to learning.

The behavioral conception of the treatment of sexual dysfunctions has produced virtually standardized procedures for eliminating or reducing sexual problems. Although the behavioral approach to treating sexual dysfunctions has been conceptualized as a reduction of performance demands (Masters & Johnson, 1970), as *in vivo* systematic desensitization (Wolpe, 1958), as a mode of helping stop the couple's attempt to control an involuntary behavior (Haley, 1973), or as a way of reducing anxiety through specific suggestions based on successive approximations (Annon, 1974), the procedures used to treat sexual problems remain much the same. This chapter will outline some of the basic similarities among the various behavioral approaches to the treatment of sexual dysfunction and then share examples of home practice assignments used during treatment.

We also want to add that this chapter focuses on heterosexual sexual behavior. While the techniques described may also be used in gay and lesbian sexual interactions, we have not focused on these interactions here.

HOMEWORK-BASED TREATMENT

Overview of Treatment

It is our view that all sexual problems are shared disorders. Thus, the wife of a husband suffering from retarded ejaculation is seen as partially responsible for the development and maintenance of his disorder. During treatment, therefore, both partners are considered responsible for future change, and systematic behavioral assignments are given to both.

Therapeutic homework is absolutely essential in the treatment of sex dysfunction. LoPiccolo and LoPiccolo (1978) state, "If there is any one procedure that is the hallmark of the treatment of sexual dysfunction it is the prescription by the therapist of a series of gradual steps of specific sexual behavior to be performed by the patients in their own home" (p. 6). Giving systematic behavioral assignments is a highly structured, client-controlled method of increasing client sexual information, effecting attitude change, eliminating performance anxiety, improving communication surrounding sexual topics, and improving sexual technique.

We view sex therapy as largely pedagogical, with the dissemination of information and subsequent practice of sexual behaviors being the primary modes of therapy. Clients learn by listening to the therapist, by doing bibliotherapeutic reading, by using educational films or audio cassettes, and by practicing. Outside practice involves the direct alteration of covert and overt sexual behaviors.

Homework Assignments

Assessment. Assessment of sexual dysfunction can take several forms. The structured interview, structured questionnaires, and tailor-made self-monitoring approaches can all be used. Within the context of the structured interview, clients should answer the questions shown in Table 10.1.

In some cases time can be saved by giving the couple a list containing these questions with instructions to answer them at home before the next session. This practice is often an excellent way of determining the couple's motivation for therapy, since couples who fail

Table 10.1
Diagnostic Questions for Sexual Dysfunction

---

1. What is the nature of the problem? How would the client behave differently if the problem were eliminated?

2. When did the problem begin?

3. How does the problem affect the sexual response of the partner?

4. What are the goals of the client and of the couple as a whole? Are the goals discrepant?

5. What is the client's concept of effective sexual functioning?

6. If the client is a woman, has she ever been orgasmic? Under what circumstances?

7. If the client is a man, has he ever had erectile or ejaculatory difficulties before?

8. What is the couple's concept of the appropriate male or female role in respect to their sexual behavior? Who is expected to initiate sexual activities?

9. Describe the first sexual relationship. Describe the first sexual contact in the current interpersonal relationship.

10. Has either partner been involved in a sexual affair outside their relationship? Is either currently involved in this manner?

11. What is the frequency of the client's masturbatory activity? How does the current frequency compare with earlier times?

12. If the client has sexual fantasies during masturbation or intercourse, what are they?

13. What is the current frequency of sexual intercourse and other sexual activities?

14. What has the greatest influence on the quantity and quality of the client's sexual activities?

15. What displeases both partners sexually? What is the most pleasing sexual behavior? Do they communicate their desires in these two areas?

16. Has the client received treatment for sexual problems before? With whom and why have they returned for additional treatment?

17. Has the couple sought psychotherapy? What was the outcome? Was a behavioral treatment used? Were home assignments given? If so, what was the extent of adherence to the prescribed activities?

18. What does the client expect will happen in treatment?

19. What is the condition of the marriage aside from the sexual relationship?

20. What was the quality of the sexual relationship in previous marriages?

---

to answer these questions typically will not follow through with assigned homework. Examples of other questions that one can ask when conducting interviews or assigning self-report homework can be found in Masters and Johnson (1970), Goldfried and Pomeranz (1968), Goldfried and Davison (1976), and Caird and Wincze (1977).

Closely related to the data obtained during initial assessment is the status of the couple's relationship. Traumatized or highly unstable marriages are not prognostic of highly successful sex therapy. In one interesting study, Leiblum, Rosen, and Pierce (1976) found that couples scoring less than 80 on the Locke-Wallace Test of Marital Adjustment did not fare well in sex therapy.

Because of the limitations inherent in interviewing, it is often difficult to objectively assess improvements in sexual arousal as a function of treatment. As a result, structured paper-and-pencil self-assessment scales, such as the Locke-Wallace test just mentioned, can be very helpful. Many of these can be given to the client with instructions to complete them at home and return them at the next therapy session.

Assignment: Complete one or more questionnaires (as assigned).

Some questionnaires that may be assigned follow.

1. *The Marriage Inventory (Knox, 1971).* This inventory can serve as a quick way of determining general information about the client's marriage or intimate relationship. It can answer questions in a number of key areas, such as family goals, decision making, child management, and sexual interaction.

2. *The Marital Pre-Counseling Inventory (Stuart, 1973).* Based on Stuart's Operant Interpersonal approach to marriage counseling, this test asks questions in a number of key areas, such as general activities, likes, dislikes, money-spending patterns, interactions with relatives, and the couple's sexual relationship.

3. *The Sexual History Form (Annon, 1971).* This test was closely patterned after the original work of the same nature first designed by Kinsey and his associates at the University of Indiana. It deals with masturbation, heterosexual and homosexual contacts, and a general history of the client's sexuality.

4. *The Sexual Knowledge Inventories (McHugh, 1955, 1967).* This psychometric instrument has both short and long forms and purports to measure knowledge of sexual anatomy, physiology, and sexual vocabulary.

5. *The Sexual Response Profile (Pion, 1975).* This checklist is especially good for helping the therapist pinpoint areas of sexual concern and attitudes that can later be discussed during the counseling session.

6. *The Sexual Fear Inventories (Annon, 1975b, 1975c).* Two forms, one for men and one for women, are designed to tap the relative degree of fear associated with various kinds of sexual activities. This inventory is especially good for helping the therapist make decisions on the need for systematic desensitization to reduce various forms of sexual anxiety.

7. *The Sexual Pleasure Inventories (Annon, 1975d, 1975e).* These two inventories, one for men and one for women, are designed to measure the number and kinds of sexual activities that male and female clients find pleasurable.

8. *The Sexual Interaction Inventory (LoPiccolo & Steger, 1972).* This instrument is designed to determine the client's attitude towards present and future sexual activities and predictions of the partner's feelings as well. This measure helps the therapist pinpoint current areas of dissatisfaction and plan future treatment directions.

9. *The Sexual Arousability Inventory (Hoon, Hoon, & Wincze, 1976).* This scale is for female clients only and measures the degree of self-reported arousal for 28 erotic experiences. It is a good aid in designing erotic homework activities.

All of the above questionnaires have strengths and weaknesses. Although many provide similar information, all perform some function potentially useful to the therapist. In addition to the information gained, the client's promptness, thoroughness, and enthusiasm for completing the questionnaires are powerful indicators of the client's likelihood of homework compliance at a later time.

In addition to the questionnaire method, informal self-monitoring procedures may be employed. The flexibility with which these procedures can be employed gives the therapist the option of focusing on many issues that structured paper-and-pencil tests might not address. The self-recording format used for the purpose of gaining information about the client's sexual responses can vary considerably. These self-monitoring approaches to assessment can range from simple frequency counts of some sexual behavior or sexual thought to elaborate and complex self-assessment homework assignments involving written or audio-taped narratives of thoughts, emotions, or behaviors surrounding the sexual expression. The following are two typical self-monitoring assignments:

Assignment: Count all sexual thoughts on a daily basis. Write down 5 thoughts per day, what preceded each thought, and what followed it.

Assignment: Count every time you are hugged, kissed, or caressed by your partner each day. Write down what happened just before the touching and what your response was.

By choosing to do assessment using self-monitoring, the therapist can assess several dimensions of the client's sexual behavior: first, the specific stimuli or situations that enhance or diminish the sexual response; second, the consequences that discourage the frequency and quality of the sexual response; third and fourth, the frequency and intensity of the sexual response; and fifth, the rate of compliance. Golf counters, 3 x 5 cards, graph paper, and occasional "reminder phone calls" can all enhance the reliability of these recordings.

At the completion of the assessment phase of treatment, the therapist, along with the client, is ready to design the behavior-change intervention.

Treatment. The particular view of sexual dysfunction expressed here borrows from the work of Annon (1974, 1975a), who conceptualized treatment as consisting of three levels of intervention: Giving Permission,

Limited Information, and Specific Suggestions.* Taken together, these three levels can be seen as brief therapy in which the client moves through each of the phases until the treatment goals are met. Not every client needs to pass through all three levels. Some may have their needs met by relatively simple interventions such as those in Level 1.

Level 1: Giving Permission. Many clients enter therapy having serious concerns over the adequacy of their sexual responses. Based on information gained through sources such as the media, many clients believe that their sexual habits are inadequate or, in some cases, "abnormal." These concerns lead to anxiety, which often diminishes sexual arousal and performance. The cycle can continue until the client's sexual responses are severely inhibited.

Individuals whose sexual behavior is adequate in every respect but who are worried about sexual matters can often profit greatly from talking with a reassuring professional who can pronounce them "normal" and can give permission for them to continue sexual activity as before. Permission giving is sufficient in some cases to resolve what might become a very major problem. Hence, it can be seen as a preventive measure as well as a treatment approach. By itself it will not solve many sexual problems, but it is a good place to start and it lays the groundwork for other, more intensive forms of therapy. Permission giving can also include permission *not* to engage in certain sexual behaviors. For example, the recently rehabilitated patient may feel compelled to engage in sexual behavior just to "prove" that he is "whole" again, or the naive college freshman may think that engaging in homosexual activities and living a "bisexual" lifestyle demonstrates maturity and social awareness.

Level 2: Limited Information. Closely related to giving permission is dispensing information. At times, giving permission and sharing information can be done simultaneously. Many clients are haunted by myths concerning breast and penis size and shape, oral genital activity, masturbation, orgasms, erectile failure, and premature ejaculation. Anxiety generated by these beliefs can diminish sexual drive and performance and activate performance anxiety which, so often, lies at the roots of sexual dysfunction.

The therapist's decision to share information can greatly reduce the client's worries and associated anxiety. Of course, in some cases, the client's fears are realistic and do reflect problems of sexual function.

---

*Annon (1974) also discussed a fourth level, Intensive Therapy, for individuals who require intensive psychotherapy in order to derive sexual satisfaction.

When such instances arise, the information confirms the client's fears but also shows him or her that similar problems have been successfully treated. Information provides encouragement, positive expectations, and enhanced motivation to continue treatment. In short, it is essential to almost all treatment of sexual dysfunction.

Information can be dispensed through several channels. Obviously, the most frequent mode is through within-the-office conversation; however, other more efficient and effective modes exist. These remaining approaches rely strongly on systematic behavioral assignments. For example, commercial audio cassettes discussing human sexuality can be purchased and then lent, rented, sold, or given to clients.

Assignment: Read assigned material from the following book(s); listen to audio cassette as assigned.

Few good guidelines exist on what information to assign and when, so there is no substitute for good clinical judgment. For example, couples or individuals with strong moralistic beliefs about sex should not be given graphic pictorials regarding sexual behavior. Many good texts are informative without being graphic, and materials focusing on sex with a religious connotation would be especially helpful for these individuals. Obviously, care regarding the education and reading levels of the client might also influence assignments involving educational materials. The amount of material covered should also be carefully tailored to each client. As is always the case, the therapist should review all materials before assigning them to clients.

Educational books we have used include material on general sexual response (Belliveau & Richter, 1970; Brecher & Brecher, 1966; Lee, 1973; Martin & Lyon, 1973; McIlvenna, 1973; McIlvenna & Vandervoort, 1972; Reubin, 1969; Smith, Ayres, & Rubenstein, 1972), books exclusively for women (Heiman et al., 1976; Reubin, 1971), specific sexual enhancement exercises (Rosenberg, 1973), and books exclusively on sexual fantasies, which may be useful in such goals as orgasmic reconditioning (Friday, 1973, 1975; Slattery, 1975).

Whether in audio cassette or book form, assignments can be given that involve permission to engage in various sexual behaviors. Such materials also provide information and serve various therapeutic functions. Systematic behavioral assignments involving bibliotherapy should involve both the client and a significant other. The client and his or her partner can discuss the materials with each other or, when anger and hostility are present, with the therapist alone. In all cases, records should be kept of what was read and what subsequent questions were raised. When giving reading assignments, the therapist should not assume the clients will derive as many benefits from the reading as the therapist thinks they can, and must take care to prime the client for what to look for while reading. In some cases, the client can be given questions to answer or particular issues to note for discussion.

Level 3: Specific Suggestions. In contrast to permission and information giving, which generally do not require the client to take active steps to change his or her sexual behavior directly, the use of specific suggestions requires active, directive, outside practice of sexual responses. This level probably constitutes the most frequent approach used by professional sex therapists. The application of specific suggestions with a number of the more frequently encountered sexual problems will be discussed next.

Male Sexual Dysfunction. Problems of male sexual dysfunction include nonarousal, premature ejaculation, and retarded ejaculation.

Problems with male sexual arousal. Problems with male sexual arousal usually begin with some precipitating event such as fatigue, worry, anger, boredom, guilt, fear of disease, or anxiety over sexual performance. Because of these and many other factors, many men lose interest in sex. In some cases, these men actually lose the ability to become sexually aroused and cannot achieve or maintain an erection. Whatever the precipitating event, it is the client's reaction to it that plays the single greatest role in the chances of repeated arousal problems. As Annon (1975a) has pointed out, cognitions play a vital role in the maintenance of sexual problems. In the case of nonarousal, if the client is able to laugh off the experience with the attitude, "Oh, well, there is always another time," then he will probably have no further problems. If, however, the experience brings to mind doubts about his "manhood," then problems may quickly appear. The next time the client enters into sexual interaction he may start to worry and observe himself closely for evidence of sexual problems. The application of specific suggestions to this problem takes several different tacks, which will now be considered.

Assignment: Masturbate _____ times over the next week.

The most typical behavioral assignment after assessment and treatment planning is completed involves self-arousal through masturbation. Self-stimulation is often accompanied by motion pictures, adult movie cassettes that can be played on the home television, erotic reading, Polaroid pictures of his nude partner, or sexual fantasies.

One procedure that is especially good for changing sexual orientation toward a target sexual behavior or specific person is known as orgasmic reconditioning. Both Davison (1968) and LoPiccolo,

Stewart, and Watkins (1972) have reported successfully using this procedure to increase sexual arousal or to change sexual arousal patterns from one target to another. The following assignment illustrates orgasmic reconditioning.

Assignment: Masturbate to orgasm, using any fantasy that you find arousing.

Clients who do not have a repertoire of sexual fantasies are asked to read some of the sources mentioned earlier to gain ideas. Once the client is regularly using his chosen sexual fantasies to accompany masturbatory activity, a behavioral assignment is given that suggests the following:

Assignment: Switch to a "preferred fantasy" at the point of ejaculatory inevitability — the point at which orgasm has been triggered and will involuntarily occur within seconds.

For example, it is important that the client imagine as clearly and vividly as possible that he is engaging in genital intercourse with a firm erection when he experiences orgasm. Polaroid pictures of his partner can be substituted for his fantasies if those are not vivid. Through classical conditioning, the image of having intercourse with his partner is paired with orgasm and soon takes on sexually arousing properties of its own.

Once the client is able to experience arousal through self-stimulation coupled with fantasies or picture of his partner, he is ready to fade her into his sexual activity. The following assignment can be given:

Assignment: Engage in a self-stimulation session with your partner in which you teach her how to arouse you to orgasm.

Frequently therapy can be terminated at this time because arousal quickly generalizes to sexual intercourse. However, in some cases, despite the early success of self-arousal, the client may still express worry over his ability to transfer his new arousal to sexual activities with his partner. This signal should be a cue to employ another type of behavioral assignment involving the reduction of performance anxiety:

Assignment (client's partner):   Initiate some kind of caressing sexual activity in a situation in which sexual intercourse is impossible.

In fact, this systematic behavioral assignment should be conducted in a situation where there is some risk of being caught. For example, the man's partner might tease him under a tablecloth at dinner or in the back seat of a friend's car. Given the socially inappropriate or "risky" conditions under which this activity occurs, the client's attention may be diverted from fear of failure to fear of being "discovered." This paradoxical procedure can eliminate the anxiety surrounding sexual functioning. Having eliminated the anxiety, the client often finds that the sexual arousal quickly occurs.

To decrease performance anxiety as well as improve the sexual communication of the couple, the following "dating" procedures, first discussed by Annon (1975a) may be assigned:

Assignment: Make a series of "dates" together.

This procedure carefully integrates increasing sexual activity into a series of "dates" involving the client and his partner. Each activity is designed to enhance communication around sexual matters and sensitivity to the partner's sexual needs and preferences and, at the same time, to decrease sexual performance anxiety. Following are some examples of activities:

Assignment (both partners):   Select a cologne or perfume that is exciting to your partner.

Assignment: Together, select a body oil to be used in later exercises.

Shortly after that, an assignment could be given that involves a quiet evening or dinner out where they can discuss sexual preferences.

Assignment: For a date, have a quiet dinner out; during the meal, discuss sexual preferences.

In this case, care must be taken in the therapist's office to make sure the couple can pinpoint behaviors that they desire and/or dislike. All of these activities are simple and straightforward. The goal is to enhance communication regarding erotic preferences and to reeducate the couple to focus on each other and their mutual needs, without having sexual intercourse. Through these activities, performance anxiety is decreased, sexual drive increases, and the chances for sexual arousal improve considerably. Most of the preceding activities can be assigned on a day-to-day basis, with several assignments being accomplished in a week or two. After this initial phase treatment proceeds into sensate focus.

Assignment: Practice sensate focus, first with the emphasis on the woman's pleasure, and then on mutual stimulation. Do not attempt intercourse.

The procedures employed in sensate focus have been discussed in a number of recent publications (see, for example, Heiman et al., 1976).

The primary goal, as the reader undoubtedly knows, is to give and receive pleasure, without having intercourse. Having reduced the anxiety of sexual performance worries, the couple is free to explore the nature of their own sexual responses in a nonthreatening manner.

When possible, sensate focus exercises are integrated into the "dating" homework format discussed earlier. As before, we insist that the partners alternate responsibility for planning the date. Hence one client selects the time, place, music, and physical surroundings for the practice session. The therapist helps prescribe the range of sexual activities. The dates need not be elaborate or costly but should endeavor to "set the tone" for each sensate focus session. When possible, there should not be one sensate focus session right after another; instead, the client should have a date in between each sensate focus session.

The first session begins with the female as the person who experiences pleasure, reducing pressure on the male. Different textures, pressures, and body parts are all varied, and the female is to communicate verbally or nonverbally what is pleasurable. The following session involves the male in the receiving role. The ban on sexual intercourse continues during this time. As sessions continue, the sensate focus activities come closer and closer to the goal of successful sexual intercourse. Activities involving kissing, blowing, nibbling, and other forms of stimulation are tried, then either discarded or used more frequently. After several sessions of pleasuring, the focus shifts again to mutual stimulation. Towards the end of homework involving sensate focus, it is a good idea to ask the woman to first stimulate the man's penis and then allow it to become flaccid. Repeating this procedure over and over successfully gives the client great confidence should he fail to gain an erection during future trials.

Assignment: Practice "quiet vagina" exercise.

Assignment: Practice "quiet vagina" exercise with increased male and female thrusting.

In these next assignments, the woman, with strict orders not to have an orgasm, is asked to straddle the client, who lies on his back. She then places his erect penis into her vagina and allows him to make whatever movements are necessary to maintain an erection. Hard and rapid thrusting is discouraged. Over the next few sessions, depending on the clients' reports of comfort, the amount of male thrusting can be increased, with orgasm still a strict "no-no." At this time or soon after the female is allowed to also begin pelvic thrusting. This procedure is continued in a low-demand manner until orgasm is reliably reached.

Premature ejaculation. Premature ejaculation has been defined as ejaculation shortly after erection is attained, ejaculation before or immediately after vaginal entry, ejaculation before the male is ready, or inability to delay ejaculation long enough for the woman to experience orgasm 50 percent of the time. This condition, which is very common, often results from a history of early sexual experiences in which hurried ejaculation was demanded. Common examples include intercourse with a prostitute whose attitude was "hurry and get it over with" and sex in situations where there was a threat of public discovery, such as in the back seat of a car. Once established, this habit dies hard.

Many homework-oriented procedures have been found helpful in the treatment of premature ejaculation. One of the simplest therapist-directed assignments follows.

Assignment: Masturbate to orgasm before making love.

Having recently experienced orgasm, the client will be less likely to have a quick orgasm with his partner. The client's partner may in some cases produce the orgasm either orally or manually before having intercourse. Being able to have sexual intercourse without rapid ejaculation will rapidly extinguish the client's fears. Another variation of this same scene calls for the couple to have a "date" in which they escape to a motel or hotel for a restful, relaxed, and unhurried weekend of lovemaking.

Assignment: Engage in repeated lovemaking.

After the client has ejaculated he can rest, swim, take a warm shower, and make love again. After repeated orgasms, he will be able to make love longer and longer without having an orgasm. After a weekend or two of such homework activity the client soon discovers that he can make love for longer intervals without having an orgasm.

Another systematic behavioral assignment involves the client in daily masturbatory exercises.

Assignment: Stimulate yourself to the point when ejaculation is imminent; then stop until the penis becomes flaccid. After a short pause of 1 minute or so, repeat the exercise without having an orgasm.

Our experience has shown that repeated attempts at masturbation without orgasms in the manner just described significantly increase the latency between intromission and orgasm. This exercise is especially good for the client without a partner. It should generally be repeated daily for three masturbatory trials until the problem is eliminated.

Systematic behavioral assignments involving changes in positions or movement may also prove useful.

Assignment: Alter positions and movement during intercourse.

Hard pelvic thrusting in the man-atop position is more likely to trigger ejaculation than most other positions for sexual intercourse. For example, maintaining deep penetration while moving slowly or in a circular movement can delay orgasm. Positions such as face-to-face with both partners on their sides, rear entry, or woman sitting above allow the male to relax and control his movements at the same time. Other behavioral assignments involving experimentation with breathing, relaxation, positions, and movement may be tailored to the specific desires of each client.

We have had a great amount of success with the use of paradoxical suggestions involving sexual homework. For example, the following assignment could be given.*

Assignment: Try to climax as quickly as possible.

In one case a man was told that the faster he produced an orgasm the sooner he could get beyond the "threshold" and begin the reversal of his rapid ejaculatory process. Primed to try hard to have a very rapid ejaculation, the man was disappointed to find that his orgasm took longer than normal. He was encouraged to try again, only harder, and reported failure again. Soon the man had "failed" enough to have experienced significant progress.

The final systematic behavioral assignment involves "interrupted stimulation" as originally discussed by Semans (1968). This assignment is for the woman.

Assignment (client's partner):   Stimulate the client until he signals the approach of orgasm. At that point, withdraw stimulation until the urge to climax subsides. Repeat several times per homework session.

After several home practice sessions, many clients find that the latency between stimulation and orgasm becomes greater and greater. After the male can tolerate stimulation up to some prearranged criterion level, such as 5 minutes, the entire procedure is repeated with vaginal containment.

Another very similar technique is based on the Masters and Johnson (1970) squeeze technique. This procedure is nearly identical to the interrupted stimulation approach.

Assignment: When reaching the prearranged point (usually the point of ejaculatory inevitability), signal your partner, who is then to place her thumb on the frenulum (head of the penis) and with her first and second fingers on the opposite side of the penis, is to apply strong pressure for approximately 5 seconds. She is

---

*The reader is again cautioned about the potential harm of paradoxical procedures that backfire.

to then release the penis for a minute's rest and subsequently resume sexual stimulation.

This procedure is repeated for about five trials per day for 2 weeks. Although great variations have been found in the amount of squeeze needed (range of 3 to 30 seconds) and in the amount of rest (range 15 to 60 seconds), usually about 60 to 90 trials are needed to produce a noticeable delay in the latency between stimulation and orgasm. At five trials per day, this adds up to about 3 weeks. After the second week, if all is going well, the next assignment is given:

Assignment: Continue the trials with vaginal containment.

In this assignment, the man does all the thrusting. At the point of ejaculatory inevitability, he signals, and his partner applies the squeeze. The next assignment is for the woman.

Assignment: During the third week, begin pelvic thrusting with appropriate stops to apply the squeeze.

The procedure continues until the couple is satisfied with the latency of his sexual response to orgasm. As just stated, about 90 trials are usually required to eliminate this problem to the client's satisfaction.

Retarded ejaculation. Retarded ejaculation, or ejaculatory incompetence, is a relatively rare type of sexual dysfunction. It is the inability to ejaculate intravaginally. We agree with Annon's (1975a) views regarding the treatment of this problem. He argues that the problem can best be conceptualized as being similar to lack of arousal in women. Hence, the treatment aims at giving homework that engages the male in self-stimulation until orgasm can be reliably reached.

Assignment: Masturbate as quickly as possible while fantasizing about intercourse.

Initially, one good means of achieving this end is to prohibit *all* sexual activity until sexual drive is very high. High drive coupled with low anxiety usually brings on a rapid sexual response.

After climax can be achieved reliably and quickly and is associated with fantasies involving sexual intercourse, homework is designed that gradually introduces the client's partner into the scene. It may begin with the following assignment:

Assignment: Engage in self-stimulation while your partner is in a nearby room involved in some activity.

Gradually the woman is brought nearer and nearer the client until she can be in the room during the time he is engaging in sexual stimulation. Rather than have her "sit and watch" while he masturbates, we often prescribe an assignment requesting that she also engage in self-stimulation parallel to his.

Assignment: Both partners masturbate.

This procedure helps reduce his anxiety. She then occupies the same bed while they both masturbate, and then she touches him while he engages in self-arousal. As therapy unfolds, other systematic behavioral assignments also involve her.

Assignment: Touch your partner while he masturbates, assisting him in stimulating himself, and then stimulate him entirely by yourself.

Treatment then proceeds to homework that involves the woman sitting atop the client and allowing him to do all the thrusting. As always, the client is told to do the following:

Assignment: Concentrate on having pleasure, not on climaxing.

If he "fails," he is to practice coping thoughts:

Assignment: Practice coping thoughts such as "I can't be perfect all the time" and "There will always be another day to practice."

At all costs, the client must be relieved of the grim determination that many clients seem to have when they are engaged in overcoming a sexual problem.

Soon after this approach has proven successful, the clients engage in mutually satisfying sexual intercourse. In some cases, we have found paradoxical procedures to be effective during this final phase of the treatment process.

Assignment: Try to refrain from having an orgasm during intercourse.

Female Sexual Dysfunction. As with men, a wide number of factors may contribute to female failure to experience sexual arousal and eventual orgasm. However, the medical or physiological variables that account for lack of arousal only constitute about 5 percent of the total. The remaining 95 percent are psychological in origin (Annon, 1975a). In fact, current research by Masters and Johnson (1970) and others suggests that nearly all women have the potential to experience orgasm on a somewhat regular basis.

Therapy involving preorgasmic women begins with the therapist trying to determine which factors may be contributing to their poor sexual arousal patterns. Attitudes about sex, religious values, fear of pregnancy, fatigue, or occupational or school worries all have an impact on the female's sexual responses. It is also helpful to know if the client has ever experienced an orgasm and, if so, under what circumstances. Determination of facts surrounding this question helps the therapist decide whether or not the client's current lack of sexual arousal is situation-specific (such as a clumsy partner) or the result of a general response pattern.

Problems with female sexual arousal. Treatment for low sexual arousal in females is generally aimed at either reducing anxiety associated with sexual activities or helping the woman learn new behaviors involving the experience of arousal and eventual orgasm. A wide number of procedures have been successfully used to achieve these ends. Relaxation training, thought modification, skill training, sensate focus, "dates," and even the use of macadamia nuts as a counter-anxiety agent (Tarter-Benlolo & Love, 1977) are but a few of the successful procedures reported in the literature.

Regardless of the exact procedures employed, we begin treatment by giving the following assignments:

Assignment: Refrain from any form of sexual activity for a period of time.

Assignment: During this time, engage in other nonsexual activities experienced as somewhat arousing in the past (such as having romantic "dates," reading erotic literature, or attending erotic movies).

Therapeutic homework is then typically prescribed that sets the groundwork for eventual orgasm via sexual intercourse. This later systematic behavioral assignment involves the Kegel Squeeze procedure and is based on the exercises first developed by Kegel (see Deutsch, 1968), who originally developed the procedure as a means of helping pregnant women gain control over urinary incontinence. The Kegel Squeeze involves gaining control over the pubococcygeus (PC) muscle, which is the main muscle used in starting and stopping the flow of urine. Only by accident was it discovered that frequent exercise involving contraction of the PC muscle led to orgasm for many women who were nonorgasmic prior to the PC muscle training.

Assignment: Practice starting and stopping urine flow each time you use the bathroom.

To pinpoint the PC muscle, Annon (1975a) argues that asking the client to spread her legs during attempts to start and stop the urine flow will aid her to more quickly identify the PC muscle. Our experience suggests that the leg-open procedure is not necessary for quick identification in all female clients, but can be useful for those who have initial trouble in making the identification. Once the PC muscle has been identified, the client is given systematic behavioral assignments that prescribe using the Kegel Squeeze procedure whenever she urinates. Annon (1975a) has suggested that a good criterion of success is the client's ability to pass 1 teaspoon of urine at a time. Larger amounts than 1 teaspoon suggest that the client still has poor vaginal control of the PC muscle. Some clients find the practice of starting and stopping urine to be unpleasant. If this situation arises, the therapist can propose an alternative homework assignment.

Assignment: Practice the Kegel Squeeze procedure for approximately 10 trials per day.

These quotas involve practice without urination. Each trial begins with a small number of squeezes (3), with 2 seconds of relaxation between each squeeze. As the client begins to develop muscle control, the therapist can increase the daily quota until the client can complete 10 trials of 10 squeezes each. The criterion for success still remains the ability to pass 1 teaspoon of urine at a time.

When the client is able to reach this criterion, the systematic behavioral assignment is modified to include twitching. The twitching exercise approximates contractions during orgasm and involves the rapid contraction of the PC muscle.

Assignment: Practice twitching (increasing numbers) times per day.

As before, the final goal is 10 trials per day and 10 twitches per trial. No relaxation pauses separate the twitches. Once the client is successfully engaging in twitching she is asked to imagine engaging in positive sexual events while practicing, with the goal being to associate PC muscle contractions with sexual images. For example, the woman may engage in her twitching program while engaged in conversation with an attractive man at a cocktail party. This program can continue in a like manner with gradually increasing exercise quotas until the client is able to complete 100 twitches a day. At that point or before, many clients begin to report a "warm sensation" during or after the Kegel Squeeze procedure. This is an excellent prognostic sign, and the woman should be encouraged to continue the exercise. Later, the Kegel Squeeze can be performed during penile containment with both partners enjoying the procedure.

Self-stimulation. For preorgasmic women, the most direct and probably the most effective manner of teaching the orgasmic response is through self-stimulation. This approach, which utilizes therapeutic home assignments, has been repeatedly shown to be effective (Annon, 1976; Barbach, 1975; LoPiccolo & Lobitz, 1972; Robinson, 1974). It has several advantages. First, it can be used even though no partner is available. Second, this procedure is very reliable: over 75 percent of all women who used this method reported orgasm within 4 minutes (Annon, 1974). Third, a number of excellent guides currently exist for teaching this skill to women.

The therapist giving therapeutic assignments involving this skill should be careful about the language used. Often it is wise to use terms like "self-stimulation" or "self-exploration" instead of "masturbation," which has a negative connotation. In addition, possible negative attitudes toward "touching myself down there" can be countered by having a female therapist disclose her own experiences with masturbation and by telling the client that the purpose of her self-exploration is to improve intercourse with her partner.

The first step is to instill a positive mental set and high expectations for success. This is accomplished by giving assignments that involve either reading or listening to material about self-stimulation.

Assignment: Listen to an audio cassette about self-stimulation.

This is a very good beginning assignment for the preorgasmic woman who is ignorant or fearful of masturbation.

Assignment: Read *Becoming Orgasmic: A Sexual Growth Program for Women* (Heiman et al., 1976).

This assignment contains an elaboration of LoPiccolo and Lobitz's (1972) 9-step masturbation plan.

Electric vibrators are often employed with this phase of orgasmic training. Their use is based on several considerations. First, many women have heard about electric vibrators for the purpose of self-stimulation and have a high expectation for success coupled with their use. High positive expectations for prudent therapeutic modalities should be supported. Second, some women dislike the thought of "touching themselves down there" and welcome the use of a vibrator as a means of not having to touch themselves. Third, some women ardently practice self-stimulation for 4 or 5 weeks without success and begin losing confidence in the therapy plan. If the woman has not been successful in reaching orgasm after 5 weeks of self-stimulation coupled with erotic reading, she should probably switch to the vibrator. After having purchased one, the client proceeds as before with systematic behavioral assignments involving self-stimulation coupled with erotic reading or viewing.

Assignment: Masturbate with vibrator and imagine sexual partner while masturbating.

Most women learn to have orgasms relatively quickly with this approach. Certainly most women will have experienced a climax by the sixth or seventh week of this regimen. Others take much longer, especially if the husband or significant other is undermining treatment. This possibility provides another reason to have him involved in therapy.

When the woman has reached an orgasm, the therapist must be careful not to switch too quickly to sensate focus with the male partner. A certain amount of overlearning is necessary before the client's ability to reliably reach orgasm is assured. Usually 1 or 2 weeks of continued practice is necessary before the man can become directly involved in pleasuring. However, once he is brought into therapy, the plan is relatively simple and straightforward. It begins with the involvement of the man in sensate-focus sessions, where the woman teaches him what she has learned through self-stimulation.

The man is initiated into this process by being told that his support and cooperation are vital to the continued success of treatment. He may be putting subtle pressure on the woman to be sexually responsive, such as asking the woman repeatedly if she has experienced a climax after every sexual practice session. It should also be stressed that it is ultimately the client's responsibility, not his, to produce an orgasm. While he should be very responsive to her suggestions for stimulation, rhythm, patterns, and areas to be caressed, it is ultimately her responsibility to reach orgasm.

Obviously one can proceed in a countless number of ways from this point.

Assignment (woman): Bring yourself to orgasm by self-stimulation while in the presence of your partner.

Based on her anxiety level, he can be in the room, reclining on the bed, touching her hand, holding her in his arms, or whatever degree of closeness she desires. The next step after gradually getting the woman to a point where she can experience orgasm with her partner near is the following assignment.

Assignment (woman): Place your hands over his and guide him in a manner of stimulation that you prefer.

As treatment progresses, he can take more and more of the responsibility for tactile stimulation. In some cases, the use of a vibrator has been incorporated into the couple's sexual play.

If the woman is experiencing orgasm through various forms of stimulation by her partner but is not able to experience orgasm through genital intercourse, further behavioral assignments are required.

Assignment (male):   Complete penile entry at the moment the woman experiences orgasm.

In this behavioral assignment the couples use a position such as the side position where the vagina is immediately adjacent to the penis. Manual or vibrator stimulation by either the man or woman is practiced until the woman is about to experience orgasm. At this point the woman signals her partner and he completes penile entry while she continues the self-stimulation regimen. If the woman loses her orgasm, the trial is repeated until she can reliably reach orgasm while having the penis inside her. At this point the time in which the penis gains vaginal entry is increased further and further back into the sexual response cycle. When the female can have an orgasm while her partner engages in full penile thrusting, she can begin to fade out the electric or manual stimulation.

Many variations of this basic tack exist in the literature (Annon, 1975a). However, regardless of the exact positions used and the order in which stimulation is paired with intercourse, a few other ideas are worth mentioning. For example, it is usually a good idea to point out to the partner that there is typically a direct relationship between the length of sexual stimulation before intercourse and the chance that the woman will experience an orgasm, and that the longer the stimulation goes on, the better the chance is. Some research suggests that if such stimulation is engaged in for 20 minutes or longer, the chances for orgasm by intercourse are very high. Another pertinent idea is the continuity of physical stimulation without interruption once a particular pattern of arousal has been found highly stimulating. When the woman becomes aroused and the male then shifts position, begins talking, or does something else, the woman usually experiences a decrease in arousal.

Vaginismus. Vaginismus is a form of sexual dysfunction in which a voluntary tightening or spasm of the outer third of the vagina makes it impossible for the woman to have intercourse without pain. Unlike many of the types of sex dysfunction discussed earlier, the causes for vaginismus are much more often due to physiological causes, and hence a thorough examination by a physician is a necessity. Having ruled out or corrected the medical basis for vaginismus, the therapist is ready to proceed with psychological treatments based on behavioral homework.

We begin work on this problem by teaching the client self-controlled relaxation skills. (This practice has been described in Chapter 4, and we will not cover it here.) After relaxation skills are mastered, a series of assignments are given involving gradual vaginal entry with different-sized objects while the client relaxes. The typical hierarchy for such an endeavor follows.

1. Intromission of one finger
2. Intromission of a small-sized dilator
3. Intromission of two fingers
4. Intromission of a larger-sized dilator
5. Masturbation with a large dilator
6. Partial intromission by the penis
7. Full intromission by the penis (without thrusting)
8. Full intromission by the penis with thrusting

In this procedure the woman obtains a set of dilators. If she is seeing a physician he or she can provide the patient with a set. If not, the client can use her own natural set of dilators—her fingers—since their variable sizes can serve the same purpose.

Assignment: Begin with the smallest set of dilators or fingers and gradually insert them into the vagina while remaining very relaxed.

Sterile lubricating jelly can often aid in the process. Larger fingers or dilators are used on successive homework trials until two or more fingers can be used together. At this point we suggest the client be treated much like one would treat the poorly aroused client. The process would consist of genital exploration, erotic reading, and masturbation with or without a vibrator. The masturbation should include some form of entry into the vagina in addition to clitoral stimulation. The partner would be gradually introduced into the sexual activity, beginning with partial intromission, followed by full intromission without thrusting, and eventually full intromission with thrusting.

A somewhat different method first reported by Wilson (1973) involves treating vaginismus with orgasmic reconditioning. This procedure relies heavily on behavioral assignments and is designed for the woman who can become sexually aroused but who cannot experience intercourse because of tight vaginal muscles.

Assignment: Bring yourself to orgasm by any means at your disposal and then imagine minimal finger insertion by your partner at the point of orgasm.

Progressive behavioral assignments would involve orgasm while imagining larger and larger vaginal entry until the woman could fantasize having intercourse while having an orgasm. Of course, this and the previous treatment can be combined. In this case, the woman would masturbate to orgasm while imagining some sexual activity. After this, she then engages in the activity she just fantasized.

COMPLIANCE ENHANCEMENT PROCEDURES

For many couples, the sexual arousal that accompanies home assignments involving some form of sexual experimentation is a powerful reinforcer that greatly enhances compliance to the prescribed task. Nonetheless, it pays to structure the treatment for sexual dysfunction to maximize compliance even more.

As always with treatments involving outside therapeutic assignments, we begin by discussing the assignment in the context of the client's own wishes, expectations, and limitations. By allowing the client to participate fully in the design of systematic behavioral assignments, the therapist is able to eliminate much of the resistance that often occurs when he or she dictates an assignment. Also, after consulting with the client regarding the form, frequency, and duration of the assignment, we then make sure the client fully understands the therapeutic assignment. Time permitting, we often encourage the client to begin roleplaying the verbal interaction leading up to a sexual encounter.

Couples' groups designed for the treatment of sexual dysfunction also have the potential for enhancing compliance. One strategy requires that each couple be paired with another couple to whom they can report. The two couples are free to communicate in any way they desire about the next week's systematic behavioral assignment. By and large, the interaction consists of encouragement, permission giving, and reinforcement for carrying out assigned homework. We cannot understate the importance of peer pressure in bringing about adherence to assigned homework tasks. If properly structured, it can pay big dividends in assignment compliance.

Another tactic we have used requires that couples pay double the normal rate at the onset of treatment. The amount collected over and above the regular rate is then refunded to the clients contingent upon completion of their homework.

ILLUSTRATIVE CASE

The Browns were a 40-year-old middle-class couple who were referred by their local minister. They had been happily married for 16 years and had two children. Both were religious and very devout in their beliefs. Both had entered into marriage as virgins and had experienced little, if any, sexual experimentation as young adults. Based on self-reports and behaviors observed during interviews, they were committed to each other, agreed eye-to-eye on most topics, and generally had an excellent marriage. The only problem area in an otherwise successful marriage was their sexual relationship.

Ms. Brown had never achieved an orgasm and was seen by herself and her husband as the central client. For the most part, their beliefs regarding Ms. Brown's sexual inadequacy stemmed from a series of lectures that they attended in their church regarding female sexuality. Having heard stories of multiple orgasms, Ms. Brown was quick to arrive at the conclusion that something was terribly wrong sexually.

As was soon discovered, the couple's sexual problem belonged to Mr. Brown as well. As the baseline data revealed, Mr. Brown was a premature ejaculator. This problem contributed a great deal to Ms. Brown's difficulties.

Assessment

Baselines and history-taking supported much of what had been described by the couple regarding their sexual activity. During 5 weeks of baseline recording (a time made inappropriately long because of the therapist's vacation plans), data were collected on several variables. Mr. Brown was asked to record the frequency of sexual intercourse, the amount of time spent in foreplay, and the length of time needed to reach climax. Ms. Brown was to record the frequency of sexual intercourse and time spent in foreplay as well. She was also asked to record the amount of arousal she experienced during sex using a 100-point scale, with 0 being no sexual feelings and 100 being the most intense sexual feelings imaginable. Figures 10.1 and 10.2 show the results of this systematic behavioral assignment.

The results of the baseline period were very interesting and ultimately proved critical for the success of therapy. In two instances (frequency of sexual intercourse and amount of foreplay), both Mr. and Ms. Brown were recording the same behavior. By looking at the data that both clients independently recorded, several interesting points can be made. First, there is some discrepancy in the number of times sexual intercourse occurred. Mr. Brown reports having had intercourse seven times during the 5-week baseline, whereas Ms. Brown reports only six. Mr. Brown reports engaging in more foreplay than does Ms. Brown. He reports times averaging nearly 6½ minutes spent in foreplay before intercourse. Ms. Brown reported several instances in which no foreplay was engaged in whatsoever and also reported an average of only 4½ minutes spent on foreplay before each instance of intercourse. Not infrequently we prescribe assignments similar to these so that we can compare the results of two observations on one behavior. Besides providing a reliability check, this procedure often brings to our attention areas in which conflict may lie. In this case, it turned out that Ms. Brown

Figure 10.1   Mr. Brown's baseline

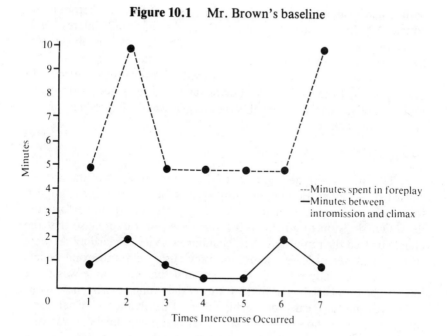

---Minutes spent in foreplay
—Minutes between
   intromission and climax

Times Intercourse Occurred

Figure 10.2   Ms. Brown's baseline

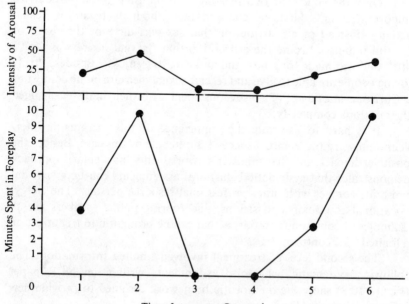

Times Intercourse Occurred

wished her husband to spend more time in sexual foreplay before intercourse. Mr. Brown viewed foreplay as "a waste of time." Interestingly, it also turned out that when Mr. Brown was able to delay his climax, Ms. Brown reported greater sexual arousal. As these facts were revealed for discussion the focus of therapy began to shift from just Ms. Brown to both spouses. In fact, the data showed, as they nearly always do if one looks closely, that the sexual dysfunction was a byproduct of the couple's interaction.

Treatment

The first step in the treatment of the sexual problems of the Browns consisted of Giving Permission. Rather than attempting to accomplish this step ourselves, we elected to ask the couple's minister to perform the task. Our decision to go this route was based on the premise that the couple trusted their minister, that the minister's views regarding sex were seen as a powerful lever against the previously held antisexual beliefs which were partially religious in origin, and that the couple was more likely to be influenced by us in the future if their minister agreed with our objectives and the means for reaching them. Luckily their minister was a progressive man who engaged in some pastoral counseling and was very supportive of our approach. By asking the couple for a release, we were able to work closely with the minister and exchange information as needed for their benefit.

Over the course of two meetings the minister accomplished two important things. First, he changed their thoughts regarding sexual activity. Instead of an attribution that sex was dirty or the result of "sinful impulses" came the attribution that "sexual desire was God's gift" and was made for a husband and wife to "enjoy." Besides, "truly loving people are able to give and receive sexual pleasure in the context of a Christian marriage." Two sessions spent with their minister changed their outlook completely.

It is hard to overstate the importance of this therapeutic intervention toward the eventual successful outcome of this case. Besides the positive impact of the minister's work, this particular approach demonstrates that systematic behavioral assignments can be given that prescribe contact with other professional resource persons. The clergy, vocational counselors, physicians, and touring public speakers are all examples of community resources that can be brought into treatment on a limited "subcontract" basis.

The second level of treatment involved Limited Information. The following systematic behavioral assignments written on NCR paper (Figure 10.3) show the therapeutic homework assigned to provide new information to the clients.

Figure 10.3   Assignments for Browns to increase sexual information

Homework for Jim and Bobbie
Spend 1 hour, four times a week, reading the Steinmetz (1972) book.
Spend 30 minutes, four times a week, discussing the reading.
Record major insights.
When finished, call for an appointment.

The Browns dove into their reading assignment with great gusto. A new communication channel was opened up to them, and they appeared to relish their discussions a great deal. Within 10 days they were back in the office, having read and discussed the Steinmetz (1972) book. The prohibition of sexual contact remained intact, and they reported compliance with this edict.

The next systematic behavioral assignment took two channels. For Ms. Brown we began the 9-step masturbation training program first described by LoPiccolo and Lobitz (1972) and expanded in Heiman et al. (1976). She was assigned sections of the Heiman et al. book to read and, over a 12-week basis, proceeded through the steps as described in the book. Each week's assignment roughly paralleled the chapters in the book. Particularly useful was the assignment prescribed during the seventh week, which involved roleplaying an orgasm. Partly because of her "Puritan" values, Ms. Brown was fearful of "how she would look" when having an orgasm. The systematic behavioral assignment involved roleplaying the most violent orgasm imaginable. Ms. Brown was encouraged to spend 15 minutes pleasuring herself in her usual fashion, and when she experienced some arousal, to roleplay an orgasm complete with cries and wild thrashing. Repeated instances of orgasm roleplaying desensitized her fears regarding the orgasmic response.

During Ms. Brown's progress through self-stimulation practice, Mr. Brown practiced as well. His practice involved masturbating to the point of ejaculatory inevitability and then practicing the squeeze technique discussed by Masters and Johnson (1970). Repeated instances of this procedure increased the latency period from masturbation to the point of ejaculatory inevitability by 200 percent; he began at about 2 minutes and progressed to 6 minutes from arousal to the point of ejaculatory inevitability.

Ms. Brown experienced her first orgasm during the seventh week. One more week was added before her husband was faded into sensate focus exercises with her. On alternate days we would focus on his problem and then on hers. Both their treatments followed closely those already described in this chapter. For example, over the next 12 weeks, Ms. Brown taught Mr. Brown her specific arousal patterns regarding self-stimulation. He learned these patterns, practiced them on her, and learned the importance of foreplay. Within 3 weeks she was able to masturbate to orgasm while her vagina contained Mr. Brown's penis. She continued to enjoy high sexual arousal during intercourse from this time forward. Although she was never able to experience an orgasm while having sexual intercourse, she was able to soon reach an orgasm during intercourse if she continued to stimulate herself. She was highly satisfied with having reached this goal.

The treatment for Mr. Brown also followed closely the outlines for individuals for whom premature ejaculation was a problem. The use of the "quiet vagina" technique coupled with the squeeze procedure discussed earlier proved very effective in increasing his latency from a mean of about 30 seconds to over 9 minutes. This change took approximately 3 months to achieve. Interestingly, as the latency between intromission and orgasm increased for Mr. Brown, Ms. Brown reported significantly increased sexual arousal. Without a doubt, the combination of Mr. Brown's greater attention to foreplay plus his greater delay in time to orgasm via sexual intercourse made a huge difference in her sexual responsiveness. A 6-month follow-up achieved by a phone call confirmed the continuation of these gains.

A summary of treatment by session is seen in Table 10.2.

Table 10.2
Summary of Treatment by Session for the Browns

Session	Major Topics	Assignments
1	Sexual histories and baselines examined.	
2-3	Rationale for treatment and guided home practice made.	
	Concerns regarding religious beliefs understood and accepted.	Make appointment to meet with minister and discuss various ideas regarding religion and sex.
	Ban on sex imposed. Goals of treatment established.	Read Steinmetz book for 1 hour each day and discuss 30 minutes. Do both four times per week.

Table 10.2   *(Continued)*

Session	Major Topics	Assignments
4	Steinmetz and talks with minister discussed.	
5-6	Two training procedures outlined, and rationales provided for sexual arousal training (Ms. B.) and premature ejaculation (Mr. B.). Compliance with homework reinforced, homework reaffirmed, and homework modified as needed.	Her: Examine yourself nude and explore "what feels good." Him: Masturbate to point of ejaculatory inevitability and then apply squeeze (twice weekly). Both: Begin reading Heiman et al. Reading assignments reflect homework progress.
7	Progress monitored, fears of failing accepted. Reassurance given. Homework compliance reinforced; new assignment given. Heiman et al. discussed.	Her: Same as before except orgasm roleplayed. Him: Same homework as before.
8	Ms. Brown has first orgasm during seventh week. Reinforcement given for practice, *not for orgasm*. Fears regarding "it will never happen again" accepted. Reassurance given.	Same behavioral assignment as last week.
9-10	Rationale of alternating practice sessions given. Homework explained.	Both: Engage in sensate focus. Her: Guide him in performing arousing stimulation behaviors. Him: Allow her to stimulate you manually to the point of ejaculation and apply squeeze procedure.
11-12	"Bugs" worked out regarding her fears of hurting him during the squeeze.	Her: Practice vaginal containment with no thrusting while stimulating yourself. Him: Practice signaling ejaculatory inevitability to her while she practices "quiet vagina."
13-15	Ms. Brown reports orgasm during penile-contained self-stimulation. Mr. Brown is jubilant over intromission without having orgasm. Reinforcement for practice given. Couple reminded that success will not always occur. Maintenance procedure reviewed.	Continue as before but with Mr. Brown gradually increasing thrusting.

SUMMARY

Noted researchers have all indicated that dysfunction of the human sexual response is extremely common. Until recently, sexual dysfunction had been treated by psychotherapeutic means, which were mostly ineffectual. However, during the '70s, Masters and Johnson and others introduced behavioral therapy for sexual dysfunction and achieved a higher level of success. The key point of this behavioral therapy is that sexual dysfunction is a result of learning, and can be treated as other learned behaviors are. Standardized procedures are now used for behavioral treatment of sexual dysfunction.

The approach outlined here assumes that all sexual problems are shared by both partners, and that the primary goal of therapy is to teach the clients about sexual behaviors and guide their practice. Homework assignments for assessment and treatment are presented.

Compliance is enhanced in several ways. The client is involved in formulating the assignments, and the assignments are made explicit by the therapist. Couples' groups can offer support or bring pressure to bear on clients, especially if each couple is paired with another to whom they report progress. A refundable deposit may also be required at the beginning of treatment, and refunding is then made contingent upon completion of assignments.

The illustrative case study concerns a middle-aged couple, the Browns. They originally sought help because Ms. Brown had never achieved orgasm, and it was later found that Mr. Brown had a problem of premature ejaculation. After recording data about their sexual activities, Mr. and Ms. Brown met with the therapist and pinpointed the underlying problems in their sexual relationship. Treatment began with the couple discussing some of their attitudes about sex with their minister, to overcome guilt feelings. They then were given information on sexual behavior to read and discuss. Each partner was taught appropriate sexual exercises for their respective problems, and then both of them followed a step-by-step progression of activities that allowed them to learn and practice sexual techniques leading up to successful intercourse. The follow-up showed that Ms. Brown had continued to experience orgasms and enjoy intercourse.

REFERENCES

Annon, J.S. The extension of learning principles to the analysis and treatment of sexual problems (Doctoral dissertation, University of Hawaii, 1971). *Dissertation Abstracts International,* 1971, *32,* 3627-B. (University Microfilms No. 72-290)

Annon, J.S. The therapeutic use of masturbation in the treatment of sexual problems. In R.D. Rubin, J.D. Brady, & J.D. Henderson (Eds.), *Advances in behavior therapy* (Vol. 4). New York: Academic Press, 1973.

Annon, J.S. *The behavioral treatment of sexual problems* (Vol. 1). Honolulu: Enabling Systems, 1974.

Annon, J.S. *The behavioral treatment of sexual problems* (Vol. 2). Honolulu: Enabling Systems, 1975. (a)

Annon, J.S. *The sexual fear inventory — female form.* Honolulu: Enabling Systems, 1975. (b)

Annon, J.S. *The sexual fear inventory — male form.* Honolulu: Enabling Systems, 1975. (c)

Annon, J.S. *The sexual pleasure inventory — female form.* Honolulu: Enabling Systems, 1975. (d)

Annon, J.S. *The sexual pleasure inventory — male form.* Honolulu: Enabling Systems, 1975. (e)

Annon, J.S. *The behavioral treatment of sexual problems: Brief therapy.* New York: Harper & Row, 1976.

Barbach, D.H. Increasing heterosexual responsiveness in the treatment of sexual deviation. *Behavior Therapy,* 1975, *8,* 655-671.

Belliveau, F., & Richter, L. *Understanding human sexual inadequacy.* New York: Bantam Books, 1970.

Bergler, E. Frigidity in the female: Misconceptions and facts. *Marriage Hygiene,* 1947, *1,* 16-21.

Brecher, R., & Brecher, E. *An analysis of the human sexual response.* New York: Bantam Books, 1966.

Caird, W.K., & Wincze, J.P. *Sex therapy: A behavioral approach.* New York: Harper & Row, 1977.

Coleman, J. *Abnormal psychology.* Glenview, Ill.: Scott, Foresman, 1964.

Davison, G.C. Elimination of a sadistic fantasy by a client-controlled counter-conditioning technique. *Journal of Abnormal Psychology,* 1968, *73,* 84-90.

Deutsch, E. Behavior therapy of sexual disorders. *Journal of Sex Research,* 1968, *3,* 49-61.

Ford, C.S., & Beach, F.A. *Patterns of sexual behavior.* New York: Harper and Brothers, 1948.

Friday, N. *My secret garden.* New York: Trident, 1973.

Friday, N. *Forbidden flowers.* New York: Pocket Books, 1975.

Goldfried, M.R., & Davison, G.C. *Clinical behavior therapy.* New York: Holt, Rinehart & Winston, 1976.

Goldfried, M.R., & Pomeranz, D. Role of assessment in behavior modification. *Psychological Reports,* 1968, *23,* 75-87.

Haley, J. *Uncommon therapy: The psychiatric techniques of Milton H. Erickson, M.D.* New York: Ballantine Books, 1973.

Hastings, D.W. *Impotence and frigidity.* Boston: Little, Brown, 1967.

Heiman, J., LoPiccolo, L., & LoPiccolo, J. *Becoming orgasmic: A sexual growth program for women.* Englewood Cliffs, N.J.: Prentice-Hall, 1976.

Hoon, E.F., Hoon, P., & Wincze, J. An inventory for the measurement of female sexual arousability. *Archives of Sexual Behavior,* 1976, *5,* 291-300.

Hunt, M. *Sexual behavior in the 1970's.* Chicago: Playboy Press, 1974.

Kinsey, A.C., Pomeroy, W.B., Martin, C.E., & Gebhard, P.H. *Sexual behavior of the human female.* Philadelphia: W.B. Saunders, 1953.

Knox, D. *Marriage happiness.* Champaign, Ill.: Research Press, 1971.

Lazarus, A.A. The treatment of chronic frigidity by systematic desensitization. *Journal of Nervous and Mental Disease,* 1963, *136,* 272-278.

Lee, R.B. *Gay men speak.* Yes books of sex. San Francisco: Multimedia Resource Center, 1973. (Available from Uniquity, P.O. Box 990, Venice, California 90291).

Leiblum, S., Rosen, W., & Pierce, R. Screening and prognosis in sex therapy: To treat or not to treat. *Behavior Therapy,* 1976, *8,* 480-486.

LoPiccolo, J., & Lobitz, W.C. The role of masturbation in the treatment of orgasmic dysfunction. *Archives of Sexual Behavior,* 1972, *2,* 163-171.

LoPiccolo, J., & LoPiccolo, L. *Handbook of sex therapy.* New York: Plenum, 1978.

LoPiccolo, J., & Steger, J.C. The sexual interaction inventory: A new instrument for the assessment of sexual dysfunction. *Archives of Sexual Behavior,* 1974, *3,* 585-595.

LoPiccolo, J., Stewart, R., & Watkins, B. Treatment of erectile failure and ejaculatory incompetence of homosexual etiology. *Journal of Behavior Therapy and Experimental Psychiatry,* 1972, *3,* 233-236.

Marquis, J.M. Orgasmic reconditioning: Changing object choice through controlling masturbatory fantasies. *Journal of Behavior Therapy and Experimental Psychiatry,* 1970, *1,* 263-271.

Martin, D., & Lyon, P. *Lesbian love and liberation.* Yes books of sex. San Francisco: Multimedia Resource Center, 1973. (Available from Uniquity, P.O. Box 990, Venice, California 90291).

Masters, W.H., & Johnson, V.E. *Human sexual response.* Boston: Little, Brown, 1966.

Masters, W.H., & Johnson, V.E. *Human sexual inadequacy.* Boston: Little, Brown, 1970.

McHugh, G. Impotence and latent homosexuality. *Archives of Sexuality,* 1955, *2,* 200-202.

McHugh, G. Erectile failure and female hostility: A conceptual issue. *Archives of Sexuality,* 1967, *14,* 109-117.

McIlvenna, T. *When you don't make it.* Yes books of sex. San Francisco: Multimedia Resource Center, 1973. (Available from Uniquity, P.O. Box 990, Venice, California 90291).

McIlvenna, T., & Vandervoort, H. *You can last longer.* Yes books of sex. San Francisco: Multimedia Resource Center, 1972. (Available from Uniquity, P.O. Box 990, Venice, California 90291).

Michelmore, S. *Sexual reproduction.* Garden City, N.J.: Natural History Press, 1964.

Pion, R.J. Conception control, birth control, and child rearing. In R. Green (Ed.), *Human sexuality and health practitioners.* Baltimore: Williams & Wilkins, 1975.

Razani, J. Ejaculatory incompetence treated by deconditioning anxiety. *Journal of Behavior Therapy and Experimental Psychiatry,* 1972, *3,* 65-67.

Reubin, D. *Everything you always wanted know about sex.* New York: David McKay, 1969.

Reubin, D. *Any woman can!* New York: Bantam Books, 1971.

Robinson, C.H. The effects of observation learning on sexual behaviors and attitudes in orgasmic dysfunctional women. (Doctoral dissertation, University of Hawaii, 1974). *Dissertation Abstracts International,* 1975, *35,* 4662-B. (University Microfilms No. 75-5040)

Rosenberg, J.L. *Total orgasm.* New York: Random House, 1973.

Semans, J.H. Premature ejaculation: A new approach. *Southern Medical Journal,* 1968, *49,* 353-362.

Slattery, W. *The erotic imagination.* Chicago: Henry Regnery, 1975.

Smith, C., Ayres, T., & Rubenstein, M. *Getting in touch.* Yes books of sex. San Francisco: Multimedia Resource Center, 1972. (Available from Uniquity, P.O. Box 990, Venice, California 90291).

Steinmetz, U.Z. *The sexual Christian.* St. Meiniad, Ind.: Abbey Press, 1972.

Stuart, R.B. *Marital pre-counseling inventory.* Champaign, Ill.: Research Press, 1973.

Tarter-Benlolo, L., & Love, W. A sexual phobia treated with macadamia nuts. *Journal of Behavior Therapy and Experimental Psychiatry,* 1977, *8,* 113-114.

Ullmann, L.P., & Krasner, L. *Case studies in behavior modification.* New York: Holt, Rinehart & Winston, 1967.

Wilson, G.T. Innovations in the modification of phobic behaviors in two clinical cases. *Behavior Therapy,* 1973, *4,* 426-430.

Wolpe, J. *Psychotherapy by reciprocal inhibition.* Stanford: Stanford University Press, 1958.

CHAPTER 11

Shyness

John L. Shelton
Department of Rehabilitation Medicine
University of Washington School of Medicine

OVERVIEW OF SHYNESS

A number of recent studies have documented the degree to which dating is a major concern for the young adult.* Zimbardo, Pilkonis, and Norwood (1975) surveyed 800 high school and college students and found that half of the subjects tested thought they could profit from therapeutic help directed at overcoming shyness. In an even more impressive survey, Arkowitz, Hinton, Perl, and Himadi (1978) studied 3,800 randomly selected undergraduates at the University of Arizona. They found that 37 percent of the men and 25 percent of the women felt anxious and inhibited about dating. Similar results have been reached by a number of investigators. Shmurak (Note 1) found that more than half of a sample of young adults reported serious concerns over dating, whereas Bryant and Trower (1974) found that 25 percent of the most

---

*Since our clinical experience is limited to heterosexual shyness, we will restrict our discussion to problems faced by the heterosexual dater. We do not mean to infer that homosexual daters do not suffer from shyness.

serious concerns expressed by a sample of college students involved heterosexual dating.

Shyness, social inhibition, social anxiety, and minimal dating also contribute to a host of other clinical problems. The notion that social incompetence plays an important role in the formation of psychopathology has been advanced by Zigler and Phillips (1960). Supporting this viewpoint have been studies by Argyle (1969) and Argyle, Trower, and Bryant (1974). In the Argyle et al. (1974) study, researchers found that 28 percent of a sample of applicants for mental health treatment were rated by their peers as being socially inadequate. Other writers, such as Annon (1974) in the area of sex dysfunction, Lewinsohn (1975) in the area of depression, and Twentyman , Zimering, and Finnegan (Note 2) in the area of assertion training, have all commented on the close relation between social skill deficits and their prospective clinical research areas.

Socially inhibited minimal daters reveal their shyness in several ways. Many blush, some report anxiety, some report poor eye contact, and others report an inability to communicate verbally. In one study (Zimbardo, 1977), 80 percent of a sample of shy subjects reported having trouble knowing what to say in social situations. In addition to having few heterosexual experiences, these people are often self-conscious about their physical appearance, are excessively critical of their own social skills, and remain in the background on social occasions. Their desire for solitude is reflected in the fact that they interact with significantly fewer persons of the opposite sex than their more gregarious counterparts and, on the whole, spend far less time with others. They often tend to marry late, if at all, and in some cases spend their adult lives in nearly total isolation from intimate social interactions.

The evidence strongly supports the contention that social inhibition is situation-specific. Zimbardo (1977) demonstrated that situations vary greatly in their power to elicit shyness. For example, 70 percent of a sample of shy subjects reported shyness when around strangers, but only 12 percent felt shy in the presence of the elderly. In addition, Zimbardo reported that 73 percent of his sample described feeling shy when they were the focus of a large group, whereas only 14 percent felt shy when engaging in one-to-one same-sex interactions.

The amount of shyness experienced also appears to vary with age, sex, and race. Zimbardo (1977) reported that adolescent women were more likely to experience shyness than adolescent males, although the overall rate of shyness in men and women was the same. Zimbardo (1977) also observed that Asian Americans were more likely to experience shyness than their Caucasian counterparts.

As the experienced clinician will observe, minimal daters have much in common with those troubled by nonassertion. In fact, some writers, such as Gambrill (1976) and Twentyman, Zimering, and Finnegan (Note 2), discuss the treatment for both in one coverage, thus suggesting the treatment for the two to be identical. Both problems do involve common social behaviors. For example, both nonassertive and shy clients often lack the ability to express their emotions, are extremely sensitive to disapproval, have trouble talking about themselves in a positive manner, and share common nonverbal mannerisms such as poor eye contact and feeble voice tone. One study by Orenstein, Orenstein, and Carr (1975) found high negative correlations between scores on an assertion inventory and scores on the Fear Inventory items relating to social fears.

Despite the similarities between nonassertion and shyness, however, important differences exist. For example, the socially inhibited client has few dates, a poor history of intimate contacts with those of the opposite sex, few close friends of the opposite sex, and difficulty making new friends, and is often socially isolated. These behaviors frequently are not true of the nonassertive client, who may have a wide range of intimate friends. Hence, the two problem areas are distinct enough to warrant separate treatment approaches.

Social skill deficits

One possible formulation of shyness or social inhibition focuses on the adequacy of the interpersonal behaviors emitted. In this model, minimal daters are viewed as lacking the social skills necessary to succeed in heterosexual interactions. According to Kanfer and Phillips (1969), a social skill deficit is a class of responses considered problematic because of any combination of the following factors: they fail to occur with sufficient frequency; they fail to occur with adequate intensity; they fail to occur in an appropriate form; they fail to occur at appropriate times and places. This model assumes that the client has not learned the appropriate skills necessary to achieve satisfactory social interactions (Arkowitz, Lichtenstein, McGovern, & Hines, 1975; Borkovec, Stone, O'Brien, & Kaloupek, 1974; Glasgow, 1974; MacDonald, Lindquist, Kramer, McGrath, & Rhyne, 1975; McGovern, 1972; Twentyman & McFall, 1975). In many cases, faulty learning can stem from numerous social interactions that have ended in rejection and failure. As is typically the case with behaviors that are frequently punished, the aversive consequences lead to avoidance of dating interactions, anxiety when forced to interact with others, and a high frequency of negative expectations about what will happen when engaging in social intercourse. A further, more long-term result is that as the client avoids social interactions, he or she fails to practice the social skills necessary to overcome his or her fears and so becomes further and further encapsulated in his or her socially isolated cocoon. Other learning paradigms, such as imitating socially unskilled models, may produce the same results.

Studies by Martinson and Zerface (1970), McGovern (1972), Eisler, Hersen, and Miller (1973), MacDonald et al. (1975), Twentyman and McFall (1975), McGovern, Arkowitz, and Gilmore (1975), and Eisler, Blanchard, Fitts, and Williams (1978) have all supported the potency of skill acquisition. Virtually without exception these studies have successfully employed various combinations of behavioral rehearsal, modeling, coaching, and feedback to produce the necessary changes in the client's behavioral repertoire. Thus, it is clear that the treatment of social inhibition based on the skill acquisition model is one effective way of treating shyness.

Several shortcomings in the research literature, however, prevent us from recommending this model as completely adequate for the treatment of shyness. For example, the typical social inhibition treatment study usually contains a carefully graduated program of outside homework practice that augments in-the-office behavioral rehearsal. Such a treatment could also be conceptualized as *in vivo* systematic desensitization. However, studies attempting to separate the relative contributions of skill modification and desensitization have not been completely adequate. Another problem is that, with few exceptions (Eisler et al., 1978), the typical subjects for a study involving the treatment or assessment of social inhibition are college students. The use of college students limits generalization to the more severely disabled clients who may not be as attractive or as skilled as typical students.

The criterion for what constitutes minimal dating also varies enormously. Zimbardo (1977) suggests allowing clients to determine for themselves what constitutes shyness. Other more empirical approaches give definitions that vary from no more than four dates in the past year (MacDonald et al., 1975) to the very liberal definition proposed by Melnick (1973) of no more than two dates in the last week.

Finally, the exact content of the target social skills has varied in this literature. As Arkowitz (Note 3) argues, most research clinicians have chosen social skills based on their own value orientation of what social behavior is appropriate and effective. A more systematic method of determining target skills is necessary. At present, no such model or methodology exists.

Social anxiety

It may be that many clients have the necessary skills to successfully engage in heterosexual social interactions but are blocked from doing so by social anxiety. In this model, cues associated with social interaction trigger anxiety, which disrupts performance much like excessive anxiety disrupts academic performance (Shelton, 1976). In turn, this anxiety leads to avoidance behaviors that are negatively reinforced by the reduction of anxiety that occurs when the person avoids or leaves the social situation.

Support for the hypothesis that anxiety plays a central role in shyness is both direct and indirect. The indirect evidence is based on two observations. First, it has been noted that researchers investigating shyness have failed to isolate consistent social skill deficits. Second, prominent shyness researchers such as Arkowitz (Note 3) have argued that behavioral assignments — which are often a strong element in successful treatment regimens — are in reality *in vivo* desensitization. Their argument is based on the fact that homework consisting of carefully graduated step-by-step exposure to a threatening stimulus is almost identical to that used in *in vivo* desensitization.

The direct evidence is more compelling. For example, Arkowitz et al. (1975) reported that anxiety measures such as heart rate were significantly different between high- and low-frequency daters. The studies using anxiety-relief procedures as a treatment for low-frequency dating are equally compelling. Mitchell and Orr (1974) showed significant changes for two groups receiving brief courses of desensitization, as compared to a relaxation-only group and a waiting-list control group. In another study, Marzillier, Lambert, and Kellett (1976) compared a social skill training group to a systematic desensitization group and a waiting-list control group. The skill training group treatment consisted of rehearsal, modeling, and receiving feedback. Although the results of this study were generally disappointing, both treatment groups produced a significantly greater range of social contacts. Other research, such as that done by Wright (1976), Hokanson (1971), Curran (1975), and Curran and Gilbert (1975) support the general finding that both social skill training and systematic desensitization are effective in decreasing shyness.

Although further investigation must be done, it appears that social skill training and anxiety reduction are both vital components of the successful treatment of shyness. Of the two, the social skill training procedure is probably the most potent because a carefully graduated program of skill practice seems to result in both a reduction in anxiety and a reduction in skill deficits, whereas anxiety-relief procedures appear to affect anxiety without directly altering social skills. However, this statement is not meant to imply that anxiety-reduction procedures are not important, for as we shall soon see, therapeutic homework assignments involving anxiety relief play a big role in the treatment of this problem.

Inappropriate cognitions

Several different cognitive models have been used to understand shyness. The assumption underlying each of them is that although the social skills of the minimal dater may be adequate, faulty cognitive appraisals and information processing may still lead to anxiety and avoidance behavior.

One of these models of shyness involves the manner in which some persons process information about themselves and their social performance. Excessively high performance standards may maintain social inhibition. Bandura's (1969) views on this point are worth quoting.

> Many of the people who seek treatment are neither incompetent or anxiously inhibited, but they experience a great deal of personal distress stemming from excessively high standards for self-evaluation, often supported by unfavorable comparison with models noted for their extraordinary achievements. (p. 37)

If Bandura is correct, it may be that the manner in which persons evaluate their social performance has an influence on their anxiety and subsequent tendency to avoid social situations, regardless of the actual effectiveness of their behaviors. In this model, the behaviors of shy persons may be reasonably adequate by external standards, but are judged inadequate by the shy client.

Other research supports Bandura's viewpoint. For example, a study by Valentine and Arkowitz (1975) provided evidence that shy subjects were more negative in their self-evaluations of their own social performance than were independent observers. This same general conclusion was reached in similar studies by Glasgow and Arkowitz (1975) and Clark and Arkowitz (1975).

Another closely related cognitive factor that may lead people to be socially inhibited is selective attention to and memory for negative information about themselves and their social performance. Thus, the extent to which clients selectively remember negative information about their social performance would influence their appraisal of these skills even though their performance might have been judged adequate by others. O'Banion and Arkowitz (1977) showed that shy men had a significantly better memory for negative feedback than nonshy men.

Other cognitive ideas have also been discussed. One paper speculates that shy clients were unable to discriminate when and when not to emit the desired responses. In the study, Melnick (1973) investigated the possibility that shy clients possessed the needed social skills required for dating but were deficient in their ability to know when to employ the necessary behavior. In short, their problem was one of response timing and selection. Other cognitive viewpoints touch on such variables as misconceptions and unrealistic thoughts about social situations (Martinson & Zerface, 1970).

Physical attractiveness

The fourth and final model seeking to describe and predict factors that produce shyness is physical attractiveness. Of the four models discussed, the least amount of research by far has been devoted to this particular conceptual model. Nonetheless, some good work has been done. A case in point is the work of Berscheid and Walster (1973), who reviewed the literature on physical attractiveness. These authors concluded that one's physical attractiveness was a very powerful determinant of interpersonal attraction. In addition, they pointed out that more positive characteristics were attributed to more physically attractive individuals and this in turn influenced the way people responded. In another study, Glasgow and Arkowitz (1975) found that the subjects' rating of physical attractiveness was predictive of interpersonal attraction. This work suggests that one problem of those suffering from shyness may be their relatively poor physical appearance. Because of this problem, their heterosexual responses are not likely to be met by success and they are less likely to be sought out for dates.

HOMEWORK-BASED TREATMENT

Overview of Treatment

Both individual client variation and therapist preference affect the process and outcome of treatments designed to reduce social inhibition. This fact is mirrored in the research literature, which shows a wide number of successful approaches to the resolution of shyness (Arkowitz, Note 3). As mentioned earlier, procedures using skill training, anxiety relief, and cognitive modification (Glass, Gottman, & Shmurak, 1976) have all been demonstrated to be effective in one or more studies involving shyness.

We view the treatment of social inhibition as a semistructured training approach with heavy emphasis on the practice of social responses in the client's natural social environment.

Assessment. The first step in the action plan is a thorough assessment of the client's complaints. Later, assessment homework involving both formal and informal measures can be given to verify hunches or client complaints. Table 11.1 lists the questions that must be answered before therapy can proceed.

The next phase in the assessment of shyness involves treatment planning. During this phase the therapist is able to construct a treatment plan that appeals to the client. Besides having face validity to the client, the chosen procedure(s) should be based on sound behavioral principles

Table 11.1

Diagnostic Questions for Social Inhibition

1. Is the client a minimal dater (fewer than one date in the last 3 months)?
2. In what situations does social inhibition occur? With whom does it occur?
3. Does the social inhibition take the form of a skill deficit? If so, which responses fail to occur with sufficient intensity, frequency, or correctness?
    a. If verbal, what is it the client can't say?
    b. If nonverbal, what is it that the client does that lessens his or her interpersonal effectiveness? Consider eye contact, body language, physical appearance, and grooming.
4. Does the client suffer from immobilizing anxiety? If so, what situations and social responses are associated with the anxiety? Is the client aware of the anxiety?
5. Do the client's cognitions interfere with the occurrence of social responses? If so, what is the content of such thoughts? What is the frequency of these cognitions?
6. Is the client physically unattractive? Are the components of the client's unattractiveness changeable?
7. What is the client's history in respect to compliance with psychological or medical regimens? Does the client intend to comply with the suggested homework?

as established by empirical investigations and should be within the client's capabilities.

Because clients respond positively to being given a role in treatment planning, we actively involve them in this process. In practice, this means that the client ranks various social target individuals in order of importance, determines which social responses he or she wishes to emit in the presence of those people, and helps choose from a number of therapeutic interventions designed to produce change. Having helped in the selection of goals and therapy procedures, the client also participates in the construction and execution of behavioral assignments and is therefore more likely to comply with the agreed-upon outside tasks.

To plan the therapeutic intervention, both client and therapist must do the following:

1. Isolate the target people with whom the client fails to interact socially.

2. Pinpoint the behaviors needed to enable the client to interact with those target people.

3. Determine which factors (skills, anxiety, thoughts, or physical attractiveness) interfere with the client's effective social behavior.

4. Enlist the client's cooperation in planning specific treatment interventions and associated behavioral assignments.

Once the information for 1, 2, and 3 is collected, the treatment plan is constructed so as to proceed from the least threatening or demanding target or situation to ones more difficult. The treatment sessions follow the problems in roughly the order presented, with each session focusing on one or more targets and corresponding problems.

Treatment. Considerable effort has been directed toward pinpointing the specific components of the treatment of shyness. Arkowitz (Note 3) and Twentyman and Zimering (1979) have provided in-depth reviews of the treatment of social inhibition. However, it should be stressed that no research to date has demonstrated the comparative effectiveness of interventions for shyness.

Step 1. In this phase of treatment, the therapist provides clients with an understanding of the rationale of social inhibition therapy, acquaints them with some of the procedures typically employed in achieving these ends, and establishes the expectation that extensive homework will be involved in treatment. The chief mode for accomplishing these goals is bibliotherapy, with either therapist-prepared handouts or commercial books or audio tapes.

Step 2. After the clients have been introduced to the notions underlying social inhibition, the therapist is ready to proceed by reducing the obstacles that prevent the occurrence of social responses. This is accomplished by instances of rehearsal, modeling, coaching, and feedback or reinforcement.

Rehearsal. As stated earlier, behavioral rehearsal is the backbone of most behaviorally oriented programs designed to change behavior. It involves the client in overt practice of new responses so that he or she can add to a limited behavioral repertoire or increase the probability that he or she will be able to perform a given social response.

Modeling. According to Twentyman and Zimering (1979), modeling is one of the most widely used treatment components in social skill training, with over 70 percent of the articles reviewed making use of this procedure. In the majority of the studies we read, the therapist or a confederate acted as the model. In a few cases the models are found in films, audio tapes, and scripts. Modeling can and usually does occur in the office, but it can occur as a form of homework in which the confederate or paraprofessional engages in some social behavior that is observed and then imitated by the client.

Coaching. In coaching, the client receives information about his or her social behavior. Coaching differs from modeling in that modeling presents a number of alternative responses, whereas coaching provides guidelines for one target response. In essence modeling is a procedure that elicits a behavior, whereas coaching occurs after the social response. It can occur in the client's natural environment as well as in the office, and it is probably more effective in the former, where the client can interact and receive immediate attention.

Feedback and Reinforcement. Giving the client feedback and reinforcement for his or her social response is very important if the client is to profit from social skill training. Feedback can only occur after the client has obtained information about the desired response through modeling or coaching and has had several practice trials. Reinforcement and feedback on the target response can also occur in the client's natural social environment.

Step 3. Step 3 consists of systematic behavioral assignments designed to augment the learning, transfer, and maintenance of skills, thoughts, and anxiety control learned during Step 2.

According to published studies, therapeutic homework appears to be a central element in the treatment of this problem. The content of the various assignments, however, varies widely across studies, with no one single type of assignment appearing most frequently. Rehearsal (Curran, 1975; Twentyman & McFall, 1975), reading (McGovern, 1972; Royce & Arkowitz, 1978), and self-monitoring (Curran, Gilbert, & Little, 1976) have been mentioned.

The first 10 or 15 minutes of each session are reserved for a discussion of the previous week's outside activity. The discussions typically focus on what happened, how the client felt and what he or she thought, what response he or she received from his or her social target, and how he or she evaluated the performance. If the client attempted the assignment but was unsuccessful in carrying it out completely (for example, if he or she asked two people each time) the session may be spent brainstorming what went wrong and what the client can do differently next time. The behavioral assignment can be reassigned or modified in keeping with the new discussion. Frequent noncompliance requires the therapist to use some of the procedures discussed in Chapter 3. New homework is then assigned.

Homework Assignments

Examples of assignments in the literature. Rehm and Marston (1968) investigated the degree to which self-reinforcement could be used to combat social inhibition. They employed graded homework assignments that were based on a hierarchy of anxiety-arousing heterosexual situations. Subjects assigned themselves points based on the adequacy of their performance, and various performance levels earned self-administered rewards. In another study, Twentyman and McFall (1975) gave homework that consisted of phone conversations with female confederates. McGovern (1972) chose to use a manual, which clients read during their treatment. Homework was structured around the activities outlined in this manual.

Bander, Steinke, Allen, and Mosher (1975) effectively used assignments to augment behavior rehearsal procedures designed to compare social skill training with desensitization. Gambrill (Note 4) conducted one of the few studies dealing specifically with women. In this study, three treatment groups were compared to a waiting-list control group. In one treatment, subjects were given a manual that contained information about behavior change. Homework was assigned to supplement the manual. Another group was given the manual plus homework and also training in self-reinforcement. A third group discussed the same topics as the first two groups but did not receive the manual-homework package. In general, the results suggest that the manual-plus-homework treatment significantly increased the range and number of social contacts over the course of treatment.

One of the most interesting trends in the use of homework in the treatment of social shyness has to do with practice dating. Prescribed practice dating was first reported by Christensen and Arkowitz (1974). Their study involved a comparison between various treatments for social inhibition, some of which involved practice dating. The results showed that significant gains were achieved by treatments involving the use of prescribed practice dates. In a later study, Christensen, Arkowitz, and Anderson (1975) required subjects to engage in six practice dates with and without immediate feedback. These two treatment groups were compared with a delayed-treatment group. The results showed that both homework-based treatments were significantly superior to delayed treatment. Surprisingly, this later study suggested that the homework group not receiving immediate feedback at times did better than the group that received immediate feedback. When assessed at the end of 3 months, both groups receiving homework practice dates were found to have maintained their gains. In another, similar study, Royce and Arkowitz (1978) randomly assigned subjects to a treatment condition involving 12 practice dates with other subjects, a treatment condition involving 12 practice dates plus 9 hours of social skill training, a minimal treatment control condition, and a delayed treatment condition. Outcomes were evaluated by several criteria, including self-report, peer rating, and behavioral measures. Results indicated no significant differences between the two treatment groups or between the two control groups. Both of the two treatment groups, however, were significantly superior to both of the control groups across a number of measures. These gains were maintained at follow-up periods of 3 and 15 months. The authors argued that practice interaction involving dating can be conceptualized as *in vivo* desensitization.

Two other studies (Ascher & Phillips, 1975; Pendleton, Shelton, & Wilson, 1976) took the notion of homework involving practice dates and included paraprofessionals in the process. Both involved the use of Guided Behavior Rehearsal, which is a treatment program involving practice dating. The program uses well-trained paraprofessionals who act as guides for socially inhibited clients. This model is useful in university and large community mental health clinics and rehabilitation programs, but it has obvious drawbacks for the therapist who works in a private practice setting and does not have access to large numbers of volunteers. To activate this program the professional recruits a number of volunteers from community or college groups. The paraprofessionals should be similar to the clients in age, socioeconomic background, and race. They must be active socially and have the ability to communicate effectively with others.

After the volunteers have received minimal training, they then meet with clients between sessions with the therapist. When interacting with clients, the volunteers can perform a number of tasks. They may accompany clients on all of their homework assignments and perform such duties as modeling appropriate behavior, rehearsing with clients before social interactions, practicing relaxation skills before interactions, giving feedback and reinforcement to clients immediately after each exchange, and providing support for clients during embarrassing or difficult interactions. Over time the volunteers' assistance and eventually their presence can be faded until the clients are able to complete assignments without any aid.

In other instances volunteers can assume the roles of "dates" and interact with the clients in a number of social situations. They can then recap each interaction, provide feedback and reinforcement, and, in some instances, ask clients to repeat the assignment until the interaction is performed up to standards. If the therapist is running social inhibition treatment groups, he or she can recruit a number of volunteers who can be rotated from client to client each week. This practice will facilitate transfer effects and lessen the chance that clients will discount their progress because they have become "used to" a particular volunteer. The difficulty of homework assignments is gradually increased, and the locations and other stimulus components of the homework scene are varied in order to enhance transfer effects. Further discussion of the use of volunteers in the treatment of social inhibition can be found in Ascher and Phillips (1975) and in Pendleton, Shelton, and Wilson (1976).

Assessment. Initial assessment of shyness involves bibliothera-peutic homework. If properly chosen, this reading homework can provide information about shyness, list some of the most common shy behaviors from which the client can identify aspects of him or herself, and provide permission for working on shyness. The best of the popular books currently available provide checklists and other aids and can be very useful to the reader. Some good bibliotherapy materials are listed in the assignment shown. Despite the face validity of these materials, at the time of this writing, no published evaluation of their impact on clients exists.

Assignment: Read one or more of the following (as assigned): *Shyness: What It Is, What To Do About It* (Zimbardo, 1977); *The Shyness Workbook* (Zimbardo & Radl, 1979); *Making Contact* (Wassmer, 1978).

Once the therapist has firmly established the presence of social inhibition, either from the interview or from the client's reaction to bibliotherapy, he or she typically is ready to engage in more precise assessment procedures, each of which may involve some form of homework assignment. This discussion begins with self-report measures useful in the assessment of shyness.

Structured paper-and-pencil inventories can add precision to the treatment plan. Since these psychometric devices can be completed at home, they can save valuable time and also serve as a compliance predictor. Clients who do not complete the inventories, who do inadequate work, or who do not meet the agreed-upon time schedule for inventory completion typically will not adhere to later treatment recommendations.

Before discussing these assessment devices we would like to issue one warning. Most of the measures currently available for minimal dating have been developed in the context of treatment-outcome studies involving middle-class, white college students. Many of these measures have inadequate validity and reliability and are not psychometrically refined. In addition, the fact that their norm group is often comprised of college students casts doubt on the power of some of these tests to make accurate predictions on other populations, such as the psychiatrically disturbed or nonwhite racial groups.

Assignment: Complete one or more questionnaires (as assigned).

The following questionnaires may be assigned.

1. *The Situation Questionnaire.* The Situation Questionnaire (SQ), developed by Rehm and Marston (1968), consists of 30 items relating specifically to heterosexual interactions. Unfortunately, the content of the scale makes it appropriate for males only. To take the test, clients are asked to rate a series of social situations on a 7-point scale of discomfort. Research suggests that this instrument has some merit. For example, Curran (1977) and Curran and Gilbert (1975) demonstrated that SQ scores reflected treatment gains, and Borkovec et al. (1974) found that scores on the SQ correlated significantly and in the expected direction with other self-report measures of social anxiety.

2. *The Social Avoidance and Distress Scale.* Developed by Watson and Friend (1969), the Social Avoidance and Distress Scale (SAD) is a

carefully constructed and well-validated self-report measure. This 28-item true-false scale measures avoidance of social interactions, group and public speaking situations, and interactions with "authority figures." As a broad measure of social inhibition, it is quite useful as a screening instrument and as an outcome measure for treatment of social inhibition. The problem with this psychometric measure center around the fact that it does not provide information about specific situations where social distress is experienced.

The SAD has been shown to discriminate between high- and low-frequency daters (Arkowitz et al., 1975) and to correlate in the expected direction of behavioral and peer-rating procedures. With the exception of a study by Marzillier, Lambert, and Kellett (1976), the SAD has been sensitive to changes due to treatment.

3. *The Fear of Negative Evaluation Scale.* The Fear of Negative Evaluation Scale (FNE) was also developed by Watson and Friend (1969). This psychometric measure is a 30-item true-false scale designed to measure the degree to which the client is fearful of receiving negative evaluations from others. The FNE and SAD were both standardized on a population of undergraduate men and women. Although the FNE overlaps with the SAD, it is still useful. Arkowitz (1977) cites evidence that the FNE was able to discriminate high- and low-frequency daters, and studies by Kramer (1975) and McGovern et al. (1975) found significant changes on the FNE with treatment.

4. *The Survey of Heterosexual Interactions.* Developed by Twentyman and McFall (1975), this promising instrument describes 20 specific heterosexual situations. Subjects rate each situation on a 7-point scale as to whether they are able to carry out the interaction. As is the case with the majority of these instruments, this scale is appropriate with men only and is not designed to measure homosexual social inhibition. The major advantage of this measure is that clients' responses to specific situations can be used to plan treatment in specific situations in which the clients express problems. The content of the items allows them to be used as the basis of anxiety hierarchies and as the platform to plan behavior rehearsal. Scores on this measure have been shown to be significantly positively related to changes brought about by treatment (McGovern et al., 1975).

Despite the excellence of the instruments just discussed, they rarely meet all the therapist's needs in assessing minimal daters. Individualized assessment homework must therefore be employed.

Self-monitoring homework can define the scope, frequency, duration, and anxiety level of the problem from information in the natural environment. The following is an illustration of an individualized assessment assignment.

Assignment: Complete a structured log.

In this method, the client is asked to record his or her heterosexual interactions in a log for some specified assessment period, usually from 7 to 10 days. The therapist should take great care to define clearly which social responses are to be recorded, perhaps providing written instructions with examples, such as the log employed by Christensen et al. (1975). Regardless of the format, we suggest that the assessment method be designed to measure the frequency and range of social interactions, since we think these criteria provide the most valid measure of treatment outcome. An illustration of a log follows in Figure 11.1.

A modification of this assignment is completion of a checklist.

Figure 11.1   Sample log for assessment of social interactions

(Front)

Date_ 12/20/80			Name_		Mary Jones			
Name	Hi	Cas	Per	Pre	Spon	Time	SUDS	Init
Bill D	✔	✔		✔		10 min	90	✔
Sondra Q			✔		✔	2 hrs	0	
Barry P	✔							
Stranger (male)	✔							
Stranger (male)	✔							
Claude	✔	✔		✔		1 hr	50	

(Back)

Instructions

This card is to be used to record any social interaction for the date specified. A social exchange is any verbal interchange between you and your peers, relatives, roommates, and anyone else with whom you may come in contact.

Name: Enter the first name and last initial of the person with whom you interacted. For each interaction check the appropriate column.

Hello (Hi): Any social interaction consisting solely of a greeting such as "hi" or "how are you."

Casual (Cas): Any social exchange that would commonly be described as small talk.

Personal (Per): Any social interaction where the intent is to develop a long-lasting, "deeper" friendship.

Prearranged (Pre): Any social interaction that is planned in advance.

Spontaneous (Spon): Any social interaction that is not planned in advance.

Time: Enter the approximate length of the interaction.

Subjective Units of Discomfort (SUDS): Enter the average amount of anxiety you experienced during the interaction with 0 equal to no anxiety and 100 equal to the most anxious you can imagine ever being.

Initiation (Init): If you said the first word, check this column; otherwise leave it blank.

Assignment: Complete a checklist of heterosexual behaviors.

A homemade checklist can be tailormade for the client from data gained during the interview or from previous assessment homework. Figure 11.2 illustrates a homemade checklist that we recently prepared for one of our clients.

Figure 11.2   A tailored social interaction checklist

SOCIAL INTERACTION CHECKLIST FOR CHRIS

Date: _____

	Day						
	M	T	W	T	F	S	S
Said positive things about yourself							
Expressed a compliment to your date							
Received a compliment without embarrassment							
Initiated a coffee break with a friend of the same sex							
Initiated a coffee break with someone of opposite sex							
Invited a woman to a basketball game							
Introduced yourself to a new person							
Dropped someone a pleasant note							

Treatment. One target that we commonly focus on when treating social inhibition is the adequacy of the clients' skills. There are few of us who couldn't profit from some improvement in our social skills. We begin therapy by (1) pinpointing deficit skills, (2) ranking skills in terms of difficulty, (3) modeling each skill, (4) having the client rehearse each skill, and (5) providing feedback, coaching, and reinforcement. This cycle is repeated until the client has mastered each of the target skills. Then behavioral assignments involving practice in the client's natural social environment are given.

Obviously the skills that require practice vary enormously, with the scope, level of difficulty, and behavioral goal being different for each client. Initial behavioral assignments are usually simple, require little time, are designed to insure success, and typically involve practice in initiating a social interaction with others. Later assignments are more complex, require more time, and often involve social responses designed to "deepen" a friendship. However, regardless of the level of complexity of the assignment, we endeavor to have the client (1) practice the skill in the office using behavioral rehearsal; (2) watch others in the natural environment emit the target response; (3) engage in the target response with immediate feedback from the therapist or a confederate; and (4) practice the target behavior without aid or feedback in his or her own natural social environment.

Some examples of behavioral assignments we have used involving practice of social skills follow.

Assignment: Sit near several couples in an informal setting and listen to their conversations. Do this for 30 minutes each day during lunch, in four different settings. Watch closely for good listeners, observing what it is they do.

Assignment: Count and observe the number of times people display affection towards one another in public, noticing what they do.

Assignment: Attend a play or movie and observe the interaction of couples there, keeping track of the number and type of topics discussed.

Assignment: Go to an arts festival and notice the eye contact between people when they talk, noting carefully the amount of gaze. Record your observations, and call for the next appointment after you have observed 50 interactions.

Assignment: Notice in your work setting how people seem to react to being touched; call for an appointment when you have made a dozen observations.

Assignment: Go to a local restaurant and notice how men and women approach each other for the first time; pick a style that fits you and try it on a nonthreatening man or woman.

Assignment: Approach four women or men in your classes during the next week, asking to see the class syllabus. Keep the interactions brief, and ask the most responsive and helpful person to have a cup of coffee.

Assignment: Approach six different single men or women in your church, asking a question regarding the Sunday night dinner. If one offers a ride, accept.

Assignment: Attend church next week and arrive early. Pick an elderly person who is nonthreatening and engage in conversation. Have some questions thought out in advance.

Assignment: Begin to identify likely prospects that you would like to invite to attend a movie, ranking them in order from least to most threatening.

Assignment: Ask someone out for an extended period of time (more than 2 hours), picking a nonthreatening time occupier such as a movie, play, or football game.

Assignment: Ask someone out for a second date, double-dating to have help with conversation.

Some clients seem to possess the necessary skills to engage in effective social interactions but are so nervous in social situations that their performance is often in jeopardy. To combat this problem we often engage in anxiety-relief procedures such as systematic desensitization, Anxiety Management Training (Suinn & Richardson, 1971), Self-Managed Deep Relaxation (Deffenbacher, 1976), and Visual Motor Behavior Rehearsal (Suinn, 1972). These last three procedures are especially applicable to treatments that use behavioral assignments.

Assignment: Couple relaxation techniques with skill practice.

Even if we do not specifically use anxiety-reduction procedures, we often achieve the same purpose by being careful to gradually increase the difficulty of the home practice involving skill modification. Hence, even a "straight skill modification" package should closely resemble *in vivo* desensitization in that it should have the client pass through a homework-focused regimen of gradually increasing difficulty.

Careful attention should also be paid to assignments involving anxiety reduction. One of the most important of these involves the practice of deep relaxation.

Assignment: Practice deep relaxation.

Although it is a good idea to begin the process of relaxation training in the office setting, for purposes of transfer and efficiency it is also good to construct home practice exercises in deep relaxation.

Assignment: Practice deep relaxation using commercial audio tapes.

Assignment: Practice deep relaxation using the therapist's own master tape.

The tapes can be loaned or rented as desired. In some cases, we even sell copies of our master tape to the satisfied client who wishes to use the tape from time to time as a booster to enhance maintenance. In other instances, we have tailored audio tapes especially for the needs of one client (see Shelton, 1976). Although the cost of cutting one tape that can't be used for other clients is high, the procedure sometimes pays off handsomely.

The first step in the relaxation practice is as follows:

Assignment: Practice daily for about 30 minutes.

After 2 weeks of practice, we ask the client to practice without the tape.

Assignment: Practice without the aid of the tape.

Soon after that, the assignment is broadened:

Assignment: Initiate your own relaxation responses in a variety of situations.

Transfer is also accomplished by asking the client to monitor his or her tension level:

Assignment: Check several times each day for your tension level.

To be effective, this homework assignment must have a cue that signals the client when to perform the self-analysis task. Any cue that occurs about 15 to 20 times a day can serve this purpose nicely. For example, clients can be instructed to gauge their level of relaxation whenever they hang up the phone or whenever they look at their wristwatch. If self-analysis reveals high tension levels, then self-relaxation procedures can be instituted immediately.

Once the client has mastered relaxation skills and has demonstrated his or her ability to use them without the aid of audio tapes, he or she is now ready to use these skills in social situations. At this point in therapy we introduce Visual Motor Behavior Rehearsal. This procedure was developed by Suinn (1972) and consists of a simple strategem useful for clients whose level of anxiety interferes with their social performance. This procedure instructs the client to follow three basic steps immediately before any social interaction:

RELAX (prior to the social response)
VISUALIZE (a successful social response)
DO (the social response)

In addition, although Suinn did not use this procedure in his original published piece, we also ask clients to reinforce themselves after each successful instance of social interaction.

Other procedures have been used as well. For example, we have used both *in vivo* and imaginal systematic desensitization in successfully reducing social contact fears. We have also had some success with Anxiety Management Training (Suinn & Richardson, 1971). This procedure is based on the premise that clients can be taught to discriminate internal visceral cues that signal the presence of anxiety. Rapid heartbeat, sweating, and "butterflies" are all examples of visceral signals that can cue the client to immediately engage in strategies to reduce anxiety.

Changing inappropriate cognitions has been attempted by procedures such as those proposed by Ellis and Harper (1975), Mahoney (1974), and Meichenbaum (1977). The procedure we most often use in the control of cognitions is based on Meichenbaum's model, which consists of four steps. Each step involves a general cognitive set that is tailored for each client. The steps are listed as follows, along with an example of how a recent client used this procedure while giving a party.

Assignment: Prepare for the social situation: Rehearse what you are going to do during the party. Think to yourself, "The purpose of my party is to get to know some of the people I work with. I want to have a relaxed, pleasant evening."

Assignment: Confront the challenge: Having given yourself the proper cognitive set, when you hear the doorbell ring, remind yourself to RELAX, VISUALIZE yourself giving the first guest a friendly greeting, saying something appropriate about the weather, and offering your guest something to drink, and then ENGAGE in the visualized behavior.

Assignment: Cope with anxiety at critical moments: At times during the evening you will suddenly become self-conscious and begin worrying about whether or not you are performing well socially and whether or not your guests are having a good time. During these times practice saying to yourself, "Don't get nervous, everything is going fine. Just relax and pay attention to what they are saying. Empathy pays."

Assignment: Reinforce self-statements: As each anxiety sensation is mastered with a self-statement, practice reinforcing yourself with such statements as "Nice going, you handled that well" and "If I stay in control of myself everything seems to work out — nice going."

Homework also plays an important part if physical attractiveness is an aspect of treatment. We often start our assessment of the client's appearance by looking at his or her weight. Frequently a behavioral program of obesity management is justified, and sometimes the client needs to see other professionals.

Assignment: Consult other professionals.

The client should see a dermatologist if his or her skin is particularly unattractive. Better-quality hair salons often can give good advice on the length of hair, whether or not to have it curled or straightened, and what style is best for the client. If the client has too much hair in the wrong places, electrolysis may be an answer. An orthodontist can work with crooked teeth even with adults, and the local ophthalmologist can prescribe soft contact lenses for those with unattractive thick glasses. Finally, reading assignments such as the following may be helpful:

> **Assignment:**   Read grooming books like *Dress for Success* (Molloy, 1975).

A theme that we have repeatedly stated in this book is the importance of therapeutic interventions designed to insure transfer of training. We endeavor to promote transfer by making assignments that vary the location and target of the social response. If confederates are used during part of the problem as social targets, we make sure that the confederate-client matches are frequently changed to eliminate the possibility that the client will become accustomed to one particular person and not be able to generalize social responses to other people.

COMPLIANCE ENHANCEMENT PROCEDURES

The particular behaviors we employ to enhance compliance follow those repeatedly outlined throughout this book. Interventions such as involving the client in treatment planning, allowing the client veto power over all behavioral assignments, using the systematic assignment format to make the assignment concrete, and building in contingencies designed to encourage the completion of the assignment have been discussed in depth. In addition to these, we also suggest making use of the confederate or paraprofessional to enhance compliance whenever possible. The use of confederates who are available to model desirable social behaviors, provide reinforcement and feedback, and act as surrogate social contacts is tremendously helpful in enhancing compliance. The establishment of a sound social relationship is often therapeutic in itself. In addition, knowing that the confederate is waiting for the client to arrive at an appointment place and to participate in some social intervention forces the client to participate out of social obligation, if nothing else.

ILLUSTRATIVE CASE

Willie was a 29-year-old Vietnam veteran who had experienced very few meaningful social interactions with women. Despite his pleasing personality and general good looks, he had had only one intimate interaction with a woman since having received his honorable discharge nearly 3 years before entering therapy. His most recent interaction seemed to typify the kind of interactions he had experienced with women over his three decades of life. Having been introduced to a mature woman by his brother, Willie was mortified to hear that his brother had described him to the woman as "nearly 30 years old and still a virgin." Determined to correct the situation, the woman quickly set out to seduce Willie. Months of gradual social interaction with the woman might have put Willie in the position where a sexual contact would have been very therapeutic; however, being seduced only days after meeting her was a catastrophe. His anxiety prevented him from performing sexually, and his clumsy, inexperienced style only served to make the situation worse. His intense chagrin at having "failed," coupled with his tendency to obsess about his personal social inadequacies, made this a tragic event in his life. Soon after this situation occurred he sought therapy.

Behavioral analysis of Willie revealed three major obstacles to his desire to have high-frequency social interactions with women. The first involved the lack of skills needed to carry out intimate social interaction. Willie was deficient in eye contact, verbal following, disclosure, and knowledge of social norms. In addition, Willie was very anxious. He had a tendency to obsess about his shortcomings and generally had a very poor opinion of himself. He had had no dates with women in years, and had had few opportunities to meet eligible women.

More than a year passed before Willie was able to participate in more satisfying social relationships with women. We proceeded on several fronts simultaneously. So limited were Willie's skills and so intense his fears that more than a month passed before he received his first systematic behavioral assignment involving social interaction with women. And even then, the interaction was limited to saying "hello" and smiling. Much work had to be done before that first simple step. The majority of the first month was spent in deep relaxation training and thought-control procedures. Especially helpful was Meichenbaum's procedure involving self-statements designed to provide the client with coping skills based on staying on the task at hand. In addition, Suinn and Richardson's (1972) procedure involving Visual Motor Behavior Rehearsal, in which the client relaxes, then visualizes successfully carrying out the task before actually completing the task, was successfully used time and time again.

After 1 month, Willie was ready for his first assignment involving social contact with women. Table 11.2 shows the step-by-step progress we followed during the early part of the task. The design is similar to that followed through the rest of the year. With the exception of an occasional vacation, we passed through one skill at a time until Willie was able to interact with women effectively. His skills were initially so limited that more than 3 months passed before he could even be placed in a social inhibition group composed of men and women who had social problems similar to his. His improvement from then on was dramatic.

Table 11.2

Partial Treatment Plan for Willie

Target	Behaviors	Obstacles to Social Effectiveness	Behavioral Assignment
			Third Week

Anyone	Say "hello" and smile.	1. Anxiety
		2. Destructive thoughts
		Antecedent event: People sometimes ignore him when he says "hello."
		Belief: I look so foolish when this happens.
		Consequence: He feels embarrassment and anxiety, and performs avoidance behaviors.
			1. Practice saying "hello" and smiling for 10 minutes each day in front of the mirror. Relax prior to practice.
			
			2. Each day smile and say "hello" to anyone you meet at work. Do this 20 times.
			
			3. If someone fails to speak:
			  a. Use thought stopping;
			  b. Counter all persistent negative thoughts, e.g., "Howard must be under great pressure if he is so harried he doesn't have time to speak."

			Fourth Week
Terri or Marti	Drop into her office and say "hello," give a compliment, and ask a question.	1. Anxiety 2. Skill deficit: He can't give a compliment without appearing artificial.	1. Continue greeting everyone 20 times a day. 2. Observe how people compliment each other; write down what you observe. 3. Practice deep relaxation for 10 minutes twice daily. 4. Note good features and behaviors of fellow workers.
			Fifth Week

			1. Continue greeting everyone.
			
			2. Note a good behavior Terri has; drop her a note telling her so.
			
			3. Follow up your note by dropping in her office for a *brief* chat.
			
			4. Before going to her office:
			  RELAX
			  VISUALIZE TASK
			  DO TASK
			
			5. Reinforce yourself afterwards.
			
			6. Repeat entire sequence with Marti.

However, it still took more than a year before he was able to relate to women in any more than the most superficial way. Constant work involving relaxation training and the cognitive control procedures discussed earlier were needed to decrease his performance anxiety.

With carefully constructed and controlled therapeutic homework, we were able to help Willie progress slowly without ever having a setback such as that suffered during his seduction by a well-meaning woman friend. In addition, we chose to conduct most homework in the context of his work situation because the women there were married and represented much less of a threat to him. Other homework assignments were conducted with female members of his therapy group because of the protection afforded by constant therapist monitoring of social activities between group members. As time progressed, female graduate students served as "dates" with whom he could practice badly needed social skills while receiving valuable feedback from socially skilled women. Only after these measures were taken was Willie able to venture out and interact socially with women whom he did not know. Such careful treatment involving homework eventually resulted in making social interaction a reinforcing and pleasant experience for a formerly shy man.

SUMMARY

Dating is a major concern of the young adult, and shyness often inhibits successful dating, as well as causing other clinical problems. Shyness seems to be situation-specific and to vary with age, sex, and race. It has much in common with nonassertiveness, although the two are not synonymous. Shyness may be attributed to social skill deficits, social anxiety, inappropriate cognitions, or a lack of physical attractiveness.

Many approaches have been used in the treatment of shyness, but the one expressed here is a semistructured training approach with emphasis on practice of social responses in the natural environment. It focuses on heterosexual dating situations. After an assessment of the client's problems, treatment is planned by the therapist in conjunction with the client. Together they isolate target persons, pinpoint the behaviors needed to deal with the target persons, determine which factors prevent the client from interacting effectively, and then lay out specific interventions and assignments. The plan is constructed to move from easier to more difficult targets or situations. Therapy consists of three steps: gaining an understanding of the rationale for treatment, usually through bibliotherapy; reducing obstacles to effective social responses through rehearsal, modeling, coaching, and feedback or reinforcement; and practicing learned thoughts and skills in the natural environment. Examples of assignments from the literature are offered, followed by sample assignments from this approach.

Actions such as involving the client in treatment planning, allowing the client to decide whether assignments are appropriate, making assignments explicit, and building in rewarding contingencies all encourage compliance. The use of a confederate for modeling, providing reinforcement and feedback, and acting as a surrogate social contact is also helpful in enhancing compliance. It places a social obligation on the client to perform certain assignments, and it gives the client a chance to establish a sound social relationship.

In the illustrative case the treatment of Willie, a 29-year-old Vietnam veteran, is examined. Willie had experienced few close relationships with women due to social skill deficits, anxiety, and low self-esteem. He sought therapy shortly after an unsuccessful sexual contact in which his performance was inhibited by anxiety. Treatment began with training in relaxation and thought-control procedures, moving on to gradual learning and practice of social skills. He also took part in a therapy group of socially inhibited men and women. By carefully proceeding, moving through assignments with married women he knew, to women in the therapy group, and then to confederates, Willie reached a point where he could interact with women confidently and pleasantly.

REFERENCE NOTES

1. Shmurak, S.H. *A comparison of types of problems encountered by college students and psychiatric inpatients in social situations.* Unpublished manuscript, Indiana University, 1973.

2. Twentyman, C.T., Zimering, R.T., & Finnegan, D. *An empirical validation of training stimuli for an assertiveness treatment program.* Unpublished manuscript, State University of New York at Binghamton, 1978.

3. Arkowitz, H. *Clinical applications of social skill training: Issues and limitations in generalization from analogue studies.* Paper read at the 10th Annual Convention of the Association for Advancement of Behavior Therapy, December 1976.

4. Gambrill, E.D. *A behavioral program for increasing social interaction.* Unpublished manuscript, University of California, Berkeley, 1975.

REFERENCES

Annon, J.S. *The behavioral treatment of sexual problems* (Vol. 1). Honolulu: Enabling Systems, 1974.

Argyle, M. *Social interaction.* New York: Atherton Press, 1969.

Argyle, M., Trower, P., & Bryant, B.M. Explorations in the treatment of personality disorders and neuroses by social skills training. *British Journal of Medical Psychology,* 1974, *47,* 63-72.

Arkowitz, H. Measurement and modification of minimal dating behavior. In M. Hersen, R.M. Eisler, & P.M. Miller (Eds.), *Progress in behavior modification* (Vol. 5). New York: Academic Press, 1977.

Arkowitz, H., Hinton, R., Perl, J., & Himadi, W. Treatment strategies for dating anxiety in college men based on real life practice. *The Counseling Psychologist,* 1978, *7*(4), 41-46.

Arkowitz, H., Lichtenstein, E., McGovern, K.B., & Hines, P. The behavioral assessment of social competence in males. *Behavior Therapy,* 1975, *6,* 3-13.

Ascher, L.M., & Phillips, D. Guided behavior rehearsal. *Journal of Behavior Therapy and Experimental Psychiatry,* 1975, *6,* 215-218.

Bander, K.W., Steinke, G.V., Allen, G.J., & Mosher, D.L. Evaluation of three dating specific treatment approaches for heterosexual dating anxiety. *Journal of Consulting and Clinical Psychology,* 1975, *43,* 259-265.

Bandura, A. *Principles of behavior modification.* New York: Holt, Rinehart & Winston, 1969.

Berscheid, E., & Walster, E. Physical attractiveness. In L. Berkowitz (Ed.), *Advances in experimental social psychology* (Vol. 7). New York: Academic Press, 1973.

Borkovec, T.D., Stone, N.M., O'Brien, G.T., & Kaloupek, D.G. Evaluation of a clinically relevant target behavior for analogue outcome research. *Behavior Therapy,* 1974, *5,* 503-511.

Bryant, B.M., & Trower, P. Social difficulty in a student sample. *British Journal of Educational Psychology,* 1974, *44,* 13-21.

Christensen, A., & Arkowitz, H. Preliminary report on practice dating and feedback as treatment for college dating problems. *Journal of Counseling Psychology,* 1974, *21,* 92-95.

Christensen, A., Arkowitz, H., & Anderson, J. Practice dating as treatment for college dating inhibitions. *Behaviour Research and Therapy,* 1975, *13,* 321-331.

Clark, J., & Arkowitz, H. Social anxiety and self-evaluation of interpersonal performance. *Psychological Reports,* 1975, *36,* 211-221.

Curran, J.P. Social skills training and systematic desensitization in reducing dating anxiety, *Behaviour Research and Therapy,* 1975, *13,* 65-68.

Curran, J.P. Skills training as an approach to the treatment of hetero-sexual-social anxiety. *Psychological Bulletin,* 1977, *84,* 140-157.

Curran, J.P., & Gilbert, F.S. A test of the relative effectiveness of a systematic desensitization program and an interpersonal skills training program with date anxious subjects. *Behavior Therapy,* 1975, *6,* 510-521.

Curran, J.P., Gilbert, F.S., & Little, L.M. A comparison between behavioral training and sensitivity training approaches to hetero-sexual dating anxiety. *Journal of Counseling Psychology,* 1976, *23,* 190-196.

Deffenbacher, J.L. Relaxation *in vivo* in the treatment of test anxiety. *Journal of Behavior Therapy and Experimental Psychiatry,* 1976, *7,* 289-292.

Eisler, R.M., Blanchard, E.B., Fitts, H., & Williams, J.G. Social skill training with and without modeling for schizophrenic and non-psychotic hospitalized psychiatric patients. *Behavior Modification,* 1978, *2,* 147-172.

Eisler, R.M., Hersen, M., & Miller, P.M. Effects of modeling on components of social skill training. *Journal of Behavior Therapy and Experimental Psychiatry,* 1973, *4,* 1-6.

Ellis, A., & Harper, R.A. *A new guide to rational living.* Englewood Cliffs, N.J.: Prentice-Hall, 1975.

Gambrill, E.D. The use of behavioral methods in a short term detention setting. *Criminal Justice and Behavior,* 1976, *3,* 53-66.

Glasgow, R.E. *The behavioral assessment of male and female social competence in dyadic heterosexual interactions.* Unpublished master's thesis, University of Oregon, 1974.

Glasgow, R.E., & Arkowitz, H. The behavioral assessment of male and female social competence in dyadic heterosexual interactions. *Behavior Therapy,* 1975, *6,* 488-498.

Glass, C.R., Gottman, J.M., & Shmurak, S.H. Response acquisition and cognitive self-statements modification approaches to dating skills training. *Journal of Counseling Psychology,* 1976, *23,* 520-526.

Hokanson, D.T. *Systematic desensitization and positive cognitive rehearsal treatment of social anxiety.* Unpublished doctoral disser-tation, University of Texas at Austin, 1971.

Kanfer, F.H., & Phillips, J.S. A survey of current behavior therapies and a proposal for classification. In C.M. Franks (Ed.), *Behavior therapy, appraisal and status.* New York: McGraw-Hill, 1969.

Kramer, S.R. *Effectiveness of behavior rehearsal and practice dating to increase heterosexual social interaction.* Unpublished doctoral dissertation, University of Texas, 1975.

Lewinsohn, P.M. The behavioral study and treatment of depression. In M. Hersen, R.M. Eisler, & P.M. Miller (Eds.), *Progress in behavior modification* (Vol. 1). New York: Academic Press, 1975.

MacDonald, M.L., Lindquist, C.U., Kramer, J.A., McGrath, R.A., & Rhyne, L.L. Social skills training: Behavior rehearsal in groups and dating skills. *Journal of Counseling Psychology,* 1975, *22,* 224-230.

Mahoney, M.J. *Cognition and behavior modification.* Cambridge, Mass.: Ballinger Publishing, 1974.

Martinson, W.D., & Zerface, J.P. Comparison of individual counseling and a social program with nondaters. *Journal of Counseling Psychology,* 1970, *17,* 36-40.

Marzillier, J.S., Lambert, C., & Kellett, J. A controlled evaluation of systematic desensitization and social skills training for socially inadequate psychiatric patients. *Behaviour Research and Therapy,* 1976, *14,* 225-238.

McGovern, K.B. *Development and evaluation of a social skills training program for undergraduate male nondaters.* Unpublished doctoral dissertation, University of Oregon, 1972.

McGovern, K.B., Arkowitz, H., & Gilmore, S.K. Evaluation of social skills training programs for college dating inhibitions. *Journal of Counseling Psychology,* 1975, *22,* 505-512.

Meichenbaum, D.H. *Cognitive-behavior modification: An integrative approach.* New York: Plenum, 1977.

Melnick, J. A comparison of replication techniques in the modification of minimal dating behavior. *Journal of Abnormal Psychology,* 1973, *81,* 51-59.

Mitchell, K.R., & Orr, F.F. Note on treatment of heterosexual anxiety using short-term massed desensitization. *Psychological Reports,* 1974, *35,* 1093-1094.

Molloy, J. *Dress for success.* New York: Warner Books, 1975.

O'Banion, K., & Arkowitz, H. Social anxiety and selective memory for affective information about the self. *Social Behavior and Personality*, 1977, *5*, 321-328.

Orenstein, H., Orenstein, F., & Carr, J.E. Assertiveness and anxiety: A correlational study. *Journal of Behavior Therapy and Experimental Psychiatry*, 1975, *6*, 203-207.

Pendleton, L.R., Shelton, J.L., & Wilson, S.E. Social interaction training using systematic homework. *The Personnel and Guidance Journal*, 1976, *54*, 484-491.

Rehm, L.P., & Marston, A.R. Reduction of social anxiety through modification of self-reinforcement: An instigation therapy technique. *Journal of Consulting and Clinical Psychology*, 1968, *32*, 565-574.

Royce, W.S., & Arkowitz, H. Multimodal evaluation of practice interactions as treatment for social isolation. *Journal of Consulting and Clinical Psychology*, 1978, *46*, 239-245.

Shelton, J.L. Homework in AT [assertive training]: Promoting the transfer of assertive skills to the natural environment. In R.E. Alberti (Ed.), *Assertiveness: Innovations, applications, issues*. San Luis Obispo, Calif.: Impact, 1977.

Suinn, R.M. Behavior rehearsal for ski racers. *Behavior Therapy*, 1972, *3*, 519-520.

Suinn, R.M., & Richardson, F. Anxiety management training: A nonspecific behavior therapy program for anxiety control. *Behavior Therapy*, 1971, *2*, 490-510.

Twentyman, C.T., & McFall, R.M. Behavioral training of social skills in shy males. *Journal of Consulting and Clinical Psychology*, 1975, *43*, 384-395.

Twentyman, C.T., & Zimering, R.T. Behavioral training of social skills. In M. Hersen, R.M. Eisler, & P.M. Miller (Eds.), *Progress in behavior modification* (Vol. 7). New York: Academic Press, 1979.

Valentine, J., & Arkowitz, H. Social anxiety and the self-evaluation of interpersonal performance. *Psychological Reports*, 1975, *36*, 211-221.

Wassmer, T. *Making contact*. New York: Dial Press, 1978.

Watson, D., & Friend, R. Measurement of social-evaluative anxiety. *Journal of Consulting and Clinical Psychology*, 1969, *33*, 448-457.

Wright, J.C. A comparison of systematic desensitization and social skills acquisition in the modification of a social fear. *Behavior Therapy,* 1976, *7,* 205-210.

Zigler, E., & Phillips, L. Social effectiveness and symptomatic behaviors. *Journal of Abnormal and Social Psychology,* 1960, *61,* 231-238.

Zimbardo, P. *Shyness: What it is, what to do about it.* New York: Harcourt, Brace, Jovanovich, 1977.

Zimbardo, P., Pilkonis, P., & Norwood, R. The social disease called shyness. *Psychology Today,* May 1975, pp. 69-72.

Zimbardo, P., & Radl, S. *The shyness workbook.* New York: A & W Visual Library, 1979.

CHAPTER 12

Nonassertion

John L. Shelton
Department of Rehabilitation Medicine
University of Washington School of Medicine

OVERVIEW OF NONASSERTION

Assertion

It is very difficult to define assertion in a manner that satisfies everyone. More than 20 books have been written on assertion training, all from a slightly different perspective.* For example, Friedman (1971) wrote that assertion is "the ability of a person to engage in behavior which indicates he has certain rights he feels he is entitled to exercise." A more popular definition, provided by Alberti and Emmons (1970), states that assertion is "behavior which enables a person to act in her (her) own best interests, to stand up for himself (herself) without undue anxiety, to express his (her) own rights without denying the rights of others." Lazarus (1971) equates assertion with "habits of emotional freedom,"

---

*A list of helpful materials in the area of assertion training is provided at the end of this chapter.

which include love, affection, and sympathy, as well as anger, pain, remorse, skepticism, fear, and sadness. A more succinct definition was given by Fensterheim (1970); he states, "assertiveness is an open and direct, honest and appropriate expression of what a person feels and thinks." More recent definitions include one by Lange and Jakubowski (1976), which states that "assertion involves standing up for personal rights and expressing thoughts, feelings, and beliefs in direct, honest and appropriate ways which do not violate another person's rights" (p. 7). Rich and Schroeder (1976) defined assertion according to its results: "assertiveness can be measured by the degree to which the behavior is effective in producing, maintaining or enhancing reinforcement from others."

Nonassertion

Nonassertion consists of numerous verbal and nonverbal behaviors common to many clients. Since many behavioral disorders, such as depression and shyness, share many common behaviors with nonassertion, it is not prudent to assume that the indices shown in Table 12.1 automatically signal the presence of nonassertion; instead, their presence should alert the professional to the possibility that nonassertion may exist.

Table 12.1
Indices of Nonassertion

Inability to express all manner of emotions, both pleasant and unpleasant, in an open, honest, and direct manner	Likelihood of being pushed around by others, for example, failure to ask loud patrons in a movie to quiet down
Inability to recognize one's personal rights	Inability to express anger
Inability to insist on fair treatment, such as equal pay	Inability to talk about oneself in a positive manner
Inability to state honest disagreements with ease	Low-frequency eye contact
Inability to say "no" or ask "why"	A weak voice or poor word fluency, which causes others to not listen to what one says
Inability to ask for what one wants	A docile, "hang-dog" look
Extreme sensitivity to disapproval	High-frequency negative thoughts regarding one's abilities and characteristics
Excessive agreement with the wishes of those older or more powerful	"Bottling up" feelings rather than creating a scene
Inability to give or accept compliments without embarrassment	Being overly eager to comply with therapeutic directives in an effort to please the therapist
Inability to express an opinion	

Assertion and Aggression

The distinction between assertion and aggression is an important skill for the therapist to acquire because clients must be taught to discriminate between the two if assertion training is to be successful. Clients frequently perceive assertion training as a flimsy disguise for aggression and will consequently be less likely to comply with outside behavioral activities that they construe as aggression. Even more common is the tendency for clients to behave aggressively during assertion-targeted homework and subsequently to experience aversive consequences from those with whom they interact.

The successful discrimination of aggression and assertion can be facilitated by comparing the two across the following five dimensions.

Behavior. The usual goal of aggression is dominating and winning, thereby forcing the other person to lose. Winning, in turn, is typically insured by humiliating, degrading, belittling, or overpowering the other person. Aggressive verbal behaviors that accomplish these ends include name-calling, accusations, ultimatums, and threats. In contrast, assertive statements typically involve far less strident and more respectful means. Assertions are simply straightforward adult-oriented responses aimed at maximizing an exchange of ideas without hurting the other party. Nonverbal aggressive behaviors include interrupting, speaking in a sarcastic or condescending tone of voice, and using parental body gestures such as excessive finger pointing. Assertive nonverbal gestures are quite the opposite. They involve a straightforward statement of one's thoughts, feelings, and desires without the use of the intimidation tactics just described.

Intent. A second factor in understanding the difference between aggression and assertion is the intent of the communication. The intent of aggression is to hurt, while the intent of assertion is to express. Admittedly, this is "a judgment call" on the part of the therapist, but frequently the client's cognitive set will provide, upon careful exploration, the intent of the response.

Effect. One manner of determining whether a behavior could be termed aggressive or assertive is the effect on the target person. If the target person receives a message and responds with reinforcement, cooperation, or compromise, then the client probably behaved assertively (Rich & Schroeder, 1976). If, on the other hand, the reaction of the target person was anger, outrage, or brooding, then the action may have been an aggressive one. Support for this premise comes from Jakubowski-Spector (1973), who showed that assertion elicits respect from others and aggression elicits responses of anger, hurt, and humiliation from the target person.

Consideration of the rights of others. Aggression usually involves directly standing up for one's personal rights while expressing thoughts, feelings, and beliefs in a way that is often dishonest, inappropriate, and disrespectful. In this sense "disrespect" implies a disregard for the rights of others. The aggressive person cares little for the rights of others as long as his or her own needs are met. On the other hand, the client displaying assertion attempts to meet his or her needs while respecting the rights of others. Exactly what rights are considered basic to humans have been discussed by a number of authors, for example, by Alberti and Emmons (1974), Fensterheim and Baer (1975), Smith (1975), and Lange and Jakubowski (1976).

Sociocultural differences. As Cheek (1976) regarding blacks, Landau and Paulson (1976) regarding Chicanos, and Hwang (1976) regarding Asian Americans have pointed out, subcultural norms, values, and expectations can greatly influence the discrimination between aggression and assertion. Although no clear-cut rules exist for taking into account sociocultural differences, the clinician should be sensitive to the problems inherent in working with minorities and culturally diverse clients and should proceed with extreme caution when deciding which behaviors constitute aggression and which constitute assertion.

Etiology of Nonassertion

Studies on assertion and designs for assertion training have sprung from three hypotheses about why some persons tend to express nonassertive behaviors. Each of these explanations generates different treatment strategies and corresponding changes in therapeutic homework.

Lack of skills. The first hypothesis, as advanced by Lazarus (1971) and McFall and Twentyman (1973), argues that nonassertion is caused by skill deficiency. The core of this argument is that people behave nonassertively because they do not know how to behave otherwise. This failure of learning may have been caused by poor models or by aversive consequences that often befall beginning attempts at assertion. Treatment generated from this model is aimed at teaching clients the requisite skills needed to successfully assert themselves. Within-the-office interventions typically include behavior rehearsal, coaching, reinforcment, and modeling. Systematic homework consists of practicing the newly acquired skills in different settings and with different targets. A major goal of homework here is to control aversive consequences that may punish and therefore lessen the frequency of assertive behaviors.

Presence of anxiety. Another compelling model argues that the client has the necessary skills but is inhibited from behaving assertively by conditioned anxiety which is triggered in situations demanding assertion responses (Salter, 1949; Wolpe, 1973). Although recent research by Thorpe (1975) and by Trower, Yardly, Bryant, and Shaw (1978) has cast doubt on the idea of anxiety as the sole cause for nonassertion, we believe that the reduction of anxiety does have merit in some cases involving nonassertion. Treatment procedures generated from this model consist of such anxiety-relief procedures as systematic desensitization, flooding, and Anxiety Management Training. Therapeutic homework consists of the self-managed application of these procedures in the client's natural environment (see Chapter 4 for additional information).

Faulty cognitions. A third model suggests that assertion may be causally related to the client's maladaptive cognitive patterns. This conceptual model argues that what a person thinks about him or herself may be an important variable in effective assertion training. Thus, for example, negative beliefs about self-worth often instill an attitude of pessimism which pervades therapy and leads to noncompliance. The thought "I'm worthless, nothing ever works for me so why try" is often the cognitive set of nonassertive clients.

This conceptual model is the newest of the theoretical views that seek to explain nonassertion, and it has not been investigated extensively. However, what research has been done has been impressive. Linehan (1979), Rich and Schroeder (1976), Schwartz and Gottman (1976), and Wolfe and Fodor (1977) have all demonstrated the strength of this conceptual model. Among the findings reported in the literature are the following results:

1. Cognitive interventions were as effective as skill training procedures in the production of assertion responses.

2. A cognitive component added to a skill training package significantly reduced assertion-associated anxiety more than anxiety-relief procedures per se.

Our experience with nonassertive clients has led us to conclude that from time to time they express all three of these modalities. Hence, some clients lack assertion skills, while others have the skills but fail to emit them because of anxiety of faulty cognitions.

HOMEWORK-BASED TREATMENT

Overview of Treatment

Treatment plans for nonassertion vary considerably. Individual client problems, as well as therapist style and training, affect both the process and the outcome of assertion procedures. The research literature shows a wide number of approaches to the successful resolution of assertion problems. For example, assertion training with psychiatric patients is likely to deal with different situations, behaviors, and beliefs than assertion training carried out with college students. Furthermore, different groups of clients may require different procedures and matching homework assignments; for example, homemakers who are returning to work after a long absence require special attention to assertion problems arising out of the work situation.

Our brand of assertion training, with its corresponding heavy emphasis on therapeutic homework, is similar to several of the most popular training methods. Succinctly stated, assertion training is a semi-structured training package with a heavy emphasis on the practice of assertion responses. Some practice is done in the formal treatment setting, but much more is conducted in the client's social environment.

Assessment. Frequently we find that clients with an assertion problem make no mention of this during initial contact. One is likely to hear complaints of emotional, cognitive, or behavioral consequences that arise as a result of nonassertion, but rarely about the behavior itself. Nonassertive clients are often not aware of the nature of their problem, but complain of unhappiness, depression, and other vague complaints that are hard to pinpoint. Unless one is sensitive to the issues associated with nonassertion, it is easy to misdiagnose the problem.

As a result, the first goal of assessment is to determine whether or not the client is nonassertive. If the initial assessment process yields evidence regarding the existence of nonassertion, then additional, more precise procedures need to be employed. The initial assessment process is conducted in the office with appropriate systematic behavioral assignments being conducted to follow up various leads. Often formal psychometric assessment will also be needed to help the therapist formulate a treatment plan. Table 12.2 illustrates the questions that must be answered before therapy can proceed.

The first question in Table 12.2 concerns the decision as to whether the client is emitting nonassertive behaviors. The therapist begins the process of answering this question by listening closely to the client's initial complaints. Questioning may also reveal the presence of negative cognitions that may interfere with interpersonal effectiveness. In addition, the therapist can often note the situations or people with whom assertion is a problem, since assertion is typically situation-specific and does not appear to be a generalized trait. Also attended to are the client's nonverbal communication patterns, since they account for a great deal of the impact of assertive communications on others (Mehrabian, 1972). Important nonverbal behaviors include eye contact,

Table 12.2
Diagnostic Questions for Nonassertiveness

---

1. Is the patient nonassertive?

2. Is the client's nonassertive behavior situational or general? If situational, in what situations does it occur?

3. What is the frequency of nonassertive behaviors in these situations?

4. Does the nonassertion take the form of a skill deficit? If so, which responses fail to occur with sufficient intensity, frequency, or correctness?

5. Is the skill deficit verbal, nonverbal, or a combination of the two? If verbal, what is it that the client won't say? Also, look for verbal characteristics such as the following:
   a. The loudness of the client's voice
   b. The fluency of the spoken words
   c. The choice of words

6. If the skill deficit is nonverbal, you should consider these behaviors:
   a. The absence of eye contact
   b. The facial expression
   c. The body expression

7. Does the client suffer from immobilizing anxiety? If so, what assertions are associated with the anxiety? In addition, is the client aware of the anxiety and ever able to control it?

8. Do the client's cognitions interfere with the occurrence of assertive behavior? If so, what is the content of such cognitions — self-talk or "mental pictures"? What is the frequency of these cognitions?

9. What is the history of the client's compliance with medical or psychological treatment regimens? Does the client think that the problem is serious? Does the client predict that he or she will comply with psychological assignments?

---

body positioning, facial expression, and the congruence between what a person says and what their nonverbal communication conveys.

Having established the hypothesis that the client may engage in nonassertion, the therapist can confirm that conclusion by asking such questions as:

1. "If you were short-changed at the supermarket, how would you respond?"

2. "If someone cut in line in front of you at the movie, how would you respond?"

3. "How often do you get angry and express your feelings to (person)?"

4. "In what situations are you most likely to be walked on?"

5. "How do you react when criticized by your boss?"

Answers suggesting the presence of nonassertion can lead to further in-the-office assessment. For example, roleplaying offers a valuable tool to further the question of nonassertion. The client can be requested to roleplay troublesome situations, with reciprocal roles assumed by the therapist after determining how significant others would act in respect to the client. Roleplaying is especially helpful in enabling the therapist to determine the extent to which nonassertion is a skill deficit, an anxiety problem, or a combination of both. In addition, asking the client to verbally describe his or her thoughts during the roleplay situation will often help clarify any dysfunctional thoughts that might impede therapy or interfere with adherence to home practice activities. Once the therapist has firmly established the presence of nonassertion by these means, he or she is ready to engage in more precise assessment procedures. Each of these involves systematic behavioral assignments that are completed by the client in his or her social environment.

The next step in the assessment of nonassertion involves treatment planning. Clients respond very positively to being given an active role in the treatment planning process. Increased self-confidence, persistence, maintenance, and adherence are just a few of the advantages gained by this approach. In addition, the ethical guidelines of the Association for Advancement of Behavior Therapy* demand that, whenever possible, clients be given a choice as to which of several treatments seem most appropriate to them.

Once the therapist has collected and analyzed the data gained during the assessment phase, he or she is ready to proceed with planning the therapeutic intervention. This particular joint endeavor contains four elements:

1. Isolate the target people with whom the client is nonassertive or aggressive.

2. Pinpoint the nonassertive behaviors to be changed with each target person.

3. Determine which factors prevent the client from behaving assertively.

4. Enlist the client's cooperation in planning specific treatment interventions and associated systematic behavioral assignments.

Obviously, the planned treatment depends entirely on the data collected during the assessment process. Incomplete or erroneous data adversely affect treatment outcome.

Treatment. The mechanics of assertion training vary enormously from trainer to trainer (Linehan, 1979). However, most experts agree that this treatment typically contains some combination of behavioral rehearsal, coaching with feedback, didactic teaching, and behavioral

---

*A copy of "Ethical Issues for Human Services" as proposed by the Association for Advancement of Behavior Therapy can be obtained by writing the association at 420 Lexington Avenue, New York, New York 10017.

assignments of one kind or another. The emphasis on any one of these factors will vary according to the therapist's orientation and the client's social environment. Our particular model incorporates many of the attributes described by Gambrill (1977) and can be used for treating both groups and individuals. The sequence of the therapeutic process in our assertion-training model follows.

Step 1: In this phase of therapy, the goal is to provide clients with an understanding of the rationale of assertion training, acquaint them with some of the procedures typically employed in achieving those ends, alert them to basic human rights—which serve as the cognitive catalyst to greater assertion—and, finally, help them make the discrimination between assertion and aggression.

Step 2: After specific assertion training goals are finalized, the therapist and client attempt to reduce the obstacles that prevent the occurrence of assertive behaviors. This task is accomplished by repeated instances of behavioral rehearsal, cognitive control, and anxiety-relief procedures.

Step 3: This step occurs after each instance of within-the-office therapy and employs systematic behavioral assignments designed to augment the learning, transfer, and maintenance of skills and cognitive control procedures learned during Step 2.

Homework Assignments

Assessment. Nonassertive behaviors and associated thoughts and emotions can be pinpointed by assignments involving bibliotherapy. Used for self-assessment purposes, several popular assertion-related books can be purchased and then rented, sold, or lent to clients. Books such as those by Salter (1949), Alberti and Emmons (1974), Fensterheim and Baer (1975), Gambrill and Richey (1976), and Lange and Jakubowski (1976) are especially useful for self-diagnostic purposes.

Assignment: Read or listen to the book or tape as assigned.

Systematic behavioral assignments involving tapes, cassettes, books, or pamphlets must be carefully given. First, it is critical that the therapist be familiar with all materials before giving therapeutic homework involving their use. Being aware of the strengths and weaknesses of each didactic piece aids the therapist in anticipating areas of confusion or misinformation. Care should also be taken to make assignments within the time and skill restraints of the client. Retention and adherence to reading or listening assignments can be greatly enhanced by giving the client tasks to perform while listening or reading.

For example, making lists, memorizing definitions, giving additional examples taken from their own lives that illustrate a point, and finding fault with various aspects of the didactic presentation are all examples of methods of compliance and retention enhancement.

The use of bibliotherapy can take many forms. Some books contain checklists and informal recording formats that enable the client to measure his or her own behavior against an assertion standard, usually idiosyncratically defined by the particular author.

> **Assignment:**   Complete the checklist (or other recording format) and bring it into therapy for discussion.

Such an assignment allows the client to read some descriptive material involving nonassertion. If the therapist's hunch regarding the presence of nonassertion is accurate, he or she will likely hear the client say something like "The book you gave me fit me to a T, you really have me pegged." Such structured self-diagnostic assignments as the one just mentioned give the client the opportunity to relabel his or her problem in an entertaining yet worthwhile manner. In addition, self-assessment that has pleasant side effects such as interesting reading is likely to be complied with. Affirmative reports of the accuracy of the bibliotherapy in describing the client are then followed up with such questions as "What exactly did you read that seemed most like you?"

> **Assignment:**   Record each of the descriptions in the book that best describes your behavior.

Whether the therapist determines the existence of nonassertion by interview of bibliotherapy or a combination of both, it is often useful to check the client's report against information gained during interviews with significant others, such as the spouse. Clients are not naturally good observers of their own behaviors and the conditions which elicit nonassertion. Hence, the importance of involving the client's spouse or a significant other in both assessment and treatment cannot be emphasized too strongly. After all, the client's behavior never occurs in a vacuum. Therefore, we simply refuse to treat individuals without the participation of the significant other(s).

Another homework-related self-assessment procedure is the use of the structured paper-and-pencil inventories available in the literature.

> **Assignment:**   Complete paper-and-pencil inventory.

These screening devices add a great deal to the precision with which the therapist can construct the treatment plan and should be used with each client. Since these psychometric devices can be taken home and completed, they can save valuable time and serve as an important compliance predictor. We have found that clients who do not complete the tests, who do inadequate work, or who do not meet the agreed-upon time schedule typically will not adhere to later treatment recommendations.

Some of the structured take-home tests we have used follow:

The Fear Inventory (Wolpe & Lang, 1964)

The Wolpe-Lazarus Assertiveness Questionnaire (Wolpe & Lazarus, 1966)

The Conflict Resolution Inventory (McFall & Bridges, Note 1)

The Rathus Assertive Inventory (Rathus, 1973)

The College Self-Expression Scale (Galassi, DeLo, Galassi, & Bastien, 1974)

The Adult Self-Expression Scale (Galassi & Galassi, 1974)

The Assertion Inventory (Gambrill & Richey, 1975)

The Interpersonal Situation Inventory (Goldsmith & McFall, 1975)

The Adult Assertion Scale (Jakubowski & Wallace, Note 2)

This list by no means exhausts the number of adequate assertion assessment devices currently available today. Competent clinicians who have combed the literature or attended workshops such as those offered by the Association for Advancement of Behavior Therapy usually develop a battery of these assessment tools. Since all fo the preceding devices have something to recommend them, the therapist must choose his or her favorite by trial and error and recommendations from colleagues. Detailed discussions of these instruments can be found in a number of publications, such as those by Galassi and Galassi (1977), Ciminero, Calhoun, and Adams (1977), Cone and Hawkins (1977), Gambrill (1977), and Mash and Terdal (1976).

The third mode of homework-focused assessment strategies to consider in the investigation of nonassertion are informal behavioral measures such as frequency, time sample, and event recording. These personalized assessment schemas are self-administered in the client's own social environment and can be tailored to the client's exact needs.

> **Assignment:** Keep a log for 1 week on your own assertive be-
> haviors and how you could have behaved more as-
> sertively.

The great advantage of self-monitoring individualized homework is that the scope, eliciting situations, frequency, and form of nonassertive behavior can be gained from information occurring spontaneously in the natural environment. For instance, the client can be requested to keep a log of relevant situations by noting what the situation was, what was said and done, and what the client could have done differently had he or she been assertive. Figure 12.1 is a fictitious log that shows what a client might record.

Figure 12.1   Sample assertion log

Name: _____ *Joe Smith* _____   Date: _____ *4/26* _____

Date	Time	Target	What Happened	What You Did	What You Should Have Done
4/26	*9:20*	*Mary*	*She asked to use my notes.*	*I said "O.K."*	*I should have said that in the past she has lost my notes and that I can't lend them anymore.*
4/26	*3:35*	*Dave*	*During our jog he kept pushing me to run harder.*	*I tried to keep up.*	*I should have told him that I was out to run for fun, not pain, and had him go on by himself.*

A modification of the preceding approach is to ask the client to complete a checklist of nonassertive behaviors.

Assignment: Record your own assertive behaviors on a checklist for 1 week.

Although this is a crude method, a homemade checklist can be tailormade for the client based on data gained during the interview or as a result of bibliotherapy. Figure 12.2 illustrates a homemade checklist prepared for one of our clients.

Figure 12.2   A tailored assertion checklist

ASSERTION CHECKLIST FOR JOE

Date: _____

	Day						
	M	T	W	T	F	S	S
Talked about yourself in a positive manner							
Expressed a compliment to a coworker							
Received a compliment without embarrassment							
Expressed your opinions directly and spontaneously							
Asked a favor of someone							
Said "no" to Dr. Lehberg							
Told Cynthia "I love you"							
Introduced yourself to a new person							

In addition to logs or tailormade checklists that yield much data but are difficult to quantify, more quantifiable approaches such as time sample or event recording can be used. The results of two self-recording homework assignments showing this more quantifiable approach are shown in Figures 12.3 and 12.4.

Figure 12.3   Sample graph

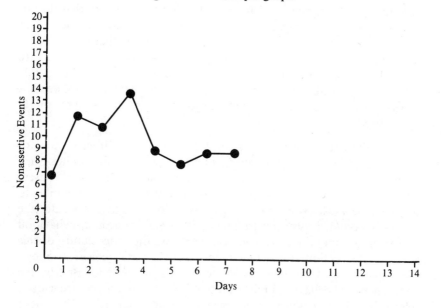

Figure 12.4   Sample time sampling

8	9	10 ✔	11 ✔
Noon ✔	1	2 ✔	3 ✔
4	5 ✔	6 ✔	7 ✔
8 ✔	9 ✔	10	11

Assignment: Count occurrence (sample or events) of nonassertive behavior for 1 week.

Figure 12.3 shows the frequency of nonassertive events for a 20-year-old college coed. After learning to observe, pinpoint, and record her nonassertive behavior, she constructed this graph. It shows that she was nonassertive on the average of 11 times per day. Figure 12.4 shows the record of a client whose rate of self-deprecatory thoughts was interfering with his ability to assert himself. In this case, we elected to use a time sample recording method. Although not as precise as event recording, it has a far lower cost and is still useful for high frequency behaviors. The client, a 17-year-old high-school senior, recorded whether or not he experienced a bad self-thought at any time during the ensuing hour. A check indicates that he had at least one negative self-thought during that hour. This method, although crude and not as accurate as event recording, is especially good for high-frequency behaviors that do not have clear-cut beginnings and endings. This point is nowhere more clear than for the client who suffers from streams of ideas that come and go and are composed of many elements. These cognitive patterns are difficult to event record but yield much more readily to time sample assessment because the only problem is to know whether or not one has experienced at least one specified category of thought during a preset time period.

Treatment. Considerable effort has been directed toward pinpointing the specific components of effective assertion training. Such researchers as McFall and Lillesand (1971), Kazdin (1974), Eisler, Hersen, and Miller (1973), and Rosenthal and Reese (1976) have all attempted to uncover the most potent elements in assertion training. To date, the generally accepted assertion training format centers around behavioral rehearsal, although not everyone can agree on the exact nature of this specific intervention either. Our model of behavioral rehearsal follows the suggestions of the most respected writers in the field. Briefly, the components of behavioral rehearsal include modeling, covert rehearsal, relaxation, live practice, reinforcement, and feedback. The entire sequence is repeated until the client and therapist are satisfied with the assertion response.

After the client has acquired the skills necessary to engage in assertive behavior, the therapist presents systematic behavioral assignments to allow the client to practice the newly acquired skills in his or her own social environment and to promote transfer and maintenance of those skills. We begin each session with a discussion of last week's assigned activity, including what the client said and did, what he or she felt and thought before, during, and after the behavior, and what response occurred as a result. Feedback and reinforcement are offered for successful homework, additional instructions given, and further homework agreed upon. The assigned tasks increase in complexity and rigor as the client progresses through within-the-office therapy.

Because assertive behavior is not always reinforced by the target people in the client's social environment, great care should be taken to insure that the selected homework as a high probability for success at a low cost of discomfort. To avoid negative outcomes, the therapist must thoroughly understand the client's limitations and environment. However, since a complete understanding of these factors is impossible, the client should have the last word on each homework activity.

Several principles should be followed when prescribing assignments with the transfer goal in mind. In treatments involving systematic homework, the therapist should endeavor to insure that the stimuli triggering the target response in the client's natural social environment are similar or identical to those that precede the response when the client is practicing in the office. This will insure the transferability of the learned skill, so the following type of assignment may be given:

Assignment: For 1 week at home, practice a particular skill (for example, positive cognitions, "I" statements, eye contact) that was roleplayed in the office.

After the client has been able to transfer skills to the outside world, the therapist should begin to gradually vary the stimulus conditions in which the assertion response is practiced. New settings, new targets, and different types of assertive responses can be programmed.

Assignment: Five times a day, five times a week, state your opinion to people, picking five different people and at least three different places each day.

At first glance this principle and assignment seem to conflict with that which we just discussed. However, if done over a time sequence, the two are complementary. At first the client should be urged to practice in settings nearly identical to those of the within-the-office-therapy arrangement. Once the assertion responses have been mastered, however, it is time to practice them under differing stimulus conditions.

Overlearning is a procedure whereby learning is extended over more trials than are necessary merely to produce initial changes in the individual's behavior. All too often in therapy the subject's ability to complete a task is considered indicative that the therapy should move on to the next assignment. What may be needed is more practice and repetition if the client is to be ultimately successful in his or her own social environment.

Assignment: Use a particular skill (for example, eye contact or a strong voice) every time you speak with someone for 1 week.

One way to increase the maintenance of behaviors acquired in therapy is to gradually lengthen the amount of time between sessions. Systematic behavioral assignments can be prescribed that require practice and self-observations over longer and longer periods of time. As time goes on the therapist can offer just booster sessions, in which the client comes in for periodic "checkups." Homework can be programmed to occur between these checkups.

Assignment: On the first Sunday of each month, reread your assertion checklist.

Assignment: On the first Sunday of each month, review assertion skills.

Assignment: On the first Sunday of each month, make a list of current problems.

Assertion training that is done in a group setting can sometimes be maintained by other group members after formal therapy has been terminated. Group contacts such as periodic phone calls and informal get-togethers can be instrumental in promoting maintenance.

COMPLIANCE ENHANCEMENT PROCEDURES

The therapist should consider occasionally calling the client. If done at random intervals, the knowledge that the therapist frequently calls to see how things are going often increases adherence. Phone calls also can provide badly needed support in those cases when assertion homework has gone poorly.

In some settings where assertion trainers have available a number of skilled paraprofessionals, it is often advisable to make use of these persons to enhance adherence. As some clinical investigators such as Pendleton, Shelton, and Wilson (1976) have shown, specifically trained paraprofessionals can accompany clients on assignments out in the clients' social environment and provide instant reinforcement and feedback for assertion attempts. In some instances paraprofessionals can serve as target individuals during the early stages of treatment, before the client has gained complete confidence in his or her abilities.

The use of consequation management to enhance adherence to behavioral home assignments involving assertion is frequently easier with assertion training done in a group context. Our belief is that the group seems to create more pressure for compliance than does the individual therapist. the natural consequences that befall the client who frequently fails to complete his or her outside therapeutic homework can be immediate and severe, even in groups composed of nonassertive clients. Conversely, we have observed few natural events as reinforcing as the assertion group applauding in unison in response to the report of a successful homework assignment completed by a fellow group member.

A final compliance enhancer is the use of recording methods. Letters, memos, and recordings of phone calls can all be brought back to therapy for discussion. The knowledge that a tangible product of assertion must be produced does aid compliance. Figure 12.5 shows an example of an assignment designed around this theme.

ILLUSTRATIVE CASE

Ed was a 47-year-old self-referred white male who came to therapy complaining of "depression." He appeared soft-spoken, avoided eye contact, and was anxious to agree with everything the therapist said. He frequently began each sentence with the phrase "this will sound stupid,

Figure 12.5   Example of a behavioral assignment requiring a tangible product

Homework for Pat
Write a letter to your mom in which you empathize with her loneliness but criticize her for not being active socially.

Xerox the letter for me to see.

Call for an appointment when you have received a reply.

Homework for John
Call if I don't hear from Pat in a week.

but..." He had been divorced for 5 years before he made the decision to seek psychotherapy. His wife of nearly 20 years had filed for divorce on the grounds of incompatibility. Ed suspected her interest in another man, which was confirmed by her marriage almost immediately following the final divorce action.

As Ed described his problems, it soon became apparent that he did not fare well with women. For example, soon after his divorce Ed began dating a partially disfigured blind woman whom he "felt sorry for." His guilt and nonassertiveness maintained their relationship for 1½ years, at which time she left him for another man.

Soon after that Ed met Mary, whom he was dating when he sought therapy. Mary was the dominant force in Ed's life. She dictated entertainment, recreational, sexual, and domestic activities most of the time. Despite her reassurance of her romantic commitment to him, she occasionally demanded the right to spend weekends with an "old friend" (Bob), when he came to town. Although she denied being sexually intimate with Bob, Ed had reason to believe otherwise. For one thing, Ed always contracted a urinary tract infection immediately after having intercourse with Mary, who, in turn, always seemed to have a urinary infection after a visit with Bob. To add insult to injury, Mary demanded that Ed not go out with other women on her weekends with Bob because he (Ed) "couldn't handle it."

Assessment

It was obvious that Ed was nonassertive from the beginning of the first interview. His low voice, frequent negative self-references, poor eye contact, inability to stand up for himself, and frequent thoughts about his inadequacies all spelled nonassertion. However, to check this perception, Ed was asked to complete the assignments shown in Figure 12.6.

Figure 12.6   First week assignment for Ed

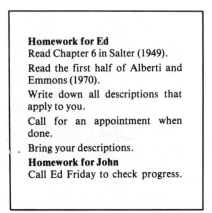

Homework for Ed
Read Chapter 6 in Salter (1949).
Read the first half of Alberti and Emmons (1970).
Write down all descriptions that apply to you.
Call for an appointment when done.
Bring your descriptions.
Homework for John
Call Ed Friday to check progress.

The second session began with a discussion of the self-assessment data obtained from the previous systematic behavioral assignment. We briefly discussed the list of adjectives Ed had copied from his readings. After 20 minutes Ed spontaneously stated that he thought of himself as nonassertive. Having accomplished the diagnosis, the treatment plan was pursued. During our interview Ed complained of nonassertion with two targets: Mary and his boss. A thorough discussion of these issues led to the second homework assignment, which determined how frequently he was nonassertive and what form his nonassertion took. The second set of homework assignments is shown in Figure 12.7.

Figure 12.7   Second week assignment for Ed

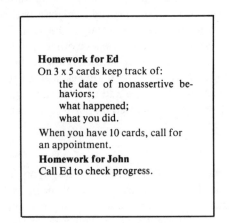

Homework for Ed
On 3 x 5 cards keep track of:
        the date of nonassertive be-
        haviors;
        what happened;
        what you did.
When you have 10 cards, call for an appointment.
Homework for John
Call Ed to check progress.

By the third week we had accumulated a great deal of information regarding Ed's nonassertion. In each case Ed had complied with the assigned home activity (nonassertive patients typically do), and had been reinforced for his efforts. On the basis of the information obtained during the treatment hour and from the homework vehicle, we constructed the treatment plan shown in Figure 12.8.

Figure 12.8   Ed's treatment plan

Target	Target's Behavior	Assertive Response
The boss	Doesn't compliment me	Make a point of telling the boss in writing or in words what you are doing that is positive.
	Doesn't promote me	Sit down with the boss, tell her you are eager for a promotion, and ask her to help you plan a course for overcoming weak areas.
Mary	Tells me what to do about everything	Develop plans for the weekend; state your opinion; initiate, don't respond; ask "why"; and say "no."
	Spends the weekend with her friend Bob	State your feelings and fears about the problem and ask to negotiate a solution. Tell her if she continues to see him you will have to reappraise your relationship.

Treatment

Treatment consisted of reviewing each target person, labeling the target's behavior, and planning assertive responses. The behavior rehearsal model discussed earlier was employed to prepare Ed for the outside practice activity. Once mastered, assertion skills were assigned to allow for practice as well as to promote transfer and maintenance.*

Ed had not been promoted in 3 years. He complained that his boss seldom paid attention to his accomplishments and therefore could not argue on Ed's behalf to the committee that made promotion decisions. It was pointed out to him that he, and not his boss, was responsible for making his accomplishments visible. The homework assignment in Figure 12.9 reflects this intent.

Complying with the last homework assignment demanded that Ed set up an appointment to discuss his future with the agency. We roleplayed a scenario that consisted of Ed sitting down with his boss and expressing his eagerness to be promoted while asking for feedback

---

*In the interest of brevity this case has been condensed.

Figure 12.9   Fourth week assignment for Ed

Homework for Ed
Drop notes two times a week into your boss's box, keeping her informed of your progress on your projects.
Keep a Xerox of notes for me to see.
Set up a meeting with your boss for next week to discuss job performance.
Call for an appointment when finished.

regarding how he might increase his chances. The next set of assignments, listed in Figure 12.10, reflects this goal.

Figure 12.10   Fifth week assignment for Ed

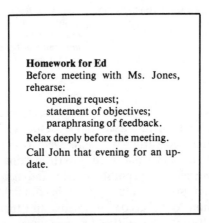

Homework for Ed
Before meeting with Ms. Jones, rehearse:
    opening request;
    statement of objectives;
    paraphrasing of feedback.
Relax deeply before the meeting.
Call John that evening for an update.

The final and more difficult target of Ed's assertion was Mary. After careful discussion, we decided that Ed's passivity accounted for much of her aggression and domination. The sixth, seventh, and eighth sessions dealt with these issues (see Fig. 12.11). In short, Ed was asked to not jump at everything Mary demanded but to slowly build in the assertion behavior in the form of requests for delays and initiations of social, sexual, and recreational ventures. His requests and initiations gradually increased in scope and intensity. Four weeks were spent completing tasks of this nature.

After one month Ed reported numerous changes. For the first time

Figure 12.11   Sixth week assignment for Ed

Homework for Ed
Call Mary and tell her you have plans for a movie. Pick one you will like.

The next time Mary tells you to vacuum, tell her you will get to it later and take your time reading a story before you vacuum.

Keep track of the results of your behavior on 3 x 5 cards.

Homework for John
Call to check progress three times.

in his adult life he began to feel confident, self-assured, and capable. His anxiety and apprehension dropped considerably and the satisfaction he gained from sexual activities increased dramatically. In addition he reported that Mary expressed feeling new respect and comfort with his newfound assertiveness.

Maintenance

Maintenance activities consisted of periodic phone calls at monthly intervals for 1 year. One booster session held at 7 months after therapy termination necessitated time spent in behavioral rehearsal with an accompanying homework assignment. Periodic phone calls after this period have confirmed the maintenance of his assertion.

SUMMARY

Nonassertiveness can be determined only by careful examination of a number of verbal and nonverbal behaviors, many of which are also common to depression and shyness. Aggression can be discriminated from assertiveness by comparing specific actions across the areas of behavior, intent, effect, consideration of the rights of others, and socio-cultural differences. there are three hypothesized causes of nonassertiveness: lack of skills, anxiety, and faulty cognitions.

Assertion training varies according to the nature of the clients involved, but the type discussed here is a semistructured training package with emphasis on the practice of assertive responses. It begins with assessment, which has two goals: determination of whether the client is nonassertive and treatment planning. Psychometric and in-the-office assessments of nonassertiveness are confirmed by appropriate assignments carried out in the client's natural environment. Treatment planning is then done jointly by client and therapist to isolate target people with whom the client is nonassertive, pinpoint the nonassertive behaviors performed with each target person, determine those problems that prevent the client from behaving assertively, and develop specific interventions and assignments. Treatment has three steps: the client is provided with information on the rationale and procedures of training, basic human rights, and the difference between assertion and aggression; the therapist and client try to eliminate obstacles to assertion through behavioral rehearsal, cognitive control, and anxiety-relief procedures; and assignments are given after each session to promote learning, transfer, and maintenance of skills and cognitive-control procedures. Typical assignments are described.

A few compliance enhancement procedures are suggested. The therapist may occasionally call the client at home to prompt adherence and to provide support. Paraprofessionals may accompany clients on assignments to provide immediate reinforcement and feedback or as surrogate target people in skill training. The social pressures and reinforcement of a group can also work effectively to increase adherence to assignments. Finally, assignments that require the client to bring in evidence of completion can encourage compliance.

The illustrative case of assertiveness training concerns Ed, an older man who came to therapy with a complaint of depression. From his history and his present behaviors, it was clear that he was nonassertive. Two target people with whom he decided to become more assertive were his lover and his boss, and assignments for approaching them assertively were worked out. Treatment consisted of considering the target person, identifying the issues Ed had been nonassertive about with that person, and planning assertive responses. Rehearsal was used to prepare Ed for outside assignments, and gradual changes in his behavior were attempted. Maintenance through periodic phone calls continued for a year, and a booster session was held at 7 months after termination. Later follow-ups confirmed that Ed had continued his assertive behavior.

ASSERTION TRAINING MATERIALS

Alberti, R.E. (Ed.). *Assert: The Newsletter of Assertive Behavior.* Impact Publishers, Inc., P.O. Box 1094, San Luis Obispo, Calif. 93406.

Alberti, R.E., & Emmons, M.L. *Your perfect right: A guide to assertive behavior* (2nd ed.). San Luis Obispo, Calif.: Impact, 1974.

Alberti, R.E., & Emmons, M.L. *Stand up, speak out, talk back!* New York: Pocket Books, 1975.

Baer, J.L. *How to be an assertive (not aggressive) woman in life, in love, and on the job.* New York: New American Library, 1976.

Bloom, L.Z., Coburn, K., & Pearlman, J. *The new assertive woman.* New York: Delacorte Press, 1975.

Bower, S.A., & Bower, G.H. *Asserting yourself.* Reading, Mass.: Addison-Wesley, 1976.

Cheek, D.K. *Assertive black. . .puzzled white.* San Luis Obispo, Calif.: Impact, 1976.

Cotler, S.B., & Guerra, J.J. *Assertion training.* Champaign, Ill.: Research Press, 1976.

Fensterheim, H., & Baer, J.L. *Don't say yes when you want to say no.* New York: David McKay, 1975.

Galassi, M.D., & Galassi, J.P. *Assert yourself! How to be your own person.* New York: Human Sciences Press, 1977.

Gambrill, E.D., & Richey, C.A. *It's up to you: Developing assertive social skills.* Millbrae, Calif.: Les Femmes, 1976.

Guerra, J.J., Cotler, S.B., & Cotler, S.M. *Assertion training series.* Champaign, Ill.: Research Press, 1976. (Cassette tape package)

Lange, A.J., & Jakubowski, P. *Responsible assertive behavior.* Champaign, Ill.: Research Press, 1976.

Lazarus, A.A., & Fay, A. *I can if I want to.* New York: William Morrow, 1975.

Liberman, R.P., King, L.W., DeRisi, W.J., & McCann, M. *Personal effectiveness.* Champaign, Ill.: Research Press, 1976.

Osborn, S.M., & Harris, G.G. *Assertive training for women.* Springfield, Ill.: Charles C. Thomas, 1975.

Phelps, S., & Austin, N. *The assertive woman.* San Luis Obispo, Calif.: Impact, 1975.

Salter, A. *Conditioned reflex therapy.* New York: Capricorn Books, 1961. (Originally published by Farrar, Straus & Giroux, 1949.)

Smith, M.J. *When I say no, I feel guilty.* New York: Dial Press, 1975.

Taubman, B. *How to become an assertive woman.* New York: Pocket Books, 1976.

REFERENCE NOTES

1. McFall, R.M., & Bridges, D.V. *Behavior rehearsal with modeling and coaching in assertive training: Assessment and training stimuli.* Unpublished manuscript, University of Wisconsin, 1970.

2. Jakubowski, P., & Wallace, G. *Adult assertion scale.* Unpublished manuscript, University of Missouri, St. Louis, 1975.

REFERENCES

Alberti, R.E., & Emmons, M.L. *Your perfect right: A guide to assertive behavior.* San Luis Obispo, Calif.: Impact, 1970.

Alberti, R.E., & Emmons, M.L. *Your perfect right: A guide to assertive behavior* (2nd ed.). San Luis Obispo, Calif.: Impact, 1974.

Cheek, D.K. Assertion behavior and black lifestyles. In R.E. Alberti (Ed.), *Assertiveness: Innovations, applications, issues.* San Luis Obispo, Calif.: Impact, 1976.

Ciminero, A.R., Calhoun, K.S., & Adams, H.E. *Handbook of behavioral assessment.* New York: John Wiley & Sons, 1977.

Cone, J.D., & Hawkins, R.P. *Behavioral assessment: New directions in clinical assessment.* New York: Brunner/Mazel, 1977.

Eisler, R.M., Hersen, M., & Miller, P.M. The effects of modeling on components of assertive behavior. *Journal of Behavior Therapy and Experimental Psychiatry,* 1973, *4,* 1-6.

Fensterheim, H. Assertive methods of marital problems. In R.D. Robin, H. Fensterheim, & L.P. Ullmann (Eds.), *Advances in behavior therapy* (Vol. 4). New York: Academic Press, 1970.

Fensterheim, H., & Baer, J.L. *Don't say yes when you want to say no.* New York: David McKay, 1975.

Friedman, P.H. The effects of modeling and role playing on assertive behavior. In C.M. Franks (Ed.), *Advances in behavior therapy.* New York: Academic Press, 1971.

Galassi, J.P., DeLo, J.S., Galassi, M.D., & Bastien, S. The college self-expression scale: A measure of assertiveness. *Behavior Therapy,* 1974, *5,* 165-171.

Galassi, J.P., & Galassi, M.D. Validity as a measure of assertiveness. *Journal of Counseling Psychology,* 1974, *21,* 248-250.

Galassi, M.D., & Galassi, J.P. *Assert yourself! How to be your own person.* New York: Human Sciences Press, 1977.

Gambrill, E.D. *Behavior modification: Handbook of assessment, intervention, and evaluation.* San Francisco: Jossey-Bass, 1977.

Gambrill, E.D., & Richey, C.A. An assertion inventory for use in assessment and research. *Behavior Therapy,* 1975, *6,* 550-561.

Gambrill, E.D., & Richey, C.A. *It's up to you: Developing assertive social skills.* Millbrae, Calif.: Les Femmes, 1976.

Goldsmith, J.B., & McFall, R.M. Development and evaluation of an interpersonal skill-training program for psychiatry inpatients. *Journal of Abnormal Psychology,* 1975, *84,* 51-58.

Hwang, P.O. Assertion training for Asian-Americans. In R.E. Alberti (Ed.), *Assertiveness: Innovations, applications, issues.* San Luis Obispo, Calif.: Impact, 1976.

Jakubowski-Spector, P. Facilitating the growth of women through assertive training. *The Counseling Psychologist,* 1973, *4*(1), 75-86.

Kazdin, A.E. Effects of covert modeling and model reinforcement on assertive behavior. *Journal of Abnormal Psychology,* 1974, *83,* 240-252.

Landau, P., & Paulson, T. Cope: A wilderness workshop in assertion training. In R.E. Alberti (Ed.), *Assertiveness: Innovations, applications, issues.* San Luis Obispo, Calif.: Impact, 1976.

Lange, A.J., & Jakubowski, P. *Responsible assertive behavior.* Champaign, Ill.: Research Press, 1976.

Lazarus, A.A. *Behavior therapy and beyond.* New York: McGraw-Hill, 1971.

Linehan, M. Structured cognitive-behavioral treatment of assertion problems. In P.C. Kendall & S.P. Hollon (Eds.), *Cognitive-behavioral interventions: Theory, research, and procedures.* New York: Academic Press, 1979.

Mash, E.J., & Terdal, L.G. *Behavior therapy assessment: Diagnosis, design, and evaluation.* New York: Springer, 1976.

McFall, R.M., & Lillesand, D.B. Behavior rehearsal with modeling and coaching in assertion training. *Journal of Abnormal Psychology,* 1971, *77,* 313-322.

McFall, R.M., & Twentyman, C.T. Four experiments on the relative contributions of rehearsal modeling and coaching to assertive training. *Journal of Abnormal Psychology,* 1973, *81,* 199-218.

Mehrabian, A. *Nonverbal communication.* Chicago: Aldine-Atherton, 1972.

Pendleton, L.R., Shelton, J.L., & Wilson, S.E. Social interaction training using systematic homework. *The Personnel and Guidance Journal,* 1976, *54,* 484-487.

Rathus, S.A. A 30-item schedule for assessing assertive behavior. *Behavior Therapy,* 1973, *4,* 398-406.

Rich, A.B., & Schroeder, H.E. Research issues in assertiveness training. *Psychological Bulletin,* 1976, *83,* 1081-1096.

Rosenthal, T., & Reese, S. The effects of covert and overt modeling on assertive behavior. *Behaviour Research and Therapy,* 1976, *14,* 463-467.

Salter, A. *Conditioned reflex therapy.* New York: Farrar, Straus & Giroux, 1949.

Schwartz, R.M., & Gottman, J.M. Toward a task analysis of assertive behavior. *Journal of Consulting and Clinical Psychology,* 1976, *44,* 910-920.

Smith, M.J. *When I say no I feel guilty.* New York: Dial Press, 1975.

Thorpe, G.L. Short term effectiveness of systematic desensitization, modeling, and behavior rehearsal and self-instructional training in facilitating assertive refusal behavior. *European Journal of Behavioral Analysis and Modification,* 1975, *1,* 30-44.

Trower, P., Yardly, K., Bryant, B.M., & Shaw, P. The treatment of social failure: A comparison of anxiety-reduction and skill acquisition procedures on two social problems. *Behavior Modification,* 1978, *2,* 41-60.

Wolfe, J.L., & Fodor, I.G. Assertiveness training for mothers and daughters. In R.E. Alberti (Ed.), *Assertiveness: Innovations, applications, issues.* San Luis Obispo, Calif.: Impact, 1977.

Wolpe, J. *The practice of behavior therapy* (2nd ed.). Elmsford, N.Y.: Pergamon Press, 1973.

Wolpe, J., & Lang, P.J. A fear inventory schedule for use in behavior therapy. *Behaviour Research and Therapy,* 1964, *2,* 27.

Wolpe, J., & Lazarus, A.A. *Behavior therapy techniques.* Elmsford, N.Y.: Pergamon Press, 1966.

CHAPTER 13

Parenting Skills

Nancy E. Hawkins
Behavior Change Center and Eugene School District 4-J

Anthony Biglan
Behavior Change Center and Oregon Research Institute

OVERVIEW OF PARENTING SKILLS

From the standpoint of social learning theory, a child's behavior develops and is maintained to a large extent by the contingencies of social reinforcement (Patterson, 1975; Patterson, Reid, Jones, & Conger, 1975). Examples of the causal role of social attention in shaping and maintaining prosocial and antisocial behavior are widespread (Becker, Madsen, Arnold, & Thomas, 1972; Greenwood, Hops, Delquadri, & Guild, 1974; Herbert & Baer, 1972; Redd, 1969; Strain & Timm, 1974). Patterson (in press) has shown that much of a child's behavior may be shaped and maintained by the cessation of aversive events. The model also suggests that for young children, parents and teachers are the primary dispensers of reinforcing and aversive consequences. Teaching appropriate behavior to children is thus a matter of helping parents or teachers acquire and maintain such skills as pinpointing the problem behavior and specifying a desirable alternative behavior, attending to the desired behavior, ignoring mildly problematic behavior, consistently give punishing serious problem behavior, and using extrinsic reinforcement when necessary to establish a child's behavior.

The most common child behavior problems we deal with involve aggression and noncompliance. A child refuses to do what he or she is asked to do. The family experiences frequent arguments and fights, with the parent(s) usually playing the role of referee. The child often whines, cries, or complains if he or she does not get what he or she wants. Predictably, one or both parents become annoyed and get angry with both the child and each other. Sometimes the frustrated parent hits the child and then feels regretful.

A second, less frequently encountered group of problems involves fears and social isolation. A child might fear school, other people, or specific objects such as cars, high places, or dogs, and may express these fears by crying, shaking, or having frequent nightmares. Usually the parents are initially sympathetic. Indeed, their sympathy may have helped shape the fearful behavior.

Somatic difficulties such as encopresis, enuresis, and asthma may be helped by training parents in the skills we described here (Conger, 1970; Neisworth & Moore, 1972). However, other behavioral interventions and medical interventions may be necessary. We recommend consulting the literature on a particular problem before proceeding (see Katz & Zlutnick, 1975).

Parents often indicate that they believe their child's problem is one of "low self-concept." If the child felt better about him or herself, these parents reason, the child would not be fearful or would not fight. To our way of thinking, the feelings are more likely products of the situation the child is in. However, since parents do not come to us for courses in philosophy of science, we simply add a goal such as "Michael will feel better about himself" and explain how such a goal could be reached through the methods we use.

Although the social learning framework stresses the importance of social consequences of behavior, it is not inconsistent with physiological and genetic hypotheses about the etiology of some child behavior problems. Although evidence is currently lacking, it is possible that some children are prone to develop aggressive or noncompliant behavior patterns because of genetic or physiological factors. Presumably such variables would interact with the reinforcement variables just described to determine the rate of problem behavior. Whatever the effects of these variables, however, the evidence that parent skill training affects common kinds of child behavior warrants the use of social learning techniques. Indeed, even where genetic variables are clearly established as causal factors in child behavior—for example, with Downs' Syndrome —the importance of modifying the child's social environment is well established (Birnbrauer, 1976).

HOMEWORK-BASED TREATMENT

Overview of Treatment

The details of our treatment plans vary depending on the specific child behavior problems we are dealing with. Nonetheless, our program includes most or all of the following components:

1. Pinpointing problems and setting goals with the parents
2. Gathering data relevant to the problems and goals
3. Helping the parents to understand the rationale for teaching them parenting skills and the specific skills we will teach them through reading assignments
4. A home visit
5. Teaching parents to praise positive behavior
6. Teaching parents to design and use point systems for increasing positive behaviors by their child, and later, ways to fade out the use of points while maintaining the positive behaviors
7. Teaching parents how to use time out to further decrease problem behavior
8. Teaching parents to use the skills they have acquired to deal with new problems that may arise

The components are typically presented in this order. We sometimes do not present all components if our initial interventions appear to have remediated the problems.

In the first session the therapist meets only with the parents and focuses on helping them define their goals for their child's behavior. The parents are asked to describe what the child does, what situations seem to prompt the most difficulty, and how they have tried to deal with the problem behavior. They are also asked to describe how they would like their child to behave and recent instances of the child's positive behaviors and their reactions at these times. At the end of this discussion the parents are presented with a summary of the goals they have described and asked if it is correct. Such a list might look like this:

1. Mike will do things when asked.
2. Mike will whine less.
3. Mike will play cooperatively with his brother.
4. The whole family will develop some enjoyable things that they do together.

Although these goals are not very specific, they are considerably more specific than those most parents have given. When it comes time to assignments, the kind of specificity that is needed to effect changes in the child's behavior is developed.

Homework Assignments

Assessment. To help them more clearly define the behaviors they want to change and to further refine their goals, parents are asked to complete three questionnaires as a homework assignment before the second session.

Assignment: Complete the three questionnaires.

The Child Behavior Checklist (Achenbach, 1978; Achenbach & Edelbrock, 1979) is a 118-item behavior problem checklist on which parents simply note which problems have been true for their child for the past year. They list the child's social competencies in activities and peer relationships, and they also rate how their child compares with age-mates in these competencies. The Positive Behavior Checklist (Hawkins & Biglan, Note 1) is designed to prompt parents to notice specific positive behaviors of their child that might otherwise go unnoticed and to help them pinpoint other positive behaviors they would like from their child. The checklist is presented in Figure 13.1. Some Questions About Your

Figure 13.1   Positive Behavior Checklist

POSITIVE BEHAVIOR CHECKLIST

Name: _____   Child's Name: _____
Date: _____

Instructions: This checklist is divided into four sections:
   A. *Morning* - from awakening to before lunch
   B. *Afternoon* - from lunch to before dinner
   C. *Evening* - from dinner to bedtime
   D. *Throughout the Day* - any time during the day or evening

Fill out Sections A, B, and C immediately after the specified period of time ends. Do this by putting a check in the appropriate box or boxes. Section D should also be referred to each time you fill out Section A, Section B, or Section C. For example, if you filled out Section A just after your child left for school, you would look over Section D.

A. *Morning:* Your child. . .	No Opportunity	Yes	No	Is this Behavior Something You Want to Have Happen More Often?
1. Got out of bed when called or before				
2. Helped prepare breakfast				
3. Came to breakfast on time				
4. Ate breakfast without complaining				
5. Helped clean up after breakfast				
6. Did necessary before-school chores promptly				
7. Brushed teeth				
8. Brushed hair				

Figure 13.1   *(Continued)*

9. Got dressed
10. Was ready for school on time
11. Other_____

B. *Afternoon:* Your child. . .

No Opportunity	Yes	No	Is this Behavior Something You Want to Have Happen More Often?

12. Helped to prepare lunch
13. Came to lunch promptly
14. Ate lunch without complaining
15. Helped clean up after lunch
16. Came home from school on time
17. Other_____

C. *Evening:* Your child. . .

No Opportunity	Yes	No	Is this Behavior Something You Want to Have Happen More Often?

18. Helped to prepare dinner
19. Helped to set the table
20. Came to dinner promptly
21. Ate dinner without complaining
22. Helped clear table after dinner
23. Helped with dishes
24. Went to bed promptly
25. Stayed in bed once there
26. Other_____

D. *Throughout the Day:* Your child. . .

No Opportunity	Number of Times Occurred	Is this Behavior Something You Want to Have Happen More Often?

27. Played *near* another child without trouble
28. Played *with* another child cooperatively
29. Talked to another child in a normal tone of voice
30. Talked to an adult without yelling, arguing, or whining
31. Laughed with another person
32. Smiled at another person
33. Complied with parents' requests
34. Stayed calm when confronted with a difficult situation
35. Shared possessions
36. Asked permission before borrowing
37. Waited for his/her turn
38. Did the following chores without complaining

_____
_____
_____

39. Other

_____
_____

Child (Hawkins, Note 2) contains questions designed to further clarify the parents' goals, the techniques they have already tried to improve the child's behavior, and the things that seem to have worked in the past. A copy of this questionnaire is in Figure 13.2.

Figure 13.2   Some Questions About Your Child questionnaire

SOME QUESTIONS ABOUT YOUR CHILD

1. How long have you been concerned about the behavior of your child?_____

2. In what situations does your child's behavior concern you most?_____

   In what situations does it not concern you?_____

3. How have you tried to handle the behavior before?
   _____ Spank
   _____ Talk to child
   _____ Send to room
   _____ Get angry
   _____ Take away privileges
   _____ Other
   How has this worked? _____
4. Have you ever had a parent training class? Yes_____ No_____ If yes, please describe what you learned. _____

5. Has your child's teacher indicated concern over his/her behavior at school? Yes_____ No_____ If yes, what has the teacher tried? _____
   How has this worked? _____
6. Is your child presently being treated by a physician or counselor? Yes_____ No_____ If yes, please fill out a permission form and sign it. This form gives us permission to talk to these people about the treatment your child has been receiving.
7. If we are completely successful in helping you and your child to change his/her behavior, what will he/she be doing differently than he/she is these days?

   _____

   What will *you* be doing differently? _____
   How will things be different in your family?_____
   How will things be different for your child at school? _____
   _____ with his/her friends?_____

Tracking behavior between sessions. Once parents have developed some tentative treatment goals, they are helped to select two behaviors to begin tracking: one problem behavior they want to reduce in frequency and one positive alternative behavior. If time allows, this selection is made in the first session. The problem behavior should occur frequently and should be easy to observe.

Having parents keep daily track of one specific problem behavior and one positive behavior in detail on the Behavior Observation Form (Figure 13.3) provides information to the therapist and the parents about possible antecedents for both positive and negative child behaviors. Becoming aware of these is the first step in setting up a procedure for changing the behaviors of concern. Keeping track of the consequences they provide for the child's behavior can help parents become more

Figure 13.3   Behavior Observation Form

BEHAVIOR OBSERVATION FORM

Behaviors to 1. _____   Person Keeping Track:_____
Be Observed: 2. _____   Date:_____
              3. _____

Times you Observe	Situation (where, who was there, what was happening)	Behavior(s) (brief description of child's behavior)	Consequence(s) (what happened as a result of this behavior) P = Praise, TO = Time out, Pt = Point, I = Ignore

For End of Day: In general, how well do you like your child today?
Strongly like   1   2   3   4   5   6   7   Strongly dislike

aware of their roles in maintaining or changing their child's behaviors. In addition, this information helps the therapist assess the parents' skills in reinforcing appropriate behaviors, so that he or she knows where to begin teaching praising and reinforcing skills.

> **Assignment (each parent):**   Observe and record the selected behaviors during a specific, agreed-upon, short period each day.

Parents are taught to observe their child's behavior by modeling and roleplaying these activities in session. They are shown the Behavior Observation Form and the use of each column is explained. They are asked to suggest a situation in which they might observe their child's problem behavior and to actually note both the situation and the behavior on the form. They are then asked how they might respond to this behavior and note their response in the appropriate column. If necessary, they go through several examples, and are guided in actually recording on the form. Both parents are encouraged to praise any positive behaviors they note and to deal with negative behaviors as they ordinarily would.

The parents are told to calmly tell their child that they will be observing and keeping track of his or her behavior and that they want to learn how to help the child behave in more positive ways more often. They are asked how they think the child might respond to this. If they think the child will react negatively, they are encouraged to avoid any arguments or prolonged discussion about their right to take data.

> **Assignment (each parent):**   Rate how well you like the child each day.

These data help us to assess whether parents come to view the child more positively as the child's behavior changes.

Some form of behavior tracking assignment will be suggested each week until fading of contact with the client begins.

Reading about social learning theory. In the first or second session with the parents we suggest that they begin reading either *Living With Children* (Patterson & Gullion, 1971) or *Families* (Patterson, 1975). There is evidence that significant changes in child behavior can result from reading these materials (Glasgow & Rosen, 1978). We generally assign *Living With Children* if the child or children are preschool or elementary school age or if the parents have less than a high-school education. *Families* is recommended for more educated parents and particularly for families with older children (Patterson, Reid, Jones, & Conger, 1975).

Assignment: Read *Living With Children* or *Families.*

We let the parents decide how much they want to read. If they are reluctant to do any reading or if repeated attempts to get them to follow through are unsuccessful, we abandon the effort, since we are aware of no evidence that knowledge of such principles is necessary to a successful treatment outcome.

If parents do follow through on reading, book assignments are suggested throughout treatment. Even when they have completed the book, suggestions may be made to reread particular chapters that are relevant to the problems they are working on at that time.

Increasing parents' attention and praise for positive behavior. Since praise and attention unquestionably increase desired behavior (Pinkston, Reese, LeBlanc, & Baer, 1973; Ward & Baker, 1968), during the second session specific assignments are introduced to increase the parents' skill in attending to and praising their child's behavior. Each parent is asked to describe a few of the positive behaviors he or she noted and praised during the week. All attempts at praising should be reinforced. Depending on the parents' skill, anywhere from a few minutes to the remainder of the session may be spent on modeling and practicing praise of positive child behaviors.

Assignment: Continue tracking the behaviors you noted the previous week, adding prompts that tended to be antecedents for positive child behaviors.

Naturally, during this week all positive behaviors that are recorded will not be praised. In these cases, parents are asked to write down a praise that could have been used, in order to provide practice in thinking up praises.

The following point system assignment can also be given:

Assignment: Establish a point system for the child whereby certain selected positive behaviors earn points. Praise each time you give points and note when praise is given.

The points in this system can be accumulated to earn activities or tangible reinforcers on a daily basis. The reward system is described more fully in the next section. The point here is that such a system prompts the parents to give praise. Assignments can also involve other family members.

Assignment: Have an older child keep track of the praises given by one or both of you.

This tracking should be done openly as a way to help prompt the parent(s) to give more praise. Finally, each parent can help the other give praise to the child.

Assignment (each parent): Keep track of praises given by your partner.

Criteria can be set such that when a parent's praise rate reaches the criteria, he or she receives some form of reinforcment from the partner. Often one parent will tend to praise more than the other because one is around the child more, or because he or she is expected to praise more. The parent who has a higher praise rate can prompt the other to praise, for example, by mentioning positive behavior that the other can praise or by having the other look at and comment on the point chart each day.

During the second session, the therapist and parents review the completed questionnaires and the records the parents have kept on the two specific behaviors. At this point any new goals the parents have decided upon are added to the previous list.

A reward system. Often helping the parents increase their praise and attention to the child's positive behaviors is not enough to effect a quick and significant change in these behaviors. Praise from the parents may not be a powerful reinforcer; the parents may have difficulty being positive with a child who is still difficult to manage; or the parents themselves may have difficulty arriving at mutually agreed-upon expectations and consequences for behaviors that are only partially positive. In most cases, a point system is a useful intervention (Christopherson, Arnold, Hill, & Quilitch, 1972). Such a system helps the child begin to behave in prescribed ways, helps the parents clarify their expectations, and also helps them provide consistent positive consequences for appropriate child behaviors. Depending on the skills of the parents, the point system can be totally developed during office sessions or can be explained and started in the office session and completed at home as an assignment.

First an overview of procedures for point systems is presented to the parents. It should be pointed out that this is a *temporary* use of points. (In light of recent writing, the reader is cautioned not to overuse or abuse a system or establish one that is hard to fade.) If the parents indicate that they understand what is entailed and want to proceed, the first steps are taken toward developing an appropriate system. Behaviors to be included on the point chart are suggested. Examples can be taken from the Positive Behavior Checklist, from positive behaviors that the parents are currently tracking and praising, or from daily chores and responsibilities that the parents would like their child to perform. While the therapist can help generate and clearly define a partial list of behaviors in the office session, usually the parents and child can decide upon the remainder of the list as a between-session assignment.

Assignment: Decide upon a complete list of behaviors for the point system.

We set the maximum number of behaviors for an initial point chart at six and make sure that at least two of the behaviors are fairly easily accomplished to insure early success and reinforcement.

After the behaviors for the chart have been chosen, point values can be assigned to each one. The behaviors can be given equal points for the first week and then be adjusted after a week of data.

Assignment (parents and child):   Decide upon behaviors for the point chart (maximum of six).

Assignment (parents and child):   Negotiate point values of each behavior.

Assignment (parents and child):   List a number of reinforcing activities that will be available daily or weekly.

Determining possible reinforcers can also be started in the office and completed at home between sessions. We give parents a list of suggested rewards that is based on work with similar-aged children (see Figure 13.4). Whenever possible, we encourage them to think of brief activities or privileges rather than tangible rewards. Our rationale for stressing nontangibles is based on our observations that positive activities between parents and a problem child are typically lacking. Providing some short fun times for the family together after the child has behaved appropriately can be a first step toward building a more positive parent-child relationship. In addition, when activities are used as reinforcers, fading the point system becomes easier. Often the activities can still be used in a less formal reinforcement system (for example, "If you clean up your room quickly, we will have time to go swimming"). Finally, the activities

Figure 13.4   Suggested rewards for children

Home Reward Possibilities for Teenagers

Having dating privileges
Participating in activities with friends
Having friends over
Taking dancing or music lessons
Redecorating your own room
Skating, especially with friends
Talking additional time on the telephone
Playing the stereo
Making a trip alone
Finding a part-time job
Taking the car to school for a day
Getting to stay out late
Having car privileges
Staying up late
Staying overnight with friends
Taking time off from chores
Having a date during the week
Getting a chance to earn money
Selecting TV programs
Being the chairman at a family meeting
Getting to use the family camera
Getting a driver's license
Driving the car on a family trip
Sewing clothes

Camping out
Going to summer camp
Getting a special haircut or hair style
Going to Disneyland or some other amusement park
Being allowed to sit alone when the family eats out
Inviting a friend to eat out with you
Getting to sleep in late on the weekend
Having your own checking account
Having a soda or a special drink with mom and dad
Getting to use make-up
Receiving a magazine subscription
Going shopping with friends
Buying a record
Having your own telephone
Selecting something special for dinner
Going to the library
Going bowling or swimming, especially with friends
Having a paper route
Going horseback riding

Home Reward Possibilities for Elementary School Children

Taking a trip to the park
Playing with friends
Having a bedtime story
Playing on the swing set
Spending the night with friends or grandparents
Going to a ball game
Eating out
Going someplace alone with dad or mom
Baking something in the kitchen
Planning a day's activities
Riding on a bicycle
Going on a fishing trip with dad or mom
Choosing a TV program
Taking time off from chores
Holding hands while walking
Using the telephone
Dressing up in parents' clothes
Setting the table
Camping in the backyard
Going to the library
Chewing gum

Telling a round-robin story
Decorating the home for the holidays
Helping to make Jello, popcorn, or something similar
Helping to take a gift to a friend
Feeding the baby
Staying up late
Going to the movies, especially with a friend
Making a trip alone
Playing a favorite record
Coloring
Riding next to the window in the car
Riding in the front seat
Listening to yourself on a tape recording
Choosing the menu for a meal
Calling grandma to tell of your successes
Getting a promise to ride the escalator three or four times in a store
Putting up schoolwork on the refrigerator door

Figure 13.4   *(Continued)*

Home Reward Possibilities for Elementary School Children

Buying something
Planting a garden
Going for a picnic
Going skating, swimming, or bowling
Making something, some special craft with mom or dad
Ordering pizza
Going for a hike
Going canoeing or camping or fishing
Sleeping in a different place in the house

Doing a jigsaw puzzle
Decorating your own room
Having a special after-school snack
Having a special treat in your school lunch
Choosing a special breakfast
Having a favorite beverage, like soft drink or hot chocolate
Playing ball with mom or dad
Playing a game with mom or dad, like checkers, marbles, or cards

Home Reward Possibilities for Preschoolers

Going to the park
Playing with friends
Getting in bed with parents
Making mud pies
Listening to a bedtime story
Playing on the swing set
Spending the night with friends or grandparents
Being lifted into the air
Feeding a pet
Rocking
Playing games
Making noises with rattles, pans, or bells
Having a horsey ride (swinging on parent's foot)
Doing a puppet play
Having parents take a Polaroid picture of you
Talking into a tape recorder
Going out for hamburgers or pizza
Wearing dress-up clothes
Playing with clay
Going someplace alone with dad or mom
Helping plan the day's activities
Helping mom or dad
Having a longer time in the bathtub
Riding on a bicycle with dad or mom

Whirling in a circle by arms
Watching a rainstorm
Playing in the sandbox
Sitting in the chair with dad or mom
Going to the library
Going for a picnic
Bouncing on the bed
Playing outside
Riding a tricycle
Staying up late
Going on a trip to the zoo
Getting a piggy-back ride
Having a bubble bath
Singing songs
Skipping
Delaying a nap
Flushing the toilet
Riding on dad's shoulders
Going outside at night
Having a family night
Helping to hold baby sister or brother
Swimming
Reading a story
Mixing cookie dough
Having a special dessert
Chewing gum
Finger painting

may help the family to establish interaction patterns that are incompatible with the ones that are bothering them.

An example of a point chart is shown in Figure 13.5. We give parents oral and written instructions for managing the point system each day (see Figure 13.6), emphasizing praising positive behaviors when points are awarded. We also model and roleplay effective ways to praise.

Figure 13.5   Point chart

Dates   From_____ to_____   Name_____

Behaviors	Points	Sun.	Mon.	Tues.	Wed.	Thurs.	Fri.	Sat.	Total Weekly points
1._____									1._____
2._____									2._____
3._____									3._____
4._____									4._____
5._____									5._____
6._____									6._____
Minimum Points Needed									
TOTAL Points Earned per Day									
Rewards Chosen Each Day									

Daily Reward Menu   Weekly Reward Menu

Figure 13.6   Instructions for point system use

HOW TO USE THE POINT CHART

I. Put the chart where you can all see it easily.
II. Each day:
   A. Early in the day—_____ (person responsible)
     1. Look at the chart with your child.
     2. Make sure the expected behaviors are clear.
     3. *Say something encouraging.*
     4. Have your child choose a reward to work for.
     5. Write down the reward chosen.
   B. As soon as a behavior is performed—_____ (person responsible)
     1. *Praise* your child.
     2. Write down the points earned.
     3. Give yourself a *star* for praising.
   C. Late in the day—_____ (person)
     1. Go over the chart with your child.
     2. Add up the behavior points earned.
     3. *Praise* the positive behaviors.
     4. If earned, give the reward.
       If not earned, do not give the reward; be matter-of-fact, and give encouragement to do better the next day.

Assignment: Manage the point system each day until the next appointment or phone call to review and change the system as needed.

In reviewing the reward system, a number of factors are examined. First, do the parents and child understand the criteria for each behavior on the chart? For example, if "having a pleasant conversation with a sibling" is one behavior, can the parents and child describe what such a conversation would be like? Second, are the rewards that are to be earned actually given when they are earned? If they are not, the points will soon not be reinforcing. Third, is the child succeeding? If not, it may be necessary to specify smaller behavioral steps, to increase the number of points that can be obtained for a behavior, or to provide more prompts for the behavior. An example of smaller behavioral steps would be reducing "clean your room" to "put dirty clothes in the laundry hamper." Fourth, are the points (and praise) being given immediately after the occurrence of the target behavior? Fifth, are the morning and evening reviews that are specified in the assignment (see Figure 13.6) being done?

If the child appears to be doing well on the reward system, the daily point criterion may be raised, and some new behaviors may be added to the system. Bonus reinforcers may also be included for earning all of the possible points in a day and for earning 80 to 90 percent of the points for the week.

Teaching parents to use time out. Time out consists of removing the child from a potentially reinforcing situation for a short period of time. The time outs are given contingent on a well-specified problem behavior such as arguing with a sibling. The child is typically put in a bathroom (once all dangerous objects have been removed) or any room isolated from reinforcement by others. Ample evidence exists that such a procedure is effective in reducing the frequency of most types of disruptive, aggressive, or noncompliant behavior (Wahler, 1969; Walker, 1979). A time out as brief as 1 minute long can be effective (White, Nielsen, & Johnson, 1972), although the typically recommended length is 5 minutes (Patterson, 1975).

Time out is introduced to parents by describing what it is, how it is used, and why it may be preferable to other negative consequences. If they agree to use it, then we help parents select a negative behavior to begin consequating with time out. If possible, the behavior is one for which positive alternative behavior is being reinforced, either by praise or by praise and points. The negative behavior is carefully defined so that both parents and child will agree that it has happened.

Rules for the use of time out are presented in Figure 13.7. We read these to the parents and child and give them a copy. The specific place in which the child will spend time out must then be determined. We recommend the bathroom or laundry room, and a time period of 5 minutes. Unless the parents seem quite confident that they can follow through, we roleplay giving a time out according to the specified rules.

Assignment: Use practiced time out procedures at home for the specified behavior.

The child is asked to cooperate (and usually agrees), and the parents are asked to note each time out and the reason it was given.

In subsequent sessions, the number of time outs that were given

Figure 13.7   Time out rules

HOW TO USE TIME OUT

1. Don't threaten use. Use immediately and for every instance of the selected behavior.

2. Be calm, ignore protests. State your expectation and the reason for time out in a brief, clear, direct, matter-of-fact way.

3. If the child argues, yells, or resists in any way add extra minutes (one at a time); if he or she balks after 20 minutes of time is accumulated, add another consequence (for example, loss of TV for the night).

4. When time out is over, start fresh; no lecturing.

5. If time out was for noncompliance, repeat the request after time out, and praise the child for appropriate behavior (reinstitute time out if the child refuses to comply again).

6. If time out is earned in a setting in which it isn't possible to administer, let the child know that he or she will have a time out upon returning home, and then *don't forget!*

7. If a child makes a mess in time out, he or she must clean it up before coming out or pay for any damages.

8. Please note any time outs you give and note the behavior that resulted in time out.

each day is reviewed. Usually the frequency of the problem behavior is decreasing and so, also, is the frequency of time out. If this is not the case, the therapist checks to be sure that time outs are being given consistently and for the same behavior each time. Parents are asked for specific descriptions of the behaviors that were timed out, whether the child balked at the application of time out, and whether the parents applied the backup loss of privileges as a result. In short, the therapist should not simply ask, "How is it going?" and trust the answer, "Fine." If necessary the parents should again roleplay giving time outs.

If there have been no problems, a negative behavior may be added to be timed out. The parents are asked to continue to track all time outs and the behaviors that prompted them.

COMPLIANCE ENHANCEMENT PROCEDURES

To enhance compliance we first state a rationale for the program so that possible parental misgivings are allayed. We describe social learning principles as they apply to the problems for which parents want help, giving simple examples of how changes in their behavior could improve the situation and alter their child's behavior as they have requested. We also stress the importance of making careful observations and of learning and practicing new skills. The skills that they develop can help them devise ways of dealing with problems that arise after treatment is completed. Only after parents indicate that they have some understanding of the importance of their own efforts are they asked to decide whether or not they want to go ahead with treatment. We continue to present rationales for all recommendations through discussions, demonstrations, and reading assignments.

The parents, and sometimes the child, determine the particular goals for treatment. We are careful to inform parents of the probability that we can succeed in reaching their goals, but we also describe possible negative effects of treatment. For example, the parents may, at least initially, become more frustrated with their child than before. At the end of the initial consultation, we offer the parents the option to seek help elsewhere, decline treatment, or go home and think about the program. Thus, clients who decide to go ahead with therapy are fully informed of the risks of treatment and the efforts that will be required.

Choice of program has been shown to play a role in the effectiveness with which people acquire skills (Kanfer & Grimm, 1978). In view of this evidence, we allow parents some choice in their between-session assignments. We do like to have some tracking of the child's problem and positive behaviors. However, we negotiate with the parents as to *who* will record the behaviors, *when* they will be noted, and *for how long*. In this way, assignments are geared to each person's time and willingness to work.

Another way to enhance compliance is to ask parents to put down a money deposit at the beginning of treatment that will be returned at termination. If they fail to comply with assignments they have agreed to do, half of their deposit is given to charity, and they must redeposit that amount to continue. The amount of money is determined by the parents. In some cases, when the child is older and will be doing assignments between sessions, he or she is asked to deposit a separate amount of money. By having a money deposit from parents or children, we can concentrate on reinforcing their efforts at keeping records and practicing new skills, rather than on cajoling them to comply with the homework.

Usually the first time a client fails to comply with an assignment, we let it go by with only a warning. The next time, the fine is applied. The first mistake could be caused by a lack of understanding of the nature of the assignment or a misjudgment as to the amount of time required for a given task. Consequently, we spend some time clarifying the assignment and perhaps making it less demanding.

Periodically clients will ask not to be required to make a money deposit. In these cases we have generally worked out an agreement that they will make a deposit if, at some point, they fail to do an assignment. In cases where no initial deposit was made, the implementation of the deposit system functions as the warning mentioned above.

We try to make each assignment small enough and easy enough so that the parents are likely to succeed. In part, this is a matter of asking parents to indicate if they feel they are being asked to do too much. For example, we might write down four things that the parents agree to do during a session. But at the end of the session, we ask the parents to look over the list and tell us if it is too much. If they appear to have any hesitation at all, we scale down one or more of the assignments. For example, we might reduce the number of behaviors to be tracked from five to three. Another way in which we try to make assignments more manageable is by suggesting ways in which both parents (if there are two) can share the work. Finally, it may be easier to follow through on these tasks if the spouse is supportive. We try to suggest assignments that the parents can do or discuss together.

Setting up assignments that are clearly defined and concrete seems to facilitate compliance. In working with parents, we explain all assignments by referring to the forms to be used and by giving concrete examples of behaviors to record in each space. We model the tracking for the parents in the office session. After we have explained and modeled, we ask the parents to do a short practice session in front of us. We can then give feedback and further clarification as necessary. When the exact nature of the homework is agreed upon, we write out a detailed assignment sheet for the parents, keeping a carbon copy of the assignment for our records.

Clients can be supported by asking for details of their activities and by paraphrasing and praising their reports of success and failure. We also stress successes they have had in carrying out the programs, for example, praising positive behaviors they noticed or ignoring negative behaviors that are difficult to ignore. Whenever possible, we relate positive changes in the child's behavior to things the parents are doing correctly, since parents do not necessarily see this connection.

Phone contacts can also provide support and encouragement early in treatment. We sometimes schedule a phone contact midway between the first and second sessions to be sure the parents get started on their assignments right away and to solve any problems that have come up.

ILLUSTRATIVE CASE

Peter was a 9-year-old boy whose parents sought help for his lack of compliance, his arguing, stubbornness, and lack of follow-through with his chores. Their usual way of dealing with Peter was to remind him repeatedly of his responsibilities, get angry at him, and spank him or lecture him when he refused to comply. Often when he argued with his mom she would give in, but would be very irritated at having done so. Dad tended to tense up when dealing with Peter's negative behaviors. He was stricter than either he or mom liked. An additional goal of the parents was that dad be more relaxed around his son.

We used the following intervention with systematic behavioral assignments for Peter and his parents.

Session 1

During the first session we focused on clarifying both Peter's behaviors and his parents' consequation skills. We had both parents describe Peter's problem behaviors in detail and asked them questions to elicit information about the situations in which his behavior was a problem and the ways in which they had tried to handle it. When we asked them to select one negative and one positive behavior to work on, they decided to start with Peter's responses to requests.

We gave each parent a copy of the Behavior Observation Form (Figure 13.3). Then we roleplayed their parent-child interactions so they could practice keeping track of these behaviors. We had each parent make a request, and one of us roleplayed Peter's response. The parents took turns actually recording the request, the response, and their own consequence on the tracking form. When they showed that they understood how to track behaviors, we asked each parent to pick specific times for recording during the week to follow. Dad agreed to keep track for a half hour on Sunday, and mom agreed to record the rest of the time. Although this seems a bit lopsided in terms of sharing responsibility, this time arrangement was acceptable to both of them.

We discussed our social learning rationale briefly in the session, emphasizing examples that would demonstrate how Peter's arguing and noncompliance could be maintained by his parents' attention and by their occasionally giving in. We recommended that they read *Living With Children* (Patterson & Gullion, 1971) to better understand the rationale. Mom agreed to read the first 50 pages of the book. Since dad was not an avid reader, mom agreed to discuss the ideas she had read with him.

For a first between-session assignment, Peter's parents agreed to do the following:

1. Complete the Child Behavior Checklist.

2. Complete the Positive Behavior Checklist (Figure 13.1).

3. Complete Some Questions About Your Child (Figure 13.2).

4. Keep track of Peter's responses to requests on the Behavior Observation Form (Figure 13.3) (dad between 3:30 and 4:00 Sunday, and mom the rest of the time).

5. Read the first 50 pages of *Living With Children* (mom read and discuss with dad).

6. Tell Peter about the observations they were going to make.

Session 2

The second session was held at the clients' house. At this time we met Peter and were given a home tour by him. We had a chance to explain our role and his parents' goals to him in a comfortable, familiar setting. After the home tour, we sat down with Peter and his parents to review the assignments the parents had completed since the previous week. We attempted to reinforce the parents for careful record keeping by going over the records in detail, and we praised their descriptions of how they had praised some of Peter's positive behavior. At the same time, we directed special attention towards any of Peter's positive behaviors that were recorded by the parents. We praised Peter, not only to try to increase his positive behaviors, but also to provide a model of appropriate praising for his parents.

After we reviewed the parents' homework, we discussed the importance of praising, provided examples of good descriptive praises, and pointed out common mistakes to avoid in attempting to praise (such as sandwiching praises in between criticisms and being too global in comments). Whenever possible, we used actual praises that the parents had used with Peter for our positive examples.

In tracking Peter's behaviors, his parents noticed that they often had to remind him several times to complete his chores. He would frequently postpone complying with a request for chore completion until he was asked again. As the parents repeated requests, they tended to be less polite and patient. At this point we concentrated on devising a chore system that would give Peter more reinforcement for completing his chores on time and would decrease the attention his parents gave to his failure to do chores.

Peter and his parents agreed on a list of five chores to begin focusing on. We entered these on a chart like the one illustrated in Figure 13.5. We also discussed rules for using the point chart and gave Peter's parents a copy of these rules to refer to each day (see Figure 13.6). Finally, we discussed possible reinforcers and gave them a list of ideas for rewards other parents had found useful (Figure 13.4). At the end of the session, although the chore chart was incomplete, Peter and his parents knew how to get it ready for use. We arranged for a phone contact in 2 days. By that time they agreed to have the chores finalized, the point values determined, and the reinforcers selected. During the phone call we planned to check that the chart was appropriate and that the parents understood how to use it.

Mom was to take the major responsibility for checking Peter's chart with him and praising him for chores done each day. Dad needed a way to become more positive with Peter, so the partners worked out an agreement as follows:

Each day at supper mom will show dad the chart and will point out at least one thing Peter has done well. Dad, in turn, will attend with interest and will praise Peter.

In addition, the weekly reinforcers that Peter could earn usually included weekend activities with dad or the whole family.

The between-session assignment for Session 2 included the following:

1. Complete the chore chart (chores defined, points determined, reinforcers selected).

2. After our phone consultation, begin using the chore chart; follow the point chart rules each day.

3. Follow the agreement for including dad as a reinforcer.

4. Continue tracking Peter's responses to requests.

Session 3

During this session we spent the majority of our time reviewing the chore chart in detail. We went over the daily instructions one at a time to make sure they were being followed; made sure the chosen activities were, in fact, reinforcing; and asked for examples of specific praises given, encouraging the parents to praise every time they gave a point. Additional time was spent roleplaying praises to try to increase dad's skill and comfort with praising. We also discussed the importance of praising as part of the social learning rationale.

Between-session assignments for Session 3 were a repeat of the ones for Session 2 except for changing two behaviors on the chore chart.

Session 4

Although the chore chart addressed many of the compliance problems they were concerned with, Peter's parents wanted some additional skills to cope with his arguing, begging, and stubbornness. After the chore chart was going well and Peter's parents were praising many of his positive behaviors, we discussed the use of time out. The parents felt that there were times when Peter's arguing was acceptable and other times when it was not. Rather than give Peter a time out to extinguish all of his arguing, the parents agreed to develop a signal. When the arguing was unacceptable, his parents would say, "This is not negotiable." If Peter persisted in arguing after that signal, he would be sent to time out. If he stopped arguing when the signal was given, he would be praised.

We went over the rules for time out as illustrated in Figure 13.7, gave the parents a copy of the rules, and made sure that they both understood them. We also checked to see that they both agreed on which behaviors would result in a time out.

The parents agreed to track all incidents of stubbornness, arguing, and begging. For each instance, they were to try to identify the positive behaviors they wanted Peter to perform.

Between-session assignments for Session 4 included the following:

1. Continue with the chore chart.

2. Continue to track compliance with requests.

3. Keep track of incidents of stubbornness, arguing, and begging—in each case, try to note what positive behavior you want instead.

4. To stop any arguing, give the signal; if Peter persists, send him to time out.

Session 5

At first, mom tended to remind Peter to do his chores so that he could earn the reinforcers. During Session 5, she expressed some frustration with having to remind him. We suggested that she stop reminding him and set a time deadline for completion of each chore. If Peter failed to do a chore by the agreed-upon time, he would earn no points for that chore. If he did the chore without being reminded, he would earn double points for the chore. We felt that by increasing both the reinforcers to Peter for completing chores on his own and the costs to him for forgetting, he would be more likely to continue succeeding.

After tracking stubbornness, arguing, and begging for a week, the parents decided to consequate arguing and begging in the same way. They decided that with either behavior they could use the "not negotiable" signal and follow it by time out if necessary. Whenever Peter was being stubborn, they agreed to model the behavior expected of him and then have him roleplay or practice it (followed by parent praise).

Between-session assignments for Session 5 included the following:

1. Continue the chore chart with specific time limits for each chore, and double points for chores Peter remembers on his own.

2. Continue to track and consequate stubbornness, arguing, and begging.

3. Use the "not negotiable" signal for arguing or begging; if Peter persists, send him to time out.

Sessions 6 and 7

During these sessions we began a slow fade-out of the chore charts. Initially we raised the number of points needed for a daily reinforcer. Then we had Peter work for 2 days' worth of points before earning a slightly more desirable reinforcer. When Peter succeeded for several 2-day blocks, we suggested moving on to the next step. He then needed to work for 3 days' accumulation of points before earning the reinforcer, then 4 days', and so on up to a week. Peter's parents decided to continue with the weekly point chart indefinitely. They felt that the minimal tracking was well worth the time and kept them all attending to Peter's positive behaviors.

Between-session assignments for Sessions 6 and 7 included:

1. Gradually fade the reinforcers for the chore chart until Peter is working for an entire week on his chores before earning the reward.

2. Continue with the signal and time out for arguing.

3. Continue to praise positive behaviors, both those on the chore chart and others you notice.

Sessions 8 and 9

During these two sessions Peter's parents identified another goal to work on. Although he was now doing well at completing his chores and complying with requests, Peter was having difficulty using what his parents termed "good judgment." They included in this category such behaviors as teasing other children and putting his hands on others without their permission. The parents agreed to assume a teaching role with Peter with regard to these behaviors. We asked them to label and praise any incidents of "good judgment" they noticed. They also began asking him each day about any times he felt he had used "good judgment" so they could praise him. Any time they felt that Peter had used poor judgment, they were able to calmly label the incident, model a better way to handle the situation, and then have him roleplay the better way. At the same time, the parents were to record instances of Peter's good and bad judgment for discussion in our sessions.

During the 2 weeks between the eighth and ninth sessions, Peter's parents devised a reward system on their own to consequate incidents in which Peter reported using good judgment or kindness. They put up a chart on which to record at least one instance of good judgment and one act of kindness each day. If Peter had filled the good judgment column by the end of the week, he would receive 50 cents. Likewise, if he reported one act of kindness each day, he earned an additional 50 cents at the end of the week. Peter's parents wrote down each report and praised it. They also looked for examples of Peter's use of good judgment and kindness, noting and praising these also. While Peter had reported only eight instances of "good judgment" in the previous month, under the new system he reported nine good judgments and eight kind acts within a 6-day period.

After the ninth session, Peter's parents felt that they were well on their way toward reaching their pinpointed goals. In addition they felt that they had the skills for dealing with new problems that might arise and for maintaining the improvements in Peter's behavior that they had already achieved.

They arranged for a couple of monthly follow-up phone contacts to support their continued efforts and to help troubleshoot if problems arose. In further contacts with them they reported that Peter continued to behave in more positive ways at home. In addition, mom was consulting with the teacher and encouraging her to attend to Peter's positive behaviors at school. This consultation was an attempt to reduce his showing off as a means of getting negative adult attention at school. Mom had arranged for daily reports of Peter's behavior from the teacher; she could then consequate these reports at home to further encourage better school behaviors from Peter.

SUMMARY

According to social learning theory, children's behavior is developed and maintained by the contingencies of social reinforcement. Thus, teaching appropriate behavior to children really means teaching parents and teachers how to handle the reinforcement contingencies they already control. Several types of inappropriate behavior often come up: aggression and noncompliance are the most common, but fears and social isolation, some somatic difficulties, and low self-concept also are problems. All these types can be treated in a social-learning framework, even if their etiology is to some extent physiological.

The treatment program shown here usually includes most or all of these things: pinpointing problems and setting goals with parents; gathering relevant data; aiding the parents in understanding the skills they are taught and the rationale behind teaching those skills; visiting the home; teaching parents to praise good behavior; showing parents how to design and use point systems to increase their children's positive behaviors and later fade those systems out; instructing parents in the use of time out to decrease unwanted behavior; and helping parents generalize their learned skills to new problems. General goals for treatment are decided upon by the parents in the first session; then further assignments in assessment and treatment are given.

A most important compliance enhancer is making sure throughout the program that parents understand the reasons behind treatment. Another is keeping parents informed of the risks and the amount of effort required to reach the goals they choose. Giving parents a choice in how assignments are carried out seems to increase adherence as well. Parents can be asked to deposit an amount of money at the beginning of treatment to be refunded or forfeited depending on whether assignments are completed or not. For better compliance, assignments should be manageable: small and easy to insure success; shared by both parents, when possible; and supported by both parents. They should also be stated clearly so they are completely understood by the parents. Finally, support and encouragement can be provided by following each family's progress closely, stressing success, and occasionally calling the home.

The parents of Peter, a 9-year-old boy, sought help in the illustrative case presented. Their son was noncompliant, argumentative, stubborn, and careless about chores, and their normal ways of handling such problems were disruptive to the family. During the first session, the parents chose treatment goals, learned how to record behaviors, and received recording, reading, and checklist completion assignments. In later sessions they learned how to praise, set up a point system for reinforcement, and use time out, and to generalize those skills to new problems. Peter's behavior at home improved, and follow-up contacts showed that he continued to behave more appropriately there. When he began to show off at school, his mother set up a system with the classroom teacher to receive daily reports of Peter's behavior that could be consequated at home.

REFERENCE NOTES

1. Hawkins, N., & Biglan, A. *The positive behavior checklist.* Unpublished checklist, Behavior Change Center, Springfield, Oregon, 1978. (Available from Behavior Change Center, 824 North A Street, Springfield, Oregon 97477).

2. Hawkins, N. *Some questions about your child.* Unpublished checklist, Behavior Change Center, Springfield, Oregon, 1977. (Available from Behavior Change Center, 824 North A Street, Springfield, Oregon 97477).

REFERENCES

Achenbach, R.M. The child behavior profile: I. Boys aged 6 through 11. *Journal of Consulting and Clinical Psychology,* 1978, *46,* 478-488.

Achenbach, R.M., & Edelbrock, C.S. The child behavior profile: II. Boys aged 12-16 and girls aged 6-11 and 12-16. *Journal of Consulting and Clinical Psychology,* 1979, *47,* 223-233.

Becker, W.C., Madsen, C.H., Jr., Arnold, C.R., & Thomas, D.R. The contingent use of teacher attention and praise in reducing classroom behavior problems. In K.D. O'Leary & S.G. O'Leary (Eds.), *Classroom management: The successful use of behavior modification.* Elmsford, N.Y.: Pergamon Press, 1972.

Birnbrauer, J.S. Mental retardation. In H. Leitenberg (Ed.), *Handbook of behavior modification and behavior therapy.* Englewood Cliffs, N.J.: Prentice-Hall, 1976.

Christopherson, E.R., Arnold, C.M., Hill, D.W., & Quilitch, H.R. The home point system: Token reinforcement procedures for application by parents of children with behavior problems. *Journal of Applied Behavior Analysis,* 1972, *5,* 485-497.

Conger, J.C. The treatment of encopresis by the management of social consequences. *Behavior Therapy,* 1970, *1,* 386-390.

Glasgow, R.E., & Rosen, G.M. Behavioral bibliotherapy: A review of self-help behavior therapy manuals. *Psychological Bulletin,* 1978, *85,* 1-23.

Greenwood, C.R., Hops, H., Delquadri, J., & Guild, J. Group contingencies for group consequences in classroom management: A further analysis. *Journal of Applied Behavior Analysis,* 1974, *7,* 413-426.

Herbert, E.W., & Baer, D.M. Training parents as behavior modifiers: Self-recording of contingent attention. *Journal of Applied Behavior Analysis,* 1972, *5,* 139-150.

Kanfer, F.H., & Grimm, L.G. Freedom of choice and behavior change. *Journal of Consulting and Clinical Psychology,* 1978, *46,* 873-878.

Katz, R.C., & Zlutnick, S. *Behavior therapy and health care: Principles and applications.* Elmsford, N.Y.: Pergamon Press, 1975.

Neisworth, J.T., & Moore, F. Operant treatment of asthmatic responding with the parent as therapist. *Behavior Therapy,* 1972, *3,* 95-99.

Patterson, G.R. *Families.* Champaign, Ill.: Research Press, 1975.

Patterson, G.R. Mothers: The unacknowledged victims. *Monographs of the Society for Research in Child Development,* in press.

Patterson, G.R., & Gullion, M.E. *Living with children: New methods for parents and teachers* (rev. ed.). Champaign, Ill.: Research Press, 1971.

Patterson, G.R., Reid, J.B., Jones, R.R., & Conger, R.E. *A social learning approach to family intervention: Vol. 1. Families with aggressive children.* Eugene, Oreg.: Castalia Press, 1975.

Pinkston, E.M., Reese, N.M., LeBlanc, J.M., & Baer, D.M. Independent control of a preschool child's aggression and peer interaction by contingent teacher attention. *Journal of Applied Behavior Analysis,* 1973, *6,* 115-124.

Redd, W.H. Effects of mixed reinforcement contingencies on adults' control of children's behavior. *Journal of Applied Behavior Analysis,* 1969, *2,* 249-254.

Strain, P.S., & Timm, M.A. An experimental analysis of social interaction between a behaviorally disordered preschool child and her classroom peers. *Journal of Applied Behavior Analysis,* 1974, *1,* 583-590.

Wahler, R.G. Oppositional children: A quest for parental reinforcement control. *Journal of Applied Behavior Analysis,* 1969, *2,* 159-160.

Walker, H.M. *How to manage the acting out child.* Boston: Allyn and Bacon, 1979.

Ward, M.H., & Baker, B.L. Reinforcement therapy in the classroom. *Journal of Applied Behavior Analysis,* 1968, *1,* 315-322.

White, G.D., Nielsen, G., & Johnson, S.M. Timeout duration and the suppression of deviant behavior in children. *Journal of Applied Behavior Analysis,* 1972, *5,* 111-120.

SUBJECT INDEX

AUTHOR INDEX

ABOUT THE AUTHORS

John L. Shelton

The use of therapeutic homework across the entire spectrum of behavioral disorders has long been the primary research and writing interest of Dr. John L. Shelton. Having received his Ph.D. in 1969 from the University of Utah and the Diplomate in Clinical Psychology in 1976, Dr. Shelton has worked in universities in Oregon, Colorado, and Washington. During that time he has written extensively regarding the utilization of therapeutic homework in the context of behavioral change. His first book (with J. M. Ackerman), *Homework in Counseling and Psychotherapy,* established practical guidelines for the use of homework in clinical practice. Other chapters and research papers have followed, with each expanding on the central theme of therapeutic homework. This current text is a result of nearly 10 years of interest in the subject of therapeutic homework.

Dr. Shelton has now left the academic life and is pursuing private practice in the Seattle area. Homework continues to be a central element in his work.

Rona L. Levy

Dr. Rona L. Levy is an Associate Professor in the School of Social Work, University of Washington, Seattle, Washington, where she teaches courses in the empirical evaluation of clinical practice and behavioral medicine. She received her M.S.W., Ph.D., and M.P.H. degrees from the University of Michigan. Dr. Levy has coauthored (with Srinika Jayaratne) *Empirical Clinical Practice* and has published numerous articles and chapters on patient compliance and the application of the single-subject design methodology in clinical settings.